The Edmonton Public Library
gratefully acknowledges the generous donation of

**Ladies Auxiliary:  Millwoods Cultural &
Recreation Facilities Association**

TO THE BOOKSTOCK CAMPAIGN

2001

in the Year _____

Edmonton
Public Library

# CONTENTS

# REPTILES

*Survivors from a prehistoric age.*

THE REPTILES THAT STILL WALK, BURROW, CLIMB AND SWIM ON OUR PLANET REPRESENT THE SURVIVORS IN A DRAMATIC EVOLUTIONARY HISTORY OF REPTILIAN EXPERIMENTATION. FROM AMPHIBIAN BEGINNINGS SOME 300 MILLION YEARS AGO, A WIDE RANGE OF MORE THOROUGHLY TERRESTRIAL FORMS OF VERTEBRATE DEVELOPED. THESE REPTILE STARTING-POINTS HAVE HAD FAR-REACHING IMPLICATIONS FOR THE REST OF VERTEBRATE EVOLUTION. FROM THESE EARLY REPTILE STOCKS OUR MODERN REPTILES CAME. FROM THEM, TOO, HOWEVER, CAME A PLETHORA OF MAGNIFICENT DEAD ENDS, INCLUDING THE ONCE-MIGHTY DINOSAURS, THE WINGED PTEROSAURS AND THE SWIMMING ICHTHYOSAURS AND PLESIOSAURS. AND FROM THE MIDST OF THE COMPLEX EARLY FAMILY TREE OF REPTILE PROTOTYPES DEVELOPED THE ANCESTORS OF THE REMAINING TWO GROUPS OF TERRESTRIAL HIGHER VERTEBRATES: THE MAMMALS AND THE BIRDS. REPTILES THUS LINK THE BEGINNINGS OF LIFE ON LAND, THE AMPHIBIANS, WITH THE MOST ADVANCED AND SOPHISTICATED VERTEBRATES.

*False Map Turtle*

Different systems exist for classifying the class Reptilia. The most recent classification by cladistic methods does not recognize "Reptiles" as a taxonomic group at all, simply as a group in which animals with different ancestries are "lumped" together. The term "reptile" will continue to be used here, however, because it is such a familiar one. Most of the existing systems, however, recognize about 16 or 17 orders, known by fossils alone or from fossils and still existing animals. Only four orders persist today: first, the chelonians – turtles and tortoises; second, the crocodilians; third, the Squamata, which includes all lizards, snakes and the amphisbaenians; fourth, with only 2 living representatives, the Sphendontia or tuatara order. Even though these four orders represent only a small fraction of past reptilian diversity, they still show something of the interesting variation of which the reptile body form is capable.

The chelonians are a varied and successful assemblage of reptiles with about 250 known species. They have short, broad bodies, enclosed by a bony box into which, to a variable extent, head, tail and limbs can be retracted for protection. The protective box consists of internal bony plates upon which is superimposed tough, horny material, similar to the scales of other reptiles. Chelonians have no teeth but consume vegetation or prey items by grasping the foods with the sharp edges of a beak, developed from the upper and lower jaws.

Crocodiles and their allies are the only remaining representatives of the archosaurian reptiles. The archosaurs, in the form of dinosaurs and pterosaurs, were the dominant terrestrial animals on earth from about 200 million years ago to approximately 63 to 70 million years ago. The characteristic elongate, heavy-headed crocodilians have been effective amphibious predators on earth for around 200 million years and are the largest living reptiles today. They are all carnivores, equipped with rows of sharp, peglike teeth which are continually replaced as they become worn.

Lizards, snakes and the burrowing amphisbaenians make up the order Squamata, meaning the scaly ones. The elongate, long-tailed bodies of lizards have become modified to enable them to live in a wide range of habitats. Lizards can be expert burrowers, runners, swimmers and climbers, and a few can manage crude, short-distance gliding on rib-supported "wings".

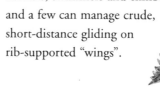

*Gavial*

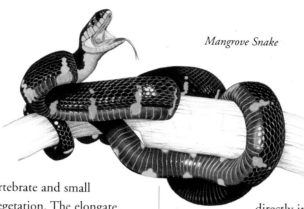

*Mangrove Snake*

Most are carnivores, feeding on invertebrate and small vertebrate prey, but others feed on vegetation. The elongate, limbless snakes have some of the most highly modified skulls to be found among vertebrates, with a high degree of flexibility to accommodate large prey and sometimes effective fang and venom systems. Other snakes use their long, powerful bodies to constrict and suffocate their prey in their embrace.

The final order of reptiles includes only the tuataras of New Zealand. They seem to have changed little in their essential details in 200 million years.

Each of the four orders of living reptiles shows different adaptations which mark a distinct advance from the amphibians. Perhaps the most crucial of these modifications relate to temperature control, skin structure and methods of reproduction.

Like the amphibians, reptiles seem not to have any significant ability to control their body temperature independently of external heat sources. They do, however, have a set of behavior patterns which enable them to regulate the effect of external heat sources (sun, hot rocks) on their own temperature. By the use of specific postures and activities in or on the heat sources, reptiles can attain high body temperatures and regulate them to some degree. But their ultimate reliance on the sun for body heat means that the main bulk of reptile species occurs in tropical and warm temperate climates.

The moist skin of the amphibians is important as a respiratory surface. Reptiles, in contrast, have waterproofed themselves with a scaly outer layer that is physically and chemically tough and relatively impermeable to water.

Compared with amphibian methods of reproduction, those of all reptiles show a great leap forward in solving the problem of sexual reproduction on land. Instead of having to return to water to breed and being dependent on the water to bring eggs and sperm together, male reptiles fertilize their mates internally by means of their one or two penises.

The great reproductive advance of the reptiles, however, is their eggs with their tough shells, sometimes doubly strengthened with mineral salts to protect them from abrasion, damage and water loss in the soil where they are normally laid. The egg contains enough yolky food reserves and enough liquid to allow the reptile to develop directly into a miniature adult, instead of passing through an intermediate larval phase as do the amphibians. Systems of blood vessels, running in special membranes enclosing the embryo, transfer the food reserves to it, exchange oxygen and carbon dioxide with the outside air via the shell, or transfer nitrogenous waste products, to be deposited in a special sac that is left behind in the shell when the reptile hatches out. The hatchling has an egg tooth which it uses to slit open the shell and which it sheds afterward.

In some reptiles, eggs are retained within the female's body and hatch within it or as they are laid, so that the female produces fully formed live young. In these species the shell is only a thin transparent membrane. A few reptiles and snakes have advanced still further, and their young develop inside the body with no shell membrane, having instead a primitive form of placenta. Young which develop inside the mother have many advantages in that they are protected from predators and physical dangers. By sunning herself, the mother can keep her body temperature as high as possible, in turn ensuring that the embryos develop rapidly. Live-bearing species occur even in predominantly egg-laying families and are often reptiles that live in particularly harsh climates or at high altitudes.

Reptiles in their evolution have produced all the basic adaptations necessary for efficient terrestrial life that the more advanced birds and mammals carry to higher levels of sophistication. Successful in their own right, they have provided the springboard for the even greater adaptive modifications of the body plans and abilities of the vertebrate animal.

*Caiman Lizard*

## KEY TO REPTILE CLADOGRAM A

1 Chelonia (turtles)
2 Sphenodontia (tuataras) and Squamata (lizards and snakes)
3 Crocodilia (crocodiles and alligators)
4 Aves (birds)
5 Mammalia (mammals)

## CLADOGRAM A

**1** Green turtle    **2** Common iguana    **3** Mississippi alligator    **4** Aves    **5** Mammalia

## KEY TO REPTILE CLADOGRAM B

1 Chelidae (matamatas)
2 Pelomedusidae (greaved turtles)
3 Chelydridae (snapping turtles)
4 Dermochelyidae (leatherback turtles)
5 Cheloniidae (marine turtles)
6 Kinosternidae (American mud and musk turtles)
7 Dermatemyidae (Central American river turtle)
8 Carettocelyidae (plateless river turtle)
9 Trionychidae (softshell turtle)
10 Testudinidae (tortoises)
11 Emydidae (emydid turtles)

*Cladogram showing possible phylogenetic relationships within the "reptiles". Traditional classification places turtles, crocodiles, lizards, and snakes, within the class Reptilia, and places the birds into a group of similar rank, the class Aves. Cladists regard the group known as reptiles as an artificial assemblage which includes members of more than one monophyletic group. This cladogram shows the possible relationships between turtles, crocodiles, and lizards and snakes. It reveals the separation of turtles, which have distinctive skulls and shells, from the other groups, the relationships between lizards, snakes and crocodiles, and the equal ranking of birds with the "reptilian" taxa shown here. The other cladograms on this page show the probable relationships within the turtles, lizards, and snakes, respectively.*

## CLADOGRAM B

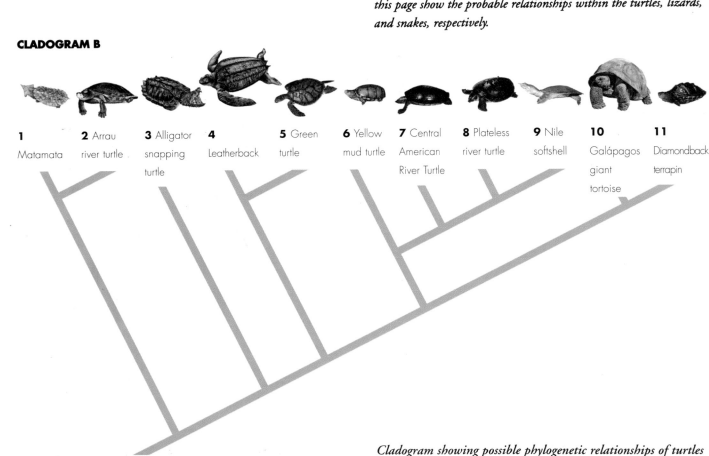

**1** Matamata    **2** Arrau river turtle    **3** Alligator snapping turtle    **4** Leatherback    **5** Green turtle    **6** Yellow mud turtle    **7** Central American River Turtle    **8** Plateless river turtle    **9** Nile softshell    **10** Galápagos giant tortoise    **11** Diamondback terrapin

*Cladogram showing possible phylogenetic relationships of turtles*

**CLADOGRAM C**

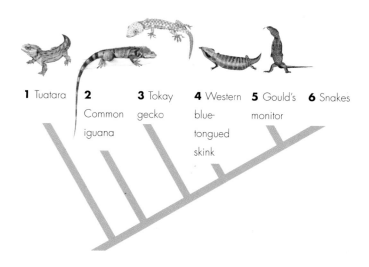

1 Sphenodontia (tuataras)
2 Iguanidae
  (iguanas, agamids,
  chameleons)
3 Gekkonidae (geckos,
  scaly-footed lizards)

4 Scincomorpha
  (teiid lizards, lacertid
  lizards, skinks)
5 Anguimorpha
  (slow worms, monitors,
  gila monsters)
6 Snakes

*Cladogram showing possible phylogenetic relationships of tuataras and lizards. Iguanidae includes iguanas, agamids, and chameleons. Gekkonidae includes geckos and scaly-foot lizards. Scincomorpha includes dibamids, teiids, lacertids, skinks, and girdled and plated lizards. Anguimorpha includes crocodile lizards, legless and alligator lizards, monitors and Gila monster.*

1 Leptotyphlopidae
  (thread snakes)
2 Typhlopidae
  (blind snakes)
3 Anomolepidae
  (dawn blind snakes)
4 Aniliidae
5 Uropeltidae
  (shieldtail snakes)
6 Xenopeltidae
  (sunbeam snake)
7 Boidae
  (boas and pythons)

8 Acrochordidae
  (wart snakes)
9 Atractaspidae (burrowing
  asps)
10 Colubridae
  (colubrid snakes)
11 Elapidae
  (cobras and sea snakes)
12 Viperidae
  (vipers and pit vipers)

**CLADOGRAM D**

**1** Western
blind snake
**2** Schlegel's
blind snake
**3** Anomalepis
sp.
**4** False
coral snake
**5** Red
blotched
shieldtail
**6** Sunbeam
snake
**7** Emerald
tree boa
**8** Elephant-
trunk snake
**9** Bibron's
burrowing
asp
**10** Common
garter
snake
**11** King
cobra
**12** Eastern
diamondback
rattlesnake

*Cladogram showing possible phylogenetic relationships of snakes*

# EMYDID TURTLES

## ORDER CHELONIA

This order contains all turtles and tortoises. There are about 230 living species. A typical chelonid has its body enclosed in a shell made of modified horny scales and bone. The shell is in two parts – on the animal's back is the carapace, and the shell underneath the body is the plastron. The ribs and most of the vertebrae are attached to the shell. Both pelvic and pectoral girdles lie within the shell and the limbs emerge sideways. The neck is long and flexible and can usually be withdrawn into the shell. In most families (the hidden-neck turtles or cryptodires) the neck bends up and down to retract, but in the greaved turtles (Pelomedusidae), and the matamata and snakenecked turtles (Chelidae), (called the side-neck turtles or pleurodires) the neck bends sideways when being retracted.

Chelonids have no teeth, but their jaws have horny beaks of varying strength. All lay eggs, usually burying them in sand or earth. Hatchlings must dig their own way out to the surface.

## EMYDIDAE: EMYDID TURTLE FAMILY

A varied group of freshwater and semi-terrestrial turtles, the emydid family is the largest group of living turtles with about 85 species. The family is closely related to land tortoises (Testudinidae). Some authorities group them as one family. The hind feet of emydids are adapted for swimming. Most species live in the northern hemisphere. Emydid turtles have a varied diet and eat both plants and animals. Some species start life as carnivores, but feed mainly on plants as adults.

### Pond Slider *Trachemys scripta* **LR:nt**

**RANGE**  USA: Virginia to N. Florida, west to New Mexico; Central America to Brazil

**HABITAT**  Slow rivers, ponds, swamps

**SIZE**  5–11¾ in (13–30 cm)

Pond sliders are highly aquatic creatures, rarely moving far from water. They bask on floating logs, often lying on top of one another. The carapace is oval and the markings variable. Males are usually smaller than females and

have elongated, curved claws. Young pond sliders feed on insects, crustaceans, mollusks and tadpoles, but as they mature they feed more on plants.

In June and July pond sliders lay up to three clutches of 4 to 23 eggs each. Millions of these turtles are raised on farms and sold as pets.

### False Map Turtle *Graptemys pseudogeographica*

**RANGE**  USA: Minnesota to Sabine River area of Louisiana and Texas

**HABITAT**  Rivers, lakes ponds

**SIZE**  3–9¾ in (8–25 cm)

False map turtles have intricate shell patterns and clear markings on their small heads. Males are smaller than females and have enlarged foreclaws. These turtles prefer habitats with plenty of vegetation and feed on aquatic plants, crustaceans and mollusks.

After a courtship ritual, during which the male swims above the female then faces her and drums her snout with his claws, the pair mate. The nesting period is from May to July. The female turtle digs a pit in the soil of the river or lake bank with her hind feet and deposits her 6 to 15 eggs. Up to three clutches are laid in a season. The numbers of this once common species have been reduced by pollution of its habitats.

### Diamondback Terrapin *Malaclemys terrapin* **LR:nt**

**RANGE**  USA: Atlantic and Gulf coasts

**HABITAT**  Salt marshes, estuaries, lagoons

**SIZE**  4–9 in (10–23 cm)

This terrapin is the only North American emydid species that is adapted for life in brackish and salt water. It is a strong, fast swimming turtle with large hind limbs. Females are bigger than males.

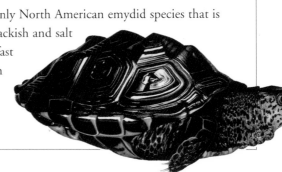

Diamondbacks spend their days on mudflats or tidal marshes, feeding on snails, clams and worms and on some plant shoots. At night they bury themselves in mud, and in the northern part of their range they hibernate throughout the winter, buried in mud. Diamondbacks mate in the spring and lay 5 to 18 eggs in cavities which they dig in the marshes or dunes.

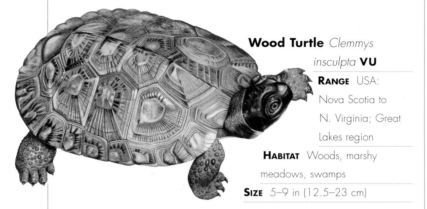

### Wood Turtle *Clemmys insculpta* **VU**

**RANGE** USA: Nova Scotia to N. Virginia; Great Lakes region
**HABITAT** Woods, marshy meadows, swamps
**SIZE** 5–9 in (12.5–23 cm)

The rough-shelled wood turtle spends most of its life on land but is usually in the vicinity of water. It is a good climber and feeds on fruit as well as on worms, slugs and insects. In May or June females lay 6 or 8 eggs, which usually hatch by October, but which may overwinter and hatch the following spring in the north. Adults hibernate in the north of the range. Wood turtles are popular pets, but they have been overhunted and are now rare and protected in some states of the USA.

### Eastern Box Turtle *Terrapene carolina* **LR:nt**

**RANGE** USA: E. states west to Texas
**HABITAT** Moist forested areas
**SIZE** 4–8 in (10–20 cm)

A poor swimmer, the box turtle stays in shallow water and spends most of its life on land. Its carapace is nearly always domed in shape and it is variable in coloration and pattern. Box turtles eat almost anything, but slugs, earthworms and fruit are favored foods; they are able to eat mushrooms that are poisonous to humans, and anyone then eating the turtle is poisoned. Usually active early in the day or after rain, box turtles may take refuge in swampy areas in the heat of the summer.

In the spring, after hibernating throughout the winter, box turtles perform prolonged courtship rituals. The female lays 3 to 8 eggs in a flask-shaped pit which she digs. The hatchlings may remain in the nest over the following winter. Females can store sperm and lay fertile eggs several years after mating.

### European Pond Turtle *Emys orbicularis* **LR:nt**

**RANGE** C. France, south to N. Africa, east to Iran
**HABITAT** Ponds, marshes, rivers
**SIZE** 5–6 in (13–15 cm)

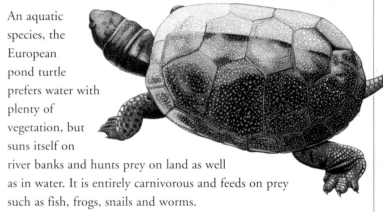

An aquatic species, the European pond turtle prefers water with plenty of vegetation, but suns itself on river banks and hunts prey on land as well as in water. It is entirely carnivorous and feeds on prey such as fish, frogs, snails and worms.

In winter these turtles hibernate burying themselves in mud or in specially built chambers in the river bank. They mate in spring and, having dug an egg pit with her tail, the female lays 3 to 16 eggs. She generally uses the same nest site every year.

### Batagur/River Terrapin *Batagur baska* **EN**

**RANGE** S.E. Asia from Bengal to Vietnam
**HABITAT** Tidal areas, estuaries
**SIZE** 23 in (58 cm)

A large herbivorous turtle with a smooth heavy shell, the batagur is often found in brackish or even salt water. It has only four claws on each foot.

Batagurs nest on sandbanks and usually lay three clutches in a season – a total of 50 to 60 eggs. Numbers have declined due to the excessive collection of eggs and killing of adults for food. The batagur has been eliminated from some parts of its range.

# LAND TORTOISES

## TESTUDINIDAE: LAND TORTOISE FAMILY

There are about 35 species of land tortoise, found in North America, Europe and Asia, and in Africa and Madagascar. All are strictly terrestrial and have stumpy, elephantine hind legs; on the front legs are thick, hard scales. The head and limbs can be retracted completely inside the shell, leaving only the soles of the hind feet, tail region and scaly fronts of the forelimbs exposed. Most depend on their armor for protection and do not usually show aggression or attempt to flee when disturbed. All species are predominantly herbivorous.

### African Pancake Tortoise *Malocochersus tornieri* **VU**

**RANGE** Africa: Kenya, Tanzania

**HABITAT** Rocky outcrops in arid land

**SIZE** 6 in (15 cm)

The African pancake tortoise is an unusual species. Its shell is extremely flat and soft, and rather than retreating into its shell when disturbed, the tortoise runs to hide in a rock crevice. Once there, it inflates its lungs, thus increasing its size, so that it is wedged in and is almost impossible to remove. Females are slightly larger than males.

The pancake tortoise feeds on dry grass. It nests in July and August, laying 1 egg at a time, and it may lay two or more times in a season. The eggs hatch after about 6 months.

### Gopher Tortoise *Gopherus polyphemus* **VU**

**RANGE** USA: South Carolina to Florida, west to Louisiana

**HABITAT** Sandy areas between grassland and forest

**SIZE** 9¼–14½ in (23.5–37 cm)

This tortoise has a domed shell and heavily scaled front legs, flattened for efficient digging. An excellent burrower, it makes a long tunnel, ending in a chamber which serves as a refuge where humidity and temperature remain relatively constant. One tunnel recorded was over 46 ft (14 m) long. Other small animals may share the tortoise's burrow.

Gopher tortoises emerge from their burrows during the day to bask in the sun and feed on grass and leaves. They mate in spring and nest from April to July. Several clutches of 2 to 7 eggs are laid in a shallow pit during the nesting period.

### Bowsprit Tortoise *Chersine angulata*

**RANGE** South Africa

**HABITAT** Coastal areas

**SIZE** 6–7 in (15–18 cm)

The bowsprit tortoise has distinctive triangular markings on its carapace. The front opening of the carapace is particularly small, providing good protection against predators. Males are bigger than females and are aggressive toward one another. Bowsprits are believed to eat plant material. They nest in August and lay 1 or 2 eggs in a hole about 4 in (10 cm) deep. Eggs take about a year to hatch.

### Galápagos Giant Tortoise *Geochelone nigra* **VU**

**RANGE** Galápagos Islands

**HABITAT** Varied, cool, moist forest to arid land

**SIZE** Up to 4 ft (1.2 m)

There are at least 13 subspecies of these giant tortoises, which may weigh over 500 lb (215 kg). Because the populations are isolated from one another on separate islands, over thousands of years subspecies have evolved. The discovery of these subspecies on the different islands was one of the observations that caused Darwin to start his speculations on the origin of species.

The tortoises vary in size, length and thickness of limbs and, most importantly, in the shape of the carapace. Some species have a "saddleback" shell which rises up above the head, allowing the tortoise to lift its head right up and enabling it to graze on a greater range of vegetation. These species occur only on those islands which have highgrowing vegetation.

Galápagos tortoises eat almost any vegetation, which they seek in the more fertile highlands.

Males are always markedly larger than females. They mate at any time of year. Nesting has been closely observed on Indefatigable Island where there is a tortoise

## Schweigger's/Serrated Hingeback Tortoise

*Kinixys erosa* **DD**

| **RANGE** | W. and C. Africa |
|---|---|
| **HABITAT** | Rain forest, marshes, river banks |
| **SIZE** | 13 in (33 cm) |

A unique hinge on the carapace of this tortoise, located in line with the junction of the second and third back plates, allows the rear of the carapace to be lowered, if the tortoise is attacked, to protect its hindquarters. This hinge is not present in young tortoises. By digging itself into plant debris, the hingeback remains hidden for much of its life. It feeds on plants and may also eat small animals. There are usually 4 eggs in a clutch.

reserve. After mating, the female descends to the lowland area where there is bare soil in full sun. She chooses a site for her nest then urinates in order to soften the earth and digs a pit up to 12 in (30.5 cm) deep with her hind feet. After laying a clutch of up to 17 eggs, she plasters the excavated soil over the cavity so that it is well closed and the soil dries again in the sun. As usual with tortoises, the young must dig themselves out of the cavity unaided after they hatch out.

## Leopard Tortoise *Geochelone pardalis*

| **RANGE** | Africa: Sudan and Ethiopia to South Africa |
|---|---|
| **HABITAT** | Savanna, woodland |
| **SIZE** | 24 in (61 cm) |

The leopard tortoise has a markedly domed, boldly patterned carapace. It feeds on a great variety of plant material, including fruit and beans.

Courting males compete for females, butting at each other until one is overturned. They nest in September and October in South Africa, but the season is longer in tropical Africa. The female prepares a nest cavity by urinating on the soil in order to soften it, then excavating a pit using her hind limbs. She lays batches of 5 to 30 eggs, and there may be several clutches in a season.

## Spur-thighed Tortoise *Testudo graeca* **VU**

| **RANGE** | N. Africa; extreme S.E. and S.W. Europe; Middle East |
|---|---|
| **HABITAT** | Meadows, cultivated land, woodland |
| **SIZE** | 6 in (15 cm) |

This tortoise has a moderately domed shell and a small spur in the thigh region of each front limb. Females are larger than males. The tortoises hibernate in winter but, in coastal areas, will emerge as early as February. They court in spring, the male butting and biting the female before mating with her. The eggs, usually 2 or 3 in a clutch, are laid in May and June and generally hatch in September and October, although this varies with the local climate. The young tortoises are similar to adults but they have more rounded shells and clearer markings. Thousands of these tortoises are collected and exported as pets, many of which die because of the unsuitable climate and conditions of their new homes.

# SOFTSHELL TURTLES, RIVER TURTLES AND MUD TURTLES

## TRIONYCHIDAE: SOFTSHELL TURTLE FAMILY

This family contains about 22 species of aquatic turtles which have only three claws on each foot. All species have rounded, flexible carapaces with no horny plates, hence their pancakelike appearance and their common name. Most species have long mobile necks. Softshells move fast in water and on land but spend most of their lives in water. Species are found in eastern North America and Southeast Asia, and there is a single species in the Middle East.

Softshells lay up to three clutches of hardshelled eggs each year. Females usually grow larger than males and, as they mature, their carapace patterns become obscured by blotches. Males tend to retain clear carapace patterns.

### Spiny Softshell *Trionyx spiniferus*

| | |
|---|---|
| **RANGE** | N. America: Ontario and Quebec, south to Florida and Colorado |
| **HABITAT** | Rivers, creeks, ponds |
| **SIZE** | 6–18 in (15–46 cm) |

Conical projections, known as tubercles, around the front edge of this turtle's shell are the origin of the species' common name. There are about six geographically distinct races found within the range and some have more pronounced spines than others. Females are notably larger than males.

Spiny softshells are highly aquatic. They feed on insects, crayfish, and some fish and plant food. They nest in summer and females lay clutches of about 20 eggs.

### Narrow-headed/Indian Softshell *Chitra indica* **VU**

| | |
|---|---|
| **RANGE** | India, Pakistan, Thailand |
| **HABITAT** | Rivers |
| **SIZE** | 36 in (91 cm) |

A fast-swimming, large turtle with flipperlike limbs, this softshell does indeed have an elongated narrow head, with eyes placed far forward near the snout. This species seems to prefer clear, sandy-bottomed water and is carnivorous, feeding in the main on fish and mollusks.

### Nile Softshell *Trionyx triunguis*

| | |
|---|---|
| **RANGE** | Africa: Egypt to Senegal |
| **HABITAT** | Ponds, lakes, rivers |
| **SIZE** | 36 in (91 cm) |

The Nile softshell can weigh up to 100 lb (45 kg) and is hunted for food by man in many parts of its range. Although it is a freshwater species, groups have been found living off the coast of Turkey. It is omnivorous and feeds on mollusks, fish, insects and fruit. In Egypt it breeds in April and lays 50 to 60 eggs; elsewhere clutches may be smaller.

### Zambesi Softshell/Zambesi Flapshell Turtle *Cycloderma frenatum* **LR:nt**

| | |
|---|---|
| **RANGE** | Africa: Tanzania, Mozambique, Zambia, Malawi |
| **HABITAT** | Ponds, lakes, rivers |
| **SIZE** | 20 in (51 cm) |

A carnivorous turtle, the Zambesi softshell feeds mainly on mollusks. It lays its clutch of 15 to 20 eggs between December and March and is most active in rainy weather. The hatchlings have pale green carapaces and dark lines on their heads. In adults these lines are outlined with white dots and become gradually fainter with age. The only other species within this genus is Aubry's softshell, *C. aubryi*, which is found in West Africa.

## CARETTOCHELYIDAE: PLATELESS RIVER TURTLE FAMILY

Fossils found in Europe, Asia and North America show that this was once a widespread family. There is now only 1 species.

### New Guinea Plateless River/Pig-Nose Turtle

*Carettochelys insculpta* **VU**

**RANGE**  New Guinea: Fly River area

**HABITAT**  Rivers

**SIZE**  18 in (46 cm)

This New Guinea species, now also found to be living in northern Australia, is better adapted for aquatic life than most freshwater turtles. Its limbs are modified into long paddles, but retain two claws and resemble the limbs of sea turtles. There are few known details about the nesting habits of this species, but it lays 17 to 27 eggs and hatchlings are about 2¼ in (6 cm) long.

## DERMATEMYIDAE: CENTRAL AMERICAN RIVER TURTLE FAMILY

A single species survives from this family, that was formerly found in North and Central America, Europe and Africa.

### Central American River Turtle *Dermatemys mawii* **En**

**RANGE**  Mexico to Guatemala and Belize (not Yucatan)

**HABITAT**  Clear rivers and lakes

**SIZE**  18 in (46 cm)

This turtle has long been hunted for its meat and is now scarce throughout much of its range. Although protected by conservation laws, there is still concern for its future.

A smooth-shelled turtle, it has a small head with a pointed, projecting snout and large nostrils. Males have a golden-yellow patch on the head, but the females and juveniles have grayish heads. It has large webbed feet and rarely leaves the water, but basks while floating. On land this turtle is awkward, but it swims

well and is able to stay submerged for long periods. Aquatic vegetation is its main food source. It nests in the flood season and lays its 6 to 16 eggs in mud near the water's edge.

## KINOSTERNIDAE: MUD AND MUSK TURTLE FAMILY

The 20 species in this family are mainly aquatic turtles living in North and Central America and northern South America. They give off a musky odor from 2 pairs of glands, positioned on each side of the body where skin and shell meet. Their heads are retractile.

### Yellow Mud Turtle *Kinosternon flavescens*

**RANGE**  USA: Nebraska to Texas; Mexico

**HABITAT**  Slow streams

**SIZE**  3½–6¼ in (9–16 cm)

The yellow mud turtle does indeed seem to prefer water with a mud bottom, but it may also be found in artificial habitats such as cattle drinking troughs and ditches. It feeds on both aquatic and terrestrial invertebrates. Breeding females lay 2 to 4 eggs.

### Common Musk Turtle *Sternotherus odoratus*

**RANGE**  USA: E. states, west to Texas

**HABITAT**  Slow, shallow, muddy streams

**SIZE**  3–5 in (8–13 cm)

Also known as the stinkpot, this turtle exudes a strong-smelling fluid from its musk glands when molested. It is a highly aquatic species, rarely found far from water, but it does emerge to bask on branches overhanging water. It feeds on carrion, insects and mollusks as well as on small amounts of fish and plants. Nesting is from February to June, depending on the latitude; females lay 1 to 9 eggs under trees, logs or dead leaves.

# LEATHERBACK AND MARINE TURTLES

## DERMOCHELYIDAE: LEATHERBACK FAMILY

There is a single living species in this family. It has many distinctive features but resembles other sea turtles in many details of skull structure and has similar nesting habits.

### Leatherback *Dermochelys coriacea* **EN**

| | |
|---|---|
| **RANGE** | Worldwide, usually in warm seas |
| **HABITAT** | Oceanic |
| **SIZE** | 61 in (155 cm) |

The world's largest turtle, the leatherback has an average weight of 800 lb (360 kg) and a maximum of 1,300 lb (590 kg). Its foreflippers are extremely long, with a span of about 9 ft (2.7 m). It has no horny shields on its shell, no scales and no claws. The carapace resembles hard rubber and has three longitudinal ridges. Leatherbacks feed mainly on jellyfish, a diet in keeping with their weak, scissorlike jaws.

Leatherbacks apparently perform long migrations between nesting and feeding sites. Most breed every other year and lay clutches of about 80 to 100 eggs. The nesting procedure is much the same as that of the other sea turtles, but after laying, the leatherback always turns one or more circles before returning to the sea. Several clutches are laid in a season at roughly 10-day intervals. Hatchlings are 2¼ in (6 cm) long and have scales on shell and skin which disappear within the first 2 months of life.

## CHELONIDAE: MARINE TURTLE FAMILY

The larger of the 2 families of marine turtles, Chelonidae contains 6 species, all generally found in tropical and subtropical waters. All have nonretractile heads and limbs. The forelimbs are modified into long, paddlelike flippers with one or two claws. The turtles swim by making winglike beats of the foreflippers. On land, the green turtle moves particularly awkwardly, heaving itself forward with both flippers simultaneously, but the others move with alternating limb movements, as most four-legged animals do.

The 6 species have become specialized for different niches and diets, to compensate for the overlap of their ranges.

### Green Turtle *Chelonia mydas* **EN**

| | |
|---|---|
| **RANGE** | Worldwide in seas where temperature does not fall below 68°F (20°C) |
| **HABITAT** | Coasts, open sea |
| **SIZE** | 40–50 in (102–127 cm) |

This large, thoroughly aquatic turtle rarely comes to land except to bask and sleep and to lay eggs. Males have slightly longer, narrower carapaces than females and enlarged curved claws on the front flippers for gripping the female when mating.

Green turtles are primarily herbivorous animals and have serrated jaw surfaces, well suited to feeding on sea grasses and seaweed; some crustaceans and jellyfish may also be eaten. The best feeding grounds, where there are vast underwater pastures of plants, are often far away from the best nesting beaches, and green turtles have evolved astounding migratory habits. At nesting time they travel hundreds of miles to the beach of their birth to lay eggs and, as a result, there tend to be a limited number of important nesting sites, to which hundreds of turtles go. One such site is Ascension Island in the mid-Atlantic.

Every second or third year, green turtles travel to their nesting site and mate. The female heaves herself up the beach well away from the tidal area. With her foreflippers she sweeps away sand to create a hollow for her body in which she lies, her shell flush with the beach. She then uses her hind flippers to dig a hole about 16 in (40 cm) deep, immediately beneath her tail. She deposits her eggs into the hole, covers the area with sand and returns to the sea. The average clutch contains about 106 eggs. Sometimes a female lays several clutches in a season at 2-week intervals.

After an incubation period of 2 to 3 months, the young turtles hatch and dig their way through the sand to the surface. Having oriented themselves, they rush for the sea, past a horde of eager predators. Mortality is high, and those which do reach the sea will have to face yet more predators.

The green turtle is now an endangered species, and the population has been eliminated in some areas although it is still reasonable in others. The turtles have been overexploited for their meat, hides and eggs, and the predictability of their nesting habits has made them easy victims. Exploitation is now strictly controlled, and imports are banned in many countries.

The closely related flatback turtle, *C. depressa*, is slightly smaller and lives off the North Australian coast.

## Loggerhead Turtle *Caretta caretta* **EN**

**RANGE** Temperate and tropical areas of the Pacific, Indian and Atlantic Oceans

**HABITAT** Coasts, open sea

**SIZE** 30–40 in (76–102 cm)

A large turtle with a long, slightly tapering carapace, the loggerhead has a wide chunky head housing powerful jaws. It can crush even hardshelled prey and feeds on crabs and mollusks as well as on sponges, jellyfish and aquatic plants.

Loggerheads usually breed every other year and lay three or four clutches of about 100 eggs each in a season.

The loggerhead population has been reduced by over collection of eggs and lack of hunting controls, but in southeast Africa, where the turtles have been protected for more than 10 years, their numbers have increased by over 50 per cent.

## Pacific Ridley *Lepidochelys olivacea* **EN**

**RANGE** Tropical Pacific, Indian and S. Atlantic Oceans

**HABITAT** Coasts, open sea

**SIZE** 26 in (66 cm)

The Pacific ridley is small and lightly built for a sea turtle. It feeds on small shrimp, jellyfish, crabs, snails and fish, which it crushes with strong jaws. Like its close relative Kemp's ridley, *L. kempi*, the Pacific ridley breeds every year and always returns to the same nesting beaches. The female lays about 100 eggs in a pit in the sand and covers them. She then begins a strange movement peculiar to ridleys, rocking from side to side so that each edge of the shell thumps the sand in turn. Both ridleys are in grave danger due to over-exploitation by man.

## Hawksbill *Eretmochelys imbricata* **CR**

**RANGE** Tropical Atlantic, Pacific and Indian Oceans; Caribbean

**HABITAT** Coral reefs, rocky coasts

**SIZE** 30–36 in (76–91 cm)

The hawksbill's beautiful carapace provides the best tortoiseshell and is the reason for the endangered status of the species. Conservation controls have been introduced after many years of hunting, and imports are now banned in some countries.

The carapace is serrated at the back and has particularly thick horny plates. The tapering head of the hawksbill is an adaptation for searching out food, such as mollusks and crustaceans, in rocky crevices and reefs.

In many areas hawksbills are opportunistic breeders, nesting on any beach convenient to feeding grounds. They lay more eggs at a time than any other turtle, usually a batch of about 150.

# SNAPPING TURTLES, GREAVED TURTLES AND MATAMATAS

## CHELYDRIDAE: SNAPPING TURTLE FAMILY

The 3 species in this family are predatory freshwater turtles. The 2 American species are large, while the Asian species is smaller. Their massive heads do not retract. The big-headed turtle is placed in a family of its own (Platisternidae) by some authorities.

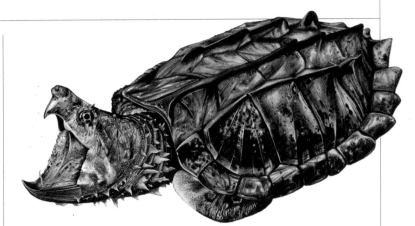

### Snapping Turtle *Chelydra serpentina*

| | |
|---|---|
| **RANGE** | S. Canada to Ecuador |
| **HABITAT** | Marshes, ponds, rivers, lakes |
| **SIZE** | 8–18½ in (20–47 cm) |

The highly aggressive snapping turtle shoots its head forward with surprising speed while snapping its strong jaws. It eats all kinds of aquatic and bankside life, including fish, amphibians, mammals and birds, as well as aquatic plants. Usually found in water with plenty of aquatic vegetation, the snapping turtle lies at the bottom, concealed among plants and is an excellent swimmer. The sexes are alike, but males are slightly larger.

Snapping turtles hibernate in winter and begin nesting in early summer. The average clutch is 25 to 50 eggs, laid in a flask-shaped cavity, dug by the female. As the eggs are laid, she pushes each one into place with movements of her hind feet. The eggs incubate for 9 to 18 weeks, depending on the area and the weather; in cooler areas, the hatchlings may remain in the nest through the winter.

### Alligator Snapping Turtle *Macroclemys temmincki* **VU**

| | |
|---|---|
| **RANGE** | C. USA |
| **HABITAT** | Deep rivers, lakes |
| **SIZE** | 13–26 in (36–66 cm) |

The alligator snapping turtle has three strong ridges on the carapace and a rough-textured head and neck. The carapace is shaped, allowing the head to be raised. A resident of dark, slow-moving water, this turtle is so sedentary that algae grow on its shell, contributing to the existing camouflage of the lumpy irregular outline. It rests, practically invisible to passing fishes, with its huge mouth gaping open to reveal a pink, fleshy appendage. Unsuspecting fish come to investigate the "bait" and are swallowed whole or sliced in half by the turtle's strong jaws. It also eats crustaceans.

These turtles continue to grow after maturity and some old specimens, at over 30 in (76 cm) long and 200 lb (91 kg) in weight, are the largest freshwater turtles in the USA. They nest between April and June and lay from 15 to 50 eggs in a flask-shaped pit dug near water. The young are born with a rough-surfaced shell and the lure already in place.

### Big-headed Turtle *Platysternon megacephalum* **DD**

| | |
|---|---|
| **RANGE** | Burma, Thailand, S. China |
| **HABITAT** | Mountain streams, rivers |
| **SIZE** | 6–7 in (15–18 cm) |

Although a relatively small species in carapace length, this turtle has a huge head, almost half the width of the carapace. The head is not retractile and the carapace is slightly shaped to allow the head and the short, thick neck to be raised. The feet of this turtle are small and only partially webbed, and there are enlarged, flattened scales on the forelimbs.

The big-headed turtle is an unusually agile climber and, using its outstretched claws, it clambers over branches and rocks in search of food or a basking spot. It lays only 2 eggs at a time.

## PELOMEDUSIDAE: GREAVED TURTLE FAMILY

This family of 19 species is one of the 2 families of side-neck turtles. A side-neck retracts its head by moving it sideways under the carapace. This leaves an undefended area of the head and neck exposed, and may have prevented the evolution of any terrestrial side-necks, since they would be too vulnerable to mammalian predators. All these turtles live in fresh water in Africa, Madagascar and South America, east of the Andes.

### Arrau River Turtle *Podocnemis expansa* **LR:cd**

| | |
|---|---|
| **RANGE** | Northern South America |
| **HABITAT** | Orinoco and Amazon river systems |
| **SIZE** | 24–30 in (61–76 cm) |

The largest of the side-necks, the Arrau turtle may weigh over 100 lb (45 kg). Females of the species have wide, flattened shells and are larger and more numerous than the males. Adults feed entirely on plant food.

The nesting habits of these turtles are similar to those of sea turtles in that they gather in large numbers in order to travel to certain suitable nesting areas. The females lay their eggs on sandbanks which are exposed only in the dry season, and there are relatively few such sites. The females come out on to the sandbanks at night and each lays as many as 90 or 100 soft-shelled eggs. They then return to their feeding grounds.

The hatchlings, which are about 2 in (5 cm) long, head straight for the sea, but they emerge to the attentions of many predators and even without man's activities, only about 5 per cent ever reach the adult feeding grounds.

Uncontrolled hunting of adults and excessive collecting of eggs have seriously reduced the population of this turtle. It is now an endangered species and is protected in most areas.

## CHELIDAE: MATAMATA AND SNAKE-NECKED TURTLE FAMILY

The other family of side-neck turtles contains 30 species, found in South America, Australia and New Guinea. This family shows a number of structural advancements over the more primitive Pelomedusids. They are carnivorous animals and live in rivers and marshes.

### Matamata

*Chelus fimbriatus*

| | |
|---|---|
| **RANGE** | N. South America |
| **HABITAT** | Rivers |
| **SIZE** | 16 in (41 cm) |

The matamata is one of the most bizarre of all turtles. Its carapace is exceedingly rough and ridged and, from above, its head is flat and virtually triangular. Its eyes are tiny and positioned close to the thin, tubelike snout. Fleshy flaps at the sides of the head wave in the water, possibly attracting small fishes. The neck is thick and muscular and its mouth wide. Its limbs are small and weak.

Well camouflaged by its irregular outline, the matamata lies at the bottom of the water. It is so sedentary that algae grow on its shell. When a fish swims by, the turtle opens its huge mouth, sucking in water and fish. The mouth is then closed, leaving only a slit for the water to flow out.

Matamatas lay 12 to 28 eggs; the young have light-tan-colored carapaces.

### Murray River Turtle *Emydura macquarri*

| | |
|---|---|
| **RANGE** | S.E. Australia |
| **HABITAT** | Rivers |
| **SIZE** | 11¾ in (30 cm) |

The Murray River turtle is a well-known Australian side-neck. The shape of its carapace alters with age – hatchlings have almost circular carapaces; in juveniles, carapaces are widest at the back; and adults have virtually oval shells. The head of the Murray River turtle is quite small, with bright eyes and a light band extending back from the mouth. It is an active species and feeds on frogs, tadpoles and vegetation.

In summer it lays a clutch of between 10 and 15 eggs in a chamber dug in the river bank. These normally hatch in 10 or 11 weeks.

# TUATARA AND IGUANAS

## ORDER SPHENODONTIA

Apart from 2 species of tuatara, living in New Zealand, this order of reptiles is known only from fossils.

### SPHENODONTIDAE: TUATARA FAMILY

The sole family in the Rhynchocephalia order contains only 2 species, which are believed to be extremely similar to related species alive 130 million years ago. The scientific name means "the wedge-toothed ones" and refers to the sharp teeth, fused into both jawbones.

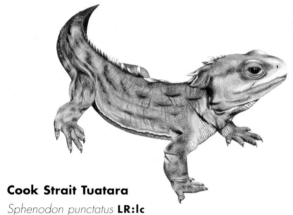

**Cook Strait Tuatara**

*Sphenodon punctatus* **LR:lc**

| | |
|---|---|
| **RANGE** | New Zealand |
| **HABITAT** | Woods with little undergrowth |
| **SIZE** | Up to 25½ in (65 cm) |

A powerfully built reptile, the tuatara has a large head and a crest running from its head down its back. The male is generally larger than the female. Active at dusk and at night, the tuatara has the least need of warmth of any reptile – it is quite content at 53°F (12°C) whereas most reptiles prefer over 77°F (25°C). Its metabolism and growth rate are correspondingly slow.

Tuataras are ground-living and shelter in burrows which they dig in loose soil or take over from shearwaters. They feed on crickets, earthworms, snails, young birds and lizards.

The female tuatara lays up to 15 eggs in a hole she digs in the soil. They hatch 13 to 15 months later – the longest development time of any reptile. She probably does not breed every year. Tuataras are long-lived and probably do not attain sexual maturity until they are about 20 years old. Once in danger of extinction from introduced predators, healthy tuatara populations now live in special island sanctuaries and are protected by conservation laws.

## ORDER SQUAMATA

The largest reptilian order, the Squamata includes all the lizards, snakes and amphisbaenians – over 6,000 species.

### IGUANIDAE: IGUANA FAMILY

There are more than 600 species in this family. The vast majority live in the Americas, though there are a few species in Madagascar and Fiji. They are the New World equivalents of the Old World agamid lizards. The two families never occur together.

Most iguanas are ground or tree-living and feed on insects and small invertebrates. Many are brightly colored and perform elaborate courtship displays.

**Common Iguana** *Iguana iguana*

| | |
|---|---|
| **RANGE** | Central and N. South America; introduced into USA: Florida |
| **HABITAT** | Forest, trees near water |
| **SIZE** | 3¼–6½ ft (1–2 m) |

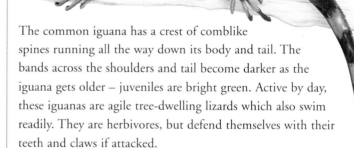

The common iguana has a crest of comblike spines running all the way down its body and tail. The bands across the shoulders and tail become darker as the iguana gets older – juveniles are bright green. Active by day, these iguanas are agile tree-dwelling lizards which also swim readily. They are herbivores, but defend themselves with their teeth and claws if attacked.

In autumn, the female lays 28 to 40 eggs in a hole she digs in the ground. The eggs hatch in about 3 months.

**Eastern Fence Lizard** *Sceloporus undulatus*

| | |
|---|---|
| **RANGE** | USA: Virginia to Florida, west to New Mexico; Mexico |
| **HABITAT** | Open woodland, grassland |
| **SIZE** | 3½–7¾ in (9–20 cm) |

This iguana occurs in many subspecies, with varying coloration over its range, but it always has a characteristic roughened surface because of its keeled scales. Either arboreal or terrestrial, depending on its habitat, it is active during the day and feeds on most insects (particularly beetles) as well as spiders, centipedes and snails.

The courting male holds a territory which he vigorously defends against competitors while he attracts his mate. The female lays 3 to 12 eggs under a log or other debris and may produce up to four clutches a season.

### Chuckwalla *Sauromalus obesus*

**RANGE**  USA: S. California, Nevada, Utah, Arizona; Mexico

**HABITAT**  Rocky desert

**SIZE**  11–16½ in (28–42 cm)

A dark-skinned, plump-bodied lizard, the chuckwalla has a thick, pale yellow tail with a blunt tip. The male tends to be darker than the female, with some red or yellow speckling on the body, while females and juveniles often have dark crossbands. The chuckwalla hides under a rock or in a crevice during the night and emerges in the morning to bask in the sun and warm its body. An herbivorous lizard, it then searches for leaves, buds and flowers to eat, often feeding on the creosote bush.

The chuckwalla is well adapted for desert life. In the folds of skin on its sides are accessory lymph glands in which it can store liquid, when it is available, for use in prolonged dry seasons. The female is thought to breed every other year and lays 5 to 10 eggs at a time.

### Green Anole *Anolis carolinensis*

**RANGE**  USA: Virginia to Florida, west to Texas

**HABITAT**  Forest edge, roadsides

**SIZE**  4¾–7¾ in (12–20 cm)

The green anole has a slender body and long toe pads as an adaptation for its tree-dwelling habits. Although usually green, it can turn brown in seconds. It is active during the day and feeds on insects and spiders.

The remarkable pink, fanlike flap on the throat of the male is used in courtship display. His display triggers sexual receptivity and ovulation in the female. She lays her eggs, one at a time, at 2-week intervals throughout the breeding season, from April to September. The eggs hatch in 5 to 7 weeks.

### Collared Lizard
*Crotaphytus collaris*

**RANGE**  USA: Utah, Colorado, south to Texas; Mexico

**HABITAT**  Rocky hillsides, forest

**SIZE**  7¾–14 in (20–35.5 cm)

The robust collared lizard has a large head and a distinctive collar of dark and light markings. Active in the daytime, this species particularly likes to bask in the sun around rocks where there are crevices where it can readily take refuge. It feeds on insects and small lizards.

The female collared lizard lays a clutch of up to 12 eggs in midsummer. The young, measuring about 3½ in (9 cm) long, hatch 2 to 3 months later.

### Texas Horned Lizard *Phrynosoma cornutum*

**RANGE**  USA: Kansas to Texas, Arizona; introduced in Florida

**HABITAT**  Arid country

**SIZE**  2¼–7 in (6–18 cm)

The well-armored Texas horned lizard has a flattened body with pointed scales fringing each side. Behind its head are two enlarged horns, flanked by enlarged scales. In its arid habitat, it may bury itself under loose soil or seek refuge under bushes. It feeds largely on ants.

The female lizard digs a hole in which she lays her 14 to 36 eggs in midsummer; the eggs hatch in about 6 weeks.

### Forest Iguana *Polychrus gutterosus*

**RANGE**  Tropical South America

**HABITAT**  Forest

**SIZE**  Up to 19¾ in (50 cm) including tail of up to 14½ in (37 cm)

A tree-dwelling iguana, this long-legged lizard lies on a branch, its flattened body pressed inconspicuously to the surface, waiting for its insect prey. It is a good climber, and is able to hold on to a branch with its hind legs alone, but it is slow-moving.

The female forest iguana lays clutches of between 7 and 8 eggs.

# IGUANAS CONTINUED

### Marine Iguana

*Amblyrhynchus cristatus* **VU**

**RANGE** Galápagos Islands

**HABITAT** Lava rocks on coasts

**SIZE** 4–5 ft (1.2–1.5 m)

The only present-day lizard to use the sea as a major habitat, the marine iguana swims and dives readily as it forages for seaweed, its main food. Vital adaptations to marine life are the nasal glands that remove the excess salt the iguana takes in with its food; the salt is expelled in a thin shower of water vapor which the iguana blows out through its nose. When swimming, the iguana uses its powerful tail for propulsion; its feet are normally held against the body, but they are sometimes used to steer a course. The iguana cannot breathe under water, but when it dives, its heart rate slows down, reducing the blood flow through the body and thus conserving the limited supplies of oxygen.

Male marine iguanas are highly territorial and fight to defend their own small areas of breeding territory on the shore. The combat is ritualistic, each individual trying to overthrow the other by butting him with his head. In one race of marine iguanas, breeding males develop green crests and red flanks. After mating, the female finds a sandy area in which to bury her eggs. She digs a hole about 12 in (30.5 cm) deep, lays 2 or 3 eggs and covers them with sand. The eggs incubate for about 112 days.

Numbers of these once abundant creatures have been reduced by predators, introduced by settlers and sailors. Previously there were no native mammalian predators to threaten their existence.

### Galápagos Land Iguana *Conolophus subcristatus* **VU**

**RANGE** Galápagos Islands

**HABITAT** Arid land coasts to volcanoes

**SIZE** Up to 4 ft (1.2 m)

Once common on all of the Galápagos islands, this iguana is now extinct in some and rare in others. Many have been shot for food or sport, and others have suffered from the ravages of introduced predators. Conservation measures have now been established in a bid to save this iguana.

A stout-bodied animal with a rounded tail, the land iguana is generally yellow or brown, sometimes with irregular spots on the body. It has a crest at the back of the neck, and older individuals have rolls of fat around the neck. It lives in arid land where there is some vegetation and where it can dig into the soil to make a burrow for shelter. Plants, including cacti, are its main food, it may also eat some small animals. Breeding females lay clutches of about 9 eggs.

### Basilisk Lizard *Basiliscus plumifrons*

**RANGE** South America

**HABITAT** Forest

**SIZE** 31½ in (80 cm)

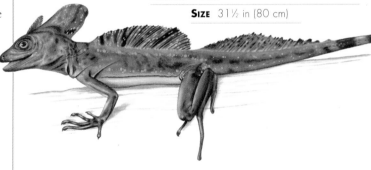

Male basilisk lizards sport prominent, impressive crests on back and tail and bony casques on the head. The 5 species in the genus are all extremely alike and can be distinguished only by the characteristic shapes of the head casques of the males; these casques are poorly developed in females and absent in juveniles.

The long-legged basilisks are among the few four-legged animals to run on two legs. They rear up on their hind legs and run in a semierect position, with the long tail held up to help balance. This counterweighting effect is vital and if too much of the tail is amputated the iguana is unable to rise up on its hind legs. Adults have achieved speeds of 6.8 mph (11 km/h) but only over short distances. Basilisks can even run a few yards over smooth water, held up by the surface film, and then swim when it is no longer possible for them to remain on the surface.

Active in the daytime, basilisks feed on fruit and small animals, often climbing into trees to find food. In the breeding season, females lay 10 to 15 eggs which incubate for about 80 days.

## Rhinoceros Iguana *Cyclura cornuta* **VU**

**RANGE** Haiti and other islands of the Lesser Antilles

**HABITAT** Arid scrub

**SIZE** Up to 4 ft (1.2 m)

The male rhinoceros iguana is easily identified by the characteristic protuberances on the tip of his snout that are formed from enlarged scales. The female has only small, inconspicuous protuberances.

A large, powerful species, this iguana has a strong tail and a somewhat compressed body. Some individuals, particularly old males, develop rolls of fat at the back of the head. There are many races of rhinoceros iguana with only minor physical variations. They are among the most primitive iguanas.

Rhinoceros iguanas live on land, among thorn bushes and cacti, and feed on plants, worms and mice. Breeding females lay clutches of about 12 eggs which incubate for 120 days or more. In some islands of the Lesser Antilles this iguana has been displaced by the common iguana which has recently become established there.

## Spiny-tailed Iguana *Ctenosaura pectinata*

**RANGE** Mexico, Central America

**HABITAT** Forest

**SIZE** 3¼ ft (1 m)

A land-dwelling lizard, the spiny-tailed iguana is so called because its tail is ringed with spiny scales, making it an effective weapon. These iguanas feed mainly on plant material, particularly on beans, but also catch some small animals. Their diet is rich in potassium salts, and they are equipped with nasal glands in order to excrete excess salt, which then collects as encrustations round the nostrils.

Highly gregarious and territorial, these iguanas live in colonies, ruled by a strict pecking order. One male in the colony is dominant and, although the other males also hold territories, they will only defend them against one another although not against the leader.

In the breeding season, females dig burrows in which to lay their clutches of about 50 eggs.

## Fijian Banded Iguana *Brachylophus fasciatus* **EN**

**RANGE** Islands of Fiji and Tonga

**HABITAT** Woodland, forest

**SIZE** 35½ in (90 cm)

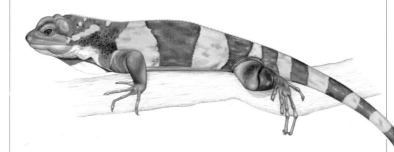

One of the few iguana species found outside the Americas, the Fijian iguana has an extremely long tail, often more than twice the length of its slender body. It sports a low crest along its back.

An arboreal iguana, its elongate fingers and toes are equipped with sharp claws for climbing. The female has a uniformly green body, while the male is banded with lighter green and has light spots on his neck. They feed on leaves and other plant material.

The Fijian iguana is a little-known species that may be nearing extinction because of the destruction of much of its forest habitat and the introduction into its range of mongooses, which prey on the iguana and its eggs.

## Madagascan Iguana *Oplurus* sp.

**RANGE** Madagascar, small offshore islands

**HABITAT** Forest

**SIZE** Up to 15 in (38 cm)

There are 2 iguana genera in Madagascar – Oplurus and Chalarodon. The 6 species of Oplurus are all similar in appearance, with rings of spiny scales on their tapering tails. Chalarodon species are easily distinguished by their small crests, which Oplurus species lack and their smooth-scaled tails.

Although primarily land-dwelling, these iguanas can climb and often take refuge in bushes and trees when danger threatens.

# AGAMID LIZARDS

## AGAMIDAE: AGAMID LIZARD FAMILY

The agamid family contains more than 300 species of plump-bodied lizards, found throughout the warmer regions of the Old World except in Madagascar and New Zealand.

Most agamids have thin tails, long legs and triangular-shaped heads. They live on the ground, in trees or among rocks and feed mainly on insects and other small invertebrates, but also on some plant matter.

### Common Agama *Agama agama*

**RANGE** Central Africa

**HABITAT** Tropical forest

**SIZE** 4¾ in (12 cm)

Agamas live in groups of 2 to 25 in a defined territory, ruled by one dominant male. They are active during the day, emerging at dawn to bask in the sun and feed, mainly on insects. If the dominant male is challenged by another male, he adopts a threat posture, bobbing his head, raising his body off the ground and spreading the folds of his neck skin as far as possible.

Mating usually coincides with the rainy season, when the earth is sufficiently moist for the female agamid to make her nest. She digs a small hole in damp soil in which she lays 4 to 6 eggs. She covers the eggs over and smooths the ground surface to conceal the nest. While they develop, the eggs absorb moisture from the soil. The young hatch in 2 or 3 months.

### Flying Dragon *Draco volans*

**RANGE** Philippines to Malaysia and Indonesia

**HABITAT** Rain forest, rubber plantations

**SIZE** 7½–8½ in (19–22 cm)

An arboreal lizard, the so-called flying dragon actually glides from tree to tree on winglike skin flaps. At each side of its body, between front and hind limbs, there is a large flap of skin supported by extended movable ribs. Usually these flaps are held folded at the sides of the body, but they can be extended to carry the lizard in an almost horizontal glide for many meters. The flying dragon feeds on insects, particularly ants.

To breed, the flying dragon descends to the ground and buries its 1 to 4 eggs in the soil.

### Frilled Lizard *Chlamydosaurus kingii*

**RANGE** Australia: N. Western Australia, N. Northern Territory, E. Queensland; New Guinea

**HABITAT** Dry forest, woodland

**SIZE** 26 in (66 cm) including tail of 17¼ in (44 cm)

This slender, long-tailed lizard has an extraordinary rufflike collar of skin around its neck which may be as much as 10 in (25.5 cm) in diameter. Normally this collar lies in folds around the neck and shoulders, but if alarmed, the lizard opens its mouth wide and at the same time the brightly colored frill erects, giving the animal a startling appearance and making it look larger than it really is in order to intimidate the enemy.

Active in the daytime, the frilled lizard forages in trees and on the ground for insects and other small animals.

### Thorny Devil *Moloch horridus*

**RANGE** Australia: W., N. and S., Queensland

**HABITAT** Arid scrub, desert

**SIZE** 6¼ in (16 cm)

The grotesque thorny devil is the only species in its genus and one of the strangest of lizards. Its body bristles with large, conical spines. It also has spines above each eye and a spiny hump behind its head. The tail, too, is covered in spines. The thorny devil is a slow-moving creature which forages for its food, mainly ants and termites, on the ground.

The female thorny devil lays 3 to 10 eggs, usually 8, in November or December. The newly hatched young are tiny, spiny replicas of their parents.

## Soa-soa Water Dragon

*Hydrosaurus amboinensis*

**RANGE** New Guinea,
Moluccas, Sulawesi

**HABITAT** Rain forest

**SIZE** 43¼ in (110 cm),
including tail of 29½ in (75 cm)

One of the largest agamids, the soa-soa is a powerfully built lizard with strong forefeet. The adult male has a showy crest on the base of the tail which can be erected, supported by bony extensions of the tail vertebrae. As its name suggests, this is an aquatic lizard, which is usually found close to rivers. It can swim well, propelling itself with its laterally compressed tail, and it will run on its hind legs on land.

Despite its formidable appearance, the soa-soa feeds largely on plants, particularly tender leaves, it also consumes insects and millipedes. It reproduces by laying eggs.

## Eastern Water Dragon

*Physignathus leseueri*

**RANGE** E. Australia

**HABITAT** Coasts, forested slopes

**SIZE** 28¾ in (73 cm), including tail 19¾ in (50 cm)

The eastern water dragon varies in coloration over its wide range, but always has a long, powerful tail and a crest running along the length of its body and tail. A semiaquatic, tree-living lizard, it lies on a branch overhanging a river or stream and, if disturbed, will tumble down into the water. It also forages on rocky seashores. Its diet is varied, including insects, small aquatic animals (such as frogs) terrestrial animals and fruit and berries. The breeding female lays about 8 eggs under a rock or in a burrow she digs in the soil. The eggs hatch in 10 to 14 weeks.

## Arabian Toad-headed Agamid *Phrynocephalus nejdensis*

**RANGE** S.W. Asia

**HABITAT** Desert, semidesert

**SIZE** Up to 5 in (12.5 cm)

The Arabian toad-headed agamid has a rounded head, long slender legs and a tapering tail. It is a burrowing lizard and digs short tunnels for shelter; it also buries itself in sand by wriggling from side to side. If alarmed it adopts a defence posture, with tail raised. It then rolls and unrolls its tail. It eats mainly insects and some flowers, fruit and leaves. Females lay several clutches of eggs during the year.

## Bearded Dragon *Amphibolurus barbatus*

**RANGE** Australia: E. and S.E. (except Cape York Peninsula and Tasmania)

**HABITAT** Arid land to forest

**SIZE** 17½ in (44.5 cm) including tail of 7¾ in (19.5 cm)

This large, formidable-looking lizard is adorned with spiny scales above its ears, at the back of its head and behind its mouth. On its body are a mixture of small and enlarged keeled scales. Adults have throat pouches or beards which are bordered with spiny scales. Most bearded dragons are semiarboreal and feed on insects, flowers and soft plant growth in low vegetation.

The female bearded dragon lays 10 to 20 eggs in a nest which she digs in the soil. She covers the eggs with soil and, warmed by the sun, they incubate in the pit for about 3 months.

## Princely Mastigure *Uromastyx princeps*

**RANGE** Africa: Somali Republic

**HABITAT** Rocky, stony land

**SIZE** About 9 in (23 cm)

A plump-bodied lizard, the princely mastigure has a short, thick tail, studded with large spines, and a small turtlelike head. It is active by day, sheltering at night in holes or crevices in the rocks. Grass, flowers, fruit and leaves are its main foods. If attacked, it defends itself against the enemy with its spiny tail, lashing it to and fro.

# CHAMELEONS

## CHAMAELEONIDAE: CHAMELEON FAMILY

The chameleons are probably the most specialized group of tree-living lizards, superbly adapted in both structural and behavioral ways. About 85 species are known; most live in Africa and Madagascar, but a few occur in Asia and there is one European species. Although primarily an arboreal group, a few species are ground-living.

Most chameleons are between 6 and 11¾ in (15 and 30 cm) long, but a few are smaller, and one species in Madagascar reaches 27½ to 31½ in (70 to 80 cm). Whatever their size, all chameleons are recognizable by certain characteristic attributes. The typical chameleon has a body which is flattened from side to side; the head often has prominent crests or horns, and the large eyes are protuberant and can be moved independently of one another to locate insect prey. The toes on hind and forefeet are arranged to provide a pincerlike grip on branches. Each foot divides clearly, with three toes on one side and two on the other. The muscular prehensile tail can be curled around a branch and helps the chameleon to stay immobile as it watches for prey.

Although several groups of lizards are able to change the color of their skins usually for camouflage purposes, the chameleon is the most accomplished. Camouflage helps the chameleon in its slow, stalking approach to prey animals and also helps to hide it from predators. The mechanism behind the chameleon's color change abilities is complex. The pattern of pigmentation in the skin cells is controlled by the nervous system, and pigment can be spread out or contracted, thus lightening or darkening the skin. The strength of the light seems to be the most important influence on the mechanism.

Perhaps, however, the most extraordinary adaptive feature of the chameleons is their protrusible tongue. It can be shot out, from its tongue-bone support, to capture insects a body-length away from the reptile; at the tip of the tongue is a sticky pad to which the insect adheres. The chameleon has superb eyesight, which enables it to take accurate aim at the prey.

Chameleons generally reproduce by laying eggs, which the mother buries in a hole in the ground. A few African species, however, give birth to live young. In these forms, completely developed young chameleons grow inside their egg membranes, but free themselves from these enclosures immediately after the eggs are laid.

## Jackson's Chameleon *Chamaeleo jacksonii*

**RANGE** E. Africa: Uganda, Tanzania to N. Mozambique

**HABITAT** Savanna vegetation

**SIZE** 4¼–4¾ in (11–12 cm)

The three prominent horns on his head make the male Jackson's chameleon instantly recognizable. The female has only one small horn on the snout and rudimentary horns by each eye. Usually colored a drab green, this chameleon resembles lichen on the bark of a tree.

One of the live-bearing species in the chameleon family, the female Jackson's chameleon may carry 20 to 40 eggs, but only 10 or so young ever actually survive. At birth, the young are about 2¼ in (5.5 cm) long and have two tiny horns in front of the eyes and a conical scale in the position of the middle horn.

## Meller's Chameleon *Chamaeleo melleri*

**RANGE** E. Africa: Tanzania, Malawi

**HABITAT** Savanna vegetation

**SIZE** 21¼–2¾ in (54–58 cm) including tail of 11–11½ in (28–29 cm)

The largest chameleon found outside Madagascar, the male Meller's chameleon has only a tiny snout horn which is also present in the female. Its body is distinctively marked with broad yellow stripes and black spots. As it sits on a branch, the chameleon often sways slightly, as a leaf might in a breeze, and this, combined with its camouflaging coloration and patterning, makes it extremely hard to detect in foliage, despite its large size. Meller's chameleons feed on small birds, as well as on insects.

## Flap-necked Chameleon *Chamaeleo dilepis*

**RANGE** Tropical and S. Africa

**HABITAT** Forest, scrubland

**SIZE** 9¾–14¼ in (25–36.5 cm)

This aggressive chameleon has lobes of membranous skin at the back of its head which it erects in threat when it meets another member of its own species. It may raise only the lobe on the side of the opponent. A tree- and bush-dwelling species, it descends to the ground only to move from one tree to another or to lay eggs. Its coloration varies with the background, being green when among leaves and yellow or reddish-brown when on bark. When angry or alarmed, for example when confronting the boomslang (tree snake), its main enemy the chameleon turns dark blackish-green with yellow and white spots and makes hissing sounds.

The female lays 30 to 40 eggs in a hole she digs in the ground and then conceals the nest with grass and twigs. The eggs hatch in about 3 months.

## European Chameleon *Chamaeleo chamaeleon*

**RANGE** S. Spain and Portugal, Crete, N. Africa, Canary Islands

**HABITAT** Bushes in dry country

**SIZE** 9¾–11 in (25–28 cm)

The only chameleon to occur in Europe, this species is usually yellowish-brown with dark bands on the body, but may turn green among grass or other green vegetation. When alarmed, it turns very dark and inflates its body with air so as to appear larger than its true size. In vegetated areas, this chameleon lives in bushes and descends to the ground only to lay eggs. In North Africa, however, in areas of sparse plant growth, it is a ground-dweller and lives in holes, which it digs itself, on the outskirts of oases. It feeds on insects, particularly locusts.

At mating time, males fight one another for females, and paired males and females may also fight. The female lays 20 to 30 eggs which she buries in the ground.

## *Brookesia spectrum*

**RANGE** Cameroon, Gabon to E. Africa

**HABITAT** Forest floor

**SIZE** 3–3½ in (7.5–9 cm)

This tiny, dusty-brown chameleon closely resembles the dead leaves among which it lives on the forest floor. The effect is enhanced by the stumpy tail, little peaks on the head and body and the irregular lines on the body which mimic leaf veins. There are two tiny appendages on the snout. Its legs are extremely thin and bony and the tail is not prehensile – as a ground-living chameleon it has no need of the fifth limb. It rarely changes color; it has little need being so well camouflaged already. Like all chameleons, it moves slowly and deliberately and may remain still for hours. It feeds on insects.

Little is known of the breeding habits, but females are believed to lay 3 to 6 eggs in a clutch.

## *Rhampholeon marshalli*

**RANGE** Africa: Zimbabwe, Mozambique

**HABITAT** Forest on mountain slopes

**SIZE** 1¼–3 in (3.5–7.5 cm)

The shape of this chameleon, with its flattened body and highly arched back, contributes to its leaflike appearance as it sits, swaying gently from side to side as if blowing in the wind. Rows of light-colored tubercles scattered over the body are particularly prominent in males. Females are usually twice the size of males. Much of this chameleon's life is spent among the leaf litter of the forest floor.

The female lays 12 to 18 eggs.

# GECKOS

## GEKKONIDAE: GECKO FAMILY

Throughout the tropical, subtropical and warm temperate zones of the world are distributed some 700 species of gecko. These lizards may inhabit forests, swamps, deserts or mountainous areas; in fact, any place with sufficient insect life for them to feed on and where nights do not become too cold. They range in size from 2 to 11¾ in (5 to 30 cm), although most are between 2¾ and 6 in (7 and 15 cm) long.

The typical gecko has a flattened head and a body with soft skin, containing many minute scales. Most are nocturnal and have enormous eyes, each with a permanently closed transparent eyelid. Many have "friction pads" of specialized scales under the toes which enable them to climb easily up vertical surfaces and even to walk upside down, on a ceiling for instance.

The males of many of the nocturnal species are among the most vocal lizards and make loud, repetitive calls. Females lay only 1 to 3 eggs at a time but may breed several times a year. The eggs of most geckos are harder shelled than those of other lizards; they are soft when laid and harden with exposure to air.

### Tokay Gecko *Gekko gekko*

| | |
|---|---|
| **RANGE** | Asia, Indonesia |
| **HABITAT** | In or near houses |
| **SIZE** | 11 in (28 cm) |

One of the largest and most common geckos, the tokay gecko is believed to bring good luck to the houses that it frequents. It eats insects, particularly cockroaches, and young lizards, mice and small birds, all of which it seizes in its powerful jaws. The male makes his loud barking call, "tokeh" or "gekoh", most frequently in the mating season; the female is mute.

The female tokay gecko lays 2 sticky-surfaced eggs, which are usually stuck fast to a perpendicular object and are almost impossible to remove without breaking. Eggs are laid in the same locations year after year, and it is common to find 8 to 10 sets of eggs together, all laid by different females and in various stages of incubation.

### White-spotted Gecko *Tarentola annularis*

| | |
|---|---|
| **RANGE** | Africa: Libya, Egypt, Sudan, Ethiopia, Somalia |
| **HABITAT** | Trees, rocks, ruins in semidesert |
| **SIZE** | 8 in (20.5 cm) |

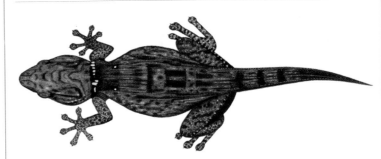

The body color of these geckos varies according to the surface that they are on. Geckos on the black rocks above the first Nile Cataract are black, however, those found on white-washed walls are almost white.

Aggressive, active creatures, they feed primarily on insects but also eat spiders and lizards. They are able to survive long periods without water, although they drink eagerly when the opportunity presents itself.

Mating is triggered by the arrival of the rains, and the female gecko lays her eggs in a crevice or hole in a rock or wall.

### Leopard Gecko *Eublepharius macularius*

| | |
|---|---|
| **RANGE** | Afghanistan, S. Turkestan, Pakistan, W. India |
| **HABITAT** | Dry, rocky regions |
| **SIZE** | Up to 11¾ in (30 cm) |

Also known as the panther gecko, this chunky lizard has a spotted body and a large head. Unlike most geckos, which have fused transparent eyelids, this species is one of the few with movable eyelids – a primitive characteristic in the gecko family. Its legs are long and thin and it holds its body well off the ground when it runs. Leopard geckos feed on grasshoppers, scorpions, beetles and spiders. They are nocturnal and hide during the day under rocks or in burrows in the sand.

During the year, the female gecko usually lays several clutches, each of 2 eggs.

### Web-footed Gecko
*Palmatogecko rangei*

**RANGE** S.W. Africa: Namib Desert

**HABITAT** Sand dunes, rocks

**SIZE** 5 in (12.5 cm)

This extremely rare species, which lives on the seaward slopes of the Namib Desert where rain is almost unknown, absorbs moisture from the sea breezes and from the mists that roll in from the sea. It laps dew from the stones and licks its own eyes for moisture.

Since this gecko lives on the ground, it has no need of friction pads on its feet for climbing vertical surfaces; instead its almost clawless toes are connected by webs which act like snowshoes in the soft sand. When running, the gecko holds its body well off the hot ground, and its feet leave little or no trace of its movements. The webbed feet are also used for burrowing into the sand to escape from predators or from the blistering sun. The gecko makes a chamber in which it lies with its head facing the entrance, waiting to pounce on the termites, beetles, flies and worms that are its main food. If a predator should try to pull it out, the gecko clings to the side of the chamber with its strong tail, engaging in a tug-of-war.

### Kuhl's Gecko *Ptychozoon kuhli*

**RANGE** S.E. Asia, Indonesia, Borneo

**HABITAT** Forest

**SIZE** 6 in (15 cm)

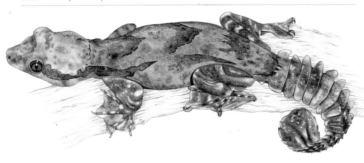

Geckos of this genus, often known as the fringed or "flying" geckos, have fringes of skin along the sides of the head, limbs, body and tail, and webs between the toes. When jumping or falling from trees, the gecko extends its legs and tail to expand the flaps and uses them like a parachute. Perhaps even more important is the camouflage the fringes give as the gecko rests on the branch of a tree. It presses the skin flaps down against the bark, thus removing any shadows and breaking up its outline.

The female Kuhl's gecko lays her eggs in November. The eggs, coated with a sticky substance when laid, adhere to each other and to the branch of the tree and gradually develop a hard shell. The young geckos hatch the following May.

### Marbled Gecko *Phyllodactylus porphyreus*

**RANGE** South Africa, Australia

**HABITAT** Arid mountain slopes

**SIZE** 4½ in (11.5 cm)

This active little gecko lives in cracks in rocks or beneath stones and varies in coloration according to its surroundings. It feeds on insects and is often parasitized by mites.

The female marbled gecko lays her eggs under a stone or on a tree, where they remain until they hatch out approximately 115 days later. The newly hatched young are about ¾ in (2 cm) long, with tails that are over half their body length.

### Brook's Gecko *Hemidactylus brookii*

**RANGE** Asia, Africa, South America, East and West Indies

**HABITAT** Coastal plains to upland savanna to 7,000 ft (2,100 m)

**SIZE** 6 in (15 cm)

This unusually widespread gecko lives under stones, in cracks in rocks, in abandoned termite mounds, beneath fallen tree trunks and even under heaps of garden debris.

With its sharply curving claws, it climbs with great agility up even vertical surfaces. It feeds on insects and at night will enter houses to prey on those which are attracted to the light.

It is difficult to ascertain the exact length of this species since adults rarely have their long tails intact, although the tail breaks off easily, muscles in the main tail artery contract speedily in order to prevent any undue loss of blood.

In the breeding season the female Brook's gecko lays 2 eggs.

# GECKOS AND SCALY-FOOT LIZARDS

**Leaf-tailed Gecko** *Uroplatus fimbriatus*

**RANGE** Madagascar

**HABITAT** Forest

**SIZE** 8 in (20.5 cm)

A flat-bodied gecko with large bulging eyes, the leaf-tailed gecko's mottled body blends excellently with bark or lichen. It lies with its body pressed against a branch or trunk of a tree and the small scales bordering its legs and sides reduce any shadow. In addition to this camouflage, it can change the intensity of its coloration, becoming darker by night and lighter again in the morning. When alarmed, it turns dark brown or black. The broad, flat tail can be rolled up dorsally – toward the back – and is used as a fifth limb for holding on to branches.

Mainly active at night, this gecko feeds on insects. Each individual has a preferred resting place where, after a meal, it retires to clean itself, using its tongue to lick over its whole body, even the eyes.

**Green Day Gecko** *Heteropholis manukanus*

**RANGE** N. New Zealand

(Marlborough Sound, Stephens Island)

**HABITAT** Forest, scrub

**SIZE** 5–6½ in (12.5–16.5 cm)

Unlike most geckos, the green day gecko is active in the daytime when it forages in trees for insects and small invertebrates. It is found mainly on the manuka, or tea tree, (*Leptospermum scoparium*). Its bright green coloration has yellow undertones, and the female's belly is yellowish green, the male's bluish green. In both sexes the soles of the feet

are a yellowish shade. The head is large in size and the snout deep and blunt.

Most geckos lay eggs, but the female of this species gives birth to 2, occasionally only 1, live young. The young are similar in appearance to the adults.

Numbers of these geckos have fallen because large areas of their forest and scrub habitat have been cleared for development.

*Phelsuma vinsoni*

**RANGE** Mauritius and neighboring islands

**HABITAT** Forest

**SIZE** 6¾ in (17.5 cm)

An unusual gecko species with its vivid coloration, the male *Phelsuma vinsoni* has bright red spots on a blue and green back and brown lines on the head and neck region. The female has similar patterning but is less vivid and is tinged with brown or gray. This gecko is also unusual in that it is active during the day; most are nocturnal. A good climber, it is often found on screwpine trees, the fruit of which attracts the insects on which it feeds. Fruit such as bananas and the nectar of flowers sometimes supplement the gecko's diet.

The female gecko lays 2 sticky-surfaced eggs which are usually left attached to a branch; several females may lay their eggs together. They hatch after 9 to 12 weeks, depending on the temperature, and the young geckos measure about 4¾ in (12 cm).

## PYGOPODIDAE: SCALY-FOOT LIZARD FAMILY

The scaly-foots, or snake lizards, are one of the groups of lizards which, although they are limbless and snakelike, are anatomically different from true snakes. There are 30 or so known species, all found in Australia or New Guinea.

Although externally so similar to snakes, the scaly-foots are, in fact, most closely related to geckos and share certain characteristics with them, such as fused eyelids and their ability to make sounds. Their hind limbs are present as vestigial scaly flaps, and the tail is extremely long. The flat, fleshy tongue is slightly forked and can be extended well out of the mouth.

**Burton's Snake-lizard** *Lialis burtonis*

**RANGE** Australia: central areas, Queensland; New Guinea

**HABITAT** Semidesert, rain forest

**SIZE** Up to 24 in (61 cm)

The most widespread species of its family, this snake-lizard is able to adapt to the contrasting habitats of rain forest and semidesert. A ground-dweller, it hides in clumps of grass or under plant debris. Its color and pattern vary but they are not related to geographical distribution, and it always has a distinctive brown stripe on each side of the head. The snout is long and pointed.

Active during both day and night, Burton's snake-lizard feeds on insects, skinks and other small lizards. Its long pointed, backward-curving teeth enable it to overcome quite large prey, which it seizes with a quick snap of its jaws and swallows whole.

Unlike other snake-lizards, which make geckolike barks or soft squeaks, this lizard emits a long drawn-out note. The female lays 2 or 3 large elongate eggs which have parchmentlike shells.

**Hooded Scaly-foot** *Pygopus nigriceps*

**RANGE** Western Australia

**HABITAT** Dry inland country, coastal forest

**SIZE** 18 in (46 cm)

Also known as the black-headed or western scaly-foot, this species has a tail that is slightly longer than its body and a rounded snout. The hind limbs are present as scaly flaps, each containing miniature leg bones and four toes. These flaps usually lie flat against the body, but when the animal is handled or injured, they are held out at right angles.

If threatened, the hooded scaly-foot mimics the poisonous elapid snake *Denisonia gouldii*, to try to deter its enemy. It draws back its head, bends its neck into an S-shape, puffs out its throat slightly and hisses. It feeds on insects and small lizards and is most active at dusk and at night. The female lays 2 eggs.

*Delma nasuta*

**RANGE** Australia: Western and Northern Territories, South Australia

**HABITAT** Sandy and stony desert, arid scrub

**SIZE** 11¾ in (30 cm) including tail of 8½ in (22 cm)

The 3 species of scaly-foot in the genus *Delma* are all slender bodied and move exactly like snakes. They resemble the smaller elapid snakes of Australia. These scaly-foot lizards feed on insects and small lizards both at night and during the day, but species living in the hot desert areas of central Australia are strictly nocturnal. The hind limbs are present as tiny but movable flaps which are held against the body.

The female lays 2 eggs.

*Aprasia striolata*

**RANGE** Australia: isolated populations in S. W. Western Australia, S. Australia to W. Victoria; Northern Territory

**HABITAT** Varied, sandy or loamy soils

**SIZE** 6 in (15 cm)

There are 4 species in the genus *Aprasia*, all of which are alike in habits and appearance. A small burrowing creature, this species has a rounded snout and inconspicuous flaps which are vestiges of its hind limbs. Its tail is short. This lizard feeds on insects and lizards and is mainly active in the daytime. The females of this genus of lizard generally lay clutches of 2 eggs at a time.

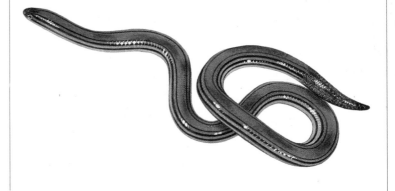

# BURROWING LIZARDS AND TEIID LIZARDS

## DIBAMIDAE: OLD WORLD BURROWING LIZARD FAMILY

This small family contains only 3 species of small, wormlike, limbless lizards, all in the genus *Dibamus*. They live in parts of Southeast Asia, the Philippines and New Guinea.

### *Dibamus novaeguineae*

**RANGE** New Guinea

**HABITAT** Forest

**SIZE** Up to 11¾ in (30 cm)

All three *Dibamus* species are blind limbless lizards, specialized for a burrowing, underground life. The body is wormlike and the eyes and ears are covered by skin. The nostrils are positioned on an enlarged scale at the tip of the snout, and the teeth are small and backward curving. The male has stumplike vestiges of hind limbs that are used for clasping the female during mating. Dibamids will burrow into rotting logs as well as soil. Little is known of their habits. Eggs, which were probably dibamid eggs, have been discovered in rotting logs and forest floor humus.

## TEIIDAE: TEIID LIZARD FAMILY

There are about 80 species in this exclusively American family, the majority of which live in South America. Teiids are slender lizards with thin, whiplike tails and characteristic long, deeply divided tongues, which they use to search for food. Most species have scales on the back and belly.

In many ways, teiids represent the New World equivalent of the lacertid lizards. Most species are ground-living, feeding on a variety of small animals, but some have become specialized for a particular way of life, for example the caiman lizard, which is semiaquatic and feeds on snails.

Teiids reproduce by laying eggs. Most must mate first in the normal way, but in a few unisexual species no mating is necessary. In these teiids, all individuals are female and can lay eggs, which do not need to be fertilized and which hatch into more females, so completely dispensing with the need for males.

### Caiman Lizard *Dracaena guianensis*

**RANGE** N.E. South America

**HABITAT** Swampy flooded ground, often woodland bordering rivers

**SIZE** 4 ft (1.2 m)

The large, powerful caiman lizard has an oarlike, laterally flattened tail and rough, horny, platelike scales along its back. It inhabits areas which are flooded for much of the time, except when the rivers are at their lowest, and frequents the resulting pools and ponds. It spends much of the day in water and dives and swims well, using its tail. At night, it finds shelter above water level, often in trees or bushes. It feeds almost entirely on aquatic snails, taking the snail in its jaws, then raising its head so that the snail slides back into its mouth, where it is broken up by the huge, crushing back teeth. The pieces of shell are spat out and the soft body swallowed.

The female caiman lizard, having mated, lays eggs which she buries, often in a deserted arboreal termites' nest.

### Common Tegu *Tupinambis teguixin*

**RANGE** Central America, N. South America

**HABITAT** Forest, woodland

**SIZE** 4–4½ ft (1.2–1.4 m), including tail of 27½–33½ in (70–85 cm)

A robust lizard with a long cylindrical tail, the tegu has prominent yellow markings on its dark body. It frequents dense undergrowth and is also found in cultivated areas where food is abundant. Chickens and their eggs are included in its diet, as well as small mammals, frogs, large insects, worms and some fruit and leaves. It hunts by day and hides in a burrow at night and in cool weather. A formidable opponent, the tegu will lash

out at an enemy with its powerful tail before attacking with its jaws. However, it will run away from danger when possible, and juveniles are able to run on their hind legs. Local tribespeople catch the tegu and use the yellow body fat as a cure for inflammations.

The female tegu lays her eggs in an inhabited arboreal termites' nest, tearing the outer wall open to deposit her 6 to 8 eggs inside. The ever-vigilant termites then repair the wall of their nest, thus sealing the tegu eggs safely away from predators and changes in temperature or humidity while they develop. The newly hatched young must break out of the termites' nest by themselves.

## Jungle Runner

*Ameiva ameiva*

**RANGE** Central America, South America, east of the Andes; introduced in USA: Florida

**HABITAT** Open grassland

**SIZE** 6–7½ in (15–20 cm)

A ground-living, extremely active lizard, the jungle runner emerges in the morning to forage for food, flicking out its long forked tongue to search for insects, spiders, snails and other small invertebrates and small lizards. The protrusible tongue is tactile and can also detect scents. In coastal regions, the jungle runner may be found in burrows, such as those made by crabs and, in Panama, it is reported to be extending its normal range by moving into areas recently cleared by man.

The male jungle runner is usually larger than the female and is marked with conspicuous light spots, whereas the female has distinctive stripes along her body. After mating, the female lays a clutch of 1 to 4 eggs.

## Teyu *Teius teyou*

**RANGE** S.E. Brazil to Argentina

**HABITAT** Open, rocky land

**SIZE** 11¾ in (30 cm)

One of the most numerous and widespread of South American teiids, the adaptable teyu lives wherever there is open land with some rock cover. For shelter, it makes a tunnel under a large stone that leads down to a small chamber, measuring about 1 in by 1½ in (2.5 cm by 4 cm). Here it lies, curled in a U-shape, its body in the chamber and its head and long tail in the tunnel. It feeds on insects and, occasionally, on spiders.

## Strand Racerunner *Cnemidophorus lemniscatus*

**RANGE** Central America to N. South America; Trinidad, Tobago

**HABITAT** Lowland plains, open regions of food-plain forest

**SIZE** 11¾ in (30 cm)

One of the fastest-moving of all the lizards, the strand racerunner is always on the move, continually darting off in different directions and sometimes running on its hind legs. Speeds of 15 to 17 mph (24 to 28 km/h) have been recorded over short distances. The racerunner is active during the day and, although mainly ground-dwelling, it also climbs low trees and bushes in search of food. A long-bodied lizard, it has an elongate, tapering, ridged tail; its snout may be blunt or pointed.

To mate, the male sits astride the female, holding the skin of her neck in his mouth. He curves his body around hers while copulating. The female lays 4 to 6 eggs which hatch some 8 to 10 weeks later.

# LACERTID LIZARDS AND NIGHT LIZARDS

## LACERTIDAE: LACERTID LIZARD FAMILY

About 180 species of lacertid lizard are distributed throughout Europe, Asia and Africa, excluding Madagascar. Within this range, they occur from the hottest tropical habitats to locations within the Arctic Circle. Most are ground-dwelling, but others live in trees or among rocks.

The elongate, longtailed lacertids are mostly small to medium-sized lizards between 4 and 29½ in (10 and 75 cm) in total length. All have large scales on head and belly. Externally, males can generally be distinguished from females by their larger heads and shorter bodies. Almost all species reproduce by laying eggs, depositing their clutches in earth or sand.

Lacertids are highly territorial in their behavior. Males in particular adopt characteristic threat postures to warn off intruders, with the head tilted upward and the throat expanded.

Lacertids feed on small, mainly invertebrate prey animals. A few species, particularly island-dwelling forms, also consume large amounts of plant material.

### Green Lizard *Lacerta viridis*

**RANGE** Europe: Channel Islands, south to N. Spain, Sicily, Greece; E. to S.W. Russia
**HABITAT** Open woodland, field edges, river banks, roadsides
**SIZE** 11¾–17¾ in (30–45 cm) including tail of 7¼–11¾ in (20–30 cm)

Also known as the emerald lizard, this is the largest lizard found north of the Alps. Males are brilliant green, finely stippled with black. Females are variable, often duller green or brownish. The color of mature adults is most vivid in the spring and fades later in the year.

An adaptable lizard, the green lizard lives almost anywhere that there is dense vegetation but avoids arid areas. It is an agile climber and can move speedily up trees, bushes and walls to find a spot in which to bask in the sun. Insects and their larvae and small invertebrates, particularly spiders, are its main foods.

Solitary creatures for most of the year, green lizards mate in the spring, when males compete fiercely for females. When copulating, the male grasps the female with his jaws. She lays 4 to 21 eggs in a hole she digs in the soil. She covers the eggs with earth and they incubate for several months. In winter, green lizards hibernate in tree hollows or other crevices.

### Viviparous Lizard

*Lacerta vivipara*

**RANGE** Europe: Arctic Scandinavia, Britain, south to N. Spain, N. Italy, former Yugoslavia; N. Asia
**HABITAT** Meadows, open woodland, marshes, any grassland
**SIZE** 5½–7 in (14–18 cm)

The viviparous lizard is the only lizard found within the Arctic Circle. Its coloration is variable over its wide range, but this lizard is commonly gray or yellowish-brown, with pale spots and dark stripes on the back. In the hotter parts of its range, it is rarely found below 1,650 ft (500 m) except in humid areas, but it basks in the sun for much of the day. Alert and agile, it is a fairly good climber and an excellent swimmer. Insects, spiders, earthworms, slugs and other small invertebrates make up its diet. It lives alone except in the hibernation and breeding seasons.

The breeding habits of this lizard are unique, hence its name meaning "live-bearing". The 5 to 8 young develop inside the mother, feeding on the yolks of their eggs, and break out of their thin membranous shells fully formed, as they are expelled from her body or shortly afterward.

### Wall Lizard *Lacerta muralis*

**RANGE** Europe: N. France to N. Spain, S. Italy, Greece, east to Romania
**HABITAT** Dry, sunny areas; walls, rocks, tree trunks
**SIZE** Up to 9 in (23 cm)

A slender, flat-bodied reptile, the wall lizard has a tapering tail which may be up to twice its body length. The coloration and markings of this species are variable over its range, but many individuals are brownish-red or gray, with dark markings. A sun-loving lizard, it spends much of the day basking on any form of wall even near human habitation; in the midday heat, it shelters in the shade. It is extremely active and alert and an expert climber. It feeds on insects such as flies and beetles, and on invertebrates such as earthworms, spiders, snails and slugs. A gregarious species, it lives in small colonies.

Soon after their winter hibernation, the lizards mate, males competing for females. The female digs a hole and lays 2 to 10 eggs which she covers with soil. The eggs hatch in 2 to 3 months. When food supplies are abundant there may be several clutches.

### Bosc's Fringe-toed Lizard
*Acanthodactylus boskianus*

**RANGE** Egypt, Saudi Arabia

**HABITAT** Desert

**SIZE** 5 in (12.5 cm)

A sand-colored, desert-living lizard, this species has long toes bordered with broad combs of scales. This arrangement enlarges the surface area of the feet and thus improves the grip on the sand. It can run quickly over sand and digs deep burrows for refuge. The female lays 2 to 4 eggs which she buries in a hole she digs in the sand.

### Algerian Sand Racer *Psammodromus algirus*

**RANGE** Spain, Portugal, S.W. France, N. Africa

**HABITAT** Dense vegetation in sandy areas, woodland, gardens, parks

**SIZE** 11¾ in (30 cm)

The reptile most commonly seen in urban areas within its range, the sand racer is metallic brown, with light stripes down its sides. Its tail is long and stiff and often orange-colored in juveniles. In the morning, the sand racer is sluggish while it basks in the sun after the cool night. When warmed up, it is an agile, fast-moving lizard which hunts for invertebrate prey among vegetation or on the ground.

The female sand racer lays 6 or more eggs which hatch in about 2 months.

### Racerunner *Eremias* sp.

**RANGE** Europe, C. Asia to Mongolia; Africa

**HABITAT** Desert, semiarid scrub, grassland, rocky desert

**SIZE** 6–8½ in (15–22 cm)

There are many species of *Eremias* lizards, many not yet properly classified. Most have scaly bodies and well-developed legs and are marked with spots, arranged in rows along the body. They tend to live in dry areas, taking refuge among rocks and in crevices, and feed on invertebrates, mainly insects and spiders.

Some *Eremias* lizards reproduce by laying clutches of 2 to 12 eggs, but others give birth to living young.

### Essex's Mountain Lizard *Tropidosaura essexi*

**RANGE** South Africa

**HABITAT** Mountains

**SIZE** 5½ in (14 cm)

A small lizard with a blunt, rounded snout, Essex's mountain lizard is marked with pale stripes, running from behind its head down its body and tail. A ground-dweller, it is active in the daytime and is quick and agile. It eats insects and small invertebrates.

## XANTUSIIDAE: NIGHT LIZARD FAMILY

As their name suggests, night lizards are nocturnal, beginning their hunting activities at dusk and spending the daylight hours hidden among rocks and under stones. There are about 18 species in the family, found in the south-west of the USA, Central America and Cuba, mostly in rocky, arid habitats. They feed on nocturnal insects.

Night lizards have a superficial resemblance to geckos, with their immobile eyelids, the lower of which have transparent "windows". Unlike the geckos, they have scales on the back and belly and shields on the head. All night lizards give birth to live young which develop inside the mother's body, nourished by a form of placenta.

### Desert Night Lizard *Xantusia vigilis*

**RANGE** S.W. USA: Nevada, Utah to California; Mexico

**HABITAT** Rocky, arid and semiarid land

**SIZE** 3¾–5 in (9.5–12.5 cm)

The desert night lizard varies in coloration over its range but is marked with many small dark spots. It frequents yucca plants and agaves and feeds on termites, ants, beetles and flies, which it finds among vegetation or rocks.

Night lizards give birth to live young. They mate in early summer, usually May or June, and 1 to 3 young are born, tail first, a few months later.

# SKINKS

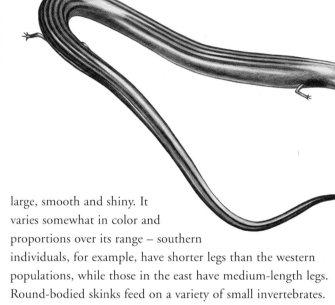

## SCINCIDAE: SKINK FAMILY

One of the largest lizard families, with many hundreds of species, skinks occur on every continent except for Antarctica. They are most abundant in Southeast Asia and the Australasian region. Skinks live on or below the ground and are normally smooth-scaled, with elongate, rounded bodies and tapering tails. Their legs are short, and some burrowing skinks have tiny legs or none at all. Many families of lizards include species with reduced or no limbs, but this is particularly common in the skink family. The majority are between 3¼ and 13¾ in (8 and 35 cm) long, although there are a few giant forms.

Most skinks feed on insects and small invertebrates; the giant forms, however, are herbivorous. Their reproductive habits vary: most species lay eggs but some give birth to live young.

### Legless Skink *Acontias* sp.

| | |
|---|---|
| **RANGE** | South Africa, Madagascar |
| **HABITAT** | Sandy regions |
| **SIZE** | 4½ in (10 cm) |

Legless skinks spend most of their lives in their underground burrows. They are indeed limbless, with long cylindrical bodies and short tails. Their eyes and ears are protected by scales, and their lower eyelids are equipped with transparent "windows", to enable them to see when burrowing without getting soil in their eyes. Their bodies are covered with hard, smooth scales, enabling them to move easily through the earth. They also move quickly on the surface, using snakelike undulations of the body. Legless skinks are largely insectivorous, but may also eat small invertebrates and frogs.

Females bear live young, producing litters of 3 or 4 at a time.

### Round-bodied Skink *Chalcides bedriagai*

| | |
|---|---|
| **RANGE** | Spain, Portugal |
| **HABITAT** | Varied, arid, sandy land, hilly areas, grassland |
| **SIZE** | Up to 6¼ in (16 cm) |

An elongate, short-legged species, this skink keeps out of sight in ground vegetation or burrows into loose sand. It is usually a buff or grayish-brown with dark-edged markings, and its scales are large, smooth and shiny. It varies somewhat in color and proportions over its range – southern individuals, for example, have shorter legs than the western populations, while those in the east have medium-length legs. Round-bodied skinks feed on a variety of small invertebrates.

Females give birth to 2 or 3 fully formed live young, which have developed inside the body, nourished during their growth by a form of placenta.

### Sundeval's Skink *Riopa sundevalli*

| | |
|---|---|
| **RANGE** | Africa: Zambia to South Africa |
| **HABITAT** | Open plains, sandy savanna |
| **SIZE** | Up to 7 in (18 cm) |

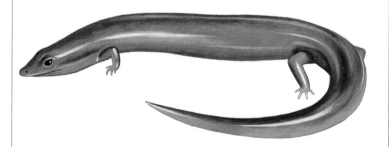

A burrowing species, Sundeval's skink has tiny limbs and smooth scales. It comes to the surface in search of food – insects and their larvae, spiders, wood lice and soft snails – and may hide under stones or leaf debris. Termite hills and manure heaps are also favorite spots for these skinks. On the ground, the skink moves in a snakelike fashion, its tiny limbs are of little use. The tail breaks away easily from the body, and adults are seldom seen with a complete tail.

Females lay a clutch of 2 to 6 eggs, usually 4, in a nest underground or in a termite mound. The newly hatched young skinks measure 2 in (5 cm).

## Sandfish *Scincus philbyi*

**RANGE** Saudi Arabia

**HABITAT** Sandy desert

**SIZE** Up to 8¼ in (21 cm)

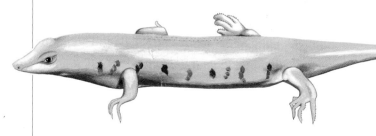

Unlike most burrowing skinks, this species retains well-developed legs and feet. Its digits are flattened and have fringes of scales in order to help it move easily over loose sand. The body of the sandfish is robust and cylindrical, and it has a broad, wedge-shaped snout. The sandfish is active through the heat of the day, for it spends most of its time under the surface of the sand, looking for prey such as beetles and millipedes. It pushes its way along, literally seeming to swim through the sand, hence its name.

The female sandfish gives birth to fully formed live young which have developed inside her body.

## *Feylinia cussori*

**RANGE** Tropical Africa

**HABITAT** Forest

**SIZE** 13¾ in (35 cm)

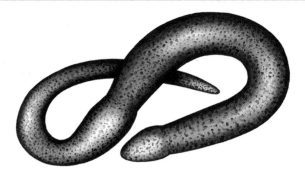

A large burrowing skink, *Feylinia cussori* has a rather flattened head, which merges smoothly with its limbless cylindrical body. There are no external eardrums and its tiny eyes are protected by transparent scales. It is often found under decaying wood and feeds largely on termites, which it locates by the sounds they make in the wood.

The female bears litters of 2 or 3 live young which have developed inside her body. There is a local superstition that *Feylinia* can enter the human body whenever it desires and, when it leaves again, the person dies.

## Great Plains Skink *Eumeces obsoletus*

**RANGE** S. C. USA: Wyoming and Nebraska to Arizona and Texas; Mexico

**HABITAT** Rocky grassland, usually near water

**SIZE** 6¼–13¾ in (16.5–35 cm)

The Great Plains skink has well-developed sturdy limbs. Its body is spotted with dark brown or black; these spots may merge to give the impression of lengthwise stripes. Active in the day, it eats insects, spiders and small lizards. It is aggressive and will bite if alarmed.

The Great Plains skink displays an unusual degree of maternal care. A few weeks after mating in April or May, the female lays 17 to 21 eggs in a nest which she makes beneath a rock. She guards the eggs while they incubate and turns them regularly to ensure even warming. When, a couple of months later, the eggs begin to hatch, the female rubs and presses them with her body, stimulating the young to move and then to wriggle free of the shell. For a further 10 days after hatching, she attends her young, cleaning them regularly. Juveniles are generally black with blue tails and some white spots. This coloration gradually fades.

## Florida Sand Skink *Neoseps reynoldsi* **VU**

**RANGE** USA: C. Florida

**HABITAT** Sandhills

**SIZE** 4–5 in (10–13 cm)

This small skink is an expert digger and burrower. Using its chisel-shaped snout, it burrows speedily into the sand, undulating its body as it goes, as if swimming. Its limbs are tiny and it has only one digit on each forelimb and two on each hind limb. It eats termites and beetle larvae, which it finds by the sound vibrations they cause. Although it is active in the daytime and comes to the surface to shelter under logs and other debris, the sand skink is a secretive species and rarely seen. If alarmed, it quickly buries itself.

Sand skinks mate in spring and the female lays 2 eggs.

# SKINKS CONTINUED

**Mabuya** *Mabuya wrightii*

**RANGE** Seychelles

**HABITAT** Granite islands with guano deposits

**SIZE** 12¼ in (31 cm) including tail of up to 7 in (18 cm)

The stocky-bodied mabuya has well-developed hind limbs with long digits. Its snout is slightly elongate and blunt. It is a fast-moving, ground-dwelling lizard. The mabuya is active in the daytime and has a great need of warmth.

Mabuyas are usually found on the smaller islands of the Seychelles, often in close association with the nesting colonies of seabirds. In the breeding season mabuyas feed on birds' eggs, especially those of terns, which they break by rolling them off rocks or branches. They then lap up the contents. Their diet is not known outside the birds' breeding season.

Most mabuya species give birth to live young, but the exact details of the breeding habits of this particular mabuya have not been observed. One South African mabuya species, *M. trivittata*, is one of the few reptiles to assist her newborn young. She helps the young to escape from the soft membranes in which they are born, by tearing the coverings open with her teeth.

**Spiny-tailed Skink** *Egernia stokesii*

**RANGE** Western Australia through arid interior to Queensland, New South Wales and South Australia

**HABITAT** Stony hills, mountains

**SIZE** Up to 10½ in (27 cm)

The spiny-tailed skink is a most unusual species, with a stout body covered with rough-edged, sometimes spiny scales. The tail is short and much flattened and particularly well endowed with spinous scales. All four limbs are strong and well developed. This skink frequents rocky areas, where it can shelter in deep crevices or underneath boulders; the spines on its tail make it virtually impossible to dislodge once it has wedged itself in such a hiding place.

The spiny-tailed skink is active during the day, when it basks in the sun and forages for insects within easy reach of its refuge. It is a gregarious species, and lives in colonies and the presence of spiny-tailed skinks in an area is signalled by their regular defecation sites, where small piles of feces accumulate.

Spiny-tailed skinks are live-bearers. The female gives birth to about 5 fully formed young, which develop inside her body, nourished during their growth by a form of placenta. The young measure about 2¼ in (6 cm) when they are born.

*Emoia cyanogaster*

**RANGE** Australia: extreme N. Queensland; Indonesia

**HABITAT** Forest, banana groves

**SIZE** Up to 10½ in (27 cm)

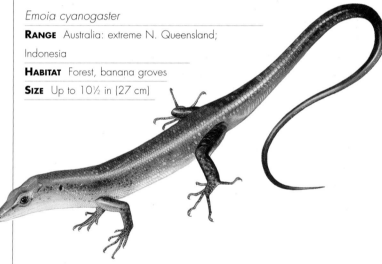

This slender, glossy skink has a slim tapering tail. The *Emoia cyanogaster* also has a pointed, somewhat flattened snout. Its limbs, particularly the hind limbs, are long and well formed, with elongate digits.

It is an agile, primarily tree-dwelling species and can jump easily from branch to branch. This skink spends much of the day basking in the sun on low vegetation or sheltering among the trailing leaves of banana trees, but it often descends to the ground in order to search for food.

These skinks breed throughout the year, although there are some seasonal fluctuations. The female usually lays a clutch of 2 eggs at a time.

*Leiolopisma infrapunctatum*

**RANGE** New Zealand

**HABITAT** Open country with some vegetation

**SIZE** 9½ in (24 cm)

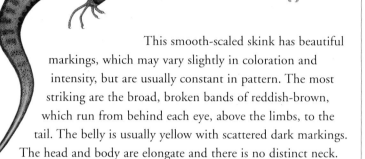

This smooth-scaled skink has beautiful markings, which may vary slightly in coloration and intensity, but are usually constant in pattern. The most striking are the broad, broken bands of reddish-brown, which run from behind each eye, above the limbs, to the tail. The belly is usually yellow with scattered dark markings. The head and body are elongate and there is no distinct neck.

Active in the daytime, this skink often lives near petrel nesting sites. It basks in the sun, but is easily scared and swiftly takes refuge at the least sign of disturbance. It feeds on small land-living invertebrates and insects. Mating takes place in spring, and the female gives birth to a litter of live young about 4 months later.

## Western Blue-tongued Skink *Tiliqua occipitalis*

**RANGE** S. Australia

**HABITAT** Arid areas

**SIZE** 17¾ in (45 cm)

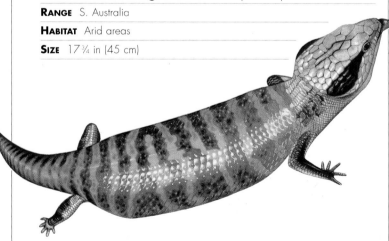

The heavily built western blue-tongued skink has a stout body and large head but its limbs are relatively small. Bands of dark brown scales pattern its body and tail and there are characteristic dark streaks behind each eye. The blue-tongued skink is active in the daytime when it forages around on the ground for insects, snails and berries. An abandoned rabbit warren may sometimes be used for shelter.

The female gives birth to about 5 live young, each of which is distinctly banded with dark brown and yellow.

## Prickly Forest Skink *Tropidophorus queenslandiae*

**RANGE** Australia: N. Queensland

**HABITAT** Rain forest

**SIZE** 5–7¾ in (13–20 cm)

The prickly forest skink is easily distinguished from other Australian skinks by its covering of strongly keeled small scales. Its rounded tail is also covered with keeled scales, and its limbs are well developed. A nocturnal skink, it lives beneath plant debris or rotting logs on the forest floor, where its dark body with irregular pale markings keeps it well camouflaged. It is a slow-moving, sluggish skink which does not like to bask in sunlight and is usually found in a rather torpid state. Worms and soft-bodied insects are its main foods.

Little is known of the breeding biology of this skink, but several of the 20 *Tropidophonts* species are known to produce litters of 6 to 9 live young. These develop inside the mother's body and break from their thin shells as the eggs are laid.

## Brown Skink *Scincella lateralis*
(previously *Lygosoma lateralis*)

**RANGE** USA: New Jersey to Florida, west to Nebraska and Texas

**HABITAT** Humid forest, wooded grassland

**SIZE** 3¼–5 in (8–13 cm)

This smooth, shiny skink, also known as the ground skink, has dark stripes on the sides of its body and a pale, often yellowish or whitish belly. Its body is long and slender and its legs well developed, with elongate digits on the hind feet. The brown skink has movable eyelids with a transparent window in each lower lid; a feature which enables it to see clearly even when it must close its eyes to avoid dirt getting into them when it is burrowing into cover. It lives on the ground and prefers areas with plenty of leaf litter in which to shelter. Active in the day, particularly in warm, humid weather, it feeds mainly on insects and spiders. The closest relatives of this species live in Central America and Australia.

A prolific breeder, the female brown skink lays a clutch of 1 to 7 eggs every 4 or 5 weeks. There is a maximum of about 5 clutches during the breeding season, which lasts from April to August in most areas.

# GIRDLED AND PLATED LIZARDS

## CORDYLIDAE: GIRDLED AND PLATED LIZARD FAMILY

The cordylid lizards are an African family of about 40 species, found largely in rocky or arid habitats, south of the Sahara and in Madagascar. Names include plated, whip, girdled, crag, snake and flat lizards, which gives some idea of the range of adaptations within the family.

The typical cordylid lizard has a body covered with bony plates which underlie the external and visible scales. This undercoat of armor, however, is not continuous over the whole body: on each side there is a lateral groove, without a plate layer, which allows body expansion, when the belly is full of food for example, or, in egg-laying females, when distended with eggs. There are many variations of form within the family. The girdle-tailed lizards have short tails, armored with rings of spines, and often have spines on the head. Flat lizards of the genus *Platysaurus* have flattened bodies and skin covered with smooth granules. Snake lizards of the genus *Chamaesaura* are very elongate, with tails up to three-quarters of their body length. Some cordylids have well-developed limbs, while in others the limbs are much reduced or even absent.

Most lizards in the family feed on insects and small invertebrates such as millipedes. Some of the larger forms also consume smaller lizards, and others are almost entirely vegetarian in their habits. Their reproductive habits vary, some species laying eggs and others bearing live young.

### *Cordylosaurus subtessellatus*

| | |
|---|---|
| **RANGE** | Africa: S. Angola, Namibia |
| **HABITAT** | Dry, rocky areas |
| **SIZE** | 6 in (15 cm) |

The greatly compressed head and body of this lizard make it easy for it to hide in crevices and crannies in the rocks, to escape enemies and intense heat or night-time cold. It may also shelter under stones. In each lower eyelid there is a transparent "window", so that the lizard can close its eyes in windy weather, when sand and dust might blow into them, but is still able to see. Under its digits are keeled scales, perhaps to help it grip on rocks. Its tail is easily shed and regenerated.

This agile, ground-dwelling lizard, eats insects and other small invertebrates. The species reproduces by laying eggs.

### Imperial Flat Lizard *Platysaurus imperator*

| | |
|---|---|
| **RANGE** | Africa: N.E. Zimbabwe, contiguous Mozambique |
| **HABITAT** | Rocky knolls of granite and sandstone in grassland |
| **SIZE** | 15¼ in (39 cm) |

The head, body, limbs and tail of this lizard are all flattened laterally; in consequence it can take refuge in narrow cracks and crevices in the rocks among which it lives. As these rocky knolls weather, many crevices are formed, ideal as hiding places; once in a crevice, the lizard expands its body with air and braces itself against the rock, making it virtually impossible for any predator to remove it. This lizard tends to frequent the tops of the knolls, whereas the other platysaurans live at the base.

The biggest species in its genus, the imperial flat lizard has large scales on its neck and a smooth back. The male, with his yellow, red and black body, is larger and more brightly colored than the female, which is largely black, with three distinctive yellow stripes on her head that taper off toward the back. Males hold territories which they compete for and defend against intruders by adopting an aggressive posture, rearing up and displaying throat and chest colors.

Active in the daytime, flat lizards hunt insects, particularly locusts and beetles. They shelter from the midday heat and emerge again to hunt in the afternoon.

The female flat lizard lays 2 eggs, elongate in shape, in a crevice in the rocks.

### Transvaal Snake Lizard *Chamaesaura aena*

| | |
|---|---|
| **RANGE** | South Africa |
| **HABITAT** | Grassland |
| **SIZE** | 15¾ in (40 cm) |

This snakelike lizard has an elongate body and a tail which is about three-quarters of its total length. It has four small limbs, each with five clawed digits; the other 3 species in this genus

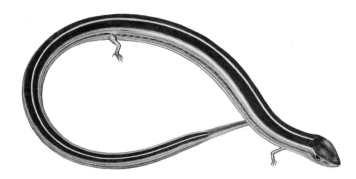

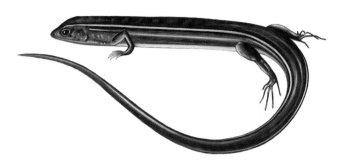

## Plated Lizard *Gerrhosaurus flavigularis*

**RANGE** Africa: Sudan, Ethiopia, south through
E. Africa to South Africa: Cape Province
**HABITAT** Grassland, scrub
**SIZE** 18 in (45.5 cm)

have at most two digits per limb, and one species, *C. macrolepsis*, has no front limbs at all. Active in the daytime, it moves quickly through the grass with serpentine undulations of its body, often with its head and forelimbs lifted off the ground. It feeds on insects, spiders, earthworms and other small invertebrates.

The female's 2 to 4 young develop inside her oviduct. The fully formed young break from their soft shells as they are expelled from her body.

## Armadillo Lizard *Cordylus cataphractus* **VU**

**RANGE** South Africa: W. Cape Province
**HABITAT** Arid rocky areas
**SIZE** 8¼ in (21 cm)

The armadillo lizard is heavily armored, with strong spiny scales which extend from its head right along its back and tail. Its head, body and clublike tail are all flattened, enabling it to wriggle easily into rock crevices for shelter. The nostrils are elongated into little tubes.

A ground-dwelling lizard, it is active in the daytime and feeds on a wide variety of insects, as well as on spiders and other small invertebrates.

This species is fairly slow moving and, rather than darting for cover when it is threatened, it may adopt a curious defensive posture which earns it its common name. It rolls itself up like an armadillo, its tail tightly held in its jaws; thus presenting a spiny defensive ring to the predator and protecting its softer, vulnerable belly area.

The 1 to 3 young of the armadillo lizard develop inside the female's body. The tiny, fully formed lizards break from their soft membranous shells as they are expelled from her body.

A ground-living and burrowing lizard, this species is usually greenish-gray or brownish, with a red or yellow throat and often a narrow stripe down each side. It is well armored, with hard body plates, and head shields fused to the skull. The tail is generally about two-thirds of the total length. Its limbs are well-developed and it has five toes on each foot. These are not specially adapted for digging, and the lizard probably does most of its tunnelling after rain when the ground is soft.

Active by day, it hunts insects and is rarely seen, despite its size. It moves rapidly through the grass and at any sign of danger darts into its burrow, usually positioned under a bush.

The female plated lizard lays clutches of 4 or 5 eggs in a shallow pit which she excavates.

## Girdled Lizard *Zonosaurus* sp.

**RANGE** Madagascar
**HABITAT** Forest
**SIZE** 15–24 in (38–61 cm)

There are 3 *Zonosaurus* species, all of which are large, strong, ground-dwelling lizards. They have well-developed limbs and distinct grooves along their sides to allow for body expansion. Little is known of their habits or biology.

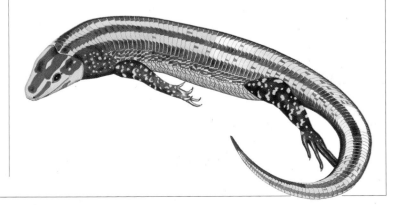

# CROCODILE LIZARDS, ALLIGATOR LIZARDS AND LEGLESS LIZARDS

## XENOSAURIDAE: CROCODILE LIZARD FAMILY

There are 4 species in this family, 3 in Central America and Mexico and 1 in south China. They are related to the anguid lizards and, under the body scales, have bony plates, which may be tiny or large but are not joined together. Unlike many anguids, however, their limbs are well developed.

*Xenosaurus* sp.

**RANGE**  Mexico, Guatemala

**HABITAT**  Rain forest

**SIZE**  About 7¾ in (20 cm)

These powerful, strong-limbed lizards have flat heads and robust bodies. They are inconspicuous creatures and are not often seen, spending much of their time in refuges beneath tree roots or in rocky crevices. They will also lie in water for long periods. Active at night, they feed on insects, particularly winged termites and ants. If alarmed, *Xenosaurus* adopts a threat posture, with mouth agape, revealing a black membrane.

The females gives birth to litters of 3 fully formed live young which are about 1½ in (4 cm) long at birth.

## ANGUIDAE: LEGLESS AND ALLIGATOR LIZARD FAMILY

There are about 80 species in this family of elongate, snakelike lizards, found in North, Central and South America, the West Indies, Europe, North Africa and Asia. Typically, they have smooth elongate bodies and tails, movable eyelids and external ear openings. Most are land-dwelling or burrowing animals and many, such as the slow worms and glass lizards and snakes, are limbless or have only vestigial limbs. The alligator lizards of North and Central America, however, have well-developed limbs.

Many of these lizards have stiff bodies, armored by bony plates under the surface skin. In order that their bodies can expand when breathing, or to accommodate food or eggs, there are grooves of soft scales along their sides. Their long tails easily become detached if seized by an attacker, usually along one of the series of fracture planes. The tail is regrown in a few weeks, but not always completely.

Most anguids feed on insects, small invertebrates and even small mammals and lizards. All but a few species reproduce by laying eggs. The others, mostly species found at high altitudes, give birth to live young.

**Galliwasp** *Diploglossus lessorae*

**RANGE**  Central America, N. South America

**HABITAT**  Forest

**SIZE**  Up to 13¾ in (35 cm)

The smooth, shiny galliwasp resembles the alligator lizards but has a more elongate body and lacks the expandable grooves along the sides of the body that the heavily armored alligator lizards possess. It is a ground-dwelling species, active in the daytime, and feeds on insects, worms and mollusks. It is believed to reproduce by laying eggs.

**Southern Alligator Lizard** *Gerrhonotus multicarinatus*

**RANGE**  W. USA: Washington; Baja California

**HABITAT**  Grassland, open woodland

**SIZE**  10–17 in (25.5–43 cm)

The agile southern alligator lizard has a strong prehensile tail, which it can wrap around branches and use like a fifth limb when climbing in bushes. There are 5 subspecies of this lizard, which vary in coloration from reddish-brown to yellowish-gray, usually with some dark markings, but all have distinct folds along their sides, where flexible scales allow the stiff, armored body to expand.

These lizards are active in the daytime, when they hunt for insects and any other small creatures that they are able to catch and swallow, including scorpions and black widow spiders.

Alligator lizards breed in the summer, females laying several clutches over the season. There are usually 12 eggs in a clutch, but there may be up to 40 on occasion.

### Glass Snake *Ophisaurus apodus*

**RANGE** Europe: Former Yugoslavia, Greece to Black Sea region, east to S.W. and C. Asia

**SIZE** Up to 4 ft (1.2 m)

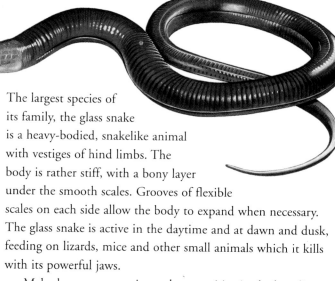

The largest species of its family, the glass snake is a heavy-bodied, snakelike animal with vestiges of hind limbs. The body is rather stiff, with a bony layer under the smooth scales. Grooves of flexible scales on each side allow the body to expand when necessary. The glass snake is active in the daytime and at dawn and dusk, feeding on lizards, mice and other small animals which it kills with its powerful jaws.

Males become aggressive and competitive in the breeding season and there is fierce rivalry for mates. The female lays 5 to 7 eggs in a hollow under a rock or log, or in a pile of rotting vegetation. She curls around her eggs and guards them from predators while they incubate. The young hatch in about 4 weeks and are about 5 in (12.5 cm) long.

### Slow Worm *Anguis fragilis*

**RANGE** Europe (not Ireland, S. Spain and Portugal or N. Scandinavia), east to central and S.W. Asia; N.W. Africa

**HABITAT** Fields, meadows, scrub, heath, up to 7,900 ft (2,400 m)

**SIZE** 13¾–21¼ in (35–54 cm)

The slow worm is a smooth, extremely snakelike creature with no visible limbs. It is reddish-brown, brown or gray above; females usually have a dark stripe on the back, while some males may have blue spots. It moves by serpentine undulations and can shed its long tail if seized by an enemy. The tail does not

fully regenerate, however, and is then stumplike. The night and heat of the day are spent under rocks or logs, and the slow worm emerges in the morning and evening in order to hunt for slugs and worms, as well as spiders, insects and larvae. It is slower-moving than most lizards but can disappear into cover with considerable speed.

In late spring, breeding males become aggressive and compete with one another for mates. As they copulate, the male holds the female's neck or head in his jaws. About 3 months later, the female gives birth to live young, usually 6 to 12, but sometimes as many as 20. The young develop in thin-shelled eggs inside her body and break out of the membranous shells as they are laid. The young slow-worms are about 2¼ to 3½ in (6 to 9 cm) long at birth.

### California Legless Lizard *Anniella pulchra*

**RANGE** USA: California; Mexico, Baja California

**HABITAT** Beaches, sand dunes, banks of streams, soft loamy soil

**SIZE** 6–9 in (15–23 cm)

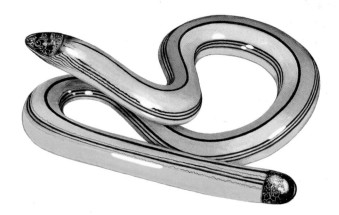

Specialized for burrowing, this legless lizard has a smooth body, which helps it to move easily through soil, and a shovel-shaped snout for digging. Its eyes are small and have movable lids. Most of this creature's life is spent underground or burrowing in leaf litter, searching for insects and insect larvae. It rarely moves in the open. One race of this species, *A. pulchra nigra*, is in danger of extinction.

These lizards are live-bearing; females produce litters of up to 4 fully formed young.

# MONITORS AND GILA MONSTER

## VARANIDAE: MONITOR LIZARD FAMILY

The monitor lizards of the Old World include within their number the largest of all lizards – the komodo dragon. This species may be as much as 10 ft (3 m) long and weigh 360 lb (163 kg); several other species within the family exceed 6½ ft (2 m) in length. There are about 30 species of monitor in a single genus and the single species of Lanthanotus (earless monitor). This species is sometimes placed in a family of its own, the Lanthanotidae. All are elongate lizards with long necks and tails and well-developed limbs. Their snakelike forked tongues can be retracted into the lizard's mouth.

Monitors occur in Africa (except Madagascar), the Middle East, southern Asia, Indonesia and Australasia. All are voracious carnivores. Male monitor lizards may perform spectacular ritualized fights to assert their dominance. They rear up on their hind legs and wrestle with their forelimbs until one contestant is pushed over and defeated. Monitors reproduce by laying eggs, and several species are known to dig pits in the ground in which the eggs are buried to incubate.

### Komodo Dragon

*Varanus komodensis* **VU**

**RANGE** Islands of Komodo, Flores, Pintja and Padar, east of Java

**HABITAT** Grassland

**SIZE** 10 ft (3 m)

The awe-inspiring komodo dragon dwarfs most present-day lizards. It has a heavy body, a long, thick tail and well-developed limbs with talonlike claws. Its teeth are large and jagged and it has a forked tongue that can be flicked in and out of the mouth. Despite its size, it is a good climber, and moves surprisingly quickly. It also swims well; and tends to live near water. It is active during the day and preys on animals as large as hog deer and wild boar, as well as on small deer and pigs.

The female komodo lays about 15 eggs which she buries in the ground to incubate.

### Nile Monitor *Varanus niloticus*

**RANGE** Africa: south and east of the Sahara to Cape Province

**HABITAT** Forest, open country

**SIZE** Over 6½ ft (2 m)

The versatile, yet unspecialized, Nile monitor is a robust, strong reptile, which is typical of the monitor group. Using its broad tail as a rudder, it swims and dives well and can climb trees with the aid of its huge claws and strong prehensile tail, which it uses to hold on to branches. It can also dig burrows.

Nile monitors tend to stay near water and do not venture into desert areas. They feed on frogs, fish and snails, as well as on crocodile eggs and young.

This is one of the most prolific egg-laying lizards. The female Nile monitor lays up to 60 eggs at a time in a termite mound. She tears a hole in the wall, lays her eggs inside and departs, leaving them to hatch unguarded. The termites then repair their nest, thus enclosing the eggs in the warm, safe termitarium. When they hatch, the young monitors must make their own way out of the nest.

## Gould's Monitor *Varanus gouldi*

**RANGE**  Australia

**HABITAT**  Coastal forest to sandy desert

**SIZE**  About 5 ft (1.5 m)

The widespread Gould's monitor, which is also known as the sand monitor, varies in size, coloration and pattern over its range. Like those of all monitors, its limbs are powerful, and its distinctly ridged tail is laterally compressed, except at the base.

Gould's monitor is a ground-dweller, sheltering in burrows, which it digs or takes over from other animals, or under logs and debris. To find food, it must roam over large areas of sparsely populated country, searching for birds, mammals, reptiles, insects, even carrion. Like all monitors, the female reproduces by laying eggs.

## Earless Monitor *Lanthanotus borneensis*

**RANGE**  Sarawak

**HABITAT**  Forest

**SIZE**  Up to 17 in (43 cm)

The earless monitor has an elongate, rather flattened body and short but strong limbs, each with five digits. On each body scale there is a small tubercle. Its eyes are tiny with movable lids, the lower of which have transparent "windows", and there are no external ear openings, which is the origin of its common name.

Much of the earless monitor's life is spent burrowing underground or swimming; it avoids bright light and does not need intense warmth. In captivity the earless monitor will eat fish, but its natural diet is not known.

## HELODERMATIDAE: GILA MONSTER FAMILY

There are only 2 species in this family which are related to the monitor lizards and the rare, earless monitor. They are the gila monster, from western North America, and the Mexican beaded lizard.

## Gila Monster *Heloderma suspectum* **VU**

**RANGE**  S.W. USA: S. Utah, Arizona to New Mexico; Mexico

**HABITAT**  Arid and semiarid areas with some vegetation

**SIZE**  17¾–24 in (45–61 cm)

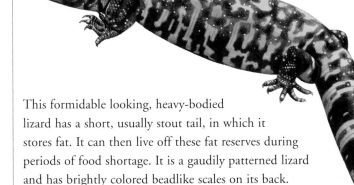

This formidable looking, heavy-bodied lizard has a short, usually stout tail, in which it stores fat. It can then live off these fat reserves during periods of food shortage. It is a gaudily patterned lizard and has brightly colored beadlike scales on its back.

The gila lives on the ground and takes shelter under rocks or in a burrow which it either digs itself or takes over from another animal. It is primarily a nocturnal creature, but it may emerge into the open during the day in spring.

The two members of the gila monster family are the only venomous lizards. The venom is produced in glands in the lower jaw and enters the mouth via grooved teeth at the front of the lower jaw. The poison flows into the gila's victim as the lizard chews. The gila will also eat the eggs of birds and other reptiles.

Gila monsters mate during the summer, and the female lays her clutch of 3 to 5 eggs some time later, in the autumn or winter.

# AMPHISBAENIANS

## AMPHISBAENIDAE: AMPHISBAENID FAMILY

The 150 or so species of amphisbaenians are extraordinary, wormlike, burrowing reptiles. Known as worm lizards, they are not true lizards and are given their own suborder within the Squamata order, on a parallel with the much larger lizard and snake groups.

There are three families of amphisbaenians – amphisbaenidae, the bipedidae (3 species) and trogonophiidae (6 species). Most species occur in Central and South America and Africa, but there are a few species that inhabit the warmer parts of North America and Europe.

These strange creatures prefer moist habitats in which they can build semipermanent tunnel systems that will not collapse after the animal has passed through. They quickly dehydrate in dry soil. Water is taken into the mouth and swallowed, not absorbed through the skin as was once believed.

Most species are limbless. The skin is loosely attached over the simple cylindrical body, which is ringed with small scales. The tail is pointed in some species and rounded in others, but it is always covered with horny scales. Amphisbaenids have no external ear openings, and their tiny eyes are covered with scales.

Amphisbaenids and the other amphisbaenians live underground in burrows which they dig themselves, often near to ant or termite colonies. Bracing their long bodies against the walls of the tunnel, they excavate new lengths by repeated battering strokes of their hard, strong heads. Like worms, they can move backward or forward in a straight line with no body undulations, a form of locomotion ideally suited to life in tunnels. Indeed, the Greek word amphisbaena means "goes both ways". This ability, combined with the similar appearance of the head and tail, has caused many to see the amphisbaenid as a two-headed monster, and it is even mentioned as such in a Roman epic poem.

Amphisbaenids find all their prey – mostly insects and worms – below the ground. Larger species may also attack and eat small vertebrate animals. Despite the lack of external ears they are able to hear their prey crawling in the ground and move accurately in its direction. The sense of smell also seems to play a part in locating prey. Once it has found its quarry, the amphisbaenid grabs it and tears it apart with its strong, interlocking teeth, set in its powerful jaws.

Little is known of the breeding habits of amphisbaenids, but most species are believed to lay eggs which incubate and hatch in their underground burrows.

### Florida Worm Lizard *Rhineura floridana*

**RANGE**  USA: N. and C. Florida

**HABITAT**  Sandy, wooded areas

**SIZE**  7–16 in (18–40.5 cm)

The only blind, limbless lizard in North America, the Florida worm lizard is just over $\frac{1}{5}$ in (0.5 cm) in diameter and has a rather shovel shaped head. It lives underground, feeding on worms, spiders and termites, and rarely comes to the surface unless driven by rain or disturbed by cultivation. Unlike an earthworm, it leaves a tunnel behind it as it burrows, pushing through the earth with its spadelike snout and compacting the soil as it goes, to form the tunnel.

In summer, the Florida worm lizard lays up to 3 long, thin eggs in a burrow. The young hatch out in autumn, when they are about 4 in (10 cm) long.

Fossil research has shown that this amphisbaenid was at one time widely distributed in North America.

### South African Shield Snout *Monopeltis capensis*

**RANGE**  Africa: C. South Africa, Zimbabwe

**HABITAT**  Sandy soil

**SIZE**  11¾ in (30 cm)

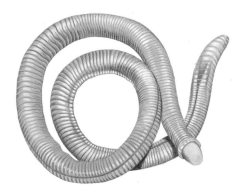

The thick horny plates on the shovellike head of this amphisbaenid enable it to burrow into harder soils than many other species. It tunnels down to depths of 7¾ in (20 cm) and only emerges above ground when driven by rains, or if attacked by ants. When they do emerge, shield snouts are preyed on by birds, such as ravens and kites. Shield snouts themselves feed on termites, beetles and other ground-living insects.

### Worm Lizard *Blanus cinereus*

**RANGE** Spain, Portugal, N.W. Africa

**HABITAT** Sandy soil or humus, often in woodland

**SIZE** 8½–11¾ in (22–30 cm)

The only European amphisbaenid, this worm lizard has a small, pointed head and a tapering tail. It spends most of its life in underground burrows and is only rarely seen above ground except after heavy rain or when it is disturbed by cultivation. It feeds on small invertebrates, particularly ants.

### White-bellied Worm Lizard *Amphisbaena alba*

**RANGE** Tropical South America; Trinidad

**HABITAT** Rain forest

**SIZE** 24 in (61 cm)

The body of this worm lizard, the most widespread in South America, is cylindrical over its entire length, the tail being almost as thick and blunt as the head. Tail and head look similar, and the species is known as the two-headed blind snake in some areas. It is over 1 in (2.5 cm) in diameter.

Although a burrowing, underground animal, this species often crawls over the forest floor, particularly after heavy rain. It eats earthworms and ants and is often found in ants' nests. Indeed some tribes call it "ant king" or "mother ant" and believe it to be reared by ants. If in danger, this worm lizard lifts its tail and moves it around as if it were a head. Presumably this tricks the enemy into attacking the tail, keeping the vulnerable head area safe and enabling the worm lizard to make a counterattack.

## BIPEDIDAE: BIPED FAMILY

The 3 species in this family are found in Mexico. They are unique among amphisbaenians in retaining forelimbs to assist with digging. Underground, the head is used for burrowing.

### Two-legged Worm Lizard
*Bipes biporus*

**RANGE** Mexico, Baja California

**HABITAT** Arid land

**SIZE** 7¾ in (20 cm)

The worm lizards of this genus are the only members of the family to possess limbs. They have two tiny front legs with five clawed toes on each limb. Despite their size, these limbs are powerful, and the digits are adapted for digging and climbing. The two-legged worm lizard spends most of its life underground in burrows and uses its limbs to start digging its tunnels. Once the burrow is begun, it pushes through with its head, compacting the soil as it goes. It may use its limbs as well as its head when digging a large tunnel.

These worm lizards eat worms and termites. Although little is known of their breeding habits, they are believed to lay eggs.

## TROGONOPHIIDAE: TROGONOPHIID FAMILY

The 6 species in this family are found in North Africa and western Asia. They use an oscillating movement of the head when digging.

### Somali Edge Snout *Agamodon anguliceps*

**RANGE** Africa: Somali Republic, S.E. Ethiopia

**HABITAT** Sandy soil

**SIZE** 4¼ in (11 cm)

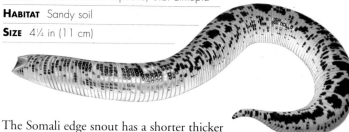

The Somali edge snout has a shorter thicker body than most amphisbaenids. Its tail is short and tapered, and its wedge-shaped head makes it a particularly efficient burrower, even in hard soils. The front of the head has a pair of sharp, vertical ridges, and by screwing motions of its head, the edge snout excavates its tunnel and compacts the soil. At night, it moves to within 2 in (5 cm) of the surface. As the daytime temperature rises, it descends again to about 6 to 11¾ in (15 to 30 cm) below ground. It occasionally moves above ground, swinging its head from side to side and pulling itself along.

# THREAD, BLIND, PIPE, SHIELDTAIL AND SUNBEAM SNAKES

## LEPTOTYPHLOPIDAE: THREAD SNAKE FAMILY

Thread snakes are small, worm-shaped, burrowing snakes that grow to about 15 in (38 cm) long. They possess minute vestiges of a pelvic girdle and hind limbs, and their tiny rudimentary eyes are hidden beneath scales. Like their relatives Typhlopidae and Anomalepidae, these snakes are specialized for a burrowing existence. The size of the mouth has become reduced, and it is only about half the length of the head, whereas in most snakes the mouth is as large as possible.

Thread snakes feed on termites and ants. The approximately 80 species live in Africa, tropical Asia and southern USA, through Central and South America to Argentina.

### Western Blind Snake *Leptotyphlops humilis*

**RANGE** S.W. USA: S.W. Utah, south to N. Mexico and Baja California

**HABITAT** Desert, grassland, scrub, rocky canyons

**SIZE** 7–15 in (18–38 cm)

A smooth, round-bodied snake, the western blind snake has a blunt head and tail. It lives almost anywhere where there is sandy or gravelly soil, and spends much of its life below ground, emerging only occasionally. It eats ants and termites which it finds by smell. With its slender body, it can slide into their nests.

The snakes mate in spring. The female lays 2 to 6 eggs. She watches over the eggs, which may be laid in a communal nest.

## TYPHLOPIDAE: BLIND SNAKE FAMILY

The 150 or so species in this family of burrowing snakes occur in tropical and warm temperate regions throughout the world. They rarely exceed 23½ in (60 cm) in length. Well adapted for burrowing, they have thin, cylindrical bodies, smooth, polished scales and narrow, streamlined heads. Their eyes are extremely small and each is covered with a translucent scale. They eat small invertebrates, particularly ants.

### Schlegel's Blind Snake *Typhlops schlegelii*

**RANGE** Africa: Kenya to South Africa

**HABITAT** Sandy or loamy soil

**SIZE** 23½ in (60 cm)

Schlegel's blind snake has a spine on the end of its tail which helps to provide leverage when it is burrowing. Although most of its life is spent underground, it will come near the surface in damp or wet weather.

The female lays 12 to 60 eggs, which are already well advanced in their development when they are laid and take only 4 to 6 weeks to hatch.

## ANOMALEPIDAE

Sometimes grouped in the Typhlopidae family, there are about 20 species in this family, all found in Central and South America. They closely resemble the blind and thread snakes.

### *Anomalepis* sp.

**RANGE** Mexico, tropical Central and South America to Peru

**HABITAT** Forest

**SIZE** Up to 15¾ in (40 cm)

There are 4 species of *Anomalepis* snakes, all little-known wormlike burrowing snakes with cylindrical bodies. They spend much of their lives buried under leaf litter in damp humus and are rarely seen on the surface, except after rain. They feed on termites, ants and other small invertebrates.

## ANILIIDAE: PIPE SNAKE FAMILY

There are 10 species in this family, all of which have a variety of primitive characteristics, including a pelvis and vestigial hind limbs, which appear as spurs, close to the vent. One species lives in northern South America and the other 9 are found in Southeast Asia. All are excellent burrowers and feed on vertebrates such as other snakes.

### False Coral Snake *Anilius scytale*

| | |
|---|---|
| **RANGE** | N. South America, east of Andes |
| **HABITAT** | Forest |
| **SIZE** | 29½–33½ in (75–85 cm) |

A burrowing species, the false coral snake has a cylindrical body, small head and smooth scales. Its tiny eyes lie beneath transparent scales. Its small mouth is not particularly flexible and it is restricted to slender prey animals such as other snakes, caecilians (limbless wormlike amphibians) and the snakelike amphisbaenids. The young develop inside the female's body and are born fully formed.

## UROPELTIDAE: SHIELDTAIL SNAKE FAMILY

There are about 40 species in this family of burrowing snakes, all found in India and Sri Lanka.

### Red-blotched Shieldtail *Uropeltis biomaculatus*

| | |
|---|---|
| **RANGE** | India, Sri Lanka |
| **HABITAT** | Mountain forest |
| **SIZE** | Up to 12 in (30.5 cm) |

The red-blotched shieldtail has the typical cylindrical body of a burrowing snake. It tunnels by forming the body into a series of S-bends, which press against the sides of the tunnel, and then thrusting the head forward into the soil. It is a secretive, inoffensive snake and feeds mainly on earthworms and grubs.

The female gives birth to 3 to 8 fully formed live young, which have developed inside her body and hatch from their membranous shells as they are laid.

### Blyth's Landau Shieldtail *Rhinophis blythis*

| | |
|---|---|
| **RANGE** | Sri Lanka |
| **HABITAT** | Forest |
| **SIZE** | Up to 14 in (35.5 cm) |

This small shieldtail burrows through the soil. Most of its life is spent beneath the ground and it feeds on earthworms. Males tend to have longer tails than females. The female gives birth to litters of 3 to 6 fully formed live young which are about ⅓ in (1 cm) long at birth.

## XENOPELTIDAE: SUNBEAM SNAKE FAMILY

Placed in a family of its own, the sunbeam snake of Southeast Asia has both primitive and advanced features. Although much of its skull structure is primitive and inflexible, its lower jaw is flexible, which permits a more varied diet. Like the more advanced snakes, it has no pelvic girdle.

### Sunbeam Snake *Xenopeltis unicolor*

| | |
|---|---|
| **RANGE** | S.E. Asia: Myanmar to Indonesia |
| **HABITAT** | Rice fields, cultivated land |
| **SIZE** | Up to 3¼ ft (1 m) |

The iridescence of its smooth, blue scales gives the sunbeam snake its name. It spends time both above and below ground and, using its head, can burrow rapidly in soft soil. With its flexible lower jaw, it is able to take a wide range of fair-sized prey, including frogs, small rodents and birds.

# PYTHONS, BOAS AND WART SNAKES

## BOIDAE: PYTHON AND BOA FAMILY

There are about 60 species of snake in this family, many of them well known. Most specialists regard the group as primitive, since its members retain characteristics which are found in lizards, but which have been lost by the more highly evolved snakes, such as vipers. For example, a pelvic girdle and diminutive hind limbs are discernible in some species. All species have two working lungs, while advanced snakes have lost the left lung.

Within the family are 2 groups – the pythons and the boas. These are sometimes placed in separate families, pythonidae and boidae. The 20 species of python inhabit the more tropical parts of the Old World. They are often found in or near water, but also spend much of their time in trees and may have prehensile tails. They lay eggs which develop and hatch outside the body. The boas are found mainly in the New World and live on the ground, in trees or in or near water. The young develop inside the body and hatch from thin-shelled eggs as the eggs are laid.

Boid snakes are predators, but they are non-venomous, capturing their prey with their teeth or killing it by constriction – wrapping the prey in the body coils until it suffocates.

adapts to widely contrasting climatic conditions but seems to prefer swampy rain forest. Primarily a ground-living snake, it does, however, climb trees and has a slightly prehensile tail which allows it to grasp branches. It kills its prey, mostly birds and mammals, by encircling them in the muscular coils of its body until the prey is suffocated or crushed.

### Emerald Tree Boa *Boa caninus*

| | |
|---|---|
| **RANGE** | South America: Guyana, south to Brazil and Bolivia |
| **HABITAT** | Rain forest |
| **SIZE** | 4 ft (1.2 m) |

This boa spends much of its life in trees, where it rests with its body flattened and pressed to a branch, which it grasps with its prehensile tail. It watches for prey, often birds and bats which it catches and kills with its strong front teeth. It is the most fast-moving of all boas and is also a good swimmer.

### Boa constrictor *Boa constrictor*

| | |
|---|---|
| **RANGE** | Mexico, Central and South America to N. Argentina; West Indies |
| **HABITAT** | Desert to rain forest |
| **SIZE** | Up to 18¼ ft (5.6 m) |

The second-largest snake in the Americas, the boa constrictor

### Rubber Boa *Charina bottae*

| | |
|---|---|
| **RANGE** | W. USA: Washington to S. California, east to Montana and Utah |
| **HABITAT** | Woodland, coniferous forest, meadows, sandy banks of streams |
| **SIZE** | 13¾–33 in (35–84 cm) |

This small boa ranges farther into the temperate zone than any other. It varies in coloration from tan to olive-green, and the confusing appearance of its broad snout and blunt tail are the origin of its other common name of "two-headed snake".

Usually active in the evening and at night, it is a good burrower and swimmer and can climb, using its prehensile tail. During the day, it hides under rocks or logs, or burrows into sand or leaf litter. It feeds on small mammals, birds and lizards which it kills by constriction. In late summer, the female gives birth to 2 to 8 live young which measure 6 to 9 in (15 to 23 cm).

## Anaconda

*Eunectes murinus*

**RANGE** South America, south to Argentina

**HABITAT** Swampy river valleys, stream banks

**SIZE** 29½ ft (9 m)

One of the world's longest snakes, the anaconda spends much of its life in sluggish fresh water but also climbs small trees and bushes with the aid of its slightly prehensile tail. It does not pursue its prey but lurks in murky water waiting for birds and animals to come to the edge to drink. It seizes its victim and then kills it by constriction. It can only remain submerged for about 10 minutes and usually glides along with the top of its head showing above the water.

In the breeding season, males court their mates by making loud booming sounds. Females produce litters of as many as 40 live young, each of which is about 26 in (66 cm) long at birth.

## Carpet Python

*Morelia argus*

**RANGE** Australia, New Guinea

**HABITAT** Forest, scrub, bush

**SIZE** 11 ft (3.4 m)

A common, widely distributed snake, the carpet python is usually found inland, less often on the coast. The dark pattern on its body mimics dead leaves and provides camouflage as it lurks among plant debris. It moves well on the ground, in trees or in water. Usually active at night, it rests during the day in a tree or hollow stump and occasionally basks in the sun.

A nonvenomous snake, the carpet python kills small mammals such as mice and rabbits, and birds, such as domestic fowl, with its sharp teeth. The female lays up to 35 eggs.

## Indian Python *Python molurus* **LR:nt**

**RANGE** India, S.E. Asia, Indonesia

**HABITAT** Estuarine mangroves, scrub jungle, cool rain forest

**SIZE** 16½–20 ft (5–6.1 m)

One of the largest species in the world, the Indian python has suffered a reduction in numbers in some areas where it is hunted for its fine skin. It is a thick-bodied, smooth snake with a head shaped like the head of a spear. Like others of its genus, it is believed to have heat sensors near the nostrils to help it find its warm-blooded prey. Coloration varies by locality, but the pale gray race found in west India is reputedly less irritable than others and is used by "snake-charmers".

By day, the Indian python basks in the sun or rests in a cave, abandoned burrow or other refuge. At night it prowls around, looking for prey, or lies in wait at a water hole or other spot where it is sure to encounter its prey – mice, civets, small deer, wild boar and birds. It stalks the animal, then grasps and encircles it with its body coils, restricting the breathing and heartbeat until they fail.

The female python lays up to 100 eggs in a hole, cave or tree hollow and, coiling herself around the eggs, incubates them for 60 to 80 days. She occasionally makes rhythmic contractions of her body muscles, and by this gradual shuffling she moves the eggs into the warmth of the sun or the protection of the shade.

## ACROCHORDIDAE: WART SNAKE FAMILY

The 3 species in this family are both aquatic, nonvenomous snakes, found in India, Southeast Asia and Australia. They are most unusual, having loose, sagging skin and distinctly tapering bodies. Highly specialized for aquatic life, wart snakes have flaps in the roof of the mouth which close off the nasal passages when they are under water. In the same way, the notch on the upper lip, through which the sensory tongue is protruded, can be closed off by a pad on the chin.

## Elephant-trunk Snake *Acrochordus javanicus*

**RANGE** India, S.E. Asia, New Guinea

**HABITAT** Rivers, streams, canals

**SIZE** 5 ft (1.5 m)

This stout, sluggish snake is almost helpless on land but an expert swimmer. It is generally more active at night and feeds exclusively on fish. The female gives birth to 25 to 30 live young which are active and able to feed immediately.

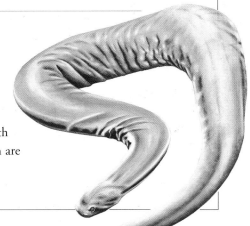

# BURROWING ASPS AND COLUBRID SNAKES

## ATRACTASPIDAE: BURROWING ASP FAMILY

These small to medium sized slender snakes have blunt heads and short tails. The 16 species of burrowing asps are found in Africa and the middle East. They are secretive snakes, living in leaf litter and burrowing into the soil.

### Bibron's Burrowing Asp/Viper *Atractaspis bibroni*

| | |
|---|---|
| **RANGE** | South Africa |
| **HABITAT** | Dry, sandy regions |
| **SIZE** | Up to 31½ in (80 cm) |

Also known as the southern mole viper, this snake is a member of a group of burrowing snakes all of which are found in Africa and the Middle East. Like its relatives, it has a shovel-shaped head, with no distinct neck, a rounded, slender body and short tail. Its eyes are small.

A venomous snake, the burrowing asp has a sophisticated venom apparatus which is similar to that of the true vipers and, because of this, it was originally believed to be a viper. Its fangs are huge, relative to the small head, and can be folded or erected independently of each other. Once swung into the attack position, the fangs eject venom which is pumped into them from the connected poison glands.

The burrowing asp burrows into the soil with its strong snout. It usually emerges at the surface only at night after rain. If it finds itself on the surface in sunlight, it coils itself into a ball and hides its head inside the coils. The burrowing asp feeds on other reptiles, such as burrowing lizards and blind snakes which it kills with its venomous bite.

The female burrowing asps reproduce by laying eggs.

## COLUBRIDAE: COLUBRID SNAKE FAMILY

The colubrid family is the largest of the three groups of advanced snakes and contains 1,600 species – two-thirds of all living snakes. Although a convenient assemblage of species, this large, diverse family may not be a natural one, and is often divided into subfamilies in order to clarify the relationships. Colubrids are found on all continents except Antarctica.

There is as much variation within the colubrid family as there is between the other two families of advanced snakes, the Vipers and Elapids, but there are a few shared characteristics. No colubrids have any vestiges of a pelvis or hind limbs, and all have the left lung reduced or even absent (for streamlining of the body). The lower jaw is flexible, but there are no hollow poison-injecting fangs. Instead there are solid teeth on both jaws and, in some cases, teeth on the upper jaw, with grooves which are connected to a poison gland (rear-fanged snakes).

Most colubrids are harmless; all those which are dangerous, such as the boomslang (*Dispholidus typus*) and the twig snake (*Thelotornis kirtlandii*), occur in Africa.

Colubrids occur in all habitats. There are ground-dwelling, arboreal, burrowing, even aquatic species. All are predators, and eat anything from insects to small mammals. Most colubrids lay eggs, but some give birth to fully formed live young.

### *Fimbrios klossi*

| | |
|---|---|
| **RANGE** | Vietnam, Kampuchea |
| **HABITAT** | Mountains with low vegetation |
| **SIZE** | 15¾ in (40 cm) |

This little-known snake is ground-dwelling and probably nocturnal. The scales around the mouth are curved, forming a fringe of soft projections the exact function of which is unknown, although they may be sensory. *Fimbrios* feeds mainly on earthworms. Like other members of its subfamily, Xenodermatinae, *Fimbrios klossi* probably lays 2 to 4 eggs.

## Slug Snake *Pareas sp.*

**RANGE** S.E. Asia

**HABITAT** Forest

**SIZE** 12–30 in (30.5–76 cm)

The slug snakes, also known as bluntheads, are mostly nocturnal and have slender bodies and short, wide heads. They feed mainly on slugs and snails, and their lower jaws are adapted for removing the snails from their shells, for they are capable of being extended and retracted independently of the upper jaws. Having seized a snail, the slug snake inserts its lower jaw into the shell so that the curved teeth at the tip of the jaw sink into the snail's soft body. It then retracts its jaw, winkling out the snail from the shell.

These snakes lack the so-called dental groove on the chin possessed by most snakes that allows the jaw to be distended when taking in large prey. Thus their diet is restricted to the small items for which they are admirably specialized. As far as is known, these snakes reproduce by laying eggs.

## Snail-eating Snake *Dipsas indica*

**RANGE** Tropical South America

**HABITAT** Forest

**SIZE** About 26¾ in (68 cm)

The snail-eating snake is a nocturnal, ground-dwelling species with a strong body, large head and blunt, short snout. Its upper jaw is short with few teeth, and its lower jaw long with elongate, curved teeth. The structure of the jaws is such that the lower jaw can be swung backward and forward without movement of the upper jaw.

It feeds entirely on snails in a manner similar to the Pareas snakes, inserting its lower jaw into the snail's shell, twisting it to sink the teeth into the soft body and then pulling it out. As it attempts to defend itself, the struggling snail produces large quantities of slime which clogs up the snake's nasal openings; while extracting the snail, the snake relies, therefore, on air stored in its lungs to breathe.

## Spotted Water Snake *Enhydris punctata*

**RANGE** Australia: coast of Northern Territory

**HABITAT** Creeks, swamps, rivers

**SIZE** 11¾–19¾ in (30–50 cm)

The spotted water snake is one of a subfamily of about 34 colubrids, all specialized for life in water. It is able to move on land as well as in water and comes ashore to bask on river banks and shores. Its small eyes are directed upward and its nostrils, too, are on the upper surface of the head. Pads of skin close off the nostrils completely when the snake is diving.

Mildly venomous, the water snake is rear-fanged – grooved teeth at the back of the upper jaw are connected to a poison gland. It preys on aquatic creatures such as fish and frogs. Females give birth to fully formed live young.

## White-bellied Mangrove Snake *Fordonia leucobalia*

**RANGE** Coast of N. Australia, S.E. Asia

**HABITAT** Mangroves

**SIZE** 2½–3¼ ft (60 cm–1 m)

A member of the subfamily of aquatic colubrids, the white-bellied mangrove snake has similar adaptations to those of the rest of its group, such as nostrils near the top of its head and upward facing eyes. Large numbers of these snakes frequent the edges of swamps, where they forage among the roots for food. It is a rear-fanged snake and feeds mainly on crabs, which seem strongly affected by its venom, unlike frogs and mammals, which are not. Fish are also included in its diet. If alarmed, the snake will take refuge in a crab burrow.

# COLUBRID SNAKES CONTINUED

### Dark-green Whipsnake

*Coluber viridiflavus*

**RANGE** Europe: N.E. Spain, C. and S. France, Italy, S. Switzerland, former Yugoslavia, Corsica, Sardinia

**HABITAT** Dry, vegetated areas: hillsides, woodland edge, gardens

**SIZE** Up to 6¼ ft (1.9 m)

A slender, elongate snake, the dark-green whipsnake has a rounded snout, large eyes and a long tapering tail. Some individuals may, in fact, be almost all black, rather than dark green. Males are generally longer than females. Usually active in the daytime, it is a ground-dwelling snake but can climb well on rocks and bushes. It locates its prey by sight and usually feeds on lizards, frogs, mammals, birds and other snakes.

Males compete fiercely for mates in the breeding season. The female lays her 5 to 15 eggs among rocks or in cracks in the soil. The young hatch in 6 to 8 weeks.

### Egg-eating Snake *Dasypeltis scabra*

**RANGE** Africa, south and east of the Sahara

**HABITAT** Woodland, scrub

**SIZE** 29½ in (75 cm)

This slender snake is one of the few snakes to exist entirely on hard shelled birds' eggs. It hunts for eggs on the ground and in trees, mainly at night, although it is sometimes active during the day. Most other snakes which eat eggs take only the softer-shelled lizard and snake eggs, since they are not able to cope with such tough, unwieldy food. The egg-eating snakes however have developed specialized equipment for dealing with hard-shelled eggs.

The egg-eating snake's mouth and jaws are extremely flexible and are hinged in such a way as to enable them to accommodate large eggs. It has only a few small teeth in each jaw, but special projections of the neck vertebrae form a serrated edge of "teeth" which pierce the wall of the snake's esophagus.

When the snake swallows an egg, which may be twice the size of its head, it pushes its mouth against the egg, gradually engulfing it in its jaws, while stretching the elastic ligament joining the two halves of the lower jaw to the utmost. The small neck scales stand apart in rows, exposing the skin beneath. The esophagus teeth slit the egg open and the contents pass into the stomach, while a specialized valve rejects the shell which is then regurgitated.

When the supply of eggs is plentiful, the snake eats as many as possible and stores up fat reserves in its body on which it is able to survive during those seasons when few eggs are available.

Females of this species lay between 8 and 14 eggs, which they deposit singly rather than in a clutch – an unusual habit for an egg-laying snake.

### Grass Snake *Natrix natrix*

**RANGE** Europe: Scandinavia, south to Mediterranean countries; N.W. Africa; Asia, east to Lake Baikal, Russia

**HABITAT** Damp meadows, marshes, ditches, river banks

**SIZE** Up to 4 ft (1.2 m); occasionally up to 6½ ft (2 m)

The grass snake swims well and spends some time in water, although it is less aquatic than some other *Natrix* species. It is one of the most common and widespread European snakes and 3 subspecies, which differ in coloration and pattern, occur over its large range. Females are generally longer and thicker-bodied than males.

The grass snake is active during the day, hunting for food in water and on land. It eats mainly frogs, toads and newts, but also takes fish and occasionally small mammals and young birds. Much of its prey is swallowed alive. It has a venomous secretion that is toxic to small animals but harmless to man.

Depending on the latitude, grass snakes start to breed from April onward. The male courts the female, by rubbing his chin over her body. He works his way up to her neck and they intertwine and mate. Some 8 or more weeks later, the female lays 30 to 40 eggs, which are fairly advanced in embryonic development. She deposits the eggs in a warm spot, preferably in decaying organic matter such as a compost or manure heap. The young hatch out after 1 or 2 months, depending on the warmth of their surroundings.

## Red-bellied Snake *Storeria occipitomaculata*

**RANGE** Extreme S. Canada; E. USA: Maine to Minnesota, south to Texas and Florida

**HABITAT** Woodland on hills and mountains, bogs

**SIZE** 7¾–16 in (20–40.5 cm)

There are 3 subspecies of this widely distributed snake which vary in coloration and the arrangement of the characteristic bright spots on the neck. In the Florida subspecies the spots may be fused, forming a collar. The red-bellied snake lives from sea level to 5,600 ft (1,700 m) and is active mostly at night, when it preys on insects and small invertebrates such as earthworms and slugs. When alarmed the snake may curl its upper lip in threat, while discharging a musky secretion from its cloacal opening.

The snakes mate in spring or autumn. Before copulation, the male throws his body into a series of waves from tail to head and rubs his chin, equipped with sensory tubercles, over the female's body. He also has sensory tubercles around the cloaca (genital opening) region which appear to help him position himself correctly. The young develop inside the female's body and are born fully formed and measuring 2¾ to 4 in (7 to 10 cm).

## Common Garter Snake

*Thamnophis sirtalis*

**RANGE** S. Canada; USA, except desert regions

**HABITAT** Damp country, often near water: marshes, meadows, ditches, farmland, woodland

**SIZE** 17¾ in–4¼ ft (45 cm–1.3 m)

The most widely distributed snake in North America and one of the most familiar, the garter snake occurs in many subspecies over its huge range. The coloration is, therefore, extremely variable, but the garter snake nearly always has distinctive back and side stripes. It is active during the day and hunts for frogs, toads, salamanders and small invertebrates among damp vegetation on the ground.

One of the few snakes to occur in the far north, the garter snake is able to withstand cold weather well and is found as far as 67° North. In the southern part of its range, it may remain active all year round, but in the north it hibernates in communal dens.

Garter snakes usually mate in spring, sometimes communally as they emerge from hibernation. They may, however, mate in autumn, in which event the sperm spend most of the winter in the female's oviduct and do not move into position to fertilize the eggs until spring. Before copulation, the male snake throws his body into a series of waves and then rubs his chin over the female's body. The tubercles on his chin must receive the right sensory responses before he will mate. As many as 80 young develop inside the female's body, nourished by a form of placenta, and are born fully formed.

## Rat Snake *Elaphe obsoleta*

**RANGE** S. Canada; USA: Vermont to Minnesota, south to Texas and Florida; N. Mexico

**HABITAT** Forest, swamps, farmland, wooded slopes

**SIZE** 33¾ in–8¼ ft (86 cm–2.5 m)

A large, powerful species, the rat snake tolerates a variety of habitats in wet and dry situations. There are 6 or more subspecies which occur in one of three main color patterns – plain, blotched or striped. It is an agile snake, good at climbing, and hunts rodents and other small mammals, birds and lizards in trees and in barns or ruined buildings. Usually active during the day, it may tend to be nocturnal in summer. In much of its range, it hibernates throughout the winter.

Rat snakes mate in spring and autumn. The female lays a clutch of between 5 and 30 eggs in leaf debris or under a rock or log. The eggs hatch in 2 to 4 months, depending on the temperature – the warmer the weather, the quicker they hatch.

# COLUBRID SNAKES CONTINUED

**Smooth Snake** *Coronella austriaca*

**RANGE** Europe: S. Scandinavia, S. England, south to N. Spain,
Italy and Greece; east to Russia, N. Iran

**HABITAT** Dry rocky areas, heathland, open woodland

**SIZE** 19¾–31½ in (50–80 cm)

The slender, round-bodied smooth snake varies in coloration
over its wide range but nearly always has a dark streak on each
side of its head. The head is fairly small and pointed and there is
no clear neck. It is a secretive snake, although active in the
daytime, and adapts to a variety of dry habitats up to 5,900 ft
(1,800 m); it is even occasionally found in moist areas. Although
it rarely basks in full sun, the smooth snake likes to retreat to
warm, shady areas under rocks or stones. Lizards, particularly
lacertids, make up the bulk of its diet and it also eats small
snakes, young mammals and insects. It holds its prey in a few
coils of its body to subdue it while it starts to swallow.

In the breeding season, males fight one another for mates.
The female gives birth to 2 to 15 live young in autumn; they
emerge in transparent, membranous shells from which they free
themselves immediately. The newly born young measure 4¾ to
7¾ in (12 to 20 cm) in length. Males mature at 3 years and
females at 4.

**Common Kingsnake** *Lampropeltis getulus*

**RANGE** USA: New Jersey to Florida in east,
Oregon to California in west; Mexico

**HABITAT** Varied, forest, woodland, desert, prairie, swamps, marshes

**SIZE** 35½ in–6½ ft (90 cm–2 m)

A large snake with
smooth, shiny
scales, the common
kingsnake usually
has alternating dark
and light rings, but
some of the many

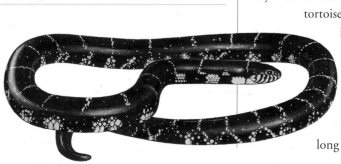

subspecies have more irregular speckled patterns. It is primarily a
ground-dwelling species, although it may sometimes climb into
small trees or bushes, and is active in the daytime, usually in the
early morning and at dusk. Found in almost every type of
habitat it will take refuge under rocks, in vegetation and under
logs. It feeds on snakes, including rattlesnakes and coral snakes,
lizards, mice and birds which it kills by constriction, holding the
prey in the powerful coils of its body until it suffocates. Indeed,
the description "king" seems to be applied only to those snakes
which feed on other snakes.

Kingsnakes mate in spring. The female lays 3 to 24 eggs
which usually hatch in 2 to 3 months, depending on the
warmth of the weather.

**Gopher Snake** *Pituophis melanoleucas*

**RANGE** S.W. Canada; USA: W. and C. states, Florida; Mexico

**HABITAT** Dry woodland, grassland, prairies, rocky desert

**SIZE** 4–8¼ ft (1.2—2.5 m)

The large, robust gopher snake is found in a
variety of habitats and is a good climber and
burrower. Its head is small and somewhat pointed and,
although the coloration varies in the many subspecies over its
wide range, most gopher snakes have pale bodies with black,
brown or reddish markings.

Usually active by day, the gopher snake may become nocturnal
in hot weather. It feeds largely on rodents, as well as on rabbits,
birds and lizards, all of which it kills by constriction – throwing
its powerful body coils around the victim until it suffocates. It
may burrow underground for shelter or take over mammal or
tortoise burrows. If alarmed, the gopher snake flattens
its head, hisses loudly and vibrates its tail
before attacking the enemy.

Gopher snakes mate in spring and the
female lays up to 24 eggs in a burrow or
beneath a rock or log. The young hatch in
9 to 11 weeks and are up to 17¾ in (45 cm)
long on hatching.

## Paradise Tree Snake
*Chrysopelea paradisi*

**RANGE** S.E. Asia: Philippines to Indonesia
**HABITAT** Forest
**SIZE** Up to 4 ft (1.2 m)

Also known as the flying snake, this species glides from tree to tree, from one branch down to another. It launches itself into the air, its body stretched out and its belly pulled in to make a concave surface with maximum resistance to the air. It glides downward at an angle of 50 or 60 degrees to the ground for 65 ft (20 m) or more and lands safely. It seems to have little control over its "flight", however, and cannot glide upward or steer with any degree of efficiency.

A further adaptation for its tree-dwelling life are the ridged scales on the snake's belly which help it to climb almost vertically up tree trunks. The ridges are thrust against the bark and enable the snake to gain a hold on every tiny irregularity of surface. Thus, it can ascend right into the trees, where few other snakes can go, and feed on the abundant tree-dwelling lizards. The closely related oriental tree snake, *C. ornata*, can glide and climb in the same manner.

The female paradise tree snake lays up to 12 eggs.

## Mangrove Snake *Boiga dendrophila*

**RANGE** S.E. Asia: Philippines to Indonesia
**HABITAT** Forest, mangroves
**SIZE** 8¼ ft (2.5 m)

The beautifully marked mangrove snake has a slender body with hexagonal scales on its back and sides. It is primarily an arboreal species, and hunts birds in the trees although it may also descend to the ground in order to prey on rodents. It is a venomous, rear-fanged snake – the grooved teeth toward the back of the jaw carry venom from the poison gland above the jaw into the prey. The female mangrove snake lays 4 to 7 eggs.

## Boomslang *Dispholidus typus*

**RANGE** Africa: central to South Africa
**HABITAT** Savanna
**SIZE** Up to 6½ ft (2 m)

The boomslang is one of only two dangerously poisonous snakes in the colubrid family. It has three large grooved fangs, set farther forward than the usual two fangs of colubrids, and extremely toxic venom which causes respiratory failure and hemorrhaging and can even kill a human being. Normally, however, it uses its venomous bites on lizards, particularly chameleons and on frogs and birds.

The boomslang is a tree-dwelling snake, usually active in the daytime. It varies in coloration but is usually predominantly black, brown or green on the upper surface.

The female boomslang lays 10 to 14 eggs.

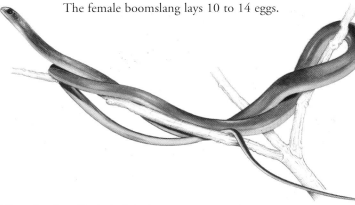

## Vine Snake *Oxybelis fulgidus*

**RANGE** Central America to N. South America
**HABITAT** Rain forest, cultivated land
**SIZE** 5–6½ ft (1.5–2 m)

Barely the thickness of a man's finger, about ½ in (1.25 cm) in diameter at the most, the vine snake is a remarkably slender, elongate species. As it lies amid the branches of forest trees, its proportions and greeny-brown coloration make it almost indistinguishable from the abundant creepers and vines. Its head, too, is thin and elongate and equipped with rear fangs and mild venom.

A slow-moving predator, active in the daytime and at night, the vine snake feeds mainly on young birds (which it steals from nests) and on lizards. If threatened, it puffs up the front of its body, revealing vivid coloration usually hidden under scales, and opens its long mouth wide. A frightened snake may also sway from side to side, like a stem in the breeze.

# COBRAS AND SEA SNAKES

## ELAPIDAE: COBRA AND SEA SNAKE FAMILY

There are about 250 species of highly venomous snake in this family, found mainly in tropical and subtropical areas of Australia, Asia, Africa (except Madagascar) and America. Elapids are most abundant in Australia.

The family is often divided into two groups – the elapids proper, including cobras, kraits, mambas and coral snakes, all of which are land- or tree-dwelling; and the sea snakes. The 50 or so species of sea snake lead entirely aquatic lives; most are marine but a few live in lakes or enter rivers. All elapids have fangs, situated near the front of the upper jaw, which are either deeply grooved for the transport of venom or have grooves the edges of which have fused to form a venom canal.

### Eastern Green Mamba *Dendroaspis angusticeps*

**RANGE** E. and S. Africa

**HABITAT** Savanna

**SIZE** 6½ ft (2 m)

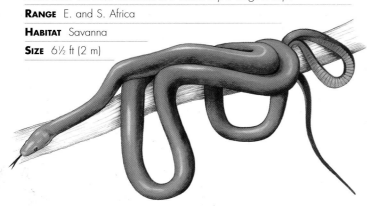

The slender, fast-moving mambas spend much of their lives in trees, where they feed on birds and lizards. Their venom is extremely toxic, but these snakes are not generally aggressive unless provoked and tend rather to flee from danger or threat.

In the breeding season, two or three males compete in ritualized fights for females. They wrap their bodies around one another and threaten with their raised heads. Mating may last for many hours. The female lays her 10 to 15 eggs in a hole in the ground or in a hollow tree stump. The young mambas hatch in 17 to 18 weeks.

### De Vis's Banded Snake *Denisonia devisii*

**RANGE** Australia: N. New South Wales, S. Queensland

**HABITAT** Dry, wooded areas

**SIZE** 19¾ in (50 cm)

A nocturnal species, De Vis's banded snake shelters under leaf litter or a log during the day and emerges at night to hunt for food, mainly lizards, which it kills with its toxic venom. It has a distinctive defense posture which it often adopts when threatened – it flattens its body, which is thrown into a series of stiff curves – and lashes out and bites if approached.

The female gives birth to about 8 live young, which have developed inside her body, nourished by a form of placenta.

### King Cobra *Ophiophagus hannah*

**RANGE** India, S. China, Malaysia to Philippines and Indonesia

**HABITAT** Forest, often near water

**SIZE** 13–18 ft (4–5.5 m)

The biggest poisonous snake in the world, the king cobra's head can be as big as a man's. It can make itself still more impressive by adopting the cobra threat posture, with the flexible neck ribs and loose skin spread out to form a wide hood. Despite its size, it is an agile, secretive snake and will flee into cover or even water if pursued. It feeds mainly on other snakes – its scientific name means "snake-eater" – but it will also eat monitor lizards.

The female king cobra constructs a nest of vegetation for her eggs, perhaps the only snake to do so. She gathers together twigs, branches and foliage with a coil of her forebody and then makes a chamber in the middle of the nest material by revolving her coiled body. She lays her clutch of between 18 and 40 eggs in this chamber, covers them and lies coiled on top of the nest to guard them while they incubate.

## Indian Cobra *Naja naja*

**RANGE** India, C. Asia, S.E. Asia

**HABITAT** Rain forest, rice fields, cultivated land

**SIZE** 6–7 ¼ ft (1.8–2.2 m)

The large, highly venomous Indian cobra eats rodents, lizards and frogs. This cobra can attack or defend itself from a distance by "spitting" venom which, can cause severe pain and damage if it reaches the eyes. The snake forces venom through its fangs, by exerting muscular pressure on the venom glands, so that it sprays out in twin jets for 6½ ft (2 m) or more. In its threat posture, it raises the front of its body and spreads its neck ribs and loose skin to form a disclike hood, which has markings resembling eyes on the back.

The female lays her 8 to 45 eggs (usually 12 to 20) in a hollow tree, a termite mound or earth. She guards them through the incubation period, leaving them only to feed. The young hatch after about 50 or 60 days.

## Eastern Brown Snake *Pseudonaja textilis*

**RANGE** E. Australia, E. New Guinea

**HABITAT** Wet forest, rocky hillsides

**SIZE** 5 ft (1.5 m)

This fast-moving, venomous snake is equally at home in dry or swampy land. It is active during the day and feeds on small mammals, frogs and lizards. Its coloration varies from yellow to dark brown with bands of varying intensity.

## Bandy-bandy *Vermicella annulata*

**RANGE** Australia (not extreme S.E., S.W. or N.W.)

**HABITAT** Varied, damp forest to desert sandhills

**SIZE** 15¾ in (40 cm)

The bandy-bandy's distinctive black and white rings vary in width and number, between the sexes and geographically. It is a nocturnal snake and eats mainly, blind snakes (Typhlopidae). Although venomous, its fangs and venom supply are too small to cause harm to anything other than small animals. An egg-laying species, the female deposits her eggs under rocks or logs.

## Eastern Coral Snake *Micrurus fulvius*

**RANGE** USA: North Carolina to Florida, west to Texas; Mexico

**HABITAT** Forest, often near water, rocky hillsides.

**SIZE** 22 in–4 ft (56 cm–1.2 m)

One of the only two elapids in North America the Eastern coral snake is a highly colorful species, with red, black and yellow or white bands ringing its body. The bright markings on the bodies of these highly poisonous snakes may serve as a warning to potential predators.

The coral snake is a secretive species, spending much of the time buried in leaf litter or sand. In the morning and late afternoon, it prowls on the surface in search of small lizards and snakes, which it kills with its highly toxic venom.

The female lays between 3 and 12 eggs which hatch out after about 3 months.

## Banded Sea Snake *Hydrophis cyanocinctus*

**RANGE** Persian Gulf, Indian Ocean, Pacific Ocean to Japan

**HABITAT** Coastal waters

**SIZE** 6½ ft (2 m)

The banded sea snake is fully adapted to aquatic life and never goes on land. Its body is laterally flattened and its tail is paddle-shaped and is used to provide propulsion when swimming. It breathes air but it can remain submerged for up to 2 hours at a time. Its nostrils are directed upward and can be closed off by pads of tissue bordering the front of the nostrils. The sea snake's body muscles have degenerated so far due to its aquatic lifestyle that if washed ashore, it collapses helplessly. Like all sea snakes, this species feeds on fish and has extremely toxic venom. The venom of one species of sea snake, *Enhydrina schistosa*, has been shown in laboratory tests to be more powerful than that of any other snake. All but one species of sea snake bear live young in the water. The banded sea snake gives birth to between 2 and 6 young.

# VIPERS

## VIPERIDAE: VIPER AND PIT VIPER FAMILY

This family has 2 subfamilies – viperinae (true vipers) and crotalinae (pit vipers).

There are about 50 species of viper, found all over the Old World except in Australia and Madagascar. Most species are short, sturdy snakes which live on the ground. A few species have become arboreal and have prehensile tails.

Vipers hide and ambush and strike their prey. The large hollow fangs fold back when the mouth is closed, then swing forward and become erect when the mouth is opened wide. Venom pumps into the fangs from venom glands at their base and the poison is injected as they pierce the prey.

The 120 species of pit vipers are highly venomous. They occur in eastern Europe and throughout mainland Asia and Japan. Although they are closely related to true vipers, they are considered by some experts to be a separate family. Unlike true vipers, pit vipers are absent from Africa and they possess some significant anatomical differences. The most important of these are the organs which give the snakes their common name – sensory pits on each side of the head in front of and just below the eyes which can detect heat and are used by these nocturnal snakes to locate warm-blooded prey. A pit viper strikes accurately at prey by moving its head from side to side and using the pit organs to discover its distance and direction. The viper kills with a rapid strike. The long, curved fangs of the upper jaw impale the target and inject venom. Small or weak creatures may be swallowed whole, but large prey is subdued with venom first.

One group of pit vipers, the rattlesnakes, has rattles on the tail which are a series of flattened, interlocking hollow segments. Each segment was once the tip of the tail, and a new one is added each time the snake sheds its skin. However, there are rarely more than 14 rattles at any time. The sound produced warns enemies to keep their distance.

### Common Viper *Vipera berus*

**RANGE** Britain, Europe to Siberia

**HABITAT** Moors, meadows, chalk hills, forest edge

**SIZE** Up to 19¾ in (50 cm)

The widely distributed common viper, or adder, is active in the day in the north of its range where it basks in the sun at every opportunity. Farther south, it is active in the evening and at night. In winter it hibernates, often using the abandoned burrow of another creature, until the temperature rises to an average of about 46°F (8°C) – the length of hibernation, therefore, varies with latitude. This viper moves slowly and does not climb but is a good swimmer. Mice, voles, shrews, lizards and frogs, all of which it kills with its venom, are its main foods, and it may occasionally take birds' eggs.

In the mating season, which may occur only every other year in areas where the hibernation period is long, males perform ritualistic aggressive dances before mating. They rear up in front of one another, swaying and trying to push each other over. The female retains her 3 to 20 eggs in the body until they are on the point of hatching. The young are about 7 in (18 cm) long when they hatch and are already equipped with venom and fangs.

### Desert Sidewinding Viper

*Vipera peringueyi*

**RANGE** Africa: Namibia

**HABITAT** Desert

**SIZE** 10 in (25.5 cm)

A small, rare viper, this species is found on the coastal sand dunes of the Namib Desert. It glides over the dunes with a sidewinding motion of lateral waves, leaving tracks like two parallel grooves where two parts of the body touch the sand and support the snake. During the day it half buries itself in the sand – a feat it can accomplish in about 20 seconds – to shelter from the sun or to lie in wait for prey such as rodents or lizards.

### Horned Viper *Vipera ammodytes*

**RANGE** Europe: Austria, Hungary, Balkan peninsula

**HABITAT** Arid, sandy regions

**SIZE** 30 in (76 cm)

Identifiable by the small horn on its snout, this viper is also called the sand viper because of its preference for sandy areas. It avoids woodland but is found in clearings, paths and often in vineyards. Its movements generally are slow, but it can strike rapidly with its fangs to kill small mammals, lizards, snakes and small birds. Horned vipers hibernate throughout the winter.

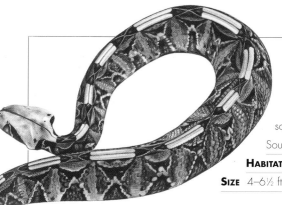

## Gaboon Viper
*Vipera gabonica*

**RANGE** W. Africa, south of the Sahara to South Africa

**HABITAT** Rain forest

**SIZE** 4–6½ ft (1.2–2 m)

One of the largest vipers, the Gaboon viper is well camouflaged, as it lies among the leaf litter on the forest floor, by the complex geometric patterns on its skin. It has a broad head, slender neck and stout body, tapering to a thin tail. Its fangs, the longest of any viper, are up to 2 in (5 cm) long and are supplied with a venom which causes hemorrhaging in the victim and inhibits breathing and heartbeat.

The Gaboon viper is nocturnal and, although it moves little, manages to find plenty of prey, such as rodents, frogs, toads and ground-living birds, on the forest floor. The female bears live young in litters of up to 30 at a time, each young snake is about 12 in (30.5 cm) long at birth.

## Aspic Viper *Vipera aspis*

**RANGE** Europe: France, Germany, Switzerland, Italy, Sicily

**HABITAT** Warm dry areas up to 9,800 ft (3,000 m)

**SIZE** Up to 30 in (76 cm)

Also known as the European asp, this species varies in coloration from area to area. A sluggish snake except when alarmed, it spends much of its time basking in the sun on a tree stump or rock, particularly in the early morning or late afternoon. It feeds on small mammals, lizards and nestling birds.

Mating takes place in the spring, after males have performed ritualistic combat displays, and females lay 4 to 18 eggs. In winter, aspic vipers hibernate singly or in groups in underground burrows or in wall crevices.

## Puff Adder *Bitis arietans*

**RANGE** Africa: Morocco, south of the Sahara to South Africa; Middle East

**HABITAT** Savanna up to 6,000 ft (1,800 m)

**SIZE** 4½–6½ ft (1.4–2 m)

Perhaps the most common and widespread African snake, the puff adder adapts to both moist and arid climates, but not to the extremes of desert or rain forest. It is one of the biggest vipers, with a girth of up to 9 in (23 cm), and can inflate its body even more when about to strike. Its fangs are about ½ in (1.25 cm) long, and the venom causes hemorrhaging in the victim.

Primarily a ground-living snake, the sluggish puff adder relies on its cryptic pattern and coloration to conceal it from both enemies and potential prey. It occasionally climbs into trees and is a good swimmer. Ground-living mammals, such as rats and mice, and birds, lizards, frogs and toads are its main prey.

The female puff adder lays 20 to 40 eggs which develop inside her body and hatch minutes after laying. The young are 6 to 7¾ in (15 to 20 cm) long when they hatch and can kill small mice.

## Saw-scaled Adder *Echis carinatus*

**RANGE** N. Africa to Syria, Iran, east to India

**HABITAT** Arid, sandy regions

**SIZE** 20¾–28¼ in (53–72 cm)

An extremely dangerous snake, the saw-scaled adder causes the majority of human deaths from snake bite in North Africa. This adder uses serrated scales on its sides to make a threatening noise; it coils its body into a tight spiral and then moves the coils so that the scales rub against one another, making a loud rasping sound. It is these scales which give the snake its common name.

The saw-scaled adder often uses a sideways motion, known as sidewinding, when on sandy ground. It throws its body, only two short sections of which touch the ground, into lateral waves. All the adder's weight is, therefore, pushing against the ground at these points, so providing the leverage to push it sideways.

During the day, the saw-scaled adder lies sheltered from the heat under a fallen tree trunk or rock, or flattens its body and digs into the sand by means of the "keeled" lateral scales.

This snake feeds at night on small rodents, skinks, geckos, frogs and large invertebrates such as centipedes and scorpions. Breeding usually takes place in the rainy season, and the female lays about 5 eggs. The young adders are about 7¾ in (20 cm) long when they hatch.

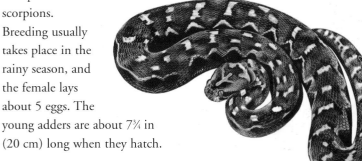

# PIT VIPERS

## Massasauga *Sistrurus catenatus*

**RANGE** USA: N.W. Pennsylvania to Arizona; N. Mexico

**HABITAT** Varied, swamp, marshland, woodland, prairie

**SIZE** 17¾ in–3¼ ft (45 cm–1 m)

The massasauga tolerates a wide range of habitat and although it seems to prefer swampy land, it also occurs even in arid grassland in the west of its range. It has up to eight rattles on its tail and is distinguished from other rattlers by the nine enlarged scales on its head. It preys on lizards, frogs, insects, small mammals and birds.

In April or May, the massasaugas mate and a litter of between 2 and 19 live young is born in the summer.

## Sidewinder *Crotalus cerastes*

**RANGE** S.W. USA: S. California, Nevada and Utah, south to Mexico

**HABITAT** Desert, rocky hillsides

**SIZE** 17–32¼ in (43–82 cm)

A small agile snake, the sidewinder has a distinctive hornlike projection over each eye. It is chiefly nocturnal and takes refuge in the burrow of another animal or under a bush during the day.

At night it emerges to hunt its prey, mainly small rodents, such as pocket mice and kangaroo rats, and lizards. A desert inhabitant, this snake moves with a sideways motion, known as sidewinding, thought to be the most efficient mode of movement for a snake on sand. It throws its body into lateral waves, only two short sections of it touching the ground. All the snake's weight, therefore, is pushing against the ground at these points, and this provides the leverage to move it sideways. As it travels, the snake leaves a trail of parallel J-shaped markings. An ideal form of movement in open, sparsely vegetated country, sidewinding has the advantage of reducing contact between the snake's body and the hot sand.

Sidewinders mate in April or May, and the female gives birth to 5 to 18 live young about 3 months later.

## Fer-de-Lance *Bothrops atrox*

**RANGE** S. Mexico to South America; West Indies

**HABITAT** Low coastal areas

**SIZE** 8 ft (2.45 m)

A common pit viper, the fer-de-lance varies in color and pattern over its wide range. A sheath of membranous flesh covers its fangs, but when the snake bites the sheath is pushed back. The fer-de-lance feeds mainly on small mammals and its venom causes rapid and severe internal bleeding. The female is an unusually prolific breeder for a pit viper, giving birth to up to 50 live young in a yearly litter.

## Eastern Diamondback Rattlesnake *Crotalus adamanteus*

**RANGE** E. USA: North Carolina to Florida Keys, west to Louisiana

**HABITAT** Woodland, farmland

**SIZE** 35¾ in–7¾ ft (91 cm–2.4 m)

The largest rattler, the eastern diamondback is the most dangerous snake in North America. Its potent venom attacks the

blood cells of its victims. Its striking diamond patterned skin provides camouflage as it lies coiled in vegetation, watching for prey such as rabbits and birds which it then ambushes.

The female diamondback bears litters of between 8 and 12 live young – each of which measures between 11¾ to 14¼ in (30 and 36 cm) – in late summer. The female defends the young snakes aggressively.

## Cottonmouth *Agkistrodon piscivorus*

**RANGE** S. and S.E. USA

**HABITAT** Marshes, streams, lakes, swamps

**SIZE** 20 in–6¼ ft (51 cm–1.9 m)

The heavy-bodied cottonmouth spends much of its life either in or near water. It swims well, holding its head up out of the water. This snake is most active at night, when it preys on amphibians, fish, snakes and birds, and it is one of the few snakes to eat carrion. The cottonmouth is an extremely dangerous species. Its venom is hemolytic – it destroys the red blood cells and coagulates the blood around the bite. The venom is actually extracted and used medically for its coagulating properties in the treatment of hemorrhagic conditions.

Female cottonmouths breed every other year and produce litters of up to 15 young which measure between 7 and 13 in (18 and 33 cm) at birth.

## Manushi/Asiatic Pit Viper *Agkistrodon halys*

**RANGE** Caspian Sea area, S. Russia, China

**HABITAT** Steppe, semidesert, taiga (coniferous forest)

**SIZE** 18–30 in (46–76 cm)

One of the few pit vipers found in the Old World, the manushi is found as far as 51° North. It is a mainly nocturnal snake and emerges at sunset in order to hunt its prey, which consists mostly of small mammals. Its venom is fatal to small creatures such as mice, but is seldom dangerous to larger animals and causes only mild temporary paralysis in humans.

The manushi hibernates through the winter, awaking in March. The males usually wake a week or more before females. Mating takes place shortly after the end of hibernation and the female lays a clutch of between 3 and 10 eggs which hatch about 3 months later.

## Bushmaster *Lachesis muta*

**RANGE** S. Nicaragua to Amazon basin of South America

**HABITAT** Rain forest

**SIZE** 8–11½ ft (2.45–3.5 m)

A rare, deadly and formidable pit viper, the bushmaster is the largest of its family. It is a strictly nocturnal snake, hiding during the day in a cave or tree hollow and emerging at night in order to hunt. It preys on small rodents and other mammals up to the size of small deer.

Although its venom is not as poisonous as that of some pit vipers, the bushmaster produces such large quantities of poison, and has such huge fangs with which to inject it, that it is one of the world's most dangerous snakes. The female bushmaster is the only New World viper to lay eggs.

# CROCODILES, ALLIGATORS, CAIMANS AND GAVIAL

## ORDER CROCODILIA

The crocodiles, alligators and caimans and the single species of gavial are the 3 families which together make up this order. All are powerful amphibious carnivores, preying on a range of vertebrate animals, although juvenile crocodiles also eat insects and other small invertebrates. Crocodilia are the most direct evolutionary descendants of the archosaurs, the dominant animal life forms from 190 to 65 million years ago. There are about 21 species alive today – 13 in the crocodile family, 7 alligators and caimans, and 1 gavial. All inhabit tropical and subtropical regions. Males and females look alike in all species, though males tend to grow larger than females.

All members of the order have elongate short-limbed bodies, covered with horny skin scales. Thickened bony plates on the back give added protection. The crocodilians have long snouts with many conical teeth anchored in deep sockets in the jaw bones. Breathing organs are highly modified for underwater predation – the external nostrils, on a projection at the snout-tip, have valves to close them off. A pair of flaps in the throat forms another valve which enables the animal to hold prey in its open jaws beneath the surface, without inhaling water.

Both crocodiles and alligators possess a pair of large teeth near the front of the lower jaw for grasping prey. In the crocodiles, these teeth fit into notches in the upper jaw and are visible when the jaws are closed, while in the alligators, the large teeth are accommodated in bony pits in the upper jaw.

### Gavial *Gavialis gangeticus* **EN**

| | |
|---|---|
| **RANGE** | N. India |
| **HABITAT** | Large rivers |
| **SIZE** | 23 ft (7 m) |

The Indian gavial has an extremely long narrow snout, studded with about 100 small teeth – ideal equipment for seizing fish and frogs underwater.

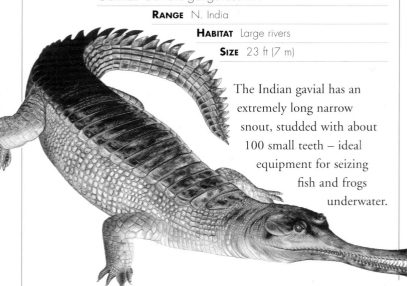

Like all crocodilians, the gavial has been hunted for its skin and it is now one of the rarest in Asia. Its hind limbs are paddlelike, and the gavial seems rarely to leave the water except to nest. The female lays her eggs at night in a pit dug in the river bank.

### American Alligator

*Alligator mississipiensis (sic)*

| | |
|---|---|
| **RANGE** | S.E. USA |
| **HABITAT** | Marshes, rivers, swamps |
| **SIZE** | Up to 18 ft (5.5 m) |

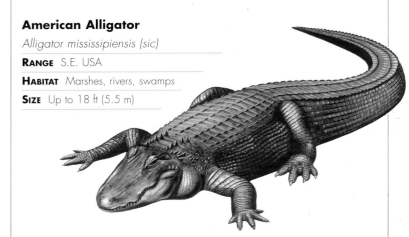

The American alligator, once struggling for survival against hunters and habitat destruction, has been so effectively protected by conservation laws that the population is now on the increase.

These alligators usually mate in shallow water in April, and courtship is slow and quiet. The male stays with the female for several days before mating, occasionally stroking her body with his forelimbs. As she nears acquiescence, he rubs her throat with his head and blows bubbles past her cheeks. The female finds a nest site near water and scrapes up whatever plant debris is available with sweeping movements of her body and tail. She packs the vegetation together to form a mound, with a cavity for the eggs. She lays 28 to 52 eggs and crawls over the mound to close the cavity with more vegetation. She guards the nest while the eggs incubate for about 65 days. The hatching young call to their mother, prompting her to open the nest and free them. They remain with her for up to 3 years.

### Spectacled Caiman *Caiman crocodilus*

| | |
|---|---|
| **RANGE** | Venezuela to S. Amazon basin |
| **HABITAT** | Slow still waters, lakes, swamps |
| **SIZE** | 5–6½ ft (1.5–2 m) |

There are several species and subspecies of this caiman and its name has been the subject of much dispute, it is often known as *C. sclerops*. Its common name derives from the ridge on the head between the eyes which resembles the bridge of a

pair of spectacles. The population of wild caimans has declined drastically since they are not only hunted for skins, but the young are also collected and sold as pets or stuffed as curios. The female caiman makes a nest of plant debris scraped together into a pile and lays an average of 30 eggs.

## West African Dwarf Crocodile *Osteolaemus tetraspis* **VU**

| | |
|---|---|
| **RANGE** | W. Africa, south of the Sahara |
| **HABITAT** | Streams and lakes |
| **SIZE** | 5 ft (1.5 m) |

Also known as the short-nosed crocodile, this animal is indeed characterized by its unusually short snout. It is now extremely rare owing to over exploitation for skins and to the destruction of its habitat. It resembles the New World alligators in appearance and size, although it is a member of the crocodile family. Little is known of its biology and breeding habits.

## Estuarine Crocodile *Crocodylus porosus* **LR:lc**

| | |
|---|---|
| **RANGE** | S. India through Indonesia; S. Australia |
| **HABITAT** | Estuaries, coasts, mangroves |
| **SIZE** | Up to 19½ ft (6 m) |

The estuarine crocodile is one of the largest and most dangerous species and has been known to attack man. It is rapidly being exterminated since its hide is considered the most valuable of all crocodiles for leather. It is now illegal to catch the estuarine crocodile in many areas, but the population is still low. Where hunting is allowed, it is restricted, and skin exports are controlled.

The most aquatic and most marine

of all crocodile species, the estuarine crocodile spends little time on land and swims great distances. The female lays 25 to 90 eggs in a mound of plant debris which she scrapes together near water. She guards the eggs for about 3 months while they incubate.

## Nile Crocodile *Crocodylus niloticus*

| | |
|---|---|
| **RANGE** | Africa (not Sahara or N.W.) |
| **HABITAT** | Large rivers, lakes, marshes |
| **SIZE** | 15–16½ ft (4.5–5 m) |

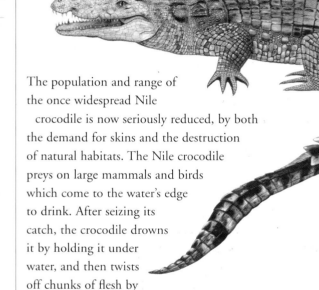

The population and range of the once widespread Nile crocodile is now seriously reduced, by both the demand for skins and the destruction of natural habitats. The Nile crocodile preys on large mammals and birds which come to the water's edge to drink. After seizing its catch, the crocodile drowns it by holding it under water, and then twists off chunks of flesh by spinning its own body in the water while holding on to the prey. Adult crocodiles swallow stones, which remain in the stomach and act as stabilizing ballast when the crocodiles are in water.

The Nile crocodile spends its nights in water and comes out on to the river banks just before sunrise in order to bask in the sun during the day. It leads a rather leisurely existence and does not need to feed every day.

The male defends a territory and enacts a courtship display at breeding time. The mated female lays 25 to 75 eggs in a pit near the water. She covers her eggs well and guards them during the 3-month incubation period. When ready to hatch, the young are sensitive to the footfalls of their mother overhead. They call to her from the nest; she uncovers them and carries them inside her mouth to a safe nursery area, where she cares for them assiduously for another 3 to 6 months. The young feed on insects, then progress to crabs, birds and fish before adopting the adult diet.

# AMPHIBIANS

*The first land vertebrates.*

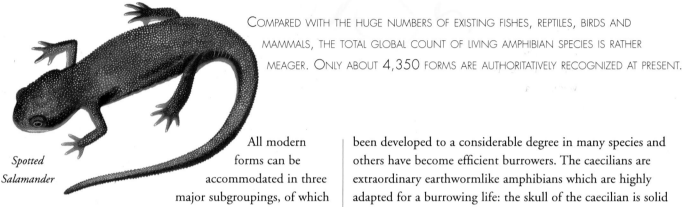

COMPARED WITH THE HUGE NUMBERS OF EXISTING FISHES, REPTILES, BIRDS AND MAMMALS, THE TOTAL GLOBAL COUNT OF LIVING AMPHIBIAN SPECIES IS RATHER MEAGER. ONLY ABOUT 4,350 FORMS ARE AUTHORITATIVELY RECOGNIZED AT PRESENT.

*Spotted
Salamander*

All modern forms can be accommodated in three major subgroupings, of which two are commonly recognizable animal types: first the Caudata or Urodela (newts and salamanders), and second, the Anura (frogs and toads). The third group is the Gymnophonia, which contains several families of limbless, elongate burrowing amphibians known as caecilians.

The amphibians were the first group of vertebrates to colonize the land. The distant evolutionary origins of amphibianlike animals from fish ancestors are a key phase in vertebrate evolution, heralding as they do all the subsequent developments of land-living vertebrates. Probably between 375 and 350 million years ago, lobe-fin fishes (crossopterygians) which already possessed lungs and four solidly constructed, downward-directed fins, began, more and more, to move out of freshwater habitats into adjacent terrestrial ones. The development of amphibians had begun.

Almost all the early amphibians must have retained fishlike habits. They were entirely or largely aquatic and were fish-eating animals like their lobe-finned fish ancestors. Only a few of these early amphibians were truly terrestrial forms.

Of the modern amphibians, it is the newts and salamanders that have kept the most fishlike appearance, with elongate bodies, sinuous swimming movements in water and dorsal and ventral fins on the body. Larval and adult newts and salamanders are relatively similar to one another in these respects, and adults frequently possess some larval characteristics.

The anuran frogs and toads all have a characteristic shortened body with no true tail. This dramatic alteration of the primitive, long-bodied amphibian has opened up a wide range of opportunities for new ways of living. In general, the limbs have become more powerful. Jumping and climbing have

been developed to a considerable degree in many species and others have become efficient burrowers. The caecilians are extraordinary earthwormlike amphibians which are highly adapted for a burrowing life: the skull of the caecilian is solid and bony, the limbs have completely disappeared.

Amphibians as a group demonstrate an interesting range of methods of locomotion, some very fishlike, others more suitable for life on land. Newts and salamanders have two basic forms of movement on land: when in haste, they move much as they do in water, by a sinuous wriggling of the body with little motion of the limbs; when moving more slowly, the body is lifted off the ground and supported on the four limbs, which move in the typical manner of four-legged vertebrates.

Frogs and toads, having lost their swimming tail, possess a completely different means of progression. Double, synchronized kicks of the long back legs are used for swimming

*Bullfrog*

in water and hopping and jumping on land. Both frogs and toads can also walk. Several groups of frogs and toads have independently developed rather similar specializations for moving in trees: they have adhesive pads on

*Fire Bellied Toad*

elongate toes enabling them to climb in vegetation. The limbless caecilians move by sinuous undulations similar to those of snakes.

Just as locomotion in amphibians is a fascinating amalgam of fishlike and terrestrial attributes, respiration shows a similar intriguing mix of "technologies". Amphibians may possess gills which are externally visible or tucked away inside a flap of skin. In both instances, the gills are developed from the outer skin and are not equivalent to the more internally placed gills of fishes. The gills are used by larval or adult amphibians for gaseous exchange (oxygen in, carbon dioxide out) in water. Amphibians on land use a mixture of two different mechanisms for the same function. Most possess lungs – paired sacs which open ultimately into the mouth cavity. This buccal cavity is used as a pump chamber to pull air in through the nostrils, before pushing it alternately a few times between lungs and mouth, then expelling it through the nostrils. The skin of the buccal cavity is itself well supplied with blood vessels and acts as a minor extension of the respiratory surface of the lungs.

In a similar way, the moist scaleless skin of the amphibians is also important for gaseous exchange. Indeed, the vital need of amphibians to keep their bodies moist for respiration is a major constraint on their utilization of habitats. Only rarely are they able to be active in potentially drying conditions. It also limits their size because, as an animal increases in size, its surface area becomes smaller in proportion to its body volume. A large

amphibian, therefore, has a correspondingly less adequate area of respiratory skin to provide for its larger body.

Like the reptiles, amphibians operate on a quite different basis of energy balance from that of birds and mammals. The latter two groups maintain a constant high temperature, somewhere between 96.8°F and 107.6°F (36°C and 42°C). Amphibians and reptiles, on the other hand, have body temperatures close to that of the air or water in which they live and gain heat by basking in the sun. They are dependent on external temperature or sunlight for full activity. They can, however, exist on smaller amounts of food than birds and mammals because of the low energy requirements of the cold-blooded condition.

Although two species of newt are known to be parthenogenetic (capable of virgin birth), all other amphibian species include both male and female forms. The females either lay eggs or produce live young. Almost all amphibians must return to water to breed, even those which are otherwise highly adapted to terrestrial conditions. A few species have sidestepped this constraint in extraordinary ways: for example, by providing a sac on the back in which egg development occurs.

In many amphibians, males and females have different appearances. In many frogs and toads, the males move to the water before the females and attract the latter with loud, species-specific calls. Males cling to the backs of the females, when mating, by means of roughened pads which develop on the hands, and fertilize the eggs externally as they are expelled.

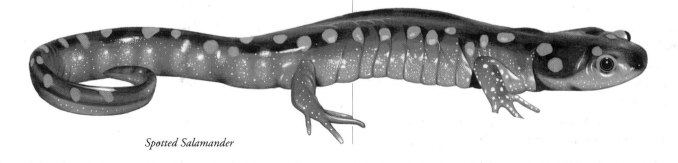

*Spotted Salamander*

Newts have complex courtship rituals. The males expel their sperm in packets, called spermatophores, which the females pick up in their genital openings (cloacas); the sperm then fertilizes the eggs internally.

Most amphibians pass through a distinctive tadpole larval stage or series of stages, after the hatching of the jelly-covered eggs. During this tadpole phase, the larvae are fully aquatic and possess prominent fins; they progressively acquire adult characteristics such as limbs and lungs. In some species of tailed amphibians, sexual maturity is reached at a stage which in other species would be regarded as larval. This process of neoteny or paedogenesis (breeding as a larva) is partly connected with effects of the hormone thyroxine, which is involved in larva-adult metamorphosis.

Although less adaptable and complex than the reptiles, birds and mammals, the amphibians in appropriate habitat conditions are clearly able to hold their own against other vertebrates. Due to their extremely low nutrient requirements, they are successful in conditions where food is sparse, seasonal or intermittent in availability.

***Cladogram showing possible phylogenetic relationships in amphibians.*** *The three lineages of amphibians – frogs, salamanders, and caecilians – despite their differences in appearance share a number of derived characters, including a moist, permeable skin, that indicate that as a group they share a single common ancestor.*

**CLADOGRAM A**

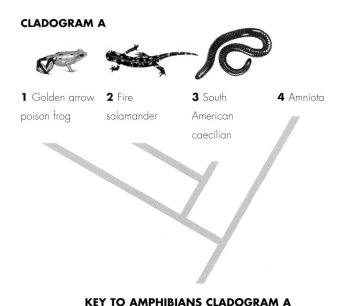

**1** Golden arrow poison frog    **2** Fire salamander    **3** South American caecilian    **4** Amniota

**KEY TO AMPHIBIANS CLADOGRAM A**

1  Anura (frogs and toads)
2  Caudata or Urodela (salamanders)
3  Gymnophonia (caecilians)

4  Amniota (turtles, lizards and snakes, crocodilians, birds, mammals)

***Cladogram showing possible phylogenetic relationships of frogs.*** *Bufonidae is a collection of families which includes glass frogs, ghost frogs, toads, gold frogs, treefrogs, mouth-brooding frogs, leptodactylid frogs, myobatrachid frogs, and sooglossid frogs. Ranidae is a collection of families which includes poison dart frogs, hyperoliid frogs, narrow-mouthed frogs, true frogs, and rhacophorid treefrogs.*

**KEY TO AMPHIBIANS CLADOGRAM B**

1  Ascaphidae (tailed frogs)
2  Leiopalmatidae (New Zealand frogs)
3  Discoglossidae (discoglossid frogs)
4  Pipidae (pipid frogs)
5  Rhinophrynidae (Mexican burrowing toads)

6  Pelodytidae (parsley frogs)
7  Pelobatidae (spadefoot toads)
8  Bufonidae (toads and treefrogs)
9  Ranidae (narrow-mouthed frogs and true frogs)

***Cladogram showing possible phylogenetic relationships in salamanders***

**KEY TO AMPHIBIANS CLADOGRAM C**

1  Sirenidae (sirens)
2  Cryptobranchidea (giant salamanders)
3  Hynobiidae (Asiatic land salamanders)
4  Amphiumidae (Congo eels)
5  Proteidae (olms and mudpuppies)

6  Plethodontidae (lungless salamanders)
7  Ambystomatidae (mole salamanders)
8  Dicamptodontidae (dicamptodontid salamanders)
9  Salamandridae (newts and salamanders)

**CLADOGRAM B**

**1** Tailed frog    **2** Hochstetter's frog    **3** Midwife toad    **4** African clawed toad    **5** Mexican burrowing toad    **6** Parsley frog    **7** Western spadefoot    **8** Spring peeper    **9** Golden arrow poison frog

**CLADOGRAM C**

**1** Greater siren    **2** Hellbender    **3** Asian salamander    **4** Congo eel    **5** Olm    **6** Red salamander    **7** Tiger salamander    **8** Pacific giant salamander    **9** Great crested newt

# TAILED, NEW ZEALAND, DISCOGLOSSID AND PIPID FROGS

## ORDER ANURA

There are over 3,500 species of frog and toad, but all are similar in appearance whatever their habits. As adults they are tailless and have well-developed limbs. Most breed in water, laying eggs which hatch into tailed tadpoles. The tadpoles live in water, feeding on vegetation, and later change to adult form.

The word "frog" was originally used only for members of the family Ranidae, and the word "toad" for members of the family Bufonidae. However the two words are also used indiscriminately for members of other families, so there is now no taxonomic implication in their use.

## ASCAPHIDAE: TAILED FROG FAMILY

This family of primitive frogs contains just one species. It shares many characteristics with members of Leiopalmatidae but is sufficiently distinct to be placed in a family of its own.

## LEIOPALMATIDAE: NEW ZEALAND FROG FAMILY

The three species found in this family are primitive frogs.

**Hochstetter's Frog** *Leiopelma hochstetteri* **LR:lc**

| | |
|---|---|
| **RANGE** | New Zealand |
| **HABITAT** | Mountains, mountain streams |
| **SIZE** | 1¾ in (4.5 cm) |

The 3 species in the genus Leiopelma are the only native frogs in New Zealand, and all are now rare and rigorously protected. Other frogs on the islands are introduced species.

First discovered in 1852, Hochstetter's frog is a robust species with partially webbed hind feet. Although it usually lives in or near water, it has also been found in mountain country some distance from streams. Like its relatives it is nocturnal and feeds on beetles, ants, earthworms, spiders and slugs.

The breeding habits of this frog are probably an adaptation to its habitat. Groups of 2 to 8 eggs are laid on moist earth under logs or stones, or in tunnels left by dragonfly nymphs. Each egg is surrounded by a water-filled gelatinous capsule and, within this capsule, the embryo passes through all the tadpole stages until it hatches out as a tiny tailed froglet, about 40 days after laying. The tail is resorbed about a month later.

## DISCOGLOSSIDAE: DISCOGLOSSID FROG FAMILY

The 14 species in this family include the fire-bellied toads, painted frogs and midwife toads, all of which live in the Old World – in Europe, North Africa and parts of Asia.

They are characterized by their disk-shaped tongues which are entirely joined to the floor of the mouth and cannot be flipped forward to capture prey. Most frogs have tongues which are fixed only at the front, leaving the back free to be swiftly flipped over and protruded.

**Midwife Toad** *Alytes obstetricans*

| | |
|---|---|
| **RANGE** | W. Europe, south to Alps, Spain and Portugal |
| **HABITAT** | Woodland, cultivated land |
| **SIZE** | Up to 2 in (5 cm) |

The small, plump midwife toad varies in coloration from gray to olivegreen or brown, often with darker markings. It is a nocturnal, land-dwelling animal, and hides by day in crevices in walls or quarries or under logs. Some individuals live in burrows, which they dig with their strong forelimbs. Midwife toads feed on insects and small invertebrates.

The midwife toad is best known for its unusual breeding habits, which are the origin of its common name. The toads mate on land at night, the male clasping the female as she lays strings of up to

60 eggs. Once he has fertilized the eggs, he then inserts his hind legs among them and twists the strings of eggs around his legs. He carries the eggs in this way while they develop, taking care that they do not dry out and moistening them at intervals in pools. After 18 to 49 days, depending on the temperature, the male deposits his eggs in shallow water, where they hatch out into tadpoles.

### Oriental Fire-bellied Toad

*Bombina orientalis*

| | |
|---|---|
| **RANGE** | Siberia, N.E. China, Korea |
| **HABITAT** | Mountain streams, rice fields |
| **SIZE** | 2 in (5 cm) |

A brilliantly colored species, the oriental fire-bellied toad's rough skin exudes a milky secretion which is extremely irritating to the mouths and eyes of potential predators. The female fire-bellied toad lays her eggs on the underside of submerged stones in small clumps, each containing 2 to 8 eggs.

## PIPIDAE: PIPID FROG FAMILY

There are 20 or more species of highly aquatic frogs in this family, found in Central and South America and in Africa, south of the Sahara. All have powerful hind limbs and large webbed hind feet but only small forelimbs and feet. As they swim, these forelimbs are held out in front of the head with the fingers spread as sensory probes, to search for food items.

### African Clawed Toad

*Xenopus laevis*

| | |
|---|---|
| **RANGE** | South Africa |
| **HABITAT** | Ponds, lakes |
| **SIZE** | 2½–5 in (6.5–12.5 cm) |

This streamlined toad is as fast and agile in water as any fish and is even able to move backward. It can change its coloration from black to gray to mottled in order to match

its background. The four digits on its forelimbs are tipped with claws, which it uses to forage in the mud around pools and streams for food, and it consumes any animal matter, even its own tadpoles.

The toads mate in water, the male making a soft buzzing sound underwater in order to attract the female. The eggs each of which is enclosed in jelly, attach to submerged plants and hatch out after 7 days.

### Surinam Toad *Pipa pipa*

| | |
|---|---|
| **RANGE** | N. South America |
| **HABITAT** | Streams, rivers |
| **SIZE** | 4¾–7¾ in (12–20 cm) |

This active, strong-swimming toad is a voracious predator and will eat almost anything it can find even carrion. It uses its slender, tactile fingers to forage for food items.

At the beginning of the Surinam toads' extraordinary mating ritual, the male clasps the female from the back, round her hind legs; this stimulates the skin on her back to swell. The clasped pair then somersault through the water and as they flip over, the female lays between 3 and 10 eggs on the male's belly. He then fertilizes the eggs and, still somersaulting, pushes them on to the female's back. This procedure is repeated until between 40 and 100 eggs have been laid. The eggs are then enveloped in the swollen skin of the female's back, each in its own separate cell. Some 2 to 4 months later, the eggs hatch out into fully formed miniature toads.

# MEXICAN BURROWING AND SPADEFOOT TOADS, PARSLEY, GLASS AND GHOST FROGS

## RHINOPHRYNIDAE: MEXICAN BURROWING TOAD FAMILY

The single species in this family, the Mexican burrowing toad is highly specialized for a burrowing existence. It enters water only in order to breed.

### Mexican Burrowing Toad *Rhinophrynus dorsalis*

| | |
|---|---|
| **RANGE** | Mexico, Guatemala |
| **HABITAT** | Woodland |
| **SIZE** | 2½ in (6.5 cm) |

This unusual frog has horny, shovellike appendages on its feet and is an expert burrower. At night, it emerges from its burrow to hunt for termites which it licks up with its tongue.

Males court the females with guttural calls. They mate in water; he clings to her back and as she lays her eggs, he fertilizes them as they are laid. The tadpoles have sensory barbels around their mouths and lack the true lips possessed by most other tadpoles.

## PELODYTIDAE: PARSLEY FROGS

This Eurasian family contains two species of small terrestrial frogs which have aquatic larvae.

### Parsley Frog *Pelodytes punctatus*

| | |
|---|---|
| **RANGE** | Europe: Spain, Portugal, France, W. Belgium, N. Italy |
| **HABITAT** | Various damp areas |
| **SIZE** | Up to 2 in (5 cm) |

A nocturnal, mainly terrestrial creature outside the breeding

season, the parsley frog is often found among vegetation near streams or by walls. It is a small, active frog with warty skin and virtually unwebbed hind feet.

Parsley frogs climb, swim and jump well and can dig shallow burrows, despite the fact that they lack the spadelike hind foot appendages that are characteristic of the rest of the family.

Parsley frogs mate in spring and may breed more than once in a season. Bands of eggs, which are held together by a thick gelatinous substance, twine round submerged vegetation, where they remain until they hatch into tadpoles.

## PELOBATIDAE: SPADEFOOT TOAD FAMILY

The 80 or so species of spadefoot toad are found in North America, Europe, North Africa and southern Asia. Many are highly terrestrial and nocturnal, spending their days in underground burrows. They are known as spadefoots because of the horny tubercle found on the inner edge of each hind foot, which is used as a digging tool.

Spadefoots breed rapidly after rains, in temporary rainpools. Because the pools will soon dry up, development must be accelerated and eggs may hatch, pass though the tadpole stage and metamorphose into frogs in only 2 weeks.

### European Spadefoot *Pelobates fuscus*

| | |
|---|---|
| **RANGE** | W., central and E. Europe to W. Asia |
| **HABITAT** | Sandy soil, cultivated land |
| **SIZE** | Up to 3¼ in (8 cm) |

The plump, European spadefoot has a large, pale-colored spade on each virtually fully webbed hind foot. Males are usually smaller than females and have

raised oval glands on their upper forelimbs. Like most spadefoots, this species is nocturnal outside the breeding season.

In the breeding season, however spadefoots may be active during the day. They breed once a year in spring, usually in deep pools or in ditches. Although spadefoots do not develop the rough nuptial pads which males of many other families have to help them grasp their mates, they clasp the females and fertilize the eggs as they are laid.

### Western Spadefoot *Scaphiopus hammondi*

| | |
|---|---|
| **Range** | W. USA: California, Arizona, New Mexico; Mexico |
| **Habitat** | Varied, plains, sandy areas |
| **Size** | 1¼–2½ in (3.5–6.5 cm) |

An expert burrower, the western spadefoot has a wedge-shaped spade on each hind foot. It is a nocturnal toad and spends the day in its burrow in conditions of moderate temperature and humidity, despite the arid heat typical of much of its range.

Temporary rainpools are used for breeding, any time between January and August, depending on rainfall. The eggs are laid in round clumps which attach to vegetation and hatch only 2 days later. Since development must be completed before the temporary pool dries up, metamorphosis from tadpole to adult form takes place in under 6 weeks.

## CENTROLENIDAE: GLASS FROG FAMILY

Glass frogs are so called because of their lightly pigmented skin that allows the internal organs to be seen through the body wall. The 70 or so species of these treefrogs are found in tropical Central and South America.

### Glass Frog *Centrolenella albomaculata*

| | |
|---|---|
| **Range** | N. South America |
| **Habitat** | Forest |
| **Size** | Up to 1¼ in (3 cm) |

The delicate glass frog behaves much like the hylid treefrogs and lives in small trees and bushes, usually near to running water. Its

digits are expanded into adhesive disks which give a good grip when it is climbing. Its eggs are laid in clusters on the underside of leaves overhanging running water and are guarded by the male. When the tadpoles hatch out they tumble down into the water below, where they complete their development and metamorphose into frogs.

## HELEOPHRYNIDAE: GHOST FROG FAMILY

Ghost frogs are so called not because of any spectral appearance, but because a species was discovered in Skeleton Gorge in South Africa. About 3 or 4 species are known, all found in southern Africa in fast-flowing mountain streams. They are long-limbed frogs with flattened bodies, enabling them to squeeze into narrow rock crevices, and expanded digits with which to grip on to slippery surfaces.

### Natal Ghost Frog *Heleophryne natalensis*

| | |
|---|---|
| **Range** | N.E. South Africa |
| **Habitat** | Forested streams |
| **Size** | Up to 2 in (5 cm) |

A nocturnal species, the ghost frog takes refuge by day among rocks and pebbles or in crevices, concealed by its mottled and speckled coloration.

In the breeding season, male frogs develop nuptial pads on the forelimbs and small spines on the fingers and armpits for grasping their mates.

The eggs are laid in a pool or even out of the water on wet gravel. Once hatched, tadpoles move to fast-flowing streams. They are able to withstand being swept away by the currents by holding on to stones in the riverbed with their suckerlike mouths.

# BUFONID TOADS AND GOLD FROG

## BUFONIDAE: TOAD FAMILY

The common name "toad" was originally applied only to the approximately 330 species in the bufonidae family, although many other anurans with warty skins and terrestrial habits tend to be called toads.

Bufonid toads are found over most of the world, except in the far north, Madagascar and Polynesia. A species has now been introduced into Australia, where previously there were no bufonid toads.

The typical bufonid toad has a compact body and short legs. The skin is not moist and is covered with characteristic wartlike tubercles. These contain the openings of poison glands, the distasteful secretions of which protect the toads to some extent, particularly from mammalian predators.

With their short legs, toads tend to walk rather than hop and are, in general, slower-moving than frogs. Breeding males develop rough nuptial pads on their three inner fingers for clasping females when mating.

### Boulenger's Arrow Poison Toad *Atelopus boulengeri*

**RANGE** South America: Ecuador, Peru

**HABITAT** Forested slopes of the Andes, near fast-flowing streams

**SIZE** About 1 in (2.5 cm)

The contrasting black and orange markings of Boulenger's arrow poison toad warn of the poisonous skin secretions that defend it from predators. An uncommon, slow-moving species, this toad is active during the day and may climb up into bushes at night.

Little is known of its breeding habits, but it is believed to lay its eggs under stones in streams. The tadpoles probably have sucking mouths in order to anchor themselves to rocks on the riverbed to prevent them being swept away in the fast-flowing water.

### American Toad

*Bufo americanus*

**RANGE** S.E. Canada: Manitoba to Labrador, south to Great Lakes; USA: south to Georgia, east to Kansas

**HABITAT** Grassland, forest, gardens

**SIZE** 2–4¼ in (5–11 cm)

A stout, broad-headed toad, the American toad is liberally covered with warts. Females are usually larger than males.

Mainly nocturnal, the American toad takes refuge during the day under stones, logs or other debris or burrows into the soil. It feeds on insects, but also eats small invertebrates such as spiders, snails and earthworms.

American toads usually breed between March and July in ponds or streams. The female lays two strings of spawn, each containing up to 8,000 eggs, which hatch into tadpoles between 3 and 12 days later. The tadpoles metamorphose into adults about 2 months after hatching.

### Giant Toad *Bufo marinus*

**RANGE** USA: extreme S. Texas; Mexico to Central and South America; introduced in many areas, including Australia

**HABITAT** Varied, near pools, swamps

**SIZE** 4–9½ in (10–24 cm)

One of the largest toads in the world, the giant toad has been widely introduced by man outside its range, often in order to feed on, and thus control, the insects which destroy crops such as sugar. It adapts well to many habitats and feeds on almost anything, including small rodents and birds and many insects, particularly beetles.

Toxic secretions from the glands at each side of its body are highly irritating to mucous membranes and in some cases may be fatal to mammalian predators.

Giant toads breed at any time of year, given sufficient rainfall and warmth. They lay strings of eggs in permanent water, where they usually hatch into tadpoles in 3 days. One female may lay up to 35,000 eggs a year.

## Green Toad *Bufo viridis*

**RANGE** Europe: S. Sweden through Germany to Italy and Mediterranean islands; N. Africa,C. Asia

**HABITAT** Varied, often lowland sandy areas, not forest

**SIZE** 3¼–4 in (8–10 cm)

A thickset species but less plump than the common toad, the green toad has warty skin and distinctive green markings. The female is larger than the male, with brighter markings, and the male has an external vocal sac. Green toads are mainly nocturnal, but they may occasionally emerge during the day to forage for their insect food. Although primarily a land-living toad, the green toad has partially webbed toes and can survive in even brackish water.

Green toads breed from April to June, males courting females with their trilling, musical calls. The mating male clasps the female under her armpits while she lays two long strings of gelatinous spawn, each containing 10,000 to 20,000 eggs.

## Natterjack Toad *Bufo calamita*

**RANGE** W. and C. Europe (including Britain), east to Russia

**HABITAT** Varied, often sandy areas

**SIZE** 2¾–4 in (7–10 cm)

The male natterjack has the loudest call of any European toad: his croak will carry 2 km (1¼ miles) or more. The female is usually larger than the male, but both are robust and relatively short-limbed. Although mainly terrestrial, natterjacks are often found near the sea and may even breed in brackish water. On land they run in short spurts and are most active at night.

The breeding season lasts from March to August. Natterjacks mate at night and the female lays several strings of gelatinous spawn, each containing up to 4,000 eggs, in shallow water. The eggs hatch in 10 days into tadpoles which metamorphose to adult form in 4 to 8 weeks. The young toads are not fully grown and mature until they are 4 or 5 years old.

## Common Toad
*Bufo bufo*

**RANGE** Europe (including Britain and Scandinavia); N. Africa, N. Asia to Japan

**HABITAT** Varied, often fairly dry

**SIZE** Up to 6 in (15 cm)

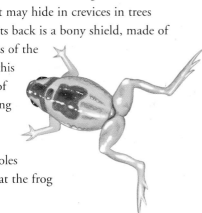

The largest European toad, the common toad varies in size over its wide range, but females are generally larger than males. It is a heavily built toad with extremely warty skin; males do not have external vocal sacs. A nocturnal species, it hides during the day, often using the same spot time after time, and emerges at dusk to feed on a variety of invertebrate prey. It usually moves by walking but, if distressed, may hop.

In much of their range, common toads hibernate in winter and then congregate in large numbers to breed at about the end of March, frequently returning to the same pond every year. Thousands of eggs are laid in gelatinous strings up to 10 ft (3 m) long. The eggs hatch in about 10 days and, if the weather is warm, the tadpoles metamorphose in about 2 months. In cold weather they take longer.

## BRACHYCEPHALIDAE: GOLD FROG FAMILY

Closely related to the bufonid toads are the 3 species of frog in this family, the gold frog.

## Gold Frog *Brachycephalus ephippium*

**RANGE** South America: S.E. Brazil

**HABITAT** Mountain forest

**SIZE** Up to ¾ in (2 cm)

This tiny, but exquisite, frog is common among the leaf litter of the forest floor, although it may hide in crevices in trees or rocks in dry weather. On its back is a bony shield, made of hard plates fused to the spines of the vertebrae. The frog may use this shield to block the entrance of its hiding place, so maintaining its humidity.

Its breeding habits are unknown but, since the tadpoles are aquatic, it is presumed that the frog lays its eggs in or near water.

# TREEFROGS AND MOUTH-BROODING FROGS

## HYLIDAE: TREEFROG FAMILY

There are approximately 600 species of treefrog, found on all continents except the Antarctic. The greatest diversity occurs in tropical areas of the New World. The majority live in trees and have a range of adaptations which make them extremely efficient insect-eating, tree-dwellers. The most important of these adaptations are on the feet. Each digit is tipped with a sticky adhesive pad to aid climbing, and inside the digit is a disk-shaped zone of cartilage before the end bone which allows the digit great mobility, while keeping the adhesive pad flat on the surface when the frog is climbing.

### European Green Treefrog *Hyla arborea* **LR:nt**

**RANGE** Most of Europe except N. Turkey, S. Russia to Caspian Sea

**HABITAT** Bushes, trees, reeds near ponds and lakes

**SIZE** Up to 2 in (5 cm)

This smooth-skinned treefrog spends most of its life in trees where it catches flying insects. It can change color rapidly, from bright green in sunlight to a dark gray in shade. In early summer, frogs congregate at night in ponds. The male grasps the female just behind the forelegs and fertilizes her eggs as they are shed into the water. Clumps of up to 1,000 eggs float on the water until they hatch into tadpoles.

### Common Gray Treefrog *Hyla versicolor*

**RANGE** S.E. Canada; USA: North Dakota, east to Maine, south to Texas and Florida

**HABITAT** Bushes, trees near water

**SIZE** 1¼–2¼ in (3–6 cm)

This treefrog's color camouflages it in trees. The orange areas on its thighs can be flashed to confuse predators. It lives high up in vegetation and is mainly active at night, when it preys on insects. It descends only to call and breed. It mates in water and the eggs are shed in small clusters of 10 to 40. The tadpoles hatch 4 or 5 days later.

### Spring Peeper *Hyla crucifer*

**RANGE** S.E. Canada; USA, south to C. Florida, west to Texas

**HABITAT** Woodland, near ponds, swamps

**SIZE** ¾–1¼ in (2–3 cm)

One of the most abundant frogs in eastern North America, the spring peeper's song does indeed herald the arrival of spring in the north of its range. This agile little frog can climb into trees and bushes, using its well-developed adhesive toe pads, and jump over 17 times its body length. It feeds mainly on small spiders and insects, including flying insects which it leaps into the air to catch.

Courting males call from trees overhanging water, making a belllike chorus. The male frog climbs on to a female who enters water and lays her 800 to 1,000 eggs, one at a time, on to stems of aquatic vegetation. He fertilizes the eggs which hatch within a few days. The tadpoles metamorphose about 3 months later and leave the pond.

### Northern Cricket Frog *Acris crepitans*

**RANGE** USA: New York, south to N. Florida, west to Minnesota and Texas

**HABITAT** Shallow ponds, slow streams

**SIZE** ½–1½ in (1.5–4 cm)

This tiny rough-skinned frog is a poor climber and spends its life on land and in water. Unlike the arboreal treefrogs which do not jump readily, the cricket frog can jump as much as 36 times its own length. Breeding starts in April in the north of its range or as early as February in the south. Thousands of frogs congregate to call and mate. The male's call is a shrill, metallic clicking sound. The eggs are shed on submerged vegetation or into the water in small clusters or singly. In warm weather, they hatch in 4 days but may take longer if the temperature is below 72°F (22°C).

## Green and Gold Bell Frog *Litoria cydorhynchus*

**RANGE** W. Australia: south coast

**HABITAT** Large ponds

**SIZE** Up to 3¼ in (8 cm)

This bell frog climbs only rarely and lives mostly in water or on reeds. It moves on land only in heavy rainfall. Active during the day, it is a voracious predator, feeding on any small animals, including its own tadpoles.

In the breeding season, males call from the water to attract mates, making a sound rather like wood being sawn. The female lays her eggs among vegetation in the pond.

## Lutz's Phyllomedusa *Phyllomedusa appendiculata*

**RANGE** South America: S.E. Brazil

**HABITAT** Forest, near moving water

**SIZE** 1½ in (4 cm)

A tree-dwelling frog, Lutz's phyllomedusa has triangular flaps of skin on each heel, which may help to camouflage its outline. Areas of red skin inside thighs and flanks can be flashed to confuse predators. It eats mainly insects.

The breeding pair selects a leaf overhanging water. They fold the leaf over, making a nest which is open at both sides, and about 50 eggs are laid in a ball of mucus in the nest. The tadpoles hatch 2 or 3 days later and drop into the water.

## Marsupial Frog *Gastrotheca marsupiata*

**RANGE** South America: Ecuador, Peru

**HABITAT** Forest

**SIZE** Up to 1½ in (4 cm)

The female frog is larger than the male and has a special skin pouch on her back. While she lays about 200 eggs, one at a time, the male sits on her back. As each egg is laid, she bends forward so that it rolls down her back; the male then fertilizes the egg before it settles into the skin pouch. When all the eggs are laid, the male helps to pack them into the skin pouch and the edges of the pouch seal over to protect them.

A few weeks later the female frog finds some shallow water – a pond or puddle – in which to release her brood. By this time her back is very swollen. She raises one hind leg and, with her fourth and longest toe, slits open the pouch and frees the young tadpoles which then complete their metamorphosis in water.

## RHINODERMATIDAE: MOUTH-BROODING FROG FAMILY

This South American family contains these 2 species of unusual mouth-brooding frogs of the genus Rhinoderma. Males of these species carry the developing eggs, and then the tadpoles, in their vocal sacs until they transform into small frogs. The species was discovered by Charles Darwin.

## Darwin's Frog *Rhinoderma darwinii* **DD**

**RANGE** S. Chile, S. Argentina

**HABITAT** Shallow, cold streams in forest

**SIZE** 1¼ in (3 cm)

The small, slender Darwin's frog has a pointed extension of skin on its head. Its digits are long and webbed on the hind feet but free on the forefeet.

Its breeding habits are unique among amphibians. The female lays 20 to 45 eggs on land. They are guarded by several males for 10 to 20 days until the embryos, which are visible from the outside, begin to move around inside the capsules. Each male then gathers up to 15 eggs and lets them slide into his large vocal sac. The tadpoles develop inside the sac, feeding on their own yolks. Once they are small adults about ½ in (1.25 cm) long, the male expels them into water and his vocal sac shrinks back to its normal size.

# LEPTODACTYLID, MYOBATRACHID, SOOGLOSSID, POISON DART AND REED FROGS

## LEPTODACTYLIDAE: LEPTODACTYLID FROG FAMILY

This is a large and varied family with several hundred species, found mainly in Central and South America, Africa and Australia. Their anatomy is similar to that of true treefrogs, but although Leptodactylid frogs may have adhesive disks on the digits, the digits are not as flexible.

### Horned Frog
*Cetatophrys cornuta*

**RANGE** N. and C. South America

**HABITAT** Litter on forest floor

**SIZE** 7 ¾ in (20 cm)

The horned frog is almost as broad as it is long and has a wide, powerful head and large mouth. Its eyes are small, with a small protuberance on each upper eyelid. The toes are partially webbed, although the frog spends much of its life half-buried in the ground. Snails, small frogs and rodents are all eaten, and it is also believed to eat the young of its own species.

### South American Bullfrog *Leptodactylus pentadactylus*

**RANGE** Central and South America: Costa Rica to Brazil

**HABITAT** Forest, close to water

**SIZE** Up to 8 in (20.5 cm)

The South American bullfrog has powerful hind legs, which are eaten by man in some areas. The male has powerful arm muscles and hard protuberances on each thumb which fit into horny structures on the female to help him grip on to her when mating.

In the winter spawning season, the sides of the bullfrog's legs turn deep orange or red. The male clasps the female in the water. She secretes a jellylike substance which he whips into foam to form a floating nest in which the eggs are laid and fertilized. Tadpoles stay in the nest until they become froglets.

## MYOBATRACHIDAE: MYOBATRACHID FROG FAMILY

This small family of frogs appears to have affinities with the bufonid toads and was previously classified with them. Members of the family tend to walk on the tips of their toes.

### Corroboree Frog
*Pseudophryne corroboree*

**RANGE** Australia: New South Wales

**HABITAT** Mountain, marshland

**SIZE** 1 ¼ in (3 cm)

The corroboree frog lives on land but near water, often at altitudes of over 5,000 ft (1,500 m), and shelters under logs or in a burrow, which it digs itself.

In summer, the frogs seek out sphagnum bogs, where they dig nesting burrows. Up to 12 large eggs are laid and one parent usually stays with the eggs while they develop. The tadpoles remain in the eggs until there is sufficient rainfall to wash them into a creek, where they hatch at once.

### *Cyclorana cultripes*

**RANGE** Australia: N. coasts, W. Australia to Queensland

**HABITAT** Underground

**SIZE** 2 in (5 cm)

This burrowing frog comes above ground only to breed and to find food. It breeds after heavy summer rains, often in temporary ponds. Eggs are laid in the water, where they attach to plants until they hatch into fat tadpoles with pointed snouts and deep tail fins.

## SOOGLOSSIDAE: SOOGLOSSID FROG FAMILY

The origins and relationships of the frogs of this family, all found in the Seychelles, have been a matter of some contention.

### Seychelles Frog *Sooglossus sechellensis* **VU**

**RANGE** Seychelles: Mahe and Silhouette Islands

**HABITAT** Moss forest on mountains

**SIZE** Up to 1 in (2.5 cm)

The tiny Seychelles frog has thin, weak front limbs but more powerful hind limbs, with long digits on its feet. It is mainly ground-dwelling and lives in rotting plant matter on the forest floor, needing water for a short phase of tadpole development only. It eats small invertebrates.

The frogs breed in the rainy season. The female lays eggs in small clumps of gelatinous substance on moist ground. The male guards the eggs and after 2 weeks incubation, they hatch. The tadpoles wriggle on to his back. They respire through their skin and do not have gills. Most of their development takes place on the male's back, but they are carried to water, where they complete their metamorphosis before returning to land.

## DENDROBATIDAE: POISON DART FROG FAMILY

Found in the forests of Central and South America, most of the 120 or so species in this family are small, brightly colored frogs. Their bright color advertises a warning to potential predators that their skin contains highly toxic alkaloids.

### Golden Arrow-poison Frog *Dendrobates auratus*

**RANGE** Central and South America: Nicaragua to Panama and Colombia

**HABITAT** Forest

**SIZE** 1½ in (4 cm)

The brilliant colors of this ground-dwelling frog warn potential enemies of its poisonous glandular secretions. This poison is extracted by local tribesmen and used on the tips of arrows.

Before mating, these frogs contest with each other until they have paired. The female lays up to 6 eggs in a gelatinous substance, on land. The male visits the clutch until, after about 2 weeks, the tadpoles hatch. They wriggle on to the male frog's back and he carries them to a hole in a tree where a little water has collected. The tadpoles complete their development in about 6 weeks.

## HYPEROLIIDAE: HYPEROLIID FROG FAMILY

The hyperoliids are climbing frogs, closely related to the ranid frogs. They differ in that they possess adaptations for climbing similar to those of the hylid frogs – each digit on the frogs' feet has a zone of cartilage which allows greater flexibility in the use of the adhesive disk at the tip when climbing. Most of the 220 species in this family live in Africa, often near fresh water.

### Arum Lily Frog

*Hyperolius horstockii*

**RANGE** South Africa: S. and W. Cape Province

**HABITAT** Swamps, dams, streams, rivers, with vegetation

**SIZE** Up to 2¼ in (6 cm)

The long-limbed arum lily frog has bands running from its snout along each side. A good climber, its feet are equipped with expanded, adhesive disks and are only partially webbed. The under-surfaces of the limbs are orange. The rest of the body changes color according to conditions, becoming a light cream in bright sun and dark brown in shade. This helps the frog control its body heat.

Courting males often climb up on to arum lilies to call to females. They then mate in water, where the small clusters of eggs are laid on submerged water plants.

### Gold Spiny Reed Frog *Afrixales brachycnemis*

**RANGE** South Africa: E., S.E. and S. coastal regions

**HABITAT** Pools, swamps

**SIZE** ¾ in (2 cm)

Also known as the golden leaf-folding frog, this tiny, slim amphibian, equipped with adhesive disks on each digit, is a good climber. Its back may be covered with tiny dark spines, hence one of its common names. This feature is common in frogs in the south of the range but rare in the north.

Breeding males take up position among reeds or on waterlily leaves in pools or vleis (temporary, rain-filled hollows) and call to females. The female lays a batch of eggs on a leaf above or below water level. Once fertilized, the leaf is folded and the edges are glued together with secretions from the female's oviduct. Tadpoles complete their development in the water.

# NARROW-MOUTHED AND TRUE FROGS

## MICROHYLIDAE: NARROW-MOUTHED FROG FAMILY

There are 300 or more species of burrowing, terrestrial and tree-living frogs in this family, found in tropical regions all over the world and extending into temperate areas in North and South America. Tree-living forms are equipped with adhesive pads on finger and toe tips to aid climbing.

### Sheep Frog *Hypopachus cuneus*

| | |
|---|---|
| **RANGE** | USA: S.E. Texas; Mexico |
| **HABITAT** | Margins of damp areas in arid country |
| **SIZE** | 1–1¾ in (2.5–4.5 cm) |

A small, stout frog with a pointed snout, the sheep frog is a nocturnal species which hides during the day under rocks or debris or in a rodent burrow; at night it emerges in order to feed on ants and termites.

Sheep frogs mate at any time of year when stimulated by sufficient rainfall. The male attracts the female to the breeding pond by making his bleating call – the origin of the common name. He clasps the female's body, and her sticky body secretions help the pair to stay together while they lay and fertilize about 700 eggs.

### South African Rain Frog *Breviceps adspersus*

| | |
|---|---|
| **RANGE** | South Africa, Namibia, Botswana, Zimbabwe |
| **HABITAT** | Savanna |
| **SIZE** | 1¼ in (3 cm) |

An extremely rotund frog, the South African rain frog has a short snout and small, sturdy limbs. Its back is covered with warty protuberances, and coloration and pattern are variable.

It burrows well, using its hind feet, and seldom emerges above ground except during rain. It feeds on insects and small invertebrates.

The courting male makes a repeated croaking chirp to attract his mate. They mate in a burrow, held together by sticky body

secretions. The few eggs are enclosed in thick jelly and lie in a compact mass in the burrow while they develop. There is no tadpole stage; metamorphosis takes place within the egg capsules and the young hatch as miniature, land-living frogs.

### Eastern Narrow-mouthed Frog

*Gastrophryne carolinensis*

| | |
|---|---|
| **RANGE** | S.E. USA: Missouri and Maryland, south to Florida, Gulf coast and Texas |
| **HABITAT** | By ponds and ditches; under moist vegetation |
| **SIZE** | ¾–1½ in (2–4 cm) |

An excellent burrower, this small smooth-skinned frog can disappear into the soil in a moment. It rests in a burrow during the day and comes out at night to hunt for its insect food, mainly ants.

Breeding is stimulated by rainfall, sometime between April and October. The dark-throated male calls to the female, usually from water, and continues to call as they mate. The eggs float on the water surface for 3 days and then hatch into tadpoles.

### Termite Frog *Phrynomerus bifasciatus*

| | |
|---|---|
| **RANGE** | Africa, south of the Sahara |
| **HABITAT** | Savanna |
| **SIZE** | 2 in (5 cm) |

The termite frog has a more elongate body than most members of its family and an unusually mobile head. Its distinctive markings warn of its toxic skin which contains substances which irritate the skin and mucous membranes of predators. A land-dwelling frog, it may climb up tree stumps and rocks or burrow in search of prey or to shelter from dry weather. Termites and ants are its main foods.

Breeding takes place in shallow pools. The small, jelly-coated eggs are laid in masses and attach to submerged plants or lie at the bottom of the water. They hatch into aquatic tadpoles.

## RANIDAE: TRUE FROG FAMILY

There are over 600 species in this family, found almost worldwide on every continent except Antarctica, but sparsely represented in Australasia and the southern parts of South America. Typically, these frogs have slim, streamlined bodies and pointed heads. Their hind legs are long and hind feet extensively webbed. They are usually smooth-skinned and often brown or green in color.

Most ranid frogs live near fresh water and enter it readily to find prey or escape danger. A few species, however, can thrive in brackish waters or warm sulfur springs and others have become adapted to a ground-living existence and can burrow like spadefoot toads. Some live in trees and have adhesive pads on their toes for grip when climbing, similar to those of the treefrogs (Hylidae). All are carnivorous as adults, feeding mainly on insects, spiders and small crustaceans.

Large numbers of ranid frogs congregate at the start of the breeding season and males chorus to attract females to the breeding site. The breeding male develops swollen pads on forelimbs and thumbs with which he grasps his mate's body. As she lays her eggs, he fertilizes them by spraying them with sperm. The eggs are usually surrounded by a jellylike substance which protects them to some degree and prevents dehydration. Although females lay thousands of eggs, many of these are destroyed by adverse conditions or eaten by predators, and relatively few survive to adulthood.

### Common Frog *Rana temporaria*

**RANGE** Europe (including Britain and Scandinavia, but excluding much of Spain and Italy), east to Asia

**HABITAT** Varied, any moist area near ponds, marshes, swamps

**SIZE** Up to 4 in (10 cm)

European frogs are divided into two groups – green and brown frogs. The brown frogs, of which the common frog is an example, tend to be more terrestrial and have quieter voices than

the green frogs. The robust common frog varies in coloration over its wide range, from brown or gray to yellow. It is tolerant of cold and is found up to the snowline in some areas. Much of its life is spent on land, and it rarely enters water except to mate or hibernate.

Breeding occurs from February to April, and males attract females to the breeding sites with their deep, rasping croaks. They mate in water and females lay 3,000 to 4,000 eggs in large clusters.

### Bullfrog *Rana catesbeiana*

**RANGE** E. and C. USA; introduced in western areas and in Mexico, Cuba and N. Italy

**HABITAT** Lakes, ponds, slow streams

**SIZE** 3½–8 in (9–20.5 cm)

The largest North American frog, the bullfrog makes a deep, vibrant call, amplified by the internal vocal sac. Although an aquatic species, it also spends time on land and is often seen at the water's edge. It is most active by night, when it preys on insects, fish, smaller frogs and, occasionally, small birds and snakes. Like all American ranid frogs, it is a good jumper and can leap nine times its own length.

In the north of their range, bullfrogs breed from May to July, but farther south the season is longer. The female lays 10,000 to 20,000 eggs in water which may float on the surface or attach to vegetation. The eggs hatch in 5 or 6 days, but the tadpoles take 2 to 5 years to transform into adults.

# TRUE FROGS AND RHACOPHORID TREEFROGS

### Northern Leopard Frog *Rana pipiens*

**RANGE** Most of northern North America except Pacific coast

**HABITAT** Varied, fresh water to brackish marshes in arid to mountain land

**SIZE** 2–5 in (5–12.5 cm)

The slim northern leopard frog is a distinctive species, with large spots on its body and prominent back ridges. It is the most widely distributed North American amphibian and the pattern and intensity of its spots vary over its large range. It adapts to almost any habitat near a permanent body of water and is equally accommodating in its diet; insects, spiders and crustaceans are its main food, but this voracious frog will eat almost anything it can find. Primarily a nocturnal species, the leopard frog may sometimes search for food during the day. If disturbed on land, it leaps away in a series of zigzagging jumps to seek refuge in water.

In the north of its range, the breeding season usually extends from March to June, but in southern, arid areas, leopard frogs are ready to breed at almost any time of year whenever there has been sufficient rainfall. Males gather at breeding sites and make low grunting calls to attract females.

Each female lays about 20,000 eggs which her mate fertilizes. The eggs then lie at the bottom of the water on submerged vegetation until they hatch about 4 weeks later. The tadpoles metamorphose into adult form in 6 months to 2 years, depending on the temperature and conditions.

### Marsh Frog *Rana ridibunda*

**RANGE** S.W. Europe: S.W. France, Spain and Portugal; E. Europe: Germany, east to Russia and Balkans

**HABITAT** Ponds, ditches, streams, lakes, rivers

**SIZE** Up to 6 in (15 cm)

The marsh frog is one of the several noisy, aquatic, gregarious green frogs found in Europe. Apart from its color, this long-legged frog is easily distinguished from the brown frogs by the external vocal sacs at the sides of its mouth. Most of its life is spent in water, but it will come out on to banks or float on lily pads. As well as catching invertebrate prey, these large frogs feed on small birds and mammals.

Marsh frogs sing night and day and are particularly vocal in the breeding season, when they make a variety of sounds. They mate in April or May, and females lay thousands of eggs in several large clusters.

### South African Bullfrog *Pyxicephalus adspersus*

**RANGE** E. South Africa

**HABITAT** Open grassland (veld); in temporary puddles when available

**SIZE** Up to 7¾ in (20 cm)

The largest South African frog, this bullfrog has a stout body and broad head. The male usually has a yellow throat while the female's is cream. On its lower jaw are toothlike projections which it uses to restrain struggling prey such as mice, lizards and other frogs. Its hind toes are webbed, but the front toes are not.

A powerful burrower, it spends much of the year underground but comes to the surface after heavy rain to breed. Males call from a breeding site in shallow water, where females then lay their many eggs, one at a time.

### Striped Grass Frog *Ptychadena porosissima*

**RANGE** Africa: central tropical areas to E. South Africa

**HABITAT** Marshy areas

**SIZE** 1½ in (4 cm)

This small, streamlined frog has a pointed snout and a ridged back. Its hind limbs are powerful, making it a good jumper and strong swimmer. Secretive in its habits, it often makes its

home among dense vegetation. Breeding males sit among aquatic vegetation and call to females with a rasping sound, which is amplified by their paired external vocal sacs. Their mates lay their eggs, one at a time, in the water. The eggs float at first and then sink to the bottom; the tadpoles swim and feed near the bottom.

## Mottled Burrowing Frog *Hemisus marmoratum*

**RANGE** N.E. South Africa

**HABITAT** Open country near pools

**SIZE** Up to 1¼ in (3 cm)

A stout, squat-bodied frog, this species has a small pointed head with a hardened snout used for burrowing. It burrows head first, pushing into the soil with its snout and clawing its way forward with its strong forelimbs. It is rarely seen above ground, although it can move rapidly on land.

Breeding males establish themselves in small holes, preferably in a mudbank, and call to attract mates. The female excavates an underground nest and lays her large eggs, each surrounded by a thick jellylike substance. When her young hatch some 10 to 12 days later, she tunnels to the nearest water, providing a canal for the tadpoles, which complete their development in water.

## Bush Squeaker *Arthroleptis wahlbergi*

**RANGE** S.E. South Africa

**HABITAT** Coastal and inland bush among leaf litter and low vegetation

**SIZE** Up to 1¼ in (3 cm)

This small, rounded frog is a land-dweller. Its legs are short but its digits, particularly the third on each foot, are elongate, well-suited to searching through vegetation for prey.

The bush squeaker's breeding habits, too, are adapted to its terrestrial existence. The eggs, each enclosed in a stiff jelly capsule, are laid among decaying vegetation. There is no tadpole stage; metamorphosis takes place within the capsule and tiny froglets emerge about 4 weeks after laying.

## RHACOPHORIDAE: RHACOPHORID TREEFROG FAMILY

The 200 or so species in this family of treefrogs are found in Africa, Madagascar, and Asia.

## Wallace's Flying Frog *Rhacophorus nigropalmatus*

**RANGE** S.E. Asia

**HABITAT** Rain forest

**SIZE** 4 in (10 cm)

This specialized frog glides from tree to tree in the forest. It has a distinctive broad head and a long slim body with elongate limbs. The feet are greatly enlarged and fully webbed, and the tips of the digits expand into large disks. Flaps of skin fringe the forelimbs and heels. All of these modifications add little to the frog's weight, but extend its surface area. It can launch itself into the air, webs with skin flaps outstretched, and glide gently down to another branch or to the ground.

The breeding habits of this extraordinary frog are little known, but are believed to be similar to those of others of its genus. Rhacophorid frogs lay their eggs in a mass of foam which makes a kind of nest to protect them from excessive heat while they incubate. The male frog grasps the female and fertilizes her eggs as they are laid. The eggs are accompanied by a thick fluid which the frogs then beat with their hind legs to form a dense light foam. Surrounded with this substance, the eggs are left on a leaf or branch overhanging water. At hatching time the bubble nest begins to liquefy, forming a miniature pool for the emerging tadpoles. In some species, the tadpoles complete their development in this custom made pool, but in others they drop down into the water beneath.

# SIRENS, CONGO EELS, OLMS AND MUDPUPPIES

## ORDER CAUDATA

There are 10 families of salamanders, newts and relatives in this order. All have elongate bodies and long tails.

### SIRENIDAE: SIREN FAMILY

The 3 species of sirens are aquatic salamanders which retain feathery external gills throughout life. Their bodies are long and eellike and they have tiny forelimbs and no hind limbs. All species occur in the USA and northern Mexico.

Sirens swim by powerful undulations of the body. They forage among water weeds for food and they are active at night. They breathe with external gills at each side of the neck.

**Dwarf Siren** *Pseudobranchus striatus*
**RANGE** USA: coastal plain of South Carolina, Georgia, Florida
**HABITAT** Ponds, swamps, ditches
**SIZE** 4–9¾ in (10–25 cm)

The smallest of its family, the dwarf siren is a slender, eellike creature which lives among dense submerged vegetation. It has no hind limbs and only tiny forelimbs with three toes on each foot. The external gills are retained throughout life. A nocturnal creature, the siren feeds on tiny invertebrate animals it finds among the plant debris near the bottom of the water. If its habitat is in danger of drying up, in a drought for example, the siren can burrow into the mud and remain there, dormant, for up to 2 months. Mucus produced by skin glands prevents the body drying out during such a period.

The female siren lays her eggs, one at a time, on aquatic plants and the larvae hatch out about 4 weeks later. There are about 5 races of dwarf siren over the range, which vary in coloration and in the shade and distribution of the stripes along the sides of the body.

**Greater Siren** *Siren lacertina*
**RANGE** USA: coastal plain from Virginia to Florida, S. Alabama
**HABITAT** Shallow, muddy fresh water with plenty of vegetation
**SIZE** 19¾–38¼ in (50–97.5 cm)

The stout-bodied greater siren has permanent external gills and a flattened tail. There are four toes on each of its front feet. During the day it hides under rocks or plant debris or burrows into the muddy bottom, emerging at night to feed on snails, insect larvae, small fish and some aquatic plants.

In drought conditions, the siren undergoes a period of dormancy; it seals itself in a cocoon made from secretions from the skin glands and buries itself in the muddy bottom until danger is past.

Sirens breed in February or March, laying eggs which hatch 2 or 3 months later into larvae, about ½ in (1.25 cm) long.

### AMPHIUMIDAE: CONGO EEL FAMILY

The 3 species of elongate, eellike creatures in this family are among the world's largest aquatic salamanders; they are all found in the southeastern USA. They have cylindrical bodies and tiny hind and forelimbs, each with one, two or three toes. These limbs are so small that they are probably of no use for moving. The skin of these amphibians is smooth and slippery.

Until 1950 there were thought to be only 2 species in this family, but a third species, the one-toed amphiuma, *Amphiuma pholeter*, was then discovered.

**Two-toed Congo Eel** *Amphiuma means*
**RANGE** USA: S.E. Virginia to Florida, E. Louisiana
**HABITAT** Swamps, bayous, drainage ditches
**SIZE** 17¾–45½ in (45–116 cm)

This aquatic salamander has tiny, virtually useless limbs, each with two toes. Mainly active at night, it hunts in water for crayfish, frogs, small snakes and fish and may occasionally come on to land in extremely wet weather. It takes refuge during the

day in a burrow that it digs in the mud or takes over the burrow of another creature.

Congo eels mate in water, and the female lays about 200 eggs in a beadlike string. The female coils around the eggs as they lie on the bottom and protects them until they hatch about 5 months after being laid. When the larvae hatch, they are about 2 in (5 cm) long; their tiny limbs are of more use to them at this stage than when they metamorphose to adult form, at about 3 in (7.5 cm) long. The three-toed amphiuma, *Amphiuma trixlactylum*, also found in the southern United States, is similar in appearance and habits but has three toes on each of its tiny limbs.

## PROTEIDAE: OLM AND MUDPUPPY FAMILY

There are 5 species of stream- and lake-dwelling mudpuppies in North America and 1 species of cave-dwelling olm in Europe. Because these amphibians live permanently in the water, they retain the external feathery gills throughout their lives, even into the adult breeding shape. They, therefore, resemble the larvae of other amphibians that do lose their gills when they become adult and leave water for at least part of the time.

### Olm *Proteus anguinus* **VU**
**RANGE** Former Yugoslavia: E. Adriatic coast; N. E. Italy
**HABITAT** Streams and lakes in underground limestone caves
**SIZE** 7¾–11¾ in (20–30 cm)

The olm is a large aquatic salamander with a pale cylindrical body and red feathery gills. Its tail is flattened and its limbs weak and poorly developed. It has three toes on the forelimbs and two on the hind limbs. It lives in total darkness in its cave home and is virtually blind,

its eyes hidden beneath the skin. It feeds on small aquatic worms and crustaceans.

The female olm lays 12 to 70 eggs at a time. The eggs are deposited under a stone and guarded by both parents. They hatch in about 90 days. Some females may reproduce in a different manner, retaining a small number of eggs inside the body and giving birth to 2 fully developed young. The young are miniature versions of the parents but have rudimentary eyes.

Once a common species, the olm is now becoming rare because of water pollution in its restricted habitat and the taking of large numbers for the pet trade.

### Mudpuppy *Necturus maculosus*
**RANGE** S. Canada: Manitoba to Quebec; USA: Great Lakes, south to Georgia and Louisiana
**HABITAT** Lakes, rivers, streams
**SIZE** 7¾–17 in (20–43 cm)

An aquatic salamander, the mudpuppy inhabits a variety of freshwater habitats, from muddy, sluggish shallows to cold, clear water. It has four toes on each limb and a flattened tail. Its feathery gills vary in size according to the water the individual inhabits: mudpuppies in cold, well-oxygenated water have shorter gills than those in warm, muddy, poorly oxygenated water, which need large, bushy gills in order to collect all the available oxygen. It hunts worms, crayfish, insects and small fish, mainly at night, but may sometimes catch fish during the day.

The breeding season is from April to June. The female lays between 30 and 190 eggs, each of which is stuck separately to a log or rock. The male guards the eggs until they hatch out about 5 to 9 weeks later. The larvae do not mature until they are 4 to 6 years old.

# LUNGLESS SALAMANDERS

## PLETHODONTIDAE: LUNGLESS SALAMANDER FAMILY

This, the most successful group of living salamanders, includes over 200 of the 350 or so known tailed amphibians. As their name suggests, these salamanders are primarily characterized by their total absence of lungs. The pulmonary artery, which would normally take blood to the lungs, is reduced to minute proportions in a lungless salamander and runs in the body wall. The animal obtains oxygen instead across its moist skin or through the internal surface of the mouth cavity, both of which are well supplied with blood vessels.

Nearly all lungless salamanders live in North or South America. Two species occur in Europe – the cave salamanders which are found in Sardinia and mainland Italy. These forms can be distinguished from all other European salamanders by their partially webbed toes.

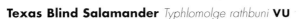

### Texas Blind Salamander *Typhlomolge rathbuni* **VU**

**RANGE** USA: extreme S. Texas

**HABITAT** Underground waters of the creek system

**SIZE** 3½–5¼ in (9–13.5 cm)

This rare species has an extremely restricted distribution. The Texas blind salamander is a typical cave-dweller, with its ghostly pale body and much reduced eyes. Its external gills are red and feathery and it has long thin legs.

Many bats roost in the caves which are the only entrance to the salamanders' habitat. Nutrients in the droppings (guano) of these bats provide food for the invertebrate animals which inhabit the caves, and these creatures, many of which are themselves unique, are in turn eaten by the salamanders.

Nothing is known about the breeding habits of this species.

### Red-backed Salamander *Plethodon cinereus*

**RANGE** S.E. Canada, N.E. USA, south to North Carolina, S. Indiana

**HABITAT** Cool, moist forest

**SIZE** 2½–5 in (6.5—12.5 cm)

This abundant, widespread salamander lives its whole life on land. The "red back" of its common name is, in fact, a stripe which may vary greatly from red to gray or yellow; some forms have gray bodies and lack the stripe altogether. It is nocturnal, hiding by day under stones or forest litter and emerging at night to search for insects and small invertebrates.

Breeding takes place every other year. The salamanders court and mate during the winter, and in June or July the female lays 6 to 12 eggs, which hang in a cluster in a crevice under a rock or in a rotten log. She coils herself around the eggs and protects them until they hatch 8 or 9 weeks later. The larvae do not have an aquatic stage and take 2 years to reach maturity.

### Slimy Salamander *Plethodon glutinosus*

**RANGE** E. and S.E. USA: New York to Florida, Missouri, Oklahoma

**HABITAT** Floodplains, cave entrances

**SIZE** 4½–8 in (11.5–20.5 cm)

The slimy salamander's skin exudes a sticky substance that may be protective. By day, it hides under rocks or logs or in a burrow. At night it searches the forest floor for invertebrate prey.

Southern females breed every year and northern females only every other year, laying 6 to 36 eggs in a burrow or a rotten log and guarding them while they develop.

### Spring Salamander *Gyrinophilus porphyriticus*

**RANGE** S. Canada: Quebec; USA: Maine, to Georgia, Mississippi

**HABITAT** Wet caves, cool, clear mountain springs

**SIZE** 4–8¾ in (10–22 cm)

The spring salamander occurs in several races, with variations of color and pattern. It spends most of its life in water but on rainy nights may come on to land to search for food. Large insects, worms and other salamanders are its main prey.

In July or August, the female lays 20 to 60 eggs, which are attached singly to the under-surfaces of submerged rocks. She guards the eggs until they hatch. Larvae do not attain adult form for about 3 years.

## Red Salamander *Pseudotriton ruber*

**RANGE** E. USA: S. New York, west to Indiana, south to Louisiana

**HABITAT** Springs, surrounding woodland, swamps, meadows

**SIZE** 3¾–7 in (9.5–18 cm)

A brilliantly colored species, the red salamander has a stout body and short tail and legs. It spends much of its life on land but is usually in the vicinity of water. Earthworms, insects and small salamanders are its main foods.

After courting and mating in summer, the female red salamander lays a clutch of between 50 and 100 eggs in autumn. The larvae hatch about 2 months later and do not transform into the adult form until some 2 years later. Females first breed when they are 5 years old.

## Yellow-blotched Salamander

*Ensatina eschscholtzi croceator*

**RANGE** USA: California

**HABITAT** Moist forest, canyons

**SIZE** 3–6 in (7.5–15 cm)

The yellow-blotched salamander is one of several subspecies of Ensatina with a wide variety of colors and patterns. All have the distinguishing feature of a tail which is constricted at its base. The male usually has a longer tail than the female.

A land-dwelling species, it shelters under rocks and logs, making forays in search of spiders and large insects such as beetles and crickets.

The female lays a clutch of between 7 and 25 eggs in spring or early summer in a burrow or rotting log. She guards the eggs while they develop. The larvae live on land and do not have an aquatic phase. They become mature at between 2 and 3 years old.

## Dusky Salamander

*Desmognathus fuscus*

**RANGE** S. Canada; N.E. USA, south to Louisiana

**HABITAT** Springs, woodland creeks, floodplains

**SIZE** 2½–5½ in (6.5–14 cm)

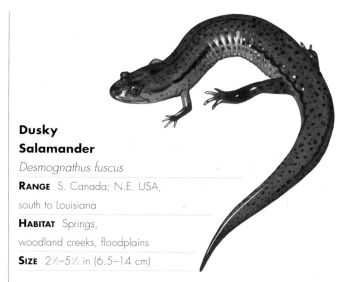

Young dusky salamanders have pairs of yellow or red spots on the back but, as they mature, these fade or become obscured. The dusky salamander can jump well when alarmed, leaping several times its own length to escape an enemy. It feeds mainly on insect larvae and earthworms.

In summer, the female lays 12 to 36 eggs in a cluster near water, usually under a rock or log. The larvae hatch in 2 to 3 months and reach maturity in 3 to 4 years.

## California Slender Salamander *Batrachoseps attenuatus*

**RANGE** USA: S.W. Oregon, California, western slopes of Sierra Nevada

**HABITAT** Redwood forest, grassland, mountains and foothills

**SIZE** 3–5½ in (7.5–14 cm)

True to its name, this salamander has a slim, elongate body and tail. Its legs and feet are tiny and narrow, with four toes on each foot. Coloration varies with area. The most common Californian salamander, it lives on land and moves with undulating movements of its body rather than by using its limbs. During the day, it hides in damp vegetation or among tree roots, and emerges at night to hunt for worms and spiders and other invertebrate prey. It is particularly active in rainy periods.

In late autumn or winter, stimulated by rainfall, the female lays 4 to 21 eggs under a rock or log. The eggs hatch in spring and the larvae do not undergo an aquatic phase.

# MOLE SALAMANDERS AND DICAMPTODONTID SALAMANDERS

## AMBYSTOMATIDAE: MOLE SALAMANDER FAMILY

There are about 32 species of mole salamander, all found in North America from Canada to Mexico. Typically, these salamanders have broad heads and a thick-bodied, sturdy appearance. Many species are ground-living, burrowing animals, rarely seen except in the breeding season when they migrate to ponds or streams to mate and lay eggs. Others have developed more aquatic habits and live in or near water most of the year. Larvae are aquatic and have feathery external gills and well-developed tail fins.

In most salamanders, the larvae remain permanently in the water while the adults spend at least part of the time on land. When the larva transforms into a mature, breeding adult, therefore, it loses such features as feathery external gills and the flattened tail, which are only useful in water. The mole salamander family is notable because some species can breed while still living in the water and still retaining these normally larval characteristics. This is known as neotenous breeding. Some geographical races of otherwise normal species are neotenous, for example, western forms of the North American tiger salamander, *Ambystoma tigrinum*, are neotenous, while the eastern relatives are normal.

Insects and small invertebrates are the main foods of all members of the family. Male and female mole salamanders look alike, but males usually have longer tails than females.

### Spotted Salamander *Ambystoma maculatum*

**RANGE** S.E. Canada, E. USA to Georgia and E. Texas

**HABITAT** Hardwood forest, hillsides near pools

**SIZE** 6–9½ in (15–24 cm)

This stout-bodied salamander is identified by the irregular spots on its back, which run from head to tail. Rarely seen, it spends most of its life underground and feeds on slugs and worms.

In early spring, heavy rains stimulate the salamanders to migrate to breeding pools. The female lays about 100 eggs at a

time, in a compact mass which adheres to submerged vegetation in the pond; she may lay more than one such mass. Some 4 to 8 weeks later, the eggs hatch into larvae ½ in (1.25 cm) long, which develop into adult form at 2 to 4 months. Spotted salamanders may live for 20 years.

In some areas these salamanders are becoming rare because acid rain is polluting their breeding ponds and preventing the successful development of eggs. Acid rain contains dilute sulfur and nitric acids from the gases released into the atmosphere by the burning of fossil fuels and is a source of increasing anxiety to biologists. In the temporary rain and snow pools used by salamanders for breeding, acidity is often extremely high, causing a high failure rate of eggs and severe deformities in those young that do survive.

### Marbled Salamander *Ambystoma opacum*

**RANGE** E. USA: New Hampshire to Florida, west to Texas

**HABITAT** Woodland: swamp areas and drier, high ground

**SIZE** 3½–5 in (9–12.5 cm)

A dark-colored, stout species, the marbled salamander has some light markings that are the origin of its common name. The male's markings are brighter than the female's; juveniles are dark gray to brown with light flecks. The salamander emerges at night to hunt for slugs and worms but before morning hides under a log or stone where it remains for the day. Marbled salamanders breed from September to December, depending on latitude, and mate and nest on land. The female lays 50 to 200 eggs, one at a time in a dip on the ground that will later fill with rain. Until the rains come, the salamander curls itself round the eggs to protect them. The larvae hatch a few days after being covered by rain. If there is insufficient rainfall to fill the nest, the eggs may not hatch until the spring. Once hatched, the larvae develop adult form at between 4 and 6 months.

male's glands. He then sheds his sperm in a small packet, known as a spermatophore, which sinks to the bottom of the water. The female settles over it and picks up the sperm packet with her cloaca (the external reproductive chamber) and is thus fertilized internally. In the wild, the axolotl lays about 400 eggs but may lay thousands in captivity.

Axolotls normally breed neotenously (in the larval state), retaining the gills and remaining in water. However, some individuals metamorphose into land-dwelling, gill-less adults.

## DICAMPTODONTIDAE: DICAMPTODONTID SALAMANDERS

The four species in this family of semiaquatic salamanders are found in the coastal forests of western North America. Like the mole salamanders, members of this family also show some neoteny, although only one species, *Dicamptodon copei*, is permanently neotenous.

### Tiger Salamander *Ambystoma tigrinum*

**RANGE** S. C. Canada, C. USA, south to N. Florida and Mexico

**HABITAT** Arid plains, damp meadows, mountain forest

**SIZE** 6–15¾ in (15–40 cm)

The world's largest land-dwelling salamander, the tiger salamander has a stout body, broad head and small eyes. Its coloration varies greatly, and it adapts to a variety of habitats, from sea level to 11,000 ft (3,350 m). Tiger salamanders live near water among plant debris or use crayfish or mammal burrows for refuge. They are often active at night and feed on earthworms, insects, mice and some small amphibians.

The timing of the breeding season varies according to area but it is usually prompted by rainfall. The salamanders mate in water and the female lays her eggs in masses which then adhere to submerged vegetation or debris.

### Axolotl *Ambystoma mexicanum* **VU**

**RANGE** Mexico: Lake Xochimilco

**HABITAT** Permanent water at high altitude

**SIZE** Up to 11½ in (29 cm)

Now rare, the axolotl is threatened by the destruction of its habitat, the introduction of predatory fishes, such as carp, and the collection of specimens for the pet trade. It has a dorsal fin, which extends from the back of its head to the tip and round the underside of its long tail, and three pairs of feathery external gills. Its legs and feet are small and weak. The name "axolotl" is an Aztec word meaning water monster.

Axolotls breed in water. The female is attracted to the male by secretions of his abdominal glands which he fans in her direction with his tail. The female approaches and noses the

### Pacific Giant Salamander *Dicamptodon ensatus*

**RANGE** Pacific coast of N. America: British Columbia to California; Idaho, Montana

**HABITAT** Cool, humid forest, rivers, streams and lakes

**SIZE** 2¾–11¾ in (7–30 cm)

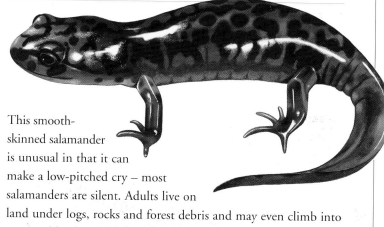

This smooth-skinned salamander is unusual in that it can make a low-pitched cry – most salamanders are silent. Adults live on land under logs, rocks and forest debris and may even climb into trees and bushes. Mainly active at night, they feed on snails, slugs, insects, mice and small snakes, and other salamanders.

In spring, adults breed in water, usually in the headwaters of a spring, and the female lays about 100 eggs on a submerged branch. The larvae live in cold clear lakes or streams; they are predatory and eat smaller larvae, as well as tadpoles and insects.

They mature into adults in their second year or become sexually mature (neotenic) larvae when about 7¾ in (20 cm) long.

# NEWTS AND SALAMANDERS

## SALAMANDRIDAE: NEWT FAMILY

There are about 49 species of salamander and newt in this family, found in temperate regions of northwest Africa, Europe, Asia and North America. All have well-developed limbs with four or five digits and movable eyelids, adults have fully functional lungs and no external gills. There are both aquatic and terrestrial forms, but most are found in or near water, at least in the breeding season.

### Sharp-ribbed Salamander *Pleurodeles waltl*

**RANGE** Portugal and Spain (except N. and N.E.), Morocco

**HABITAT** Slow rivers, ponds, ditches

**SIZE** 6–11¾ in (15–30 cm)

One of the largest European amphibians, the sharp-ribbed salamander has a stout body and a broad, flat head. Its skin is rough and there is a row of small protuberances along each side which lie at the tips of the ribs; the ribs are often distinct and may even protrude through the skin. A powerful swimmer, it is usually active at night when it searches for small invertebrate animals to eat.

A courting male carries his mate on his back in the water before depositing his package of sperm on the bottom. He then lowers the female on to the sperm and she collects it with her reproductive organ and is fertilized internally. She lays her eggs on a submerged stone.

### Fire Salamander
*Salamandra salamandra*

**RANGE** Central, W. and S. Europe; N.W. Africa, parts of S.W. Asia

**HABITAT** Forest on hills and mountains

**SIZE** 7¾–11 in (20–28 cm)

A heavily built species with a rather short tail, the fire salamander has bright markings, which may be in the form of spots or stripes. These markings provide warning to potential predators of the salamander's unpleasant body secretions, which irritate the mouth and eyes of enemies and may even be fatal to small mammals. Although a land-dweller, it prefers moist areas and is seldom far from water. It emerges from daytime refuges to hunt for its invertebrate prey at night.

Fire salamanders mate on land. The male carries the female around on his back, then deposits his sperm package on the ground and lowers her on to it. She collects the sperm with her reproductive organ and is fertilized internally. The eggs develop inside the female's body and about 10 months after fertilization she gives birth to 10 to 50 live young in the water.

### Warty/Great crested Newt *Triturus cristatus* **LR:cd**

**RANGE** Europe (not S. and S.W. France, Iberia, Ireland or S. Greece)

**HABITAT** Still or slow water, woodland

**SIZE** 5½–7 in (14–18 cm)

A large, rough-skinned newt, the male warty newt develops a jagged crest on his back in the breeding season. Females are often larger than males, but do not develop crests. Warty newts eat invertebrates. They will also take some small fish and other amphibians and their eggs.

The courting male performs an energetic display for his mate then deposits his sperm, over which the female either walks or is led, and which she collects with her reproductive organ. She lays between 200 and 300 eggs, one at a time, which hatch out after 4 or 5 months.

**Eastern Newt**

*Notophthalmus viridescens*

**RANGE** S.E. Canada, E. USA: Great Lakes area to Florida and Texas

**HABITAT** Ponds and lakes with vegetation, ditches, swamps

**SIZE** 2½–5½ in (6.5–14 cm)

The eastern newt occurs in several different patterns and colors over its wide range. Adults are aquatic and are eager predators, searching in shallow water for worms, insects, crustaceans and the eggs and young of other amphibians.

The breeding season begins in late winter or early spring. The female lays from 200 to 400 eggs, one at a time, on submerged plants and, after an incubation of up to 2 months, the eggs hatch into larvae. In later summer, these larvae transform into subadults, known as efts, and leave the water to spend up to 3 years living on land and feeding primarily on insects. They then return to the water and become mature, fully developed adults.

## Rough-skinned Newt

*Taricha granulosa*

**RANGE** W. North America: Alaska to California

**HABITAT** Ponds, lakes, slow streams and surrounding grassland or woodland

**SIZE** 2½–5 in (6.5–12.5 cm)

The most aquatic of Pacific newts, the rough-skinned newt is identified by its warty skin and its small eyes with dark lower lids. It searches for its invertebrate prey both on land and in the water, and its toxic skin secretions repel most of its enemies.

In the breeding season, the male's skin temporarily becomes smooth and his vent swells. Unlike other western newts, the female rough-skinned lays her eggs one at a time, rather than in masses, on submerged plants or debris. The eggs hatch into aquatic larvae.

## CRYPTOBRANCHIDAE: GIANT SALAMANDER FAMILY

This family contains the largest amphibians alive in the world today. Only 3 species are known – the Chinese and Japanese giant salamanders and the hellbender of the eastern USA. The Asiatic giant salamanders can reach lengths of over 5 ft (1.5 m).

**Hellbender** *Cryptobranchus alleganiensis*

**RANGE** E. USA: S. New York to N. Alabama, Missouri

**HABITAT** Rocky-bottomed streams

**SIZE** 12–29 in (30.5–74 cm)

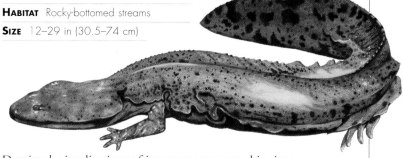

Despite the implications of its common name, this giant salamander is a harmless creature which feeds on crayfish, snails and worms. It has the flattened head characteristic of its family and loose flaps of skin along the lower sides of its body.

A nocturnal salamander, the hellbender hides under rocks in the water during the day. It depends on its senses of smell and touch, rather than on sight, to find its prey, since its eyes are set so far down the sides of its head that it cannot focus on an object with both eyes at once.

Hellbenders breed in autumn – the male makes a hollow beneath a rock or log on the stream bed and the female lays strings of 200 to 500 eggs. As she lays the eggs, the male fertilizes them and then guards the nest until the eggs hatch 2 or 3 months later.

## HYNOBIIDAE: ASIATIC LAND SALAMANDER FAMILY

The 35 species in this family are considered the most primitive of living salamanders. All occur in central and eastern Asia.

## Asian/Amber-colored Salamander

*Hynobius stejnegeri* **DD**

**RANGE** Japan

**HABITAT** Mountain streams

**SIZE** 5½ in (14 cm)

Like all members of its family, the Asian salamander's methods of breeding are primitive, involving external fertilization. The female lays her eggs in water in paired sacs, each sac containing 35 to 70 eggs. The male then takes the sacs and fertilizes the eggs but shows no interest in the female.

# CAECILIANS

## ORDER GYMNOPHONIA

This order contains 6 families of caecilians, over 170 species in all. Caecilians are limbless amphibians with cylindrical, ringed bodies and resemble giant earthworms. One family is aquatic, but the others are blind, burrowing creatures, rarely seen above ground. They burrow into the rich, soft soil of tropical or warm temperate forests in search of their prey, usually earthworms, insects and other invertebrates. Adults have a sensory tentacle beneath each eye which is probably used for finding prey. Many species have small scales embedded in the surface of the skin. This is probably a primitive feature which all other amphibian groups have since lost.

### ICHTHYOPHIDAE

There are 43 species in this family of terrestrial caecilians, found in Southeast Asia, Central America and tropical South America. They have short tails and scales on the body.

#### Sticky Caecilian *Ichthyophis sp.*

**RANGE** S.E. Asia

**HABITAT** Forest

**SIZE** Up to 15 in (38 cm)

Adult caecilians of this Southeast Asian genus live in burrows and feed on earthworms and small burrowing snakes. They breed in the spring. The female lays 20 or more eggs in a burrow she makes in moist ground near to water. She coils around her eggs while they develop, in order to protect them from predators. As they incubate, the eggs absorb moisture and gradually swell until they are double their original size. On hatching, the larva is four times the weight of a newly laid egg and has a pair of breathing pores on its head. The larvae undergo a prolonged aquatic phase before becoming land-based adults.

## SCOLECOMORPHIDAE

The 6 species of caecilian in this family are all of the same genus and occur only in central Africa. They are tailless and have no primitive body scales. All species live on land in burrows.

*Scolecomorphus kirkii*

**RANGE** Africa: Tanzania, Malawi, Zambia

**HABITAT** Mountain forest

**SIZE** Up to 16½ in (41 cm)

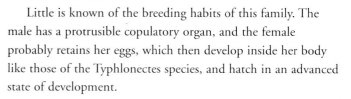

This caecilian lives in burrows it digs under the leaf mold on the forest floor. Unlike other caecilians, it does not even come to the surface after rain. Termites and worms are its main foods.

Little is known of the breeding habits of this family. The male has a protrusible copulatory organ, and the female probably retains her eggs, which then develop inside her body like those of the Typhlonectes species, and hatch in an advanced state of development.

## CAECILIAIDAE: CAECILIAN FAMILY

There are 90 species in this family, all of which are land-dwelling burrowers. Many species have scales on the body. Females reproduce either by laying eggs, which develop and hatch outside the body, or by producing eggs, which are retained to develop and hatch inside the body, and are then born as live young. The young have external gills and may spend some time as free-swimming larvae. Species occur in Old and New World tropics.

#### Panamanian Caecilian *Caecilia ochrocephala*

**RANGE** Central and South America: E. Panama, N. Colombia

**HABITAT** Forest

**SIZE** Up to 24 in (61 cm)

The Panamanian caecilian has a small slender head and a wedge-shaped snout. It burrows into soft, usually moist earth and seldom appears above ground except when heavy rains flush

it from its burrow. It eats mainly insects and earthworms. Snakes often enter the burrows of these caecilians and devour them.

Little is known of the breeding habits of this rarely seen creature, but females are thought to lay eggs which then develop and hatch outside the body.

### South American Caecilian *Siphonops annulatus*

**RANGE** South America, east of Andes to Argentina

**HABITAT** Varied, often forest

**SIZE** 13¾ in (35 cm)

This widespread caecilian has a short thick body and no scales. It spends most of its life underground and feeds largely on earthworms. The female lays eggs, but it is not known whether the young pass through a larval stage.

### São Tomé Caecilian

*Schistometopum thomensis*

**RANGE** São Tomé Island in Gulf of Guinea, off W. Africa

**HABITAT** Forest

**SIZE** Up to 12 in (30.5 cm)

The body of this brightly colored caecilian is usually about ½ in (1.25 cm) in diameter. Its snout is rounded and it has no tail. It lives underground, feeding on whatever invertebrate prey it can find, mainly on insects and worms. The female retains her eggs in her body where they develop and hatch; the young are then born in an advanced state of development.

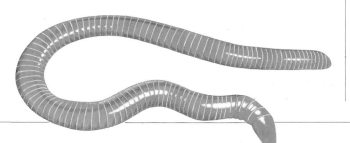

### Seychelles Caecilian *Hgpogeophis rostratus*

**RANGE** Seychelles

**HABITAT** Swampy coastal regions

**SIZE** 7½ in (20 cm)

The Seychelles caecilian has a slightly flattened body which tapers at both ends. The body darkens as the caecilian matures. It burrows wherever the soil is moist. It often lives beneath rocks or logs or digs into rotting trees. It eats small invertebrates and frogs.

Mating takes place at any time of year when there is plenty of rain. The female lays 6 to 30 eggs and coils her body around them to guard them. The young do not have a larval stage, but hatch as miniature adults.

## TYPHLONECTIDAE

There are 18 species of aquatic caecilian in this family, all found in tropical South America. They live in freshwater. Although they have no tails, the end of the body is laterally flattened for propulsion in water. This family lacks the primitive body scales, present in other families.

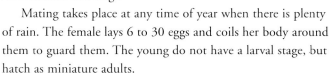

### *Typhlonectes compressicauda*

**RANGE** Guianas, Brazil

**HABITAT** Rivers, streams, pools

**SIZE** 20½ in (52 cm)

This aquatic caecilian swims with eellike movements of its compressed tail. The sexes look similar, but the male has a protrusible copulatory organ with which he fertilizes his mate internally. The female retains her eggs inside her body while the young develop. Having eaten all the yolk that surrounds them in their eggs, the young hatch and distribute themselves along the mother's oviduct. They feed on cells and drops of oil from the uterine wall which they obtain with the rasping plates in their mouths. More nutrients are obtained through the thin delicate skin which the young possess; they also have broad, baglike, external gills which disappear before they hatch. When the young are born; their thin skin is replaced by firmer, stronger skin, and the rasping plates by teeth.

# FISH

## *The first vertebrates.*

MORE THAN 45,000 OR SO KNOWN SPECIES OF VERTEBRATE ANIMALS ARE FISHES, WHICH IN THEIR AQUATIC ENVIRONMENT HAVE EVOLVED INTO A HUGE RANGE OF SPECIALIZED FORMS, AT LEAST AS DIVERSE AS THAT OF FOUR-LEGGED ANIMALS. THE FIRST MAJOR DIVISION IN THIS GROUP IS BETWEEN JAWLESS AND JAWED FISHES, WITH THE FORMER GROUP TODAY CONSISTING OF ONLY LAMPREYS AND HAGFISHES, REMNANTS OF AN EARLY STAGE OF VERTEBRATE EVOLUTION. THE JAWED FISHES, WHICH AROSE JUST UNDER 400 MILLION YEARS AGO, ARE THEMSELVES DIVIDED INTO VASTLY DIFFERING GROUPS. FIRST ARE THE CARTILAGE-SKELETONED FISH (CHONDRICHTHYES) SUCH AS SHARKS, SKATES AND RAYS, RATFISH, RABBITFISH AND ELEPHANTFISH. SECOND, THERE ARE THREE MAIN TYPES OF BONY-SKELETONED FISHES: THE RAY-FINNED FISHES, WITH NARROW-BASED FINS AND FIN RAYS WHICH SUPPORT THEM (ACTINOPTERYGIAN FISHES); AND TWO TYPES OF FLESHY- OR LOBE-FINNED FISHES, NAMELY, THE LUNGFISHES AND THE COELACANTHIMORPHS, REPRESENTED TODAY ONLY BY THE COELACANTH (LATIMERIA).

*Imperial
Angelfish*

Lampreys and hagfishes, like the earliest vertebrates before them, have no jaws. They have only the most rudimentary vertebrae and cylindrical bodies, with small unpaired fins at the rear end. Only about 30 species of lamprey and 32 of hagfish survive today. The former are found in the cool areas of the world both in the sea and in fresh water; the latter are marine fishes of worldwide distribution. Lampreys live parasitically on other fishes, hanging on to their outer surfaces with a sharply toothed sucker that bears a small mouth and a rasping tongue at its center. The lamprey uses its tongue to make a wound in the host's body and then feeds on its blood. Larval lampreys are bottom-dwelling filter-feeders, and lamprey life cycles sometimes involve both marine and freshwater stages. Hagfishes are an entirely marine group, and although well known as scavengers which suck out the body contents of dead or dying fishes, they feed mainly on crustaceans and worms.

Both lampreys and hagfishes swim by lateral undulations of the body, produced by the contractions of repeating blocks of muscles along the flanks. These simplest living vertebrates possess what is basically a prototype of the water-breathing gill apparatus used by all higher fishes. The side walls of the pharynx are perforated to provide gill openings from the gut cavity to the outside world; there are seven such openings on each side in lampreys. Because of the lamprey's sucker, respiratory water cannot usually pass through the mouth. Instead, when the sucker is in action, water passes both in and out through the gill openings and oxygenates the blood, which is pumped from the heart to the gills through 8 pairs of

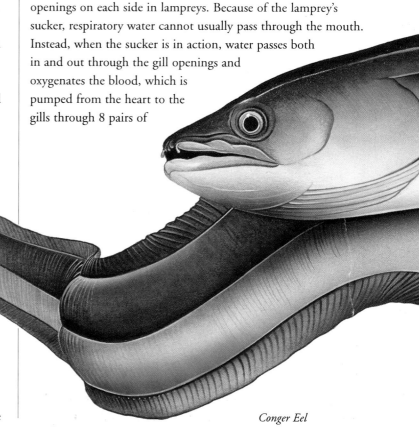

*Conger Eel*

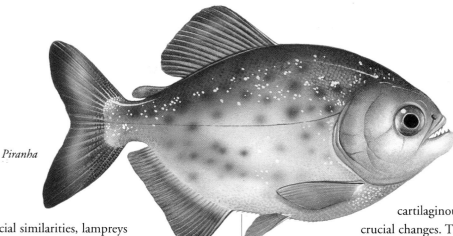

*Piranha*

branchial arteries.

Despite their superficial similarities, lampreys and hagfishes are very different. Some biologists even exclude hagfishes from the vertebrates altogether and place them within a separate group within the chordates.

The cartilaginous fishes, of which about 850 species are known, are marine fishes, which vary in size between the huge sharks of more than 49 ft (15 m) in length and tiny forms about 11¾ in (30 cm) long. Most are active predators on other fish and are equipped with sharp-edged teeth in both jaws. Although their skeletons are made of cartilage, not bone, these fishes conform to the orthodox body plan of jawed fishes, with paired fins and proper vertebrae. The body is beautifully streamlined, with the greatest width some way down it, a pointed anterior end and a tapering rear part, terminating in a two-vaned propulsive tail. This is moved from side to side, using muscles similar to those which produce undulations of the body in the jawless fishes.

In many cartilaginous fishes the upper vane of the tail is larger than the lower one, and the front pair of paired fins, the pectorals, act as winglike control surfaces for changing directions. Like the large, unpaired dorsal fins, they also provide directional stability against rolling, pitching and yawing when the fish is swimming. Cartilaginous fishes have between 5 and 7 pairs of gill slits, opening to the outside world, on each side of the head. Typically the respiratory current passes in through the mouth and out through the gill slits.

There are 24,000 or so species of bony fish – about half the known total of living vertebrate species – and, unlike the cartilaginous fishes, they thrive in fresh as well as salt water. The body plan of these successful animals is similar to that of the cartilaginous fishes, but with some crucial changes. The skeleton, including the fin rays, is made of bone; the tail vanes are characteristically, but not always, equal in size, and there is often a gas-filled swim-bladder in the body for buoyancy control. This can be adjusted to make the fish weightless in the water so that it can rest or stay motionless – a great advance over the cartilaginous fishes, which must keep moving or sink. There is also a difference in the gill system. In bony fishes there are usually four respiratory gills on each side of the pharynx, but the openings associated with them are enclosed by a large flap, the operculum, which effectively produces a single, ultimate opening on each side of the fish. The bodies of most bony fishes are covered with overlapping scales, set in the skin, which form a protective armor.

Bony fishes feed in a wide variety of ways and fill every underwater feeding niche. Some are herbivorous, living on aquatic vegetation and microscopic plant plankton. Others catch small invertebrate animals or strain them from the water by means of gill rakers, comblike structures attached to the gill bars. Still others are active, fast-moving predators, equipped with sharp teeth; while species such as flatfishes and angler fishes rely on their camouflage to keep them hidden while they lie in wait for prey.

Many fishes reproduce by simply shedding vast numbers of eggs into the water, where they are fertilized by the male depositing sperm on to them. There is rarely any parental care, and although most eggs hatch, few survive to maturity. Some

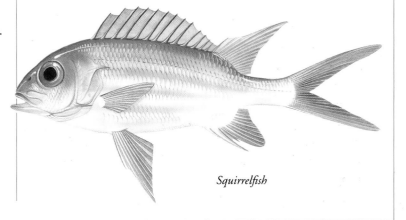

*Squirrelfish*

male fishes, notably sharks, fertilize their mates internally and have clasping organs, developed from modified pelvic fins, which help them hold the female while depositing sperm in her genital opening. These internally-fertilized females may retain their eggs and developing young inside the body and give birth to fully formed young.

Most bony fishes are marine and freshwater forms of actinopterygians (ray-finned fishes), but there is also the single marine genus of lobe-finned coelacanth and the 3 surviving genera of lungfishes that all live in fresh water. Lungfishes

*Sheepshead*

***Cladogram showing possible phylogenetic relationships in fishes.*** *Although we use the term "fish" to refer to any fish-shaped aquatic vertebrate, the term in fact covers a diverse assortment of vertebrates that have arisen along different evolutionary pathways.*

**KEY TO FISH CLADOGRAM A**

1 Myxini (hagfishes)
2 Cephalaspidomorphi (lampreys)
3 Chondrichthyes (cartilaginous fish)
4 Actinopterygii (ray-finned fishes)
5 Coelacanthiformes (coelacanth)
6 Dipnoi (lungfishes)
7 Tetrapoda (land vertebrates)

**CLADOGRAM A**

**1** Hagfish  **2** Lamprey  **3** Porbeagle  **4** Sweetlip emperor  **5** Coelacanth  **6** Australian lungfish  **7** Tetrapoda

breathe air, and most make burrows, in which they live when the rivers and lakes of their tropical habitats seasonally dry up. In these fishes the swimbladder is connected to the gut cavity via a tube and operates as an air-breathing lung.

The huge number of fish species and the proportionately large number of fish families have made it impossible to treat them in the family-focused format of the rest of this book. Consequently the section on fishes is completely comprehensive at order level, but with mention of families only in the largest orders.

*Clown Triggerfish*

*Cladogram showing possible phylogenetic relationships in the Actinopterygii (ray-finned fishes). Bony fishes form the largest of all fish groups, and most bony fishes are ray-finned. There are two evolutionary groups within the Actinopterygii: the Chondrostei, which include the bichirs and sturgeons and the Neopterygii, the more advanced group that includes most modern bony fishes. Apart from the gars and bowfins, most fish in this group belong to the Teleostei, the group that contains the dominant bony fishes.*

**KEY TO FISH  CLADOGRAM B**

1  Polypteriformes (bichirs)
2  Acipenseriformes (sturgeons)
3  Lepisosteiformes (gars)
4  Amiiformes (bowfin)
5  Osteoglossiformes (bony-tongues)
6  Elopomorpha (eels)
7  Clupeimorpha (herrings)
8  Ostariophysi (carps, catfish)
9  Protacanthopterygii (pikes, salmon)
10 Stenopterygii (cods, anglerfishes)
11 Atheriniformes (flying fishes, silversides)
12 Percomorpha (perch, mullets)

**CLADOGRAM B**

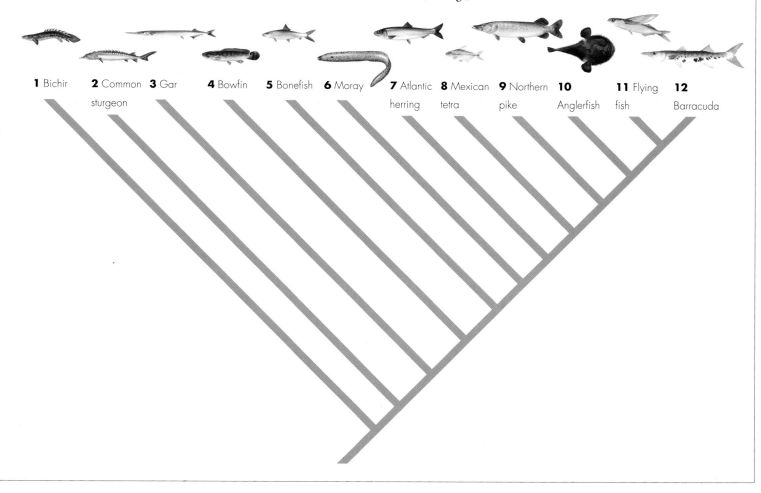

1 Bichir   2 Common sturgeon   3 Gar   4 Bowfin   5 Bonefish   6 Moray   7 Atlantic herring   8 Mexican tetra   9 Northern pike   10 Anglerfish   11 Flying fish   12 Barracuda

# HAGFISH, LAMPREYS AND SHARKS

## MYXINIFORMES: HAGFISH ORDER

The 43 species of hagfishes make up the only living family in this order. They are all marine and occur in temperate and subtropical waters of the Atlantic, Indian and Pacific Oceans. They are jawless fishes and have slitlike mouths surrounded with fleshy filaments. Some zoologists do not regard hagfish as vertebrates because they lack vertebrae, placing them instead in their own chordate subphyllum.

**Hagfish** *Myxine glutinosa*

| | |
|---|---|
| **RANGE** | N. Atlantic, Arctic Oceans |
| **HABITAT** | Ocean bed |
| **SIZE** | 24 in (61 cm) |

Hagfishes live in fairly deep water where there is a soft muddy bottom into which they can burrow. They have no paired fins nor scales; their eyes are hidden under skin and they are almost blind. The surface of the skin is particularly slimy since it is copiously supplied with mucus-secreting glands.

Hagfishes feed on some marine worms and crustaceans, but they are best known for attacking dead and dying fish, or fish that are trapped in nets. Using the toothlike plates on the tongue and the single tooth in the mouth, the hagfish bores into the prey's body and eats away all its flesh and intestines, leaving only skin and bone.

## PETROMYZONIFORMES: LAMPREY ORDER

This order includes only 1 family, the lampreys, with about 41 species. All are primitive fishes which have no true jaws, but only sucking, funnellike mouths lined with small teeth. Many are parasitic and live on the blood of other fishes. Some are freshwater species, others are anadromous – they live in salt water but travel to fresh water in order to spawn. Most lampreys occur in the northern hemisphere, but there are some species which occur in and around southern South America, south Australia and New Zealand.

**River Lamprey/Lampern** *Lampetra fluviatilis* **LR:nt**

| | |
|---|---|
| **RANGE** | Britain, N.W. Europe |
| **HABITAT** | Rivers, coastal waters |
| **SIZE** | 11¾–20 in (30–50 cm) |

The parasitic lampern feeds on the blood of other fishes. It attaches itself to the host's body by its round suckerlike mouth and rasps away the skin and scales with its sharp teeth.

At spawning time, lamperns leave the coast and migrate upriver. They lay their eggs in spring in shallow pits excavated in the river bed. The larvae hatch then move downstream and bury themselves in mud. They stay her for up to 5 years, filter-feeding on microorganisms until they reach maturity.

**Sea Lamprey** *Petromyzon marinus*

| | |
|---|---|
| **RANGE** | Atlantic coasts of Europe and N. America; W. Mediterranean Sea |
| **HABITAT** | Coastal waters, rivers |
| **SIZE** | 35½ in (90 cm) |

Adult sea lampreys are blood-feeding parasites. The lamprey attaches itself to its victim so firmly that it is almost impossible to remove. A secretion in the lamprey's mouth prevents the host's blood from clotting, allowing the lamprey to feed. Victims often die from blood loss or from infection of the wound.

Adults leave the sea and travel up into rivers to spawn. They make a shallow pit in a stony-bottomed area by moving stones with their mouths, the eggs are deposited in this nest. The blind, toothless larvae live buried in mud, filter-feeding for 4 to 6 years, until as juveniles, they migrate to the sea. Lampreys also occur in inland lakes where they prey on commercial fish, but efforts are made to control their numbers in such waters.

## HETERODONTIFORMES: BULLHEAD SHARK ORDER

This is a small order containing one family of 8 primitive species of shark, found in the tropical Indian and Pacific Oceans. All have two dorsal fins preceded by a thick spine.

## Port Jackson Shark

*Heterodontus portusjacksoni*

**RANGE** S. Pacific Ocean, Southern Ocean: coasts of Australia from S. Queensland to S.W. Western Australia

**HABITAT** Coastal waters to depths of 600 ft (180 m)

**SIZE** Up to 5 ft (1.5 m)

The Port Jackson shark has the large, heavy head, prominent forehead and ridge over each eye that are typical of all bullhead sharks. Other characteristic features are the dark-brown markings encircling its grayish-brown body and the stout spines in front of each dorsal fin. The shark's small mouth has sharp, pointed teeth at the front and broader, crushing teeth farther back, suggesting that it eats hardshelled items such as mollusks and crustaceans. Most feeding takes place at night.

Year after year, these sharks are believed to migrate to the same shallow, reef areas to breed. Like all bullheads they are egg-laying, producing eggs protected by strong, horny cases with spirally twisted edges. This formation helps the egg-case to lodge in a rock crevice, where it remains until the young shark hatches out.

# LAMNIFORMES: LAMNIFORM SHARK ORDER

This order contains 7 families of sharks, 16 species in all. Lamniformes have skeletons made of cartilage. Almost all these species have two dorsal fins, one anal fin and five gill slits.

## Sand Tiger *Odontaspis taurus*

**RANGE** Atlantic Ocean: N. American and African coasts

**HABITAT** Coastal waters

**SIZE** 10½ ft (3.2 m)

The sand tiger is a predatory shark which tends to live at the bottom of shallow water, feeding on fish. It has characteristic yellow spots on its body, and dorsal, pelvic and anal fins are much the same size. Its long pointed teeth project forward noticeably. The female gives birth to 2 young which develop inside her body for 12 months while feeding on the yolks of unfertilized eggs. The young are about 39 in (1 m) long at birth.

A similar species, the raggedtooth shark, *O. ferox*, is found in the Mediterranean and off European Atlantic coasts, as well as the Pacific coast of the USA.

## Thresher Shark *Alopias vulpinus*

**RANGE** Temperate and tropical oceans

**HABITAT** Surface waters in open sea

**SIZE** 19½ ft (6 m)

The distinctive thresher shark has a tail as long as the rest of its body which it uses to advantage when hunting. The sharks feed mainly on schooling fish and, working in pairs or alone, they lash their tails to herd the fish into a compact mass where they make easy prey. A thresher may also strike and stun an individual fish with its tail. Threshers sometimes hunt in coastal waters, particularly in summer, when they are seen along the American Atlantic coast.

Females give birth to litters of 2 to 4 fully formed young, which may be as long as 5 ft (1.5 m) at birth.

In Australian waters, the thresher shark is known by different scientific names – *A. caudatus* and *A. grayi*.

## Basking Shark *Cetorhinus maximus* **VU**

**RANGE** Worldwide, outside the tropics

**HABITAT** Oceanic

**SIZE** 34 ft (10.4 m)

The basking shark is the second-largest living species of fish. It shares the streamlined body shape of other sharks but is distinguished by its extra large gill slits. It feeds entirely on plankton which it sieves from the water by means of comblike bristles on its gill arches. The shark simply swims with its mouth agape, taking in a vast quantity of water and plankton and filtering it through the gill slits. As the name implies, basking sharks often float sluggishly at the surface of the water.

Little is known of the basking shark's breeding habits, but its eggs are believed to develop inside its body, hatching as they are expelled. The young sharks are about 5 ft (1.5 m) long at birth.

# SHARKS CONTINUED

## Porbeagle *Lamna nasus* **VU**

**RANGE** N. Atlantic Ocean: Newfoundland, south to South Carolina, Iceland, south to N. Africa; Mediterranean Sea

**HABITAT** Open sea; coastal waters

**SIZE** 6–9¾ ft (1.8–3 m)

The porbeagle is a swift-swimming, heavy-bodied shark with five gill slits. It feeds on surface-dwelling fish, such as mackerel and herring, and on squid and some bottom-dwelling fish. Identifying characteristics are the position of the dorsal fin (above the base of the pectoral fin) and of the second dorsal fin (directly above the anal fin). This species and the related sharks (mako and great white) have body temperatures higher than the surrounding water, an adaptation linked with great muscular activity that improves their swimming efficiency.

The eggs hatch inside the mother and remain there for a short time before she gives birth to fully formed live young. Litters usually contain 1 to 5 young, which are sustained for a few weeks by the yolks of unfertilized eggs that they eat before birth.

The closely related salmon shark, *L. ditropis*, which lives in the Pacific, is similar to the porbeagle both in its appearance and habits.

## Mako *Isurus oxyrinchus*

**RANGE** Atlantic, Pacific and Indian Oceans: temperate and tropical areas

**HABITAT** Open sea

**SIZE** 9¾–13 ft (3–4 m)

A powerful, streamlined shark, with a slender body and a pointed snout, the mako is a fast-swimming predator. Distinguishing features are the slightly rounded tip to the first dorsal fin, which is positioned in line with the rear edge of the base of the pectoral fin, and the small second dorsal fin, positioned just in front of the anal fin. The mako is usually deep blue above and white below.

An active surface-dweller itself, the mako usually feeds on surface-living fish, such as tuna, mackerel, herrings and sardines, and on squid.

It is renowned for its habit of leaping clear of the water, and, although known to be dangerous and aggressive, the mako is a popular sporting fish with shark fishermen because of the spectacular struggle that it puts up and the leaps it performs when it is hooked.

The female mako gives birth to live young, which develop and hatch inside her body.

## White Shark *Carcharodon carcharias* **VU**

**RANGE** Atlantic, Pacific and Indian Oceans: warm temperate and tropical coastal areas

**HABITAT** Open sea; seasonally enters coastal waters

**SIZE** 19¾ ft (6 m)

The white shark, also known as the great white shark, is not actually white, but ranges in color from gray to brown with white underparts. Its long snout is pointed, and its large, powerful teeth are triangular and serrated. The top lobe of its tail is slightly longer than the lower lobe.

It feeds on a variety of aquatic animals, such as fish (including other sharks), seals and dolphins, and it also scavenges on dead animals and refuse. This is an extremely large and aggressive fish, and it has acquired the formidable reputation of a maneater and has, indeed, been involved in many attacks on humans.

Little is known of its breeding habits other than that it bears litters of up to 9 live young.

# CARCHARINIFORMES: REQUIEM SHARK ORDER

With 210 species in 8 families, the requiem or ground sharks make up more than half of the 350 shark species. Many of the order have the "typical" shark shape.

## Bull Shark *Carcharhinus leucas*

**RANGE** W. Atlantic Ocean: North Carolina to S. Brazil

**HABITAT** Inshore waters, rivers and connecting lakes

**SIZE** 8¼–11½ ft (2.5–3.5 m)

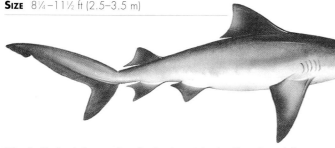

The bull shark has a chunky body, with the first dorsal fin placed well forward. Normally quite slow-moving, it is usually found in shallow water and regularly swims into rivers. Bull sharks eat a wide range of fish, including rays and small sharks, and they also eat shrimps, crabs, sea-urchins and refuse.

The female produces live young, generally born from May to July in brackish, inshore waters.

## Smooth Hammerhead *Sphyrna zygaena*

**RANGE** Atlantic, Pacific and Indian Oceans: tropical and warm temperate areas

**HABITAT** Coastal and inshore waters

**SIZE** 14 ft (4.3 m)

This is one of 10 species of hammerhead shark, all of which have flattened projections at the sides of the head. The eyes are on the outer edges of these lobes, and the nostrils also are spread far apart. The advantages of this head shape are not clear, but it may be that the shark gains some improvement of its sensory abilities by the spacing out of eyes and nostrils, or that the head shape improves manoeuvrability or simply increases lift.

The smooth hammerhead feeds on fish, particularly rays, and also scavenges on occasion. In summer, it makes regular migrations to cooler waters. Hammerheads have been known to attack man, and are thought to be aggressive sharks.

## Sandy Dogfish *Scyliorhinus canicula*

**RANGE** N. Atlantic Ocean: coasts of Norway, Britain, Europe, N. Africa; Mediterranean Sea

**HABITAT** Sandy or gravel bottoms

**SIZE** 23½ in–3¼ ft (60 cm–1 m)

A common fish, the sandy dogfish is one of a family of 60 species of small, shallow-water sharks. Its dorsal fins are placed well back toward the tail, which is long, with the lower lobe barely developed. Usually light sandy-brown in color, this dogfish is boldly marked with dark-brown spots and has a creamy or white belly. Primarily a bottom-dweller, it occurs in shallow water to depths of 330 ft (100 m), but may sometimes be found in deeper water, down to 1,300 ft (400 m). Its diet consists of many types of bottom-living invertebrates as well as fish.

Reproduction may take place throughout the year, but in the northern hemisphere most eggs are laid between November and July. The female deposits her eggs, each of which is encased in a horny capsule with tendrils at each corner, among seaweed in shallow water. The tendrils anchor the eggcase to weeds or other objects, where it remains for 5 to 11 months. The newly hatched young are 4 in (10 cm) long; they are sexually mature when about 19¾ in (50 cm) long.

## Blue Shark *Prionace glauca*

**RANGE** Atlantic, Pacific and Indian Oceans: temperate and tropical areas

**HABITAT** Open sea, surface waters

**SIZE** 9–12½ ft (2.7–3.8 m)

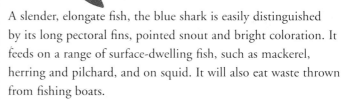

A slender, elongate fish, the blue shark is easily distinguished by its long pectoral fins, pointed snout and bright coloration. It feeds on a range of surface-dwelling fish, such as mackerel, herring and pilchard, and on squid. It will also eat waste thrown from fishing boats.

Females give birth to live young, and litters of as many as 50 to 60 at a time have been reported. Blue sharks make regular migrations to warmer waters in the winter months.

# SHARKS CONTINUED

## ORECTOLOBIFORMES: CARPET SHARK ORDER

This diverse order of sharks contains 31 species in 7 families including the bottom-dwelling wobbegongs and the whale shark, the largest of all fishes.

**Whale Shark** *Rhincodon typus* **DD**

**RANGE** All tropical seas

**HABITAT** Surface waters

**SIZE** 50 ft (15.2 m)

The huge whale shark is the largest living fish, growing up to 60 ft (18 m) long. It eats small fish and plankton which it filters from the water. The shark opens its mouth to take in a rush of water. The water is filtered out through the gills and plankton is retained. Little is known of this species' breeding habits.

## SQUATINIFORMES: ANGEL SHARK ORDER

The 13 species of angel sharks look more like rays because they are flattened. Unlike rays, the large pectoral fins are not attached to the head.

**Monkfish** *Squatina squatina*

**RANGE** North Sea; E. Atlantic Ocean: Scotland to N. Africa and Canary Islands; Mediterranean Sea

**HABITAT** Coastal waters, seabed

**SIZE** 6 ft (1.8 m)

The monkfish appears to be almost a cross between a shark and a ray, but the gills, positioned at the sides, the mouth at the end of its head and well-developed dorsal fins all reveal it to be a true shark (rays have mouth and gill slits positioned on their undersides). Its broad pectoral fins strongly resemble those of rays. Female monkfishes are larger than males.

The monkfish lies almost buried in sand or mud much of the time, but it can swim well. It feeds on bottom-living fish, such as dab plaice, sole and rays, and on crabs and mollusks. It bears live young, in litters of 9 to 20, from eggs which develop and hatch inside the mother.

## HEXANCHIFORMES: COW AND FRILL SHARK ORDER

The 5 species in this order are all primitive sharks, with long bodies and only one dorsal fin. All have six or seven pairs of gill slits – sharks generally have only five pairs. Most are deep-sea species, and relatively little is known of their habits.

**Bluntnose Six-gilled Shark** *Hexanchus griseus* **VU**

**RANGE** Atlantic, Pacific and Indian Oceans: temperate and warm temperate areas

**HABITAT** Open sea, inshore waters

**SIZE** 6–16½ ft (1.8–5 m)

An elongate shark, with a long tail fin and one dorsal fin positioned near the tail, this species has six pairs of gills.

Although apparently fairly sedentary and sluggish, it is a powerful shark and feeds on a wide range of bottom-living fish, such as rays, as well as on crustaceans. It is thought to mate in spring; the eggs develop and hatch inside the mother, and the young are 18 to 24 in (46 to 61 cm) long when they are born. There are often 40 or more in a litter, depending on the size of the female.

# SQUALIFORMES: SQUALIFORM SHARK ORDER

This order includes 74 species of shark in 3 families – dogfish sharks, bramble sharks and sleeper sharks. All have two dorsal fins, no anal fin and five or six pairs of gill slits. The species occur worldwide, and the order contains the world's smallest sharks.

## Spurdog/Spiny dogfish *Squalus acanthias*

**RANGE** N. Atlantic Ocean: coasts of Norway, Britain to N. Africa, W. Greenland to Florida; Mediterranean Sea; N. Pacific Ocean

**HABITAT** Inshore waters, near seabed

**SIZE** 3¼–4 ft (1–1.2 m)

A common shark, which is easily identified by the large spine in front of each dorsal fin, the spurdog has a long, slender body, a pointed snout and large eyes. Females are longer and heavier than males and do not become sexually mature until they reach 19 or 20 years of age. Males mature at 11 years.

Spurdogs feed on schooling fish, such as herrings and whiting, and on bottom-living fish and invertebrates. They themselves move in schools sometimes numbering thousands of individuals and often of only one sex. These schools may be migrating to warmer or cooler waters or, if females, to shallow water in order to give birth.

The spurdog bears live young, which develop for 18 to 22 months. From 3 to 11 young are born at a time, but the exact number and development time depend on the size of the mother. The combination of a small litter, long gestation and late maturity make this species particularly vulnerable to fishing pressure, and at one time it was fished in considerable quantities.

## Greenland Shark *Somniosus microcephalus*

**RANGE** N. Atlantic Ocean: inside Arctic Circle, south to Gulf of Maine and Britain

**HABITAT** Seabed at depths of 600–1,800 ft (180–550 m)

**SIZE** 21 ft (6.4 m)

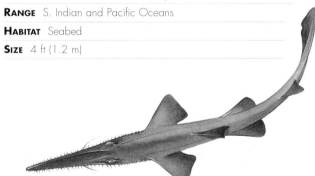

The Greenland shark is the giant of its group, but unlike other Atlantic squalid sharks, it has small dorsal fins with no spines in front of them. It appears to be a sluggish bottom-dweller, but will come to the surface in search of food, particularly during the winter. It preys on many kinds of fish, both surface and bottom-living, and also feeds on mollusks, crustaceans and squid and, reputedly, on seals, porpoises and seabirds. In Arctic whaling stations, it was well known as a scavenger.

Female Greenland sharks bear live young, from eggs which develop and hatch inside the mother's body. The usual litter is believed to be about 10 young.

# PRISTIPHORIFORMES: SAW SHARKS FAMILY

The single family in this order contains 5 species of saw sharks. The extended snout of the saw shark has teeth attached to it, forming a long blade. This is used by some species for slashing at fish, cutting them into pieces which are then eaten.

## Common Saw Shark *Pristiophorus cirratus*

**RANGE** S. Indian and Pacific Oceans

**HABITAT** Seabed

**SIZE** 4 ft (1.2 m)

The common saw shark, one of 5 species of saw shark, has a distinctive, bladelike snout with sharp teeth, which are alternately large and small, along each side. The fish's slender body and fin shapes show its relationship to the sharks, despite its strangely adapted snout.

This sedentary shark probes in the mud of the seabed with its saw, searching for invertebrates and bottom-living fish, which it detects with the aid of sensitive barbels on its snout.

The young are born well developed, but their teeth are enveloped within the skin and do not erupt until after birth.

# SKATES, RAYS AND CHIMAERAS

## RAJIFORMES: SKATES AND RAY ORDER

There are 12 families of cartilaginous fishes in this order, about 456 species in all. Most are marine fishes of temperate and tropical waters. All, except for the sawfish, have broad, flattened bodies and greatly expanded pectoral fins which extend along the head and trunk, giving the fishes a diamond shape. Tails are small and whiplike and dorsal fins tiny. Gill openings and the slit mouth are on the underside of the body, but there are small openings, or spiracles, on the upper surface through which they breathe when on the seabed. Most skates live on or near the seabed and eat mollusks and crustaceans.

Eggs are either deposited in egg cases, or develop and hatch inside the mother, who gives birth to fully formed live young.

### Smalltooth/Greater Sawfish *Pristis pectinata* **EN**

**RANGE** Temperate and tropical oceans

**HABITAT** Shallow coastal waters

**SIZE** 25 ft (7.7 m)

The smalltooth is the largest of the 6 sawfish species and is well known off the Atlantic coast of the USA and the East African coast. It has a bladelike snout, each side studded with 24 to 32 large teeth of equal size. Its body is more sharklike than raylike, apart from the enlarged pectoral fins and the gill openings on its underside.

Sawfishes live on the seabed in shallow water and use their saws to probe the sand and mud for small invertebrate prey. It is claimed that sawfishes also lash out with their snouts at schools of fish to obtain food. This is unconfirmed, but they can seriously wound other fish, and fishermen, if caught.

### Atlantic Guitarfish *Rhinobatus lentiginosus*

**RANGE** W. Atlantic Ocean

**HABITAT** Shallow waters, bays, estuaries

**SIZE** 30 in (76 cm)

A common fish along the American Atlantic coast from North Carolina to Yucatan, the guitarfish is halfway between sharks and rays in body shape. Its body is long and rounded with well-developed dorsal fins, but the pectoral fins are enlarged and the gill slits are on the underside of the body. It is a bottom-dweller and feeds mainly on crustaceans and mollusks. There are about 45 species of guitarfish.

### Skate *Raja batis*

**RANGE** E. Atlantic Ocean: Arctic Ocean to Madeira; Mediterranean Sea

**HABITAT** Deep waters

**SIZE** 8 ft (2.4 m)

Large numbers of skate are caught for food. Skates live in waters 98 to 2,000 ft (30 to 600 m) deep; only young fishes are found in the shallower part of this range. The skate has a flat body, broad pectoral fins and a tiny tail. There are small spines on the tail and on the underside of the body; adult females also have spines on the front edge of the body, while males have spines on their backs.

Skates are bottom-dwellers; they eat fish, crabs, lobsters and octopuses. Their eggs, deposited on the seabed, are encased in horny capsules which have long tips at each corner. Hatchlings are about 80 in (21 cm) long.

### Southern Stingray *Dasyatis americana*

**RANGE** Atlantic coast: New Jersey to Brazil; Gulf of Mexico; Caribbean

**HABITAT** Shallow coastal waters

**SIZE** 5 ft (1.5 m) wide

Stingrays are almost rectangular and have long thin tails; they have no dorsal or anal fins. The stingray has a sharp spine near the base of the tail which has venom-secreting tissue in its underside and can inflict a serious wound that may be fatal, even to humans. The stingray wields its tail with great speed and force to drive the spine into its victim.

Stingrays usually live buried in sand on the seabed; they feed on fish, crustaceans and mollusks which they crush with their strong, flattened teeth. The 3 to 5 young of the stingray develop inside the mother and are about 7 in (18 cm) wide at birth. All stingray species have much the same habits.

### Eagle Ray *Myliobatis aquila*

**RANGE** E. Atlantic Ocean: Britain to Senegal;
Mediterranean and Adriatic Seas

**HABITAT** Coastal waters

**SIZE** 6 ft (1.8 m)

Eagle rays are large, graceful fishes, with pointed, winglike pectoral fins and long thin tails. They feed on the seabed on crustaceans and mollusks, but are more active than stingrays.

In the north of its range, the eagle ray is seen only in summer; in winter it moves south to breed. The female produces up to 7 live young which are nourished before birth by secretions of her uterine membrane.

### Atlantic Manta *Manta birostris*

**RANGE** Atlantic Ocean: North Carolina to Brazil,
Madeira to W. Africa

**HABITAT** Coastal waters, open sea

**SIZE** 17 ft (5.2 m); 22 ft (6.7 m) wide

The gigantic manta, also known as the giant devil ray, is the largest ray. It has huge pointed pectoral fins, a fairly short tail and a short dorsal fin. Two fleshy appendages at each side of the mouth act as scoops for food. Mantas feed on tiny planktonic creatures which they filter from the water on to their gill arches. They also swallow fish and large crustaceans. The young hatch inside their mother and are born well developed.

### Atlantic Torpedo/Electric Ray *Torpedo nobiliana*

**RANGE** Atlantic Ocean: Scotland to South Africa, Nova Scotia
to North Carolina; Mediterranean Sea

**HABITAT** Seabed

**SIZE** 6 ft (1.8 m)

Torpedo rays can give electric shocks of 70 to 220 volts, sufficient power to kill or stun a prey fish or to throw a man to the ground. The electric discharges of these fishes are produced by modified muscle cells. Torpedos eat fish, which they trap and

envelop in their pectoral fins while delivering the shock. Females produce live young which are about 94 in (25 cm) long when they are born.

## CHIMAERIFORMES: CHIMAERA ORDER

This is the third major group of cartilaginous fishes. It includes 31 species of marine fishes distributed throughout the world. Chimaeroids are long-bodied fishes with long thin tails. Their gills open into a single external opening on each side, covered by a flap. Male chimaeroids have pelvic claspers for internal fertilization of females at spawning time.

### Ratfish *Chimaera monstrosa*

**RANGE** E.N. Atlantic Ocean: Iceland
to Azores; Mediterranean Sea

**HABITAT** Deep water

**SIZE** 5 ft (1.5 m)

The ratfish has a prominent dorsal fin, large pectoral fins and large eyes. The spine on the dorsal fin is linked to a venom gland. Males have a clublike appendage on the head and are often slightly smaller than females. Ratfishes often occur in one-sex schools. Ratfish are generally found close to the seabed and eat starfish, mollusks and crustaceans. In summer the ratfish breeds and lays eggs in shallow water.

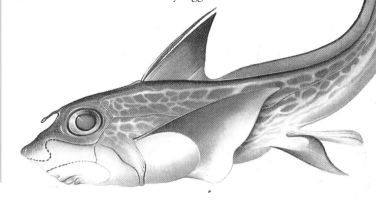

# BICHIRS, STURGEONS, GARS AND BOWFIN

## POLYPTERIFORMES: BICHIR ORDER

This order contains a single family of 11 species, all found in African freshwater habitats. The fishes strongly resemble the earliest fossil fishes and have primitive features, such as a swimbladder which can be used as a means of breathing air.

**Bichir** *Polypterus weeksi*

| | |
|---|---|
| **RANGE** | C. Africa: upper Congo |
| **HABITAT** | Lakes, rivers |
| **SIZE** | 15¾ in (40 cm) |

A long-bodied fish covered with hard diamond-shaped scales, this bichir, like the rest of its family, inhabits overgrown water margins. Its distinctive dorsal fin is made up of small flaglike fins, each supported by a bony ray. The fan shaped pectoral fins are mounted on fleshy lobes. Bichirs feed on fish and amphibians.

## ACIPENSERIFORMES: STURGEON ORDER

There are 2 families in this order. First there are the 24 species of sturgeon which are mainly freshwater and coastal fishes of temperate regions, the marine species of which migrate into rivers to spawn. All have five rows of bony plates along the sides of the body. Second there is the paddlefish family, in which there are 2 species of sturgeonlike freshwater fishes with long paddlelike snouts and no bony plates.

**Beluga** *Huso huso* **EN**

| | |
|---|---|
| **RANGE** | Basins of Caspian and Black Seas; Adriatic Sea, Sea of Azov |
| **HABITAT** | Sea, rivers |
| **SIZE** | 16½ ft (5 m) |

Huge heavy fishes, belugas certainly weigh up to 2,645 lb (1,200 kg), sometimes more. They are now relatively uncommon, partly because of river pollution interfering with their migrations, and partly because of pressure of fishing. The taking of eggs for caviare from mature females is damaging to stocks, particularly because these fishes mature late – males at 14 years and females at 18 years. A single ripe female may contain up to 7 million eggs.

Belugas migrate into rivers in winter or spring and spawn on rocky river beds. The newly hatched young immediately start moving towards the sea, feeding on small bottom-living invertebrates. At sea, the adult belugas feed on fish, particularly herringlike species and members of the carp family.

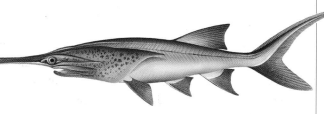

**Paddlefish** *Polyodon spathula* **VU**

| | |
|---|---|
| **RANGE** | USA: Mississippi river system |
| **HABITAT** | Large rivers and lakes |
| **SIZE** | 6½ ft (2 m) |

The paddlefish has a long flattened snout and a large head. It swims with its large mouth agape and lower jaw dropped, filtering any planktonic creatures from the water on to the comblike gill rakers; it closes its mouth periodically to swallow. Its skeleton is mostly cartilage and there are only a few small scales on the skin.

Paddlefish spawn in April and May in gravel or sandy-bottomed areas. As the female deposits the eggs, the male fertilizes them. The eggs then develop an adhesive coating which makes them sink and attach to the first object they touch. The newly hatched larva lacks a long snout, but it starts to develop in 2 to 3 weeks. The only other species *Psephurus gladius*, lives in China, where it is critically endangered.

**Common Sturgeon** *Acipenser sturio* **CR**

**RANGE** European coastline: Norway and Baltic Sea
to Mediterranean and Black Seas

**HABITAT** Shallow sea, rivers

**SIZE** 10 ft (3 m)

Sturgeons are increasingly rare fishes and are in need of
protection in Europe. They have been used by man for centuries
as food fish, and the female's unshed eggs are collected, salted
and eaten as caviare. Overfishing, combined with pollution and
man-made obstructions in spawning rivers, has led to the
sturgeon's decline.

A bottom-dwelling species, the sturgeon feeds on invertebrates,
such as worms, mollusks and crustaceans, and on some fish. In
spring, breeding sturgeons migrate into rivers to spawn. A large
female may contain from 800,000 to 2,400,000 sticky black
eggs which she sheds on to the gravel of the river bed. The eggs
hatch in about a week. The young fishes remain in the river for
up to 3 years, feeding on insect larvae and crustaceans. A closely
related, if not identical species, *A. oxyrhynchus*, occurs along the
Atlantic coast of North America.

# LEPISOSTEIFORMES: GAR ORDER

The single surviving family in this previously abundant and
widely spread order occurs in North and Central America.
It contains 7 species of gars or garpikes, all with some primitive
characteristics. They are mostly freshwater fishes, although
sometimes found in brackish or salt water. All have long bodies
and jaws, and anal and dorsal fins which are placed well back.
Their bodies are covered with hard scales.

**Longnose Gar** *Lepisosteus osseus*

**RANGE** N. America: Quebec and the Great Lakes
to Florida and New Mexico

**HABITAT** Rivers, lakes

**SIZE** 5 ft (1.5 m)

The most abundant and
widely distributed of the gars, the
longnose has particularly long jaws, studded with
sharp teeth. It is a predatory fish, waiting concealed among

vegetation for fishes and crustaceans to come
near; it then thrusts forward and seizes its prey.

In spring gars congregate in shallow water in order to
spawn. The eggs are adhesive and stick to weeds or stones.
The newly hatched young have adhesive suckers under their
mouths and they attach themselves to floating objects
until their yolk sacs have been absorbed and they must start to
hunt for food.

# AMIIFORMES: BOWFIN ORDER

Only 1 family with a single species remains in this order that
once contained at least 7 other families, all now extinct.
The modern bowfin possesses many of the features of its fossil
relatives, which have been found in Europe and Asia as well as
in North America.

**Bowfin** *Amia calva*

**RANGE** N.E. America

**HABITAT** Quiet streams and ponds

**SIZE** 3 ft (91 cm)

A stout-bodied fish with a long dorsal fin and a rounded tail, the
bowfin has the primitive feature of two bony plates under the
throat. Males are usually smaller than females and have an
orange bordered dark spot at the base of the tail.

The bowfin generally lives in densely vegetated sluggish
waters which are poor in oxygen, but by using its swim bladder
as a lung and breathing oxygen from the air, it can withstand
such conditions. Bowfins feed on fish and some crayfish.

In spring, the male bowfin clears a hollow in the riverbed,
making a nest from small roots and gravel. The eggs are then
laid in the nest and the male guards them for 8 to 10 days until
they hatch out. Each larva attaches itself to the
nest by the cement gland on its head and is
nourished by its yolk sac. After
about 9 days, the larvae are able to
swim and feed themselves, but
they are still guarded and herded
by their male parent until they are
about 4 in (10 cm) long.

# OSTEOGLOSSIFORMS, ELOPIFORM FISHES, BONEFISH AND SPINY EELS

## OSTEOGLOSSIFORMES

This group of freshwater fish includes bonytongues, butterflyfishes, mooneyes, knifefishes and elephantfishes. They are distributed in South America, Africa, Southeast Asia, and Australasia, with 2 species of mooneye in North America. They eat fish and insects and have well-developed bony tongues. Of the 220 or so species in the order, about 200 belong to one African family, the Mormyridae (elephant fish), so called because of the trunklike appendage on the snout. Many species of elephantfish have muscles at the base of the neck that are modified into electric organs that set up an electric field in the water. The fish can detect any disturbances in this field, such as an obstruction or prey, and can navigate and hunt even at night. *Gymnarchus niloticus* uses electricity in a similar way.

### Pirarucu *Arapaima gigas* **DD**
**RANGE** Tropical South America
**HABITAT** Rivers, swamps
**SIZE** Up to 13 ft (4 m)

Said to be the largest freshwater fish in the world, this bonytongue may weigh up to 441 lb (200 kg) and reach 16½ ft (5 m) long. It has large body scales, but a scaleless head, and long, low dorsal and anal fins, set back near the tail. The pirarucu has a large swim bladder which can be used as a lung. Pirarucus breed in sandy-bottomed water and make a small hollow in the river bed, where the eggs are laid and guarded.

### Aruana *Osteoglossum bicirrhosum*
**RANGE** Tropical South America
**HABITAT** Freshwater lakes, quiet rivers
**SIZE** 3¼ ft (1 m)

The aruana has prominent chin barbels and an upward-slanting mouth. Its back forms a virtually straight line with the head, and the dorsal and anal fins are long and low.

Thought to incubate its eggs in its mouth, the aruana has a pouchlike structure on its lower jaw.

### Goldeye *Hiodon alosoides*
**RANGE** N. America: S. Canada to Mississippi basin
**HABITAT** Rivers, lakes
**SIZE** 12–16 in (30.5–41 cm)

The goldeye is one of the small family of mooneyes, characterized by their large golden eyes, adapted for night vision, and the many small teeth. This silvery fish is herringlike in appearance, with a long anal fin. Insects and their larvae, as well as small fish, are its main foods. It is generally active at night.

### Elephant-snout Fish *Mormyrus kannume*
**RANGE** Africa: Nile river system
**HABITAT** Rivers, lakes
**SIZE** 31½ in (80 cm)

The elephant-snout fish has an elongated snout. All these mormyrid fishes appear to have good learning abilities and well-developed brains; relative to their body size, the brain is comparable in size to that of humans. This species can produce weak electric impulses, which set up an electric field around the body. Via specialized pores in the head region, it can detect any disturbances caused to this field. It feeds mainly on insect larvae.

### *Gymnarchus niloticus*
**RANGE** Africa: upper Nile, W. Africa
**HABITAT** Swamps, lakes, still water
**SIZE** 35½ in–5 ft (90 cm–1.5 m)

An elongate, slender fish, *Gymnarchus* has no anal, pelvic or tail fins, the dorsal fin is long and low, and the body tapers to a point. The fish swims by undulations of its dorsal fin and can swim backward by reversing the direction of the undulations. Capable of generating an electric field around its body, *Gymnarchus* is sensitive to any disturbance within it, so is able to navigate and hunt for prey fish in turbid waters.

Breeding fishes build a nest of plant fibers, in which about 1,000 eggs are laid. The parents guard the eggs for a few days just before they hatch. The young fishes feed on insects and other small invertebrates.

# ELOPIFORMES

There are 8 species in this order, grouped in 2 families – tenpounders and tarpons. All are marine fishes, but some may enter fresh or brackish water. Related to eels and herrings, they are slender-bodied fishes, with deeply forked tails. The order includes several important game fishes.

**TARPON** *Tarpon atlanticus*

**RANGE** W. Atlantic Ocean: Nova Scotia to Gulf of Mexico and Brazil; E. Atlantic: off W. Africa

**HABITAT** Coastal and oceanic waters

**SIZE** 4–8 ft (1.2–2.4 m)

The tarpon is a huge, silvery fish, its body covered with large scales. It is characterized by its compressed body and flattened sides, protruding lower jaw and pointed dorsal fin, with an elongate last ray. Tarpons feed on many types of fish and on crabs.

One of the most prolific breeders of all fishes, a large female may contain more than 12 million eggs. These are shed out at sea, but the larvae drift to inshore waters and live in estuaries, swamps and river mouths while they grow. Tarpons are not sexually mature until about 6 or 7 years of age.

**Ladyfish** *Elops saurus*

**RANGE** Tropical Atlantic, Indian and W. Pacific Oceans

**HABITAT** Shallow inshore waters, estuaries

**SIZE** 4 ft (1.2 m)

A slender, silvery-blue fish, with fine scales, the ladyfish has dark, fairly small fins and a deeply forked tail. Fishes and crustaceans are its main foods. The ladyfish is a popular game fish because of its habit of leaping and struggling fiercely when it is hooked.

Ladyfishes spawn offshore, but the larvae then drift inshore and live in bays and salt marshes while they develop; they may also enter fresh water.

# ALBULIFORMES

The 29 species in this group divide into 2 groups. Bonefishes (*Albulidae*) are predators that resemble tarpons, and are found in shallow seas in the tropics. The 25 species of spiny eels (*Notacanthidae*) and halosaurs (*Halosauridae*) have an eellike body shape, and are mostly deep-sea fishes that live on the bottom eating small invertebrates extracted from the seabed.

**Bonefish** *Albula vulpes*

**RANGE** Worldwide in tropical seas

**HABITAT** Inshore waters, especially over sand flats

**SIZE** 35½ in (90 cm)

The bonefish has a slender, body, with dark, silvery scales and a deeply forked tail. Its snout projects slightly beyond its mouth. Shoals of bonefishes feed together, foraging over the seabed, with heads down and tails near or above the surface, for bottom-living invertebrates such as clams, crabs and shrimps.

The thin, eellike larvae drift to inshore waters, where they metamorphose to adult form.

**Spiny-eel** *Notacanthus chemnitzii*

**RANGE** N. Atlantic Ocean: temperate areas; possibly temperate areas of all other oceans

**HABITAT** Deep sea

**SIZE** 4 ft (1.2 m)

The spiny-eel has a slender, elongate body and a rounded snout that projects beyond the ventrally placed mouth. On its back are a series of short, sharp spines, and there are similar spines preceding the anal fin. The fish is usually brown to grayish-brown in color. Spiny-eels are thought to eat bottom-living invertebrates, especially sea anemones, and they probably feed in a head-down position on the seabed. Few details are known of the biology of this rarely seen fish.

# EELS, SNIPE-EELS AND GULPER EELS

## ANGUILLIFORMES: EEL ORDER

There are more than 730 species of eel, grouped into about 15 families. They occur worldwide, except in polar regions. Most are marine, but there are some freshwater eels. All have long slender bodies and long dorsal and anal fins; pelvic fins are absent. All species produce eggs which hatch into thin, transparent larvae.

**Chain Moray** *Echidna catenata*

**RANGE** W. Atlantic Ocean: Bermuda to Brazil, including Caribbean

**HABITAT** Coastal waters

**SIZE** 35½ in (90 cm)

Moray eels of this genus are most abundant in the Indian and Pacific Oceans, but some occur in the tropical Atlantic. The chain moray is common in the Caribbean, where it leads a retiring life among rocks or rocks and sand, usually in shallow water. A striking fish, it is distinctively patterned with brownish-black and yellow or white; young fishes have more light than dark areas.

Unlike most morays, which have sharp, pointed teeth, the chain moray has blunt teeth resembling molars. It feeds mainly on crustaceans and, on occasion, can be seen chasing crabs at the water's edge and even out of water.

**Moray** *Muraena helena*

**RANGE** Mediterranean Sea; E. Atlantic Ocean: Azores and Cape Verde Islands, north to Bay of Biscay

**HABITAT** Rocky shores

**SIZE** 4¼ ft (1.3 m)

The most abundant eels, the 100 species of moray are widely distributed in tropical and warm temperate oceans. This moray is typical of the group, with its scaleless, boldly patterned body, which is somewhat laterally compressed. It has no pectoral fins but it does have well-developed dorsal and anal fins, and its large mouth is equipped with strong, sharp teeth.

A voracious predator, the moray habitually lurks in underwater rock crevices with only its head showing, watching for prey – largely fish, squid and cuttlefish. When it is disturbed, it is a vicious fish and can deliver savage bites.

Morays breed between July and September, and their eggs float at the surface of the sea until they hatch.

**European Eel** *Anguilla anguilla*

**RANGE** N. Atlantic Ocean: coasts from Iceland to N. Africa; Mediterranean and Black Seas; fresh water in Europe and N. Africa

**HABITAT** Coastal waters, estuaries; fresh water: rivers, streams

**SIZE** 19¾ in–3¼ ft (50 cm–1 m)

The European eel is easily identified in fresh water, where it is the only eellike fish, but elsewhere it is characterized by its rounded pectoral fins, the dorsal fin that starts well back from the head, and its small teeth. Its body is covered with tiny scales.

As they approach sexual maturity, European eels migrate from their fresh water homes to the mid-Atlantic, where they spawn and then die.

The eggs hatch, and the larvae drift in surface waters for some 3 years, gradually being brought back to coastal waters by ocean currents. Here they metamorphose into elvers and then enter estuaries and rivers, where they grow and mature, feeding on insects, crustaceans and fish. During the freshwater stage, the eels are yellowish-brown in color, but as they mature, they become darker, until they are almost black, with silvery bellies.

The European eel is a valuable traditional food fish and is caught by man in large quantities.

The American eel, *A. rostrata*, found along the Atlantic coasts of North America, closely resembles the European species. It spawns in the west-central Atlantic and the larvae take only 1 year to drift back to coastal waters.

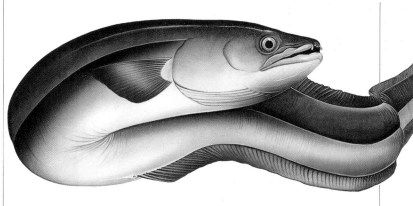

## Conger Eel *Conger conger*

**RANGE** N. Atlantic Ocean: coasts from Iceland to
N. Africa; Mediterranean Sea

**HABITAT** Shallow waters, often close to rocks

**SIZE** 9 ft (2.7 m)

This large fish is fairly common on rocky shores, the conger eel
has a large scale-less cylindrical body, with prominent pectoral
fins and a long-based dorsal fin, which originates well forward
near to the eel's head. The conger-eel's upper jaw overlaps the
lower one, giving its face a brutish appearance.

The conger feeds on fish and crustaceans, particularly
crabs, and octopus.

Though they are usually found hiding in rock crevices in
shallow water, adult congers migrate into deeper water in order
to mate and spawn. The eggs hatch out into transparent larvae,
which then drift in the ocean's surface waters for between 1 and
2 years before they develop into small eels.

## SACCOPHARYNGIFORMES

This order of deep sea eels includes among its 26 species the
bobtail snipe eels, swallowers, gulpers, and pelican eels.
Many species in the order have a large mouth and pharynx,
probably an adaptation to catching prey larger than themselves.

It is thought that saccopharyngiformes may attract prey in
the darkness of the deep ocean by using a light-producing organ
located on the tip of the tail to lure them within striking range.

## Snipe Eel *Nemichthys scolopaceus*

**RANGE** Atlantic, Pacific and Indian Oceans:
temperate and tropical areas

**HABITAT** Open ocean to depths of
3,300 ft (1,000 m)

**SIZE** 3¼–4 ft (1–1.2 m)

Snipe eels are deep-sea fishes with immensely
long, slender bodies and dorsal and anal fins
that run most of the length of the body.
The narrow, elongate jaws are beaklike and
equipped with pointed, backward-facing
teeth, which the eel uses to trap prey,
such as crustaceans and fish,
extremely efficiently.

Even though the snipe eel
is a fairly common species,
very little is known of
their biology.

## Gulper Eel *Eurypharynx pelecanoides*

**RANGE** All oceans (particularly Atlantic):
warm temperate and tropical areas

**HABITAT** Deep sea at 4,500 ft (1,400 m) or more

**SIZE** 24 in (61 cm)

The gulper eel has a highly unusual appearance, with its long,
delicate body and its relatively huge, gaping jaws. Clearly too
thin and fragile to be a very powerful swimmer, the gulper eels
nevertheless does manage to feed on quite large fish. It is
thought that the gulper may swim with its large jaws held wide
open, thus engulfing any fish or crustaceans that swim
unwittingly into its gaping mouth.

# HERRINGS

## CLUPEIFORMES: HERRING ORDER

The herring order contains 5 families – one, the denticle herring has only a single species, while another, the wolf herrings, contains 2 species. The two major families are the anchovies, and the largest family of about 180 species that includes all the true herrings, shads, sardines and menhadens. Over 350 species are known. It is one of the most important groups of food fish – the herring, sardine and anchovy alone account for a large proportion of the total world fish tonnage. Indeed some populations, such as that of the North Sea herring, provide the clearest examples of commercial fish stocks that have been overfished to the point of declining catches.

Most clupeoid fishes are marine and live in schools near the surface of the open sea or in inshore waters. Local populations of some species return to traditional spawning grounds, and the partial genetic isolation thus produced leads to recognizable races. Typically, clupeoids eat plankton which they filter from the water through long gill rakers. Their bodies are considerably flattened laterally, and covered with large, reflective, silvery scales. One set of specialized scales found in most clupeoids is the group of enlarged scales (scutes) that form a jagged series of backward-pointing teeth along the middle line of the belly.

### Twaite Shad *Alosa fallax* **DD**

**RANGE** Europe, Icelandic coasts, Baltic to Mediterranean Seas

**HABITAT** Open sea, coastal waters, estuaries

**SIZE** 22 in (55 cm)

The twaite shad is a heavy-bodied fish with large fragile scales. It is similar to the allis shad, *A. alosa,* but can be easily distinguished by the number of gill rakers on the first gill arch – 40 to 60 in the twaite, and 80 to 130 in the allis. Crustaceans and small fish are its main diet. To spawn, the fishes migrate from coastal waters to the tidal reaches of rivers, but river pollution and man-made obstructions have affected these journeys badly in some areas. The shads spawn at night, spreading their eggs over the gravel of the river bed. The young fishes move slowly downriver to the sea.

### Alewife *Alosa pseudoharengus*

**RANGE** N. American Atlantic coast, Great Lakes

**HABITAT** Coastal waters, rivers

**SIZE** 15 in (38 cm)

Although primarily a marine fish, the alewife, like all shads, enters rivers to spawn, so is often found in fresh water. The fishes start their journey in February and most have returned to the sea by May.

There are some landlocked, freshwater populations which spend their whole lives in lakes, including the Great Lakes. The freshwater alewife is only about half the size of the marine form. Alewife feed mainly on plankton and also take small fish.

### Sardine/Pilchard *Sardina pilchardus*

**RANGE** European coasts; Mediterranean and Black Seas

**HABITAT** Open sea, coastal waters

**SIZE** 10 in (25 cm)

The sardine is a herringlike fish but has a more rounded body and larger scales. Its gill covers are marked with distinct radiating ridges. Shoals of sardines move in surface waters and make seasonal migrations northward in summer, south in winter. They spawn in spring and summer and after spawning generally move farther inshore.

Young sardines feed mainly on plant plankton, adults on larger types of animal plankton.

Sardines are extremely valuable food fish. Species of sardine in the closely related genus *Sardinops* are found off the coasts of Chile and Peru, South Africa, Japan, Australia and along the Pacific coast of the USA.

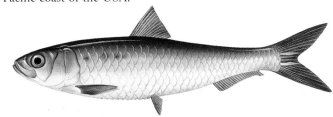

## Atlantic Herring *Clupea harengus*

**RANGE** N. Atlantic Ocean

**HABITAT** Open sea, coastal waters

**SIZE** 16 in (41 cm)

The Atlantic herring can be divided into a number of races, each with its own characteristics and breeding season. Some races spawn in shallow inshore bays, others offshore on ocean banks and the eggs form a layer over the seabed. The larvae swim in surface waters in large schools and are generally found inshore during the first year of life. Adults, too, swim in surface waters.

Herrings select different items of planktonic food as they grow and also eat other small crustaceans and small fish. The herrings are preyed on by birds, other fish, dolphins and seals and are an important link in many marine food chains. Atlantic herring has long been an important food fish, and it is one of the top commercial species. The Pacific herring, *C. pallasi*, is closely related to the Atlantic species and has similar habits.

## Wolf Herring *Chirocentrus dorab*

**RANGE** Indo-Pacific Oceans: Red Sea to Australia

**HABITAT** Surface waters, shallow sea

**SIZE** 12 ft (3.7 m)

A herringlike fish of dramatic size, the wolf herring has a long cylindrical body and fanglike teeth. Unlike other members of the order, it does not filter-feed but hunts for its food. Its flesh is of little commercial value.

## Atlantic Menhaden *Brevoortia tyrannus*

**RANGE** N. American Atlantic coast

**HABITAT** Surface waters

**SIZE** 18 in (46 cm)

Menhaden are abundant fishes and travel in huge schools of hundreds of thousands, moving north in spring and summer, and south to warmer waters in winter. Also known as the mossbunker, the adult has a large head and straight-edged body scales with comblike teeth at their free edge. There is always a definite black spot behind the menhaden's head and a number of smaller spots on its upper sides.

The menhaden does not select particular items of plankton, but eats whatever planktonic creatures it filters from the water.

It has extremely oily flesh and is used to produce fishmeal, oil and fertilizer rather than as food for humans. Many other creatures, such as birds, whales, porpoises, sharks, cod and bluefishes eat the menhaden and it is often used as a baitfish.

## European Anchovy *Engraulis encrasicolus*

**RANGE** European seas

**HABITAT** Surface waters

**SIZE** 8 in (20 cm)

The 110 species of anchovy are found all around the world in temperate to tropical seas. The shape of the anchovy head is distinctive and characteristic, with the snout overhanging the huge mouth. The body is rounded. Anchovies are important food items for many creatures including tuna, and many species are valuable commercial fish, which are caught in large quantities, especially in the seas off the coast of Peru.

The European anchovy is a slender fish with large, fragile scales. It moves in schools of many thousands of individuals and feeds on plankton, particularly small crustaceans, and the larvae of fish and invertebrates. Found in offshore waters in winter, anchovies move farther inshore in summer to spawn. Eggs and larvae float in surface waters.

The northern anchovy, *E. mordax*, is a common Pacific form, similar to the European species in appearance.

# GONORYNCHIFORM FISHES AND CYPRINIFORM FISHES

## ORDER GONORYNCHIFORMES

This order contains only about 35 species of mostly freshwater fish, which occur in tropical Africa and the Indian and Pacific oceans.

The milkfish, the single species in the family Chanidae, is the largest and most important member of the order, but it also includes the family Kneriidae, with 27 species of small, loachlike fish. These fishes live in tropical areas of Africa in swift-flowing water and feed on plant matter. Male kneriids develop horny protuberances on their gill covers, which they rub over the females to stimulate them sexually.

**Milkfish** *Chanos chanos*

**RANGE** Indian and tropical Pacific Oceans

**HABITAT** Open sea, coasts, estuaries; occasionally fresh water

**SIZE** 6 ft (1.8 m)

A large, silvery fish, with a pointed tail and a prominent dorsal fin, the milkfish is a fast-swimming species. It is toothless and feeds on planktonic plant material.

Normally a fish of the open sea, it enters coastal waters to breed and may venture into fresh water. One female may shed as many as 6 million eggs in a season.

Milkfishes are important food fish in Southeast Asia and are the centre of a considerable industry in some areas of Indonesia and the Philippines, where newly hatched young are caught and reared in coastal ponds.

## ORDER CYPRINIFORMES

An enormously successful group of freshwater fish, this order contains nearly 2,700 species and includes the carps, minnows, barbs, algae eaters, suckers, and loaches. Cypriniform fish dominate the streams, rivers, and lakes of Eurasia and North America, and are also found in Africa. They have scaled bodies and scaleless heads, a single dorsal fin, and their swim bladders are connected to the inner ear, which gives them acute hearing abilities. Of the 5 families in the group, the carp family (Cyprinidae) is the largest with over 2,000 species.

**Dace** *Leuciscus leuciscus*

**RANGE** N. Europe and Asia: Ireland to Siberia, north to Sweden, south to S. France

**HABITAT** Rivers, streams

**SIZE** 6–11¾ in (15–30 cm)

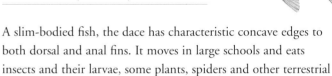

A slim-bodied fish, the dace has characteristic concave edges to both dorsal and anal fins. It moves in large schools and eats insects and their larvae, some plants, spiders and other terrestrial invertebrates which fall into the water.

Although normally a river fish, some dace occur in lakes. Dace spawn in spring, often in gravel-bottomed shallow streams, and shoals gather in the breeding areas a few days before spawning. The eggs lodge among the gravel where they remain until they hatch about 25 days later.

**Carp** *Cyprinus carpio*

**RANGE** Originally S. Europe and Black Sea area; introduced in N. Europe, N. and South America, Australia, New Zealand, parts of Asia and Africa

**HABITAT** Lowland lakes, and rivers

**SIZE** 20 in–3¼ ft (51 cm–1 m)

Now an extremely widely distributed fish, the carp belongs to the large, freshwater family, Cyprinidae. Carp are robust, fairly deep-bodied fishes; some are fully scaled, but there are other varieties, such as leather carp, which are scaleless, and mirror carp (illustrated here), which have some exceptionally large scales on the sides and at the base of the dorsal fin.

Inhabitants of slow-moving waters with much vegetation, carp are able to tolerate low oxygen levels, which would be fatal for many other fish species.

They feed mostly on crustaceans, insect larvae, mollusks and some vegetation. Breeding occurs in spring and summer. The eggs are laid in shallow water, where they adhere to aquatic plants until they hatch.

### Goldfish *Carassius auratus*

**RANGE** Native from E. Europe across to China; introduced in temperate areas worldwide

**HABITAT** Well-vegetated pools, lakes

**SIZE** Up to 12 in (30.5 cm)

An extremely familiar species, the goldfish is bred in a variety of forms as an ornamental fish. It is typical of the family Cyprinidae, to which it belongs, in its body shape and its teeth on the pharyngeal bones, but it has strong spines at the front of both dorsal and anal fins.

Goldfishes spawn in summer over aquatic vegetation. The eggs adhere to the plants and hatch in about a week.

### Barbel *Barbus barbus*

**RANGE** Europe: Britain, south to Alps and Pyrenees, east to Hungary

**HABITAT** Lowland rivers, streams

**SIZE** 19¾–35¾ in (50–91 cm)

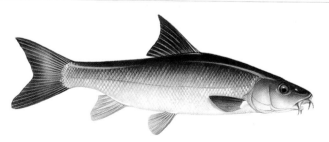

A slender, long-bodied fish, the barbel has a characteristic high dorsal fin and two pairs of sensory barbels around its fleshy lips. It is a bottom-living fish, which is most active at night and at dusk. It feeds on insect larvae, mollusks and crustaceans. It is a member of the family Cyprinidae.

Barbels breed in late spring, often migrating upstream before spawning. They shed their eggs in shallow, gravel-bottomed water, where they lodge among the stones until they hatch from 10 to 15 days later.

### Mahseer *Barbus tor*

**RANGE** N. India

**HABITAT** Varied, sluggish rivers, fast hill streams

**SIZE** 4 ft (1.2 m)

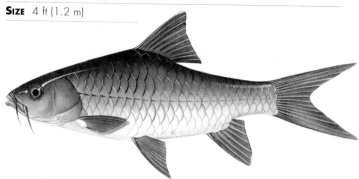

A heavily built fish, with large body scales, the mahseer is a member of the family Cyprinidae and is a common species in its range. It feeds on invertebrates, particularly mollusks, as well as on algae and other aquatic plants.

### Tiger Barb *Barbus tetrazona*

**RANGE** Sumatra, Borneo

**HABITAT** Rivers, streams

**SIZE** 2¾ in (7 cm)

This tiny fish, with four black bands ringing its body, is a distinctive member of the family Cyprinidae. Although it is rather aggressive, the tiger barb is a popular aquarium species.

### Tench *Tinca tinca*

**RANGE** Europe: Britain, S. Sweden and Denmark to Mediterranean, east to C. Asia; introduced in New Zealand, Australia, North America

**HABITAT** Lakes, ponds; sometimes in slow, lowland rivers

**SIZE** Up to 27½ in (70 cm)

The tench, a member of the family Cyprinidae, is identified by its thickset body, rounded fins and extremely small scales; these scales are plentifully covered with mucus. In males, the second ray in the pelvic fin is swollen and the fin may be longer than that of a female, but otherwise the sexes look alike. Tench feed mostly on the bottom on insect larvae, mollusks and crustaceans and are able to thrive in poorly oxygenated water.

Tench breed in shallow water in spring and summer. Eggs are often shed onto aquatic vegetation, and hatch in 6 to 8 days.

# CYPRINIFORM FISHES

**Bream** *Abramis brama*

**RANGE** N. Europe: Britain, France, E. to C. Russia

**HABITAT** Slow rivers, lakes, ponds

**SIZE** 16–24 in (40.5–62 cm)

The bream has a deep body, flattened at the sides, and a curving, high back. Its anal fin has a distinctly concave edge. The bream's head is rather small for its size and its mouth protrudes into a tubelike structure with which it gathers insect larvae, mollusks and worms from the river bottom. It lives in shoals and usually feeds at night.

Bream breed in late spring or in summer, usually in shallow water where there is plenty of vegetation. The eggs adhere to submerged plants and take up to 12 days to hatch, depending on the temperature.

**Roach** *Rutilus rutilus*

**RANGE** Europe, W. Asia: England to C. Russia; N. Sweden to Black and Caspian Sea areas

**HABITAT** Lowland rivers, lakes

**SIZE** 13¾–18 in (35–46 cm)

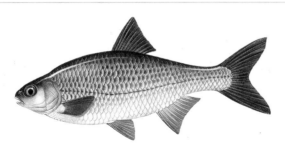

An abundant, adaptable fish, the roach can survive in poorly oxygenated and even slightly polluted water and has an extremely wide distribution; it can also tolerate brackish water. Its abundance and presence in otherwise sparsely populated

waters make it an important prey for fish-eating birds and mammals, as well as for other fishes.

An attractively colored fish, the roach has a fairly deep body and small head. Its diet is varied, insects, larvae, crustaceans and other small invertebrates, as well as plants, being consumed. It breeds in well-vegetated shallow water, where its eggs stick to plants while they develop. The eggs hatch in under 2 weeks but, from then on, growth rates of the young vary enormously, according to conditions.

**Gudgeon** *Gobio gobio*

**RANGE** Europe: Britain to S. Sweden, south to France, east to Russia

**HABITAT** Rivers, streams, lakes, ponds, marshes

**SIZE** 4–7¾ in (10–20 cm)

A round-bodied fish, the gudgeon has a large head for its size and a sensory barbel at each side of its thick-lipped mouth. Found in a wide variety of habitats, it is always a bottom-dweller and feeds on insect larvae, mollusks and crustaceans.

Gudgeons spawn at night in early summer. The sticky eggs adhere to plants or rocks and take up to 4 weeks to hatch. Young gudgeons feed largely on planktonic crustaceans.

**Bitterling** *Rhodeus sericeus*

**RANGE** N. and E. Europe: N. France, Germany, east to Black and Caspian Sea basins; introduced in N. America

**HABITAT** Lakes, ponds, slow rivers

**SIZE** 2¼–3½ in (6–9 cm)

The bitterling is a small, rather deep-bodied fish. It lives in densely vegetated areas and can tolerate poorly oxygenated water. It feeds on plants and small invertebrate animals.

The breeding habits of the bitterling are most unusual. The female develops a long egg-depositing tube that extends from her genital opening. Using this tube, she lays her eggs inside the gill chamber of a freshwater mussel. The male, who develops brilliant, iridescent coloration in the breeding season, sheds his sperm by the mussel's gills so that it is inhaled by the mussel and fertilizes the eggs. Safe from predators, the eggs develop inside the mussel for 2 or 3 weeks, and the young leave it about 2 days after hatching. The mussel is unharmed by this invasion.

### Minnow *Phoxinus phoxinus*

**RANGE** Europe, N. Asia: British Isles,
east to Siberia, south to the Pyrenees,
north to Sweden

**HABITAT** Streams, rivers, lakes

**SIZE** 3½ in (9 cm); rarely 4¾ in (12 cm)

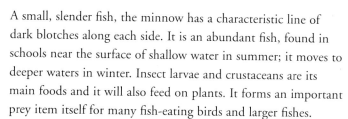

A small, slender fish, the minnow has a characteristic line of dark blotches along each side. It is an abundant fish, found in schools near the surface of shallow water in summer; it moves to deeper waters in winter. Insect larvae and crustaceans are its main foods and it will also feed on plants. It forms an important prey item itself for many fish-eating birds and larger fishes.

Breeding takes place in late spring, when courting males develop brilliant red bellies. Minnows spawn in gravel-bottomed water and the eggs lodge among the stones. They hatch within 5 to 10 days.

### Grass Carp *Ctenopharyngodon idella*

**RANGE** China; introduced in S.E. Asia, Russia, parts of Europe and USA

**HABITAT** Rivers

**SIZE** 3¼–4 ft (1–1.25 m)

A native of China, the grass carp has been introduced into many other areas for two reasons. In China and Southeast Asia it is a valuable commercial species, and in Europe and Russia, this plant-eating fish is used to control vegetation in canals and reservoirs. Although, as an adult, the grass carp is entirely herbivorous, young fishes feed on insect larvae and crustaceans once their egg sacs have been absorbed.

Grass carp spawn in rivers in summer. The eggs float at the surface and must have warm water to grow well.

### Stoneroller *Campostoma anomalum*

**RANGE** E. USA, west to Minnesota and Texas

**HABITAT** Clear creeks, streams, rivers

**SIZE** 4–7 in (10–18 cm)

Typically, the stoneroller lives in small streams in riffle areas (shallow areas of water where the flow is broken by the stones and gravel on the stream bed). It feeds at the bottom on tiny plants, insect larvae and mollusks.

In spring, the dorsal and anal fins of breeding males turn bright orange and black, and tubercles develop on the upper half of the body. The male makes a shallow nest in the gravel of the stream bed in which the female lays her eggs.

### Pearl Dace *Semotilus margarita*

**RANGE** Canada; N. USA, south to Virginia, Wisconsin, Montana

**HABITAT** Streams, lakes

**SIZE** 6 in (15 cm)

The pearl dace is a small fish which, with its blunt, rounded snout, resembles the European minnow. It feeds on insects, planktonic invertebrates and even other tiny fish.

During the breeding season, males establish territories on the stream bed which they defend against other males. Females are attracted to the territories, where spawning takes place.

### Northern Squawfish *Ptychocheilus oregonensis*

**RANGE** N. America: Columbia river system, coastal streams of Oregon and Washington

**HABITAT** Lakes, slow streams and rivers

**SIZE** 35½ in–4 ft (90 cm–1.2 m)

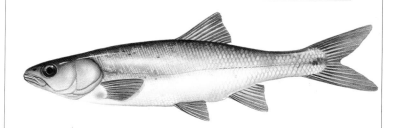

Squawfishes are the largest North American minnows. A long, slender fish, the northern squawfish lives close to the bottom of streams, lakes and rivers. It is a voracious predator, feeding largely on fish, including young trout and salmon.

# CYPRINIFORM FISHES CONTINUED

**Common Shiner** *Notropis cornutus*

**RANGE** S. Canada; N. USA, south to Colorado and Virginia

**HABITAT** Clear streams

**SIZE** 2¼–4 in (6–10 cm)

Shiners are the largest group of American minnows. The common shiner is a round-bodied fish, usually found in fast-flowing water, but sometimes in lakes with tributary streams. It eats aquatic and terrestrial insects and some algae.

Common shiners spawn in spring or early summer in streams. Schools of breeding adults congregate in the breeding areas; male fishes develop bright blue coloration with pinkish fins at this time. Females shed their eggs into shallow nests, excavated in the gravel of the stream bed, where they are fertilized by the males.

**Fallfish** *Semotilus corporalis*

**RANGE** S.E. Canada; USA: Atlantic coast, south to Virginia

**HABITAT** Clear streams, lakes

**SIZE** 4–12 in (10–30.5 cm)

The fallfish is similar in appearance to another American minnow, the creek chub, *S. atromaculatus*, but can be distinguished by the lack of a dark spot on the base of the dorsal fin. Aquatic insects are the main diet of the fallfish, but some small invertebrates are also eaten. Young fallfishes move in schools in shallow waters, while adults inhabit deeper waters.

In spring, breeding males develop some pinkish coloration on their sides and small wartlike projections on the head. In a quiet shallow area, each pair makes a nest of stones which they carry in their mouths. Once the eggs are laid, more stones are added to the nest by the male. The nest protects the eggs while they develop and hatch.

**Harlequin Fish** *Rasbora heteromorpha*

**RANGE** Thailand, Malaysia, E. Sumatra

**HABITAT** Streams, lakes

**SIZE** 1¾ in (4.5 cm)

A tiny but attractive fish, the harlequin fish is a popular aquarium species. In its natural habitat, it moves in shoals and feeds on insect larvae.

Having been courted by her mate, the breeding female searches out a broadleaved water plant and lays her sticky-surfaced eggs on the underside of a leaf where they remain until they hatch.

**White Sucker** *Catostomus commersoni*

**RANGE** Canada: Labrador to Nova Scotia; N. USA, south to Georgia and New Mexico, west to Montana

**HABITAT** Large streams, lakes

**SIZE** 12–20½ in (30.5–52 cm)

The most common of the suckers, the white sucker is typical of its family, with its mouth positioned behind the point of the snout and its thick, suckerlike lips. Found in a variety of conditions, the white sucker tolerates some pollution and poorly oxygenated waters. It is a bottom-living fish and feeds on insect larvae, crustaceans and mollusks, as well as plant material.

Breeding takes place in spring. White suckers spawn at night, depositing their eggs in rocky or gravel-bottomed streams. The eggs, which are slightly sticky, sink to the bottom and are lightly covered by gravel which is stirred up by the vigorous spawning movements.

**Northern Redhorse** *Moxostoma macrolepidotum*

**RANGE** E. and C. Canada; USA: Great Lakes to New York, south to Arkansas and Kansas

**HABITAT** Rivers, streams, lakes

**SIZE** Up to 24 in (61 cm)

The northern redhorse is one of 18 or more in this genus of sucker. All are silvery to reddish-brown fishes, with round

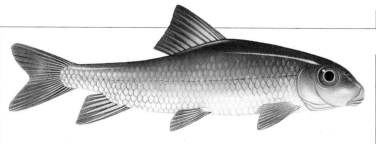

bodies, large heads and suckerlike mouths. They feed mainly on insect larvae and mollusks. Northern redhorses have a preference for clear, swift-flowing water and cannot tolerate muddy or polluted rivers – a characteristic which has led to a decline in their population.

In April or May, northern redhorses migrate up small streams or into shallow areas of lakes to spawn. Each breeding female lays from 10,000 to 50,000 eggs, which she leaves at the spawning site to develop. The eggs hatch in about 2 weeks. Young redhorses feed on tiny planktonic creatures until they are big enough to take the adult diet.

## Bigmouth Buffalo *Ictiobus cyprinellus*

**RANGE** S. Canada; USA: North Dakota, east to Pennsylvania, south to Gulf Coast

**HABITAT** Large rivers, lakes

**SIZE** 3¼ ft (1 m)

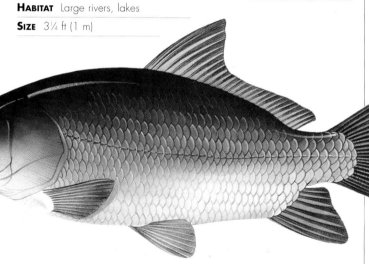

The powerful, deep-bodied bigmouth buffalo is the largest of the American suckers and, in suitable conditions, may become extremely abundant at the expense of other fishes. Distinguishing characteristics are its long-based dorsal fin and its large, slanting mouth, the upper lip of which is almost level with the eyes. It feeds on crustaceans and plant material as well as on small quantities of insect larvae.

Bigmouth buffalo spawn in April or May. Groups of breeding adults gather in shallow well-vegetated water where females shed as many as 500,000 eggs randomly into the water. The eggs adhere to plants or other debris and take up to 2 weeks to hatch. The young fishes remain in the shallow breeding areas for some months, feeding on plankton. They are mature at about 3 years old.

## Stone Loach *Noemacheilus barbatulus*

**RANGE** England, south to S. France, across Europe and N. Asia to Siberia and Korea

**HABITAT** Small fast-flowing rivers, lakes

**SIZE** 4–6 in (10–15 cm)

The sluggish stone loach is a bottom-living fish. It spends the day hidden among stones, where it is well camouflaged by its irregular markings and is active at night or in dull daylight. It eats bottom-living creatures such as crustaceans, insect larvae and worms.

In April or May, the stone loach breeds, shedding its sticky-surfaced eggs over stones or plants. The eggs usually hatch in just over 2 weeks.

## Coolie Loach *Acanthopthalmus kuhlii*

**RANGE** Thailand, Singapore, Sumatra, Java

**HABITAT** Streams

**SIZE** 3¼ in (8 cm)

A tiny, elongate fish, the coolie loach has striking dark markings  which vary in number. Its eyes are covered with transparent skin. It lives near the bottom, often lurking in dense vegetation, and is a shy, rarely seen fish in the wild. It is a popular aquarium species.

## Spined Loach *Cobitis taenia*

**RANGE** E. England across Europe (including Mediterranean countries and S. Sweden) and C. Asia to China and Japan

**HABITAT** Lakes, canals, slow rivers

**SIZE** 4½ in (11.5 cm)

The spined loach has a long, laterally compressed body and a small head, with a few sensory barbels around the mouth. Beneath each eye is a tiny spine which is usually buried in the skin. A slow-moving fish, the spined loach spends much of its time buried in mud or weed and feeds on small bottom-living crustaceans. It is thought to be most active at night or at dusk.

The breeding season begins in April. The eggs are shed over aquatic plants and algae but few details of the spawning behavior are known.

# CYPRINIFORM FISHES CONTINUED

## ORDER CHARACIFORMES

The 1,400 or so species of characins and their relatives are found in freshwater habitats in Central and South America, and Africa. Most are predators with large eyes and numerous teeth, and many have an adipose fin, a small fleshy fin between the dorsal fin and the tail. The 10 families in the order show considerable diversity. The largest family (Characidae) includes the characins and tetras, as well as the South American piranhas. Although several piranhas are notorious for their carnivorous habits and have formidable teeth, their close relatives eat fruit and seeds fallen from the trees into the streams.

### Jaraqui *Semaprochilodus insignis*

| **RANGE** | N. South America: Amazon basin |
| **HABITAT** | Rivers, tributaries |
| **SIZE** | Up to 14 in (35.5 cm) |

The jaraqui belongs to the South American family Corimatidae. The fishes in this family are similar to the related characins but lack their complex dentition. The jaraqui feeds on the bottom on detritus and other fine material.

Around the time of the annual floods, the adults descend from tributaries to spawn in the muddy waters of the main river, where the poorer visibility may give the eggs and young a better chance of escaping predatory fishes. They then move back into the tributary, and the flooded forest, to feed. Later in the year the adults migrate again, this time moving down to the main river and upstream to yet another tributary. The vacated tributary is restocked by the arrival of young fishes, which are swept downstream by strong currents at spawning time.

### Curimbata *Prochilodus platensis*

| **RANGE** | Central South America |
| **HABITAT** | Rivers |
| **SIZE** | 20 in (51 cm) |

A member of the family Curimatidae, the curimbata is an abundant fish, which lives in huge schools. It feeds on bottom detritus and

fine plant matter and has a small mouth with fine teeth well suited to this diet.

Curimbatas make regular migrations upstream to spawn. When the males reach the spawning areas, they emit sounds, which may attract the females, though this is not confirmed. The eggs drift downstream, where young fishes find suitable shallow, nursery areas, in which they remain while they grow.

### Red Piranha
*Serrasalmus nattereri*

| **RANGE** | N. South America: Amazon basin |
| **HABITAT** | Rivers |
| **SIZE** | Up to 12 in (30.5 cm) |

The red piranha is not a large fish but swims in such large shoals that, together, the fishes form a formidable hunting group. They are armed with strong jaws and razor-sharp triangular teeth, which can chop pieces of flesh from a victim with alarming efficiency. Despite their very bloodthirsty reputation, carnivorous piranhas feed largely on fish and on seeds and fruit but will attack larger, usually wounded animals, which they quickly devour by their combined efforts.

### Giant Tigerfish *Hydrocynus goliath*

| **RANGE** | Africa: Congo basin, Lake Tanganyika |
| **HABITAT** | Streams, rivers, lakes |
| **SIZE** | 5–6 ft (1.5–1.8 m) |

One of the largest characins, the giant tigerfish has an elongate, fully scaled body and a well-developed, forked tail fin. It has a small number of large, sharp teeth, with half-grown replacement teeth behind them, and is a voracious predator, taking a wide variety of smaller fish.

## Pacu *Colossoma nigripinnis*

**RANGE** N.E. South America

**HABITAT** Rivers

**SIZE** 27½ in (70 cm)

The pacu is a plant-eater but is similar in appearance to the carnivorous piranhas. It has become adapted to feeding on the many fruits and seeds that fall into the forest bordered water and is equipped with strong jaws and teeth for crushing them.

## Flame Tetra *Hyphessobrycon Flammeus*

**RANGE** South America:
Rio de Janeiro area of Brazil

**HABITAT** Swampy areas

**SIZE** 1¾ in (4.5 cm)

The flame tetra has brilliant red fins and some red coloration on the body. Males and females differ slightly. The male has a black edge to the anal fin that is reduced or absent on the female's fin.

## Mexican Tetra *Astyanax mexicanus*

**RANGE** USA: Texas, New Mexico; Mexico,
Central America, south to Panama

**HABITAT** Coastal streams

**SIZE** 3–4 in (8–10 cm)

The only characin to occur in the USA, the Mexican tetra is plain compared to the brilliantly colored tetras from South America. It is sometimes considered to be a subspecies of *A. fasciatus*, some races of which are eyeless and found in caves.

## Neon Tetra *Pracheirodon innesi*

**RANGE** N. South America: upper Amazon river system

**HABITAT** Rivers, streams

**SIZE** 1¾ in (4 cm)

The striking neon tetra has a bright blue or bluish-green stripe along its body and a band of red toward the tail. Like all tetras, it is a member of the characin family.

## Sardinha *Triportheus elongatus*

**RANGE** N. South America: Amazon basin

**HABITAT** Rivers, streams, flooded forest

**SIZE** 7¾–11 in (20–28 cm)

Popularly known as sardinhas because of their resemblance to marine sardines, the fishes of this genus have long, compressed bodies and extended pectoral fins. This species is an adaptable surface-dwelling fish, able to eat fruit and seeds and invertebrate animals. Its small mouth, equipped with many fine teeth, fits it well for taking invertebrates from the surface, but means that it is unable to crush hard nuts and seeds and must take softer items. When fruit is scarce, it also eats leaves and flowers. When the forest is flooded and the fish has access to plenty of vegetation sardinhas lay down body fat, which sustains them in times of shorter supplies.

## *Boulengerella lucius*

**RANGE** N. South America: Amazon basin

**HABITAT** Rivers

**SIZE** 24 in (61 cm)

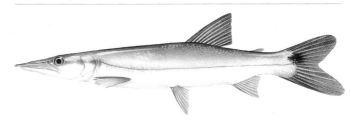

Related to the characins, *Boulengerella* is a member of the family Ctenoluciidae, a small group of South American freshwater fishes. It is a predatory fish, with a pointed snout, long jaws, the upper of which has an extended tip, and many sharp teeth.

## Hatchetfish *Gasteropelecus sternicla*

**RANGE** N. South America

**HABITAT** Rivers

**SIZE** 2½ in (6.5 cm)

The highly distinctive hatchetfish is a small fish, with an almost straight back but a dramatically curved belly. This body shape makes room for greatly enlarged shoulder muscles, which power the long pectoral fins and enable the fish to fly above the water surface for a short distance, beating its "wings" noisily. These hatchetfishes of the South American family Gasteropelecidae are the only fishes actually to use propulsive force while in the air.

Hatchetfishes feed at the surface of the water. They mainly feed on insects and crustaceans.

# SILURIFORM FISHES

## ORDER SILURIFORMES

The bottom-living catfishes, with clusters of sensory barbels around their mouths, have been remarkably successful in their "mud-grubbing" way of life. They have spread into many freshwater habitats throughout the world, being absent only from western Europe, Arctic regions of the northern hemisphere, the tip of South America, New Zealand and parts of Australia. Over 2,400 species have been described, ranging from tiny forms, only a few centimeters in length, to some giant forms, which can reach 5 ft (1.5 m) or more and weigh as much as 100 lb (45 kg).

Catfishes do not have ordinary scales, but some have bony plates, which cover them like jointed armor. Food is sought by a combination of touch and taste, by probing the bottom sediment until the sensory barbels locate small prey items.

### Tadpole Madtom *Noturus gyrinus*
**RANGE** S. Canada, USA: North and South Dakota to Texas, New York to Florida
**HABITAT** Lakes, quiet streams, ponds, marshes
**SIZE** 4 in (10 cm)

Madtoms are small catfishes which have poison glands at the base of the pectoral spines. The tadpole madtom, like other species, has a characteristic, long fleshy fin on its back that virtually merges with the upper lobe of the tail. A species which favors muddy-bottomed, well-vegetated water, the tadpole madtom often hunts under stones or logs. It feeds on small fish, crustaceans and insect larvae. In early summer, it spawns, laying its eggs in a shallow hollow, which it excavates in the stream bed.

### *Bagrus docmac*
**RANGE** W. and C. Africa
**HABITAT** Slow-running rivers, backwaters, lakes
**SIZE** 3¼ ft (1 m)

This species is one of a family of African and Asian freshwater catfishes, most of which are slender bodied, with well-developed barbels and strong dorsal and pectoral spines. *Bagrus docmac* has a long, fleshy fin on its back, a flattened head and a narrow extension of the upper lobe of its tail.

A bottom-living predator, the adult feeds mainly on other fish, but the young eats insect larvae and crustaceans. It is a valuable commercial species in its range.

### Blue Catfish *Ictalurus furcatus*
**RANGE** USA: Minnesota and Ohio, south through Mississippi river system and Gulf states; Mexico
**HABITAT** Rivers, lakes
**SIZE** 5 ft (1.5 m)

One of the largest catfishes in North America, the blue catfish can grow to over 100 lb (45 kg) in weight and is an important commercial species. It is a slender-bodied fish, generally a dull silvery-blue in color with a whitish belly, and has a deeply forked tail, long anal fin and small, fleshy adipose fin. There are several pairs of sensory barbels around its mouth. Often found in swifter, clearer waters than is usual for other catfish species, the blue catfish will even frequent rapids and waterfalls; it feeds largely on fish and crayfish.

Blue catfishes shed their eggs in a nest made in the shelter of a rock or submerged log on the river or lake bed. Both parents guard the nest and the young once they hatch.

### Brown Catfish *Ictalurus nebulosus*
**RANGE** S. Canada, E. USA to Florida; introduced in W. USA, New Zealand, Europe
**HABITAT** Muddy-bottomed ponds and rivers
**SIZE** 11¾–18 in (30–46 cm)

The brown catfish is one of a group of North American catfishes known as bullheads,

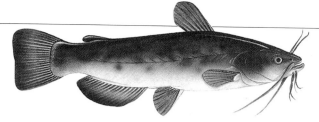

although they are most easily distinguished from other catfishes by their rounded tails. A slender, medium sized catfish, the brown bullhead has a mottled, mainly brownish body, lighter on the underparts. It has a long-based anal fin, a small adipose fin and several sensory barbels around the mouth.

Generally a bottom-dwelling fish, it is usually found in well-vegetated waters, where it feeds mainly on invertebrates, such as insect larvae and mollusks, although it will consume anything from plant material to fish. It feeds at night, feeling for prey with its sensitive chin barbels.

In the spring, these catfishes scrape a shallow hollow in the mud, where they spawn, and the male then stands guard over the clusters of sticky-surfaced eggs. Once hatched, the young swim in schools, defended by one or both parents until they are about 2.5 cm (1 in) long.

Although it is not fished for commercially, the brown catfish has been widely introduced outside its native range.

### Wels *Silurus glanis*

**RANGE** Central and E. Europe to S. Russia; introduced in Britain

**HABITAT** Rivers, lakes, marshes; brackish water in Baltic and Black Seas

**SIZE** 3¼–9¾ ft (1–3 m)

A large, long-bodied catfish, with a broad head and a long anal fin, the wels lives in slow-moving or still waters. It is chiefly nocturnal, remaining close to the bottom during the day, concealed among vegetation or in a hollow.

Fish are its main food, but it also eats frogs, birds and small mammals such as water voles. It spawns in early summer. The male makes a hollow in the river bottom in which the female lays her eggs, and he then guards the eggs until they hatch. Young wels feed on plankton.

### Glass Catfish *Kryptopterus bicirrhis*

**RANGE** Malaysia, Indonesia

**HABITAT** Rivers, streams

**SIZE** 4 in (10 cm)

Unlike most catfishes, the glass catfish moves in small schools in surface and mid-waters during daylight hours. As its common name suggests, its body is virtually transparent, with some iridescent coloration on the sides. It has a long anal fin, a tiny dorsal fin and an apparently lop-sided tail fin.

Glass catfishes have been observed to balance themselves on the lower lobe of the tail fin, standing either obliquely or vertically in the water. These attractive fishes are a popular aquarium species.

### Butterfish *Schilbe mystus*

**RANGE** W. and C. Africa

**HABITAT** Lakes, rivers

**SIZE** 14¼ in (36 cm)

One of a family of catfishes found in Africa and Asia, the butterfish has a scaleless body and four pairs of barbels around its mouth. Its anal fin is long and its dorsal fin tiny. It usually lives in shallow water and feeds on small fish and insect larvae. Spawning takes place during the rainy season.

This species is caught as a food fish, and small specimens are kept in aquariums.

### African Glass Catfish *Physailia pellucida*

**RANGE** Africa: upper Nile basin

**HABITAT** Fresh water

**SIZE** 4 in (10 cm)

The body of the African glass catfish is so transparent that much of its internal structure, such as its organs, blood vessels and spine, are clearly visible. Its anal fin is long, and there is a tiny, fleshy fin on the back but it has no true dorsal fin. This catfish is a popular aquarium species.

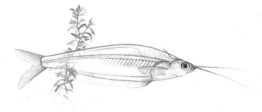

# SILURIFORM FISHES CONTINUED

### Mekong Catfish *Pangasianodon gigas* **EN**

**RANGE** China, S.E. Asia

**HABITAT** Lakes, rivers

**SIZE** Up to 8 ft (2.4 m)

The huge Mekong catfish is one of about 25 species in the family Pangasiidae, a group of Asian freshwater fishes. It is a distinctive fish, with its flattened back and deeply curving belly, and differs from the rest of its family in having extremely low-set eyes, which give it a rather upside-down look. It has no teeth. These catfishes migrate upstream to breed, spawning in lakes and tributaries.

### Pungas Catfish *Pangasius pangasius*

**RANGE** India, Burma, Thailand, Java

**HABITAT** Rivers, estuaries

**SIZE** 4 ft (1.2 m)

The pungas catfish, a member of the catfish family Pangasiidae, is fairly slender, with a rather flattened back and curving belly. Its dorsal fin is high but short based, and its tail is deeply forked. It has one pair of sensory barbels near its mouth. Believed to be active mainly at night, the pungas catfish feeds on the bottom, on detritus and invertebrate animals.

### Walking Catfish *Clarias batrachus*

**RANGE** India, Sri Lanka, S.E. Asia; introduced in USA: Florida

**HABITAT** Slow-moving, often stagnant waters

**SIZE** 12 in (30.5 cm)

The walking catfish is, indeed, capable of moving on land and, when it does so is able to breathe air. It belongs to the family Clariidae, whose members have additional, specialized breathing organs opening off the gill arches. These are saclike structures, containing many-branched extensions, well supplied with blood vessels for respiration.

An elongate fish, this catfish has longbased dorsal and anal fins and several pairs of sensory barbels; its skin is scaleless but liberally supplied with mucus which protects the fish when it is out of water. These catfishes live in ponds or temporary pools, some of which may disappear in prolonged dry spells. When this happens, the catfish can move overland to another body of water, making snakelike movements and using its pectoral fins as "legs". If necessary, the walking catfish can bury itself in mud at the bottom of a pond and remain dormant throughout a dry season until the rains return. It feeds on aquatic invertebrates and fish.

### Electric Catfish *Malapterurus electricus*

**RANGE** Tropical Africa

**HABITAT** Swamps, reedbeds in rivers

**SIZE** 8 in–4 ft (20.5 cm–1.2 m)

The electric catfish is a plump, scaleless fish, with no dorsal fin; it does, however, have a fleshy adipose fin near the tail. Its body is mottled with irregular black blotches, and its mouth bristles with several pairs of sensory barbels. Young fishes have a conspicuous black band near the tail fin. This catfish belongs to the family Malapteruridae, which is thought to contain only 1 other species, *M. microstoma*, also found in Africa. Capable of producing charges of several hundred volts, the electric catfish has well-developed electrical organs under its skin, which occupy much of the length of the body. This catfish uses its electrical powers to defend itself and can render even a human being unconscious. It is also thought to catch its prey by stunning it, and is certainly a sluggish fish that would probably find it hard to catch prey any other way.

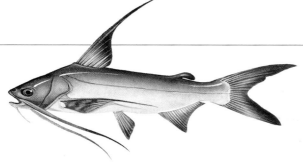

**Gafftopsail Catfish** *Bagre marinus*

**RANGE** W. Atlantic Ocean: Cape Cod to Panama, including Gulf of Mexico

**HABITAT** Coastal waters, bays, estuaries

**SIZE** 24 in (61 cm)

One of the large family of sea catfishes, Ariidae, the gafftopsail catfish is distinguished by its high dorsal fin, the first ray of which is extended into a long, thin filament. The first rays of the pectoral fins are also extended into spines, which can inflict painful wounds. There are two pairs of barbels, one short and one elongate and ribbonlike.

Although a more active fish than many of its freshwater relatives, the gafftopsail catfish still does much of its feeding on the bottom, taking crabs, shrimps and fish.

The breeding habits of this catfish are remarkable. It spawns in summer, and as the eggs are laid, the male fertilizes them and takes them into his mouth where they remain until they hatch. There may be between 10 and 30 eggs, and the male is not able to eat during the incubation period. Even after hatching, the young use their parent's mouth as a refuge for several weeks.

**Sea Catfish** *Arius felis*

**RANGE** W. Atlantic Ocean: Cape Cod to Panama (rare north of Virginia)

**HABITAT** Coastal waters, estuaries

**SIZE** 12 in (30.5 cm)

The sea catfish, one of the Ariidae family of marine catfishes, is slender and elongate, with a high, but not extended, dorsal fin and a deeply forked tail. It is most active at night, feeding on crabs, as well as on some shrimps and fish.

Large shoals swim together and the fishes are capable of making quite loud sounds by vibrating their swim-bladders with specialized muscles.

Spawning takes place in summer, and as the eggs are laid, the male takes them into his mouth, where they incubate. He must fast during the incubation period. The young fishes also use the male's mouth as a refuge after they hatch.

**Upside-down Catfish** *Synodontis nigriventris*

**RANGE** Africa: Congo basin

**HABITAT** Streams

**SIZE** 2¼ in (6 cm)

The upside-down catfish belongs to the family Mochokidae, a group of scaleless catfishes that are found in fresh waters in Africa. There are about 150 species. Most species in the Mochokidae family have long fins, forked tails and several pairs of sensory barbels.

As its name suggests, this fish swims on its back, belly upward, for long periods. Although many others in the family swim upside down for part of the time, it is the usual method of movement for this species. It is thought to adopt the posture in order to feed on the algae that grow on the underside of leaves. Young fishes swim the right way up at first, gradually spending more and more time in the upside-down position.

The interesting habits of this little catfish have made it a popular aquarium species.

**Cuiu-cuiu** *Oxydoras niger*

**RANGE** South America: Amazon basin

**HABITAT** Rivers, lakes, flooded forest

**SIZE** 4 ft (1.2 m)

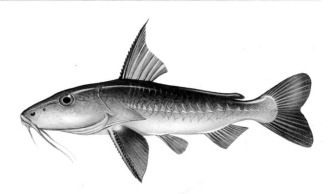

The cuiu-cuiu is one of about 130 species in the South American family of catfishes, Doradidae. Known as thorny catfishes, these fishes have rows of bony plates, most bearing spines, along the sides of the body and toothed spines at the front of both dorsal and pectoral fins.

A slow-moving, bottom-living fish, the cuiu-cuiu is toothless and feeds on detritus, extracting insect larvae from the mud and rotted leaves.

# SILURIFORM FISHES CONTINUED

**Barber-eel** *Plotosus lineatus*

**RANGE** Indian and Pacific Oceans: E. Africa to Sri Lanka and S.E. Asia

**HABITAT** Coastal waters, estuaries, reefs

**SIZE** 11¾ in (30 cm)

The barber-eel is one of a family of eeltail catfishes, all found in Indo-Pacific areas. Its body is elongate and eellike, and there are two dorsal fins, one just behind the head, the other continuous with the tail and anal fins. As in many other catfishes, spines on the dorsal and pectoral fins can inflict painful wounds. There are several pairs of sensory barbels around the mouth.

Young barber-eels are particularly distinctive fishes, with light bands running the length of the body from snout to tail. Older fishes have brown backs, shading to light brown or white on the belly.

**Australian Freshwater Catfish** *Tandanus tandanus*

**RANGE** S. and E. Australia

**HABITAT** Rivers

**SIZE** 24 in (61 cm)

The Australian freshwater catfish is a member of the same family (Plotosidae) as the barber-eel and has a similar fin pattern; its first dorsal fin is high and short based and the second is continuous with the tail and anal fins. Spines on the dorsal and pectoral fins can cause painful wounds. Its body may be brownish or dull green in color but is always mottled with dark markings.

Several pairs of sensory barbels around the mouth help the catfish find food, mainly invertebrates such as mussels, prawns and worms. In the breeding season, the eggs are laid in a circular nest, made in sand or gravel and tended by one of the parents, usually the male.

**Mandi** *Pimelodus blodii*

**RANGE** South America: Amazon basin

**HABITAT** Rivers, streams, flooded forest

**SIZE** 7¾ in (20 cm)

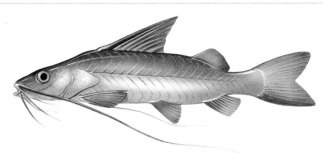

The mandi is a member of a family of South American catfish, known as the fat, or longwhiskered, catfishes (Pimelodidae). Typical of its family, it has a scaleless body and three pairs of sensory barbels, one pair of which is almost as long as the fish itself. Mostly active at night or at dusk, the fish uses these barbels to search for food. Although catfishes are generally bottom-dwellers, the mandi feeds both at the surface, on fruit and seeds, which drop into the water, and on detritus and old leaves at the bottom; it also eats invertebrate animals at both levels.

**Surubim** *Pseudoplatystoma fasciatum*

**RANGE** South America: Amazon basin

**HABITAT** Rivers, lakes, flooded forest

**SIZE** 19¾–35½ in (50–90 cm)

A distinctive fish, the surubim belongs to the Pimelodidae family of South American catfishes. It has an elongate snout, a slender body, marked with irregular dark stripes, and dark blotches on the fins and nose. There is considerable variation in the exact distribution of these markings.

Like most catfishes, the surubim is a bottom-dweller and is thought to feed mostly on invertebrate animals. It has several pairs of sensory barbels around its mouth which help it find food. Unlike many of the Amazonian fishes, the surubim does not appear to have adapted to feeding on the plant material that falls into the water.

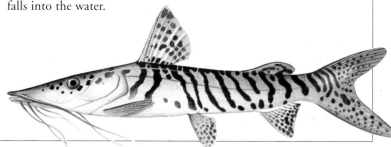

## Vieja *Plecostomus commersonii*

**RANGE** South America: S. Brazil, Uruguay, Paraguay, N. Argentina

**HABITAT** Rivers

**SIZE** 20¾ in (53 cm)

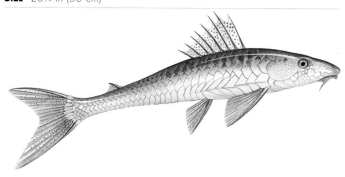

The vieja is one of a large South American family of heavily armored catfishes (Loricariidae). Its long, slender body is covered with overlapping bony plates, but unlike other members of its family, it has no such plates on the belly.

The fins of this species are well developed, with some dark spots on the high dorsal fin; the tail is large, and the lower lobe longer than the upper one. The rounded mouth is on the underside of the snout.

Viejas spawn in spring. The adults feed on worms and crustaceans, as well as aquatic plants, while the young fishes feed on algae.

## Cascarudo *Callichthys callichthys*

**RANGE** Tropical South America: Guyana, south to Paraguay and Uruguay

**HABITAT** Rivers

**SIZE** 7 in (18 cm)

This widely distributed fish belongs to a South American family of armored catfishes (Callichthyidae). As the name suggests, their bodies are heavily armored with overlapping bony plates. The cascarudo has a more slender body than is usual in its family, a neat, pointed head, and two pairs of barbels around the mouth. It lives on the river bottom and is most active at dawn and dusk.

When the cascarudos spawn the male makes a nest, usually placed among floating plants, by blowing bubbles of air and mucus, which form a foamy mass. The eggs are then deposited in these protective bubbles.

## Cascadura *Hoplosternum littorale*

**RANGE** South America: Venezuela, Guyana, south to Peru and Argentina; Trinidad

**HABITAT** Rivers, marshes, swamps

**SIZE** 7¾ in (20 cm)

The cascadura belongs to the armored catfish family (Callichthyidae), and its body is covered with neatly overlapping bony plates. It is a heavily built fish, greeny-gray in coloration and with several pairs of long barbels. Like many of its family, it lives on the bottom, often in oxygen-poor, swampy water. In such conditions, it is able to utilize atmospheric oxygen by gulping in air at the water surface that is then taken into its hind-gut. It is even believed to be able to travel short distances on land while using the air in its vascular gut. Cascaduras feed on aquatic plants.

Spawning cascaduras blow a bubble nest from air and mucus, which is placed among floating vegetation. The eggs are laid in this protective nest, and the male guards the nest and then the young fishes when they hatch.

## Candirú *Vandellia cirrhosa*

**RANGE** South America: Amazon basin

**HABITAT** Rivers, streams

**SIZE** 1 in (2.5 cm)

The tiny, delicate candirú belongs to a family of parasitic catfishes, Trichomycteridae, all found in South America. Its scaleless body is slender, elongate and virtually transparent, and its dorsal fin is placed well back near the tail. It has two pairs of rather short sensory barbels.

Like other members of its family, the candirú is a parasite, living on the blood of other fishes. With small fishes, it simply pierces the skin with its sharp teeth to obtain blood, but it may penetrate the gill system of large fishes and live there, sucking blood. Its tiny body can swell considerably when gorged with food. It is generally active at night or at dawn and dusk and, when not feeding, may bury itself in the sand at the bottom of the river.

The candirú is notorious for its habit of entering the urethra of human bathers or of other mammals, which urinate in the water. It is thought that the fish mistakes the urine for the respiratory water flow of a large fish. Once in the urethra, it becomes lodged by the barbs on its gill covers that normally help it stay in the gill chambers of large fishes, and it is extremely difficult and painful to remove.

# GYMNOTIFORM FISHES, PIKES, OSMERIFORM FISHES AND SALMON

## ORDER GYMNOTIFORMES

The 62 species of freshwater fish in this order are all found in the South American tropics. There are six families including one, the Electrophoridae, whose sole member is the electric eel. Like the elephantfish of Africa, the gymnotiforms, or knifefishes, have evolved, albeit independently, electric organs that can generate an electric field for use in navigation, and the detection and capture of prey, in turbid waters.

### Electric Eel *Electrophorus electricus*

| | |
|---|---|
| **RANGE** | N.E. South America, including Amazon basin |
| **HABITAT** | Muddy streams and pools |
| **SIZE** | 8 ft (2.4 m) |

The electric eel is the only species in its family, Electrophoridae. It is not a true eel, but has a similar long and cylindrical body. Its anal fin runs much of the length of its body, to the tip of its tail, and it has no dorsal, tail or pelvic fins. An inhabitant of turbid, oxygen-poor water, the fish is able to gulp extra air at the surface, from which it absorbs some oxygen via specialized areas of blood vessels inside its mouth.

Much of its bulky body is occupied by its electric organs – modified muscles, which can release high-voltage charges, used for killing prey or for defence. Each organ is made up of many electroplates, each of which produces only a tiny charge but which together may amount to a charge of 500 volts. Such charges kill smaller fish easily and can give a human being a severe shock. The fish can produce slow pulses of low voltage to help it navigate in murky water, where vision is of little use. Young electric eels feed on bottom-living invertebrates, but adults eat mostly fish, many of which they stun before eating.

### Banded Knifefish *Gymnotus carapo*

| | |
|---|---|
| **RANGE** | Central and South America: Guatemala to N. Argentina |
| **HABITAT** | Creeks, slow murky water |
| **SIZE** | 24 in (61 cm) |

The banded knifefish is an elongate, eellike fish, which has an anal fin running the length of its body and small pectorals, but no other fins. It moves backward or forward by wavelike motions of the anal fin but is generally fairly sluggish. Usually active at dawn and dusk, in rather cloudy water, it relies on weak electrical pulses for navigation. Adults eat fish and crustaceans.

## ORDER ESOCIFORMES

This small order of Eurasian and North American freshwater fish has just two families – Esocidae contains 5 species of pikes, while Umbridae has 5 species of mudminnows. All are predators that lie in wait for their prey. Pikes are large fish with long snouts. They hide in weeds then dart out to capture their prey. Mudminnows are smaller and feed on invertebrates.

### Northern Pike *Esox lucius*

| | |
|---|---|
| **RANGE** | Circumpolar: Britain, N. Europe, Russia, Alaska, Canada, N. USA |
| **HABITAT** | Lakes, quiet rivers |
| **SIZE** | 5 ft (1.5 m) |

The long-bodied northern pike has large jaws with sharp teeth and a pointed snout. The dorsal and anal fins are positioned near the tail and opposite one another. Females are larger than males and individuals may weigh 50 lb (23 kg) or more. The pike lurks among vegetation at the water's edge, then shoots out to trap prey. It feeds mainly on invertebrates when young, and then on fish, but also birds and even mammals.

In early spring, as soon as any ice has melted, northern pikes spawn at the water's edge or even in meadows flooded by melted snow. Females shed thousands of eggs over the vegetation.

# ORDER OSMERIFORMES

This is a diverse order of 13 families and nearly 240 species of smelts and their relatives. These silvery, elongate fish include marine and freshwater species as well as anadromous forms (fish that migrate between the sea and freshwater). Most smelts are predators that feed on plankton and small fish.

## Smelt *Osmerus eperlanus* DD

**RANGE** N. Atlantic Ocean: northern coasts of France, Britain, Holland, Germany, Scandinavia

**HABITAT** Coastal waters, estuaries, rivers, fresh water

**SIZE** 11¾ in (30 cm)

Smelts are marine fishes which breed in fresh water. This species is similar to the trout in shape and has a small, fleshy fin on its back, behind the dorsal fin that is itself set well back. Its mouth is large with powerful teeth. It eats small crustaceans and large smelts may eat young fish.

In winter, mature smelts leave the sea to travel up rivers to breed. In spring, they spawn, shedding the eggs on gravel on the river bed or on aquatic plants. Eventually the young fish descend to the sea to grow and mature.

There are isolated populations of smelts in freshwater lakes in Scandinavia which do not migrate. These are slow-growing fishes, smaller than the migratory race.

## Jollytail *Galaxias maculatus*

**RANGE** New Zealand, Tasmania, Australia, S. America

**HABITAT** Rivers, estuaries, coastal waters

**SIZE** 7¾ in (20 cm)

The jollytail has a slender-body, a small head and dorsal and anal fins set close to the tail. Mature fish migrate downstream to spawn among estuarine vegetation, which is flooded by high spring tides at the time of the new moon. The eggs remain stranded among the vegetation, above the reach of the tides, until the next high spring tides two weeks later. If that tide does not reach them, the young are able to survive inside the eggs for a further 2 weeks. When immersed in water they hatch, and the larvae are swept out to sea. After spending some months at sea, the young fish travel up rivers, where they grow and mature.

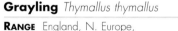

# SALMONIFORMES SALMON ORDER

This order contains 1 family, the salmonidae, with approximately 76 species, including salmon, trout, whitefishes, graylings and charrs. Members of the order occur in freshwater and marine environments, mainly in the northern hemisphere. Some migrate from the sea into rivers to spawn. Most species are predatory.

## Powan *Coregonus lavaretus* DD

**RANGE** Baltic and North Sea basins; Britain, N. Europe, N. Russia, Swiss Alps

**HABITAT** Marine, brackish water, lakes

**SIZE** 8–27½ in (20–70 cm)

The powan is a member of the whitefish family, all of which have large scales, no teeth and forked tails. Whitefishes tend to vary enormously in size and appearance according to habitat, for example, lake-dwellers are generally much smaller than ocean-dwellers because their food supply is often poor. Many lake populations have been isolated since the last ice age and have evolved their own characteristics.

Powan feed on planktonic crustaceans. They spawn in winter, ocean-dwellers migrating into rivers to spawn.

## Grayling *Thymallus thymallus*

**RANGE** England, N. Europe, Scandinavia, Russia

**HABITAT** Rivers, large lakes

**SIZE** 18 in (46 cm)

The 4 species of grayling have high, saillike dorsal fins, forked tails, and small fleshy adipose fins near the base of the tail. Graylings have small teeth in both jaws, and they feed on insects and their larvae, crustaceans and mollusks.

In spring the male oftens displays before breeding; the female makes a hollow in shallow, gravel-bottomed water for her eggs. The eggs hatch 3 to 4 weeks after laying.

The American grayling, *T. arcticus*, is similar in appearance and habits.

# SALMON AND STOMIIFORM FISHES

## Arctic Charr *Salvelinus alpinus*

**RANGE** Circumpolar: Arctic and N. Atlantic Oceans, Britain, Europe, Russia, N. America

**HABITAT** Open sea, rivers, lakes

**SIZE** 10–38 in (25–96 cm)

The Arctic charr is a highly variable species, according to its environment. In the north of its range, it lives in the sea, growing large on the rich supplies of fish, mollusks and crustaceans, and enters rivers to spawn. Farther south, Arctic charr live in mountain lakes, and because of their long isolation, populations have become quite unlike one another and the migratory form. The lake fishes are much smaller and feed on planktonic crustaceans, insects and larvae, and mollusks.

Migratory charr breed in gravel-bottomed rivers. The female makes a nest in the male's territory and lays her eggs; he then fertilizes them in the nest. Lake populations spawn in a similar manner on the lake bed or in streams. Growth is slow, although the rate varies from population to population. Migratory fish do not attain full size until they are about 20 years old.

Charr is a good food fish of particular importance to the people of arctic Canada.

## Lake Trout *Salvelinus namaycush*

**RANGE** Canada, N. USA

**HABITAT** Lakes, rivers

**SIZE** 4 ft (1.2 m)

A popular sport-fishing species in North America, the lake trout is a charr, not a true trout. It has been introduced into lakes out of its natural range. It has pale spots on head, back and sides. Lake trout eat fish, insects, crustaceans and plankton.

From late summer to December, lake trout spawn in shallow gravel-bottomed water. There is no nest, but males clear the spawning ground of debris. Eggs are laid on the

gravel and settle among the stones; they remain there for the winter and hatch in early spring.

## Trout *Salmo trutta*

**RANGE** Europe; introduced worldwide

**HABITAT** Marine; lakes, rivers

**SIZE** 9 in–4½ ft (23 cm–1.4 m)

There are two forms of this well-known food- and angling-fish: the sea trout, which migrates from river to sea and back to river to breed, and the smaller brown trout, which spends all its life in fresh water. They are alike physically, but sea trout have silvery scales with scattered black markings, and brown trout have numerous dark spots. Both forms feed on fish and crustaceans.

Trout spawn in winter in gravel-bottomed fresh water; the female makes a shallow nest for her eggs. The young hatch in spring and remain in the gravel for a few weeks.

## Rainbow Trout *Salmo gairdneri*

**RANGE** N.W. America, E. Pacific; introduced worldwide

**HABITAT** Marine; rivers

**SIZE** Up to 3¼ ft (1 m)

Now farmed in large quantities, rainbow trout are extremely popular with anglers and are an important food fish. There is a large migratory form, known as the steelhead, which bears the same relationship to the rainbow as the sea trout does to the brown trout. Both forms feed mainly on insect larvae, mollusks and crustaceans.

In their natural range, rainbow trout spawn in spring in shallow, gravel-bottomed streams. The female makes a shallow nest in the gravel and deposits her eggs which are then fertilized by the male and covered over.

## Atlantic Salmon *Salmo salar*

**RANGE** N. Atlantic Ocean: Greenland to Cape Cod;
Arctic coast of Russia, south to N. Spain

**HABITAT** Open sea; rivers

**SIZE** Up to 5 ft (1.5 m)

The Atlantic salmon is a long-bodied, rounded fish with a slightly forked tail. There are some salmon in inland lakes, but most are migratory, moving from their natal river out to sea and then back to the river to spawn. The salmon enter the river at different times but all spawn in the winter. Breeding males develop hooked protuberances on their lower jaws. Having excavated a shallow nest in the gravel of the river bed, the female lays her eggs while the male lies next to her fertilizing them. The eggs overwinter and hatch the following spring. After 2 to 6 years in the river, the young salmon go out to sea, returning to spawn from 1 to 4 years later. Unlike Pacific salmon, Atlantic salmon can spawn more than once in their lifetime.

## Sockeye Salmon *Oncorhynchus nerka*

**RANGE** N. Pacific Ocean: N. American coast: Alaska to California;
coast of Russia to Japan: Hokkaido

**HABITAT** Open sea, coastal waters, rivers and lakes

**SIZE** 33 in (84 cm)

The sockeye salmon lives in the ocean, eating small shrimplike creatures, until it is 4 to 6 years old. In late spring, mature adults enter rivers to ascend to their breeding areas, sometimes 1, 500 miles (2 ,400 km) inland. They breed in lakes or small adjacent streams. Breeding males develop bright red skin on back and sides, and the back becomes humped and jaws hooked. Females show some red color.

At their breeding grounds the female digs a shallow pit in the stream bed with her tail and body, and lays her eggs. They are then fertilized by the male. After spawning the adults die. The eggs hatch after 6 to 9 weeks, and the young spend 1 to 3 years in the lake before migrating to the sea.

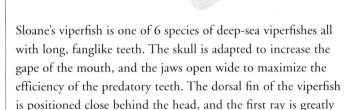

# ORDER STOMIIFORMES

The 320 or so species of stomiiforms are deep sea fishes and include bristlemouths, marine hatchetfishes, lightfishes, dragonfishes, and viperfishes. Bristlemouths are some of the most abundant fishes in the oceans. Most stomiiforms have large mouths, long teeth, and light organ used to attract prey in the dark, deep ocean.

## Hatchetfish *Argyropelecus aculeatus*

**RANGE** Atlantic, Pacific and Indian Oceans:
tropical and subtropical areas

**HABITAT** Open sea at 330–2,000 ft
(100–600 m)

**SIZE** 2¾ in (7 cm)

The hatchetfish is a common species which forms a major item of diet for many larger fishes. Its silvery body is deep and laterally compressed, with a sharp-edged belly. Its eyes are large, and its capacious mouth is nearly vertical. On the fish's belly there are rows of light-producing organs, which are arranged in a characteristic pattern in each species, enabling the hatchetfishes to recognize their own kind from below.

Hatchetfishes normally live at depths of 1,300 to 2,000 ft (400 to 600 m) by day, but migrate nearer to the surface each night in search of food.

## Sloane's Viperfish *Chauliodus sloani*

**RANGE** Atlantic, Pacific and Indian Oceans:
temperate and tropical areas

**HABITAT** Deep sea

**SIZE** 11¾ in (30 cm)

Sloane's viperfish is one of 6 species of deep-sea viperfishes all with long, fanglike teeth. The skull is adapted to increase the gape of the mouth, and the jaws open wide to maximize the efficiency of the predatory teeth. The dorsal fin of the viperfish is positioned close behind the head, and the first ray is greatly elongated and bears a light-producing organ to attract prey in the darkness of the deep sea. Viperfishes feed on smaller fish, such as lanternfishes, which they follow when they make their nightly migrations to waters nearer the surface, where they feed on plankton.

# AULOPIFORM FISHES, LANTERNFISHES AND TROUT-PERCHES

## ORDER AULOPIFORMES

Most of the 219 species in this order are deep sea fishes, although one family, the lizardfishes, live in shallower waters. The aulopiforms form a diverse group. The deep sea members are mostly small predators, and include the 55 or so species of barracudinas, that resemble miniature barracudas, as well as bizarre-looking forms such as the telescopefishes and spiderfishes.

Lizardfishes are found in the shallow tropical and subtropical seas and are common inhabitants of coral reefs where they conceal themselves in order to ambush passing prey.

### Red Lizardfish *Synodus synodus*
**RANGE** Atlantic Ocean: Florida, through Gulf of Mexico to Uruguay
**HABITAT** Coastal waters
**SIZE** 12½ in (32 cm)

The red lizardfish is one of a family of about 34 lizardfishes, all found in shallow areas of tropical and warm temperate seas. It has a large head and wide jaws, set with long sharp teeth. With its heavy, shiny scales, it is thought to have a reptilian appearance – hence its common name – and it has some reddish coloration on its tail.

The pelvic fins are unusually long, and the fish has the habit of lying on the seabed, supported on these fins. It is also able to partly bury itself. A voracious carnivore, it catches its prey by ambushing – suddenly darting upward from where it is concealed on the seabed.

### Bummalow *Harpadon nehereus*
**RANGE** N. Indian Ocean
**HABITAT** Estuaries, shallow coastal waters
**SIZE** 16 in (41 cm)

The bummalow is one of a small family of 4 or 5 species, all of which are found in the Indian Ocean. It has an elongate body and large jaws with sharp curving teeth, It also has long pelvic and pectoral fins. This species is often found near the mouths of large rivers such as the Ganges, where it eats small fish and crustaceans, though it breeds farther out to sea.

This fish is better known as Bombay Duck, its name when it has been split, dried in the sun and served with curry. It is a valuable commercial species.

## ORDER MYCTOPHIFORMES

Most of the 240 species in this family are found in one of the two families – the lanternfishes. They are small fish with blunt heads, large eyes, and photophores (light-producing organs) which are arranged in rows on the body and head. The photophores are arranged in patterns characteristic to each different species and are an important means of distinguishing between species in the darkness of the deep ocean.

Myctiforms are deep sea fishes that are found in all oceans from the Arctic to the Antarctic. They are important prey species for many other fish and also for some marine mammals.

**Lanternfish** *Myctophum punctatum*

**RANGE** N. Atlantic Ocean; Mediterranean Sea

**HABITAT** Deep sea

**SIZE** 4 in (10 cm)

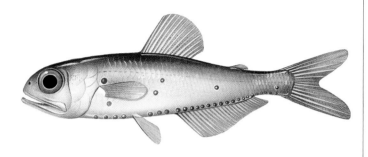

This species is typical of its family; with its blunt, rounded head and very large eyes, the lanternfish also has many light-producing organs, known as photophores, which are arranged in short rows and groups on its body.

Young fish start to develop their light-producing organs when they are about 4 in (2 cm) long, and the arrangement differs between males and females of the species.

The function and value of these photophores are not yet fully understood. They may help the fish to illuminate the dark depths and find prey, or they may be used to confuse predators; the lanternfish has photophores on its tail and it is said to lash its tail to and fro in order to dazzle an enemy.

Lantern-fishes feed on tiny planktonic animals, making vertical migrations from the ocean depths of as much as 1,300 ft (400 m) or more, in order to follow the nightly movements of the plankton to the ocean's surface waters.

Lanternfish move in large schools and, in the Mediterranean area, they are known to breed betweeen April and July.

# PERCOPSIFORMES
# TROUT-PERCH ORDER

There are 9 species, grouped in 3 families, that are known to belong to this order. All percopsiformes are freshwater fishes, and are found in North America in larger streams, deep clear lakes and cave water, and have common names such as sand-roller, pirate-perch and the cavefish.

Trout-perches, as their name suggests, show some structural similarities to both the trout and perch, but they are never more than 6 in (15 cm) long. They are not actually related to either the trout or the perch.

Most species in the order feed on aquatic insects and crustaceans, but the pirate-perch preys on small fish.

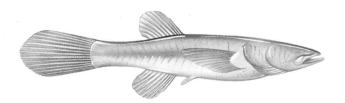

**Northern Cavefish** *Amblyopsis spelaea*

**RANGE** USA: Kentucky, Indiana

**HABITAT** Fresh water in limestone caves

**SIZE** 4 in (10 cm)

One of a small family of 10 species, many of which live in limestone caves, the northern cavefish was first discovered in 1842. It is a slender-bodied fish, with no scales on its head but small irregular scales on its body. Its eyes are rudimentary and covered with skin, since it has no need of vision in its dark cave habitat and has adapted accordingly. To compensate for its virtual blindness, its body is covered with tiny sensory protuberances with which it can detect even slight movements in water and thus find its prey and avoid obstacles.

The male cavefish fertilizes the female internally with a specially adapted genital organ. She has an unusual way of guarding her eggs – once they are fertilized and shed, she carries them in her gill chamber until they hatch.

**Trout-perch** *Percopsis omiscomaycus*

**RANGE** N. America: Alaska to Quebec; Great Lakes to Kentucky, Missouri, Kansas

**HABITAT** Lakes, muddy rivers

**SIZE** 7¾ in (20 cm)

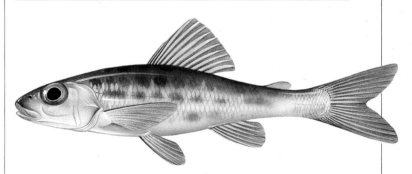

One of the 2 species of trout-perch, this fish has a silvery body, translucent in parts. Its head is scaleless, but the rest of its body is covered with rough, sawtoothed scales. The nocturnal trout-perch eats aquatic insects, crustaceans and mollusks. It spawns in spring or early summer in streams or shallow lakes. The eggs sink to the bottom, where they stay until they hatch.

The other trout-perch, the sandroller, *P. transmontana*, lives only in the Columbia River system in northwest USA. It is similar to *P. omiscomaycus*, but is usually greenish-yellow.

# OPHIDIIFORM FISHES AND CODFISHES

## ORDER OPHIDIIFORMES

The 355 species of ophidiiforms are mainly eellike fish with long tapering tails. The 6 families include cusk-eels and brotulas that live in a wide range of habitats from the brackish water of caves to the depths of the ocean. The 27 species of pearlfish are inquilines ("tenants") living inside the body cavities of marine invertebrates including starfish, clams, sea squirts, and sea cucumbers.

### Pearlfish *Carapus acus*

**RANGE** Mediterranean and Adriatic Seas

**HABITAT** Seabed

**SIZE** 7¾ in (20 cm)

Pearlfishes are small, slender fishes with translucent, spotted skin, found in tropical and warm temperate waters. Many of them spend much of their lives inside other marine animals such as clams, sea urchins, starfish, sea cucumbers and even pearl oysters – hence the common name.

This species is a typical pearlfish, with its elongate tapering body and long, low dorsal and anal fins which form a continuous border to the body. The adult fish lives inside a sea cucumber. It enters the animal through its anus, inserting its tail first and then wriggling backward until it is inside the body cavity. Several pearlfishes may occupy one host, feeding on its internal organs until the host is destroyed.

Young pearlfishes pass through two larval stages before taking up residence in this way; in the first phase, the young fishes float in surface waters, in the second, they live near the seabed. Adult pearlfishes can live outside a host, feeding on small crustaceans.

### New Providence Cusk-eel *Lucifuga spelaeotes* **VU**

**RANGE** Bahamas: near Nassau

**HABITAT** Freshwater pools in limestone

**SIZE** 4¼ in (11 cm)

This species was first discovered in 1967 and is known only from this one location, although it is believed to be related to 3 species in the same genus, found in cave pools in Cuba.

A small but distinctive fish, the body of the new providence cusk-eel curves upward sharply behind the broad, flattened head and its long-based dorsal and anal fins are continuous with the tail fin. Much of its head is scaleless, but the body is covered with small scales. The Cuban species are blind, but *L. spelaeotes* has small yet well-developed eyes.

In view of its apparently extremely restricted distribution, it seems that this species may be in danger of disappearing only years after its discovery.

### New Zealand Ling *Genypterus blacodes*

**RANGE** Seas off S. Australia, New Zealand

**HABITAT** Coastal waters

**SIZE** 35½ in (90 cm)

Not to be confused with the North Atlantic lings (*Molva*), this ling is one of a group known as cusk-eels, which belong to the cod order. A long, tapering fish, its dorsal, tail and anal fins are joined to form one continuous strip around the body. The head is flattened, and there are two thin pelvic fins under the lower jaw. The anus is positioned behind the head.

## GADIFORMES COD ORDER

This order contains about 480 species only 5 of which are freshwater fishes. They are grouped into 12 families, and some of the most familiar forms, such as cod, haddock, whiting, hake, saithe and ling, are extremely valuable food fish.

The majority of the cod species lives in the northern

hemisphere in the relatively shallow waters of the continental shelves. Some species in the order, however, notably the grenadiers, which are also known as rat-tails, live in deep oceanic water. All species are carnivorous, feeding on fish, crustaceans and other forms of marine life.

The body of the codfish is covered with small scales, and the fins contain soft rays. Many members of the order have a sensory barbel on the chin. The barbel is equipped with additional taste buds.

Most cod spawn simply by coming together into large shoals. Then both sexes discharge their eggs and sperm into the water. The eggs are then abandoned by the parents and, although many millions of eggs are produced in each spawning, so many are destroyed by the elements or are eaten by other fishes that relatively few survive. In the case of the cod, for example, it is estimated that only about one egg in a million survives to adulthood.

### Rough-head Grenadier *Macrourus berglax*

**RANGE** N. Atlantic Ocean: Nova Scotia to Greenland, Iceland, Norway

**HABITAT** Deep water, 650–3,300 ft (200–1,000 m)

**SIZE** 35½ in–3¼ ft (90 cm–1 m)

The rough-head grenadier is one of a family of about 15 species belonging to the cod order which are found in deep water; all are known as grenadiers or rat-tails. The males of many of these species can make surprisingly loud sounds by vibrating their swim-bladders with specialized muscles. Such sounds may be used for communication, particularly during the breeding season.

The rough-head grenadier has the characteristic appearance of its family, with its large, heavy head and tapering, pointed tail. It has a high first dorsal fin, but its second dorsal fin and anal fin are continuous with the tail. The head is ridged beneath the eyes and the body scales are rough and toothed.

The grenadier feeds on crustaceans, mollusks and brittle stars. It is believed to breed in winter to early spring.

### Three-barbed Rockling *Gaidropsarus mediterraneus*

**RANGE** European coasts: S. Norway, W. British Isles to Mediterranean and Black Seas

**HABITAT** Rocky shores

**SIZE** 6–13¾ in (15–35 cm)

One of several species of rockling, the three-barbed is typical of the group, with its long slender body and two dorsal fins. The first of these fins has short, fine rays and the second fin is long based. The anal fin is also long based and, as the common name implies, there are three barbels, one on the chin and two on the fish's snout.

This is an abundant fish on many shores. The rockling nearly always occurs on rocky bottoms where it feeds on crustaceans, worms and small fish.

It spawns offshore, and eggs and larvae float on surface waters. When the young fishes measure about 1½ in (4 cm) long, they adopt the bottom-living habits of the adult rocklings.

### Burbot *Lota lota*

**RANGE** Canada, N. USA, N. Europe, Asia

**HABITAT** Rivers, lakes

**SIZE** 20–39 in (51–99 cm)

One of the few fishes in the cod order that lives in fresh water, the burbot is similar to many marine codfishes, with its long body, chin barbel and long-based dorsal and anal fins.

It is a fairly sluggish fish, hiding among aquatic vegetation by day and emerging at dawn and dusk to feed. Adults eat fish, crustaceans and insects, while the young burbot feed on insect larvae and small crustaceans.

Burbot spawn at night in shallow water during the winter. They are prolific egg-layers – one female may shed up to 3 million eggs which then sink to the bottom, where they remain while development takes place.

# CODFISHES CONTINUED

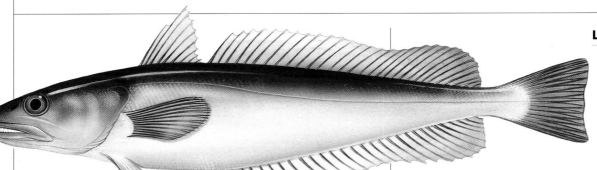

## European Hake *Merluccius merluccius*

**RANGE** N. Atlantic Ocean: Iceland, Norway to N. Africa; Mediterranean

**HABITAT** Deep water, 550–1,800 ft (165–550 m)

**SIZE** 3¼–6 ft (1–1.8 m)

True hakes are a small family of codlike fish, all in the genus *Merluccius.* The European hake is typical with its slender body, large head and two dorsal fins, the first of which is triangular and the second long based and curving. It lives near the seabed migrating upward nightly to feed nearer the surface.

Hakes spawn in spring or summer. The eggs and larvae drift in surface waters, gradually being carried inshore, where young fish remain for the first year, eating mainly crustaceans.

The Pacific hake, *M. productus,* is similar to the European species in appearance and habits.

## White Hake *Urophycis tenuis*

**RANGE** N.W. Atlantic Ocean: Gulf of St. Lawrence to North Carolina

**HABITAT** Inshore and offshore waters to depths of 3,300 ft (1,000 m)

**SIZE** 4 ft (1.2 m)

An elongate fish, the white hake has only two dorsal fins, the second of which is long based, a small, rounded tail and one long anal fin. It is commonly found near soft muddy bottoms where it feeds on crustaceans, squid and small fish. Spawning begins in late winter and eggs and larvae float at the surface.

Large quantities of white hake and the closely related red hake, *U. chuss,* are taken by commercial fisheries. Even though, confusingly, their common names are the same, these hakes are a quite separate group from the true hakes (*Merluccius* species).

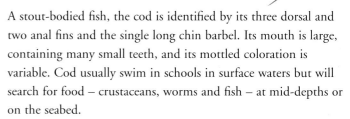

## Ling *Molva molva*

**RANGE** N.E. Atlantic Ocean: Iceland, Norway to Bay of Biscay

**HABITAT** Deep water: 980–1,300 ft (300–400 m)

**SIZE** 5–6½ ft (1.5–2 m)

Ling are valuable commercial fish in some European waters. A long slim fish, the ling has two dorsal fins, the second of which is long based, and one long anal fin. It has a barbel on its chin. It is most common in rocky-bottomed areas and eats fish and large crustaceans. Although mainly a deepwater species, the ling may be found in shallower areas, where the bottom is suitable. It breeds from March to July, and a female may shed up to 60 million eggs which float in surface waters while they develop.

## Cod *Gadus morhua* **VU**

**RANGE** N. Atlantic Ocean: Greenland and Hudson strait to North Carolina; Baltic sea to Bay of Biscay

**HABITAT** Coastal waters

**SIZE** 4 ft (1.2 m)

A stout-bodied fish, the cod is identified by its three dorsal and two anal fins and the single long chin barbel. Its mouth is large, containing many small teeth, and its mottled coloration is variable. Cod usually swim in schools in surface waters but will search for food – crustaceans, worms and fish – at mid-depths or on the seabed.

Breeding takes place between February and April, and some cod populations make long migrations to specific spawning areas. Eggs drift in surface waters, at the mercy of currents and predators, while they develop and hatch into larvae. The young cod feed on small crustaceans.

The cod is an extremely valuable food fish which has been exploited by humans for centuries.

## Haddock *Melanogrammus aeglefinus* **VU**

**RANGE** N. Atlantic Ocean: Barents Sea and Iceland to Bay of Biscay; Newfoundland to Cape Cod

**HABITAT** Coastal waters, near seabed

**SIZE** 30 in (76 cm)

The haddock resembles the cod, with its three dorsal and two anal fins, but the first dorsal fin is triangular and pointed and there is a distinct black mark on each dusky side. Haddock live near the seabed and feed on bottom-living animals such as brittle stars, worms, mollusks and some small fish.

Spawning takes place between January and June and eggs are left to float in surface waters while they hatch into larvae. Young haddock often shelter among the tentacles of large jellyfishes. Some haddock populations migrate south in winter or move from shallow inshore waters to deeper waters.

## Blue Whiting *Micromesistius poutassou*

**RANGE** N. Atlantic Ocean: Barents Sea to Mediterranean and Adriatic Seas

**HABITAT** Oceanic

**SIZE** 13¾–16 in (35–41 cm)

Shoals of blue whiting move in surface and mid-waters to depths of about 980 ft (300 m). They have three well spaced dorsal fins and two anal fins, the first of which is long based. They eat mainly crustaceans and some small fish. They are an important item of diet for many larger fishes.

## Whiting *Merlangius merlangus*

**RANGE** European coasts, Iceland to Spain, Mediterranean and Black Seas

**HABITAT** Shallow inshore waters to 330 ft (100 m)

**SIZE** 11¾–15¾ in (30–40 cm)

The whiting has three dorsal and two anal fins, the first of which is long based. The upper jaw is longer than the lower and there is a characteristic black mark at the base of each pectoral fin. Adult whiting eat fish and crustaceans, while young feed mainly on small crustaceans. They spawn in spring in shallow water.

A common species, it is a valuable commercial food fish for humans and is also hunted and eaten by many larger fishes and also birds.

## Walleye Pollock *Theragra chalcogramma*

**RANGE** N. Pacific Ocean: N.W. Alaska to California; Sea of Japan

**HABITAT** Surface to mid-waters, 1,200 ft (360 m)

**SIZE** 35½ in (90 cm)

The widely distributed walleye pollock has a tapering body, three well-spaced dorsal fins and two anal fins. Its head and mouth are large, and its eyes bigger than those of most codfishes. Unlike most codfishes, it spends little time near the seabed and feeds mainly in mid-depths on crustaceans and other marine invertebrates and some small fish.

## Saithe *Pollachius virens*

**RANGE** N. Atlantic Ocean: Iceland, Greenland and Barents Sea to Bay of Biscay; Labrador to North Carolina

**HABITAT** Surface waters: coastal and offshore

**SIZE** 27½–31½ in (70–80 cm)

Although it has the typical cod fin pattern, the saithe is characterized by its slightly forked tail, the lower jaw, which protrudes slightly beyond the upper, and the lack of a chin barbel. Saithe usually move in small schools and feed on fish, particularly other cod species and herring; young saithe feed on crustaceans and small fish.

Saithe migrate to offshore breeding grounds to spawn in deep water between January and April. The eggs and then the larvae drift at the surface gradually being carried to shallower inshore waters, where the young fishes are found the following summer. Large numbers are caught commercially, and it is a popular species with sea anglers.

# TOADFISHES AND ANGLER FISHES

## BATRACHOIDIFORMES TOADFISH ORDER

There are about 69 species of bottom-dwelling toadfish, found in many of the oceans of the world, mostly in tropical or warm temperate areas. The common name comes from the resemblance of the broad, flattened head, with its wide mouth and slightly protuberant eyes, to that of a toad.

### Atlantic Midshipman *Porichthys porosissimus*
**RANGE** W. Atlantic Ocean: coasts of Brazil to Argentina
**HABITAT** Inshore waters
**SIZE** 11¾ in (30 cm)

The bottom-dwelling Atlantic midshipman has a large, flattened head and eyes near the top of the head. The body is scaleless, and on each side there are rows of hundreds of light-producing organs, which are arranged in a regular pattern. Midshipmen are among the few shallow-water fishes to possess such organs.

Also known as the singing fish, this species can make a variety of sounds. Specialized muscles in the walls of the fish's swim bladder contract producing grunts and whistles.

## LOPHIIFORMES ANGLER FISH ORDER

There are about 300 species of angler fish known. They are found at all depths in tropical and temperate seas. All have large heads, wide mouths filled with many rows of sharp teeth and small gills. The body is rounded in deep-water forms and flattened in shallow-water forms.

Most anglers have a fishing lure, which is a modified dorsal fin spine, tipped with a flap of skin. It can be positioned in front of the mouth. The shallow-water angler lies camouflaged on the seabed, gently moving its lure. Prey, mistaking the lure for food, approaches to investigate and is engulfed in the fishes' huge jaws.

In a number of deep-sea angler species, males, which are relatively tiny, attach themselves to females so intimately that their tissues fuse.

### Angler *Lophius piscatorius*
**RANGE** European coasts from Scandinavia and Iceland to N. Africa; Black and Mediterranean Seas
**HABITAT** Coastal waters
**SIZE** 3¼–6½ ft (1–2 m)

A large, highly distinctive fish, the angler has a flattened body, dominated by its broad, flattened head. The mouth is extremely wide with well developed teeth. The head and mouth are fringed with small skin flaps that help conceal the fish's outline as it lies on the seabed. The pectoral fins are placed on the small fleshy limbs, and on the first elongated dorsal spine is a flap of skin, used as a fishing lure. The angler is a bottom-living fish found from shallow water down to 1,650 ft (500 m) or more. Half-buried in the sand or shingle of the seabed, it watches for prey and moves its lure to attract fish within easy reach of its capacious mouth. Once the angler opens its mouth, powerful water currents are created, sucking in the unfortunate prey.

Anglers move farther out to sea in spring and early summer to spawn over deep water. The eggs are shed enclosed in ribbonlike trails of gelatinous mucus which keeps them together as they float near the surface. The larvae, too, float near the surface, aided by their enlarged dorsal fins. The closely related goosefish, *L. americanus*, of the Atlantic coast of North America is similar in appearance and habits.

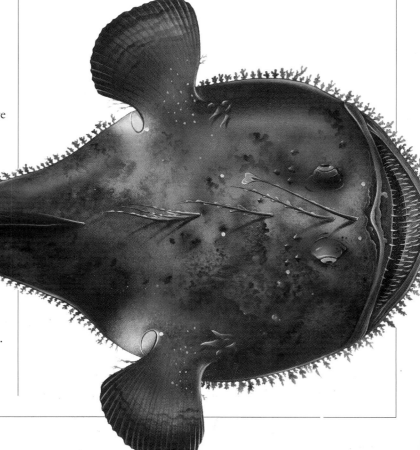

## Sargassumfish *Histrio histrio*

**RANGE** Atlantic, Indian, Pacific
Oceans, tropical areas
**HABITAT** Surface waters
among sargassum weed
**SIZE** 7½ in (19 cm)

The sargassumfish is one of the family of anglers known as
frogfishes which, typically, have a balloon-shaped body covered
with bumps and flaps of skin. It is perfectly camouflaged to
blend with the sargassum weed in which it lives and, while its
coloration is variable, it always matches its own particular weed
patch. Frondlike rays on the snout mimic the weed itself, and
white dots on the body resemble the white encrustations of
tiny animals that live on sargassum plants. The fish's pectoral
fins are flexible and can be used actually to grasp the weed as
it clambers around.

Small invertebrates are the main food of the sargassumfish,
and it attracts prey with the small lure on its snout. If it is
attacked by a predator, the sargassumfish may rapidly take in
water, pumping itself into a ball too big to swallow.

## Longlure Frogfish

*Antennarius multiocellatus*

**RANGE** Tropical W. Atlantic Ocean,
Caribbean
**HABITAT** Seabed
**SIZE** 6 in (15 cm)

The longlure frogfish has a stout
body typical of its family and a
pronounced "fishing line" on its snout.
Its coloration is variable but always merges well with its
surroundings, whether rock, coral or seaweed. A bottom-living,
slow-moving fish, it crawls around the seabed with the aid of its
limblike pectoral fins, feeding on small fish and crustaceans.

## Shortnose Batfish *Ogcocephalus nasutus*

**RANGE** Caribbean
**HABITAT** Seabed
**SIZE** 11 in (28 cm)

The shortnose batfish is typical of
the 55 or so species of batfish, with its
almost triangular body, dramatically flattened
from top to bottom. Its pectoral fins are large and
flexible and positioned on armlike stalks. Its snout is
pointed and mouth small, and the upper surface of its body is

studded with hard tubercles – rounded projections.

A slow-moving, awkward swimmer, the batfish
crawls over the seabed on its pectoral and pelvic fins,
using its tail as support. It eats fish, mollusks, crustaceans
and worms.

## Football-fish

*Himantolophus groenlandicus*

**RANGE** Worldwide (but uncommon)
**HABITAT** Deep sea: 330–980 ft (100–300 m)
**SIZE** 24 in (61 cm)

The football-fish is a deep-sea angler. Its extremely rotund body
is studded with bony plates, each bearing a central spine, and
the modified ray on the head makes a thick "fishing rod", tipped
with a many-branched lure and with a central luminous bulb. It
preys on fish attracted to the lure in the sparsely inhabited dark
depths. Males are smaller than females but are not parasitic.

*Linophryne arborifera*

**RANGE** Atlantic, Pacific, Indian Oceans
**HABITAT** Deep sea
**SIZE** 2¾ in (7 cm)

One of a family of deep-sea anglers,
*Linophryne* has
a rounded
body and
a branched chin barbel, resembling a
piece of seaweed. The prominent "fishing rod" on its snout
is branched and bears a luminous lure. The tiny adult
males are believed to live parasitically on the females,
losing their own powers of vision and smell.

# BELONIFORM FISHES

## ORDER BELONIFORMES

This diverse order of about 190 species of mostly marine fishes includes 5 families – flyingfishes, halfbeaks, needlefishes, sauries, and medakas. Most are active near or above the surface of the water. Flyingfishes are tail-powered gliders, different species gaining lift from enlarged, winglike pectoral fins, but all propelling themselves forward with their rapidly beating tails to glide short distances over the water. Halfbeaks skip along the surface of the sea but do not become fully airborne like the flyingfishes. Flyingfishes usually "fly" to escape from predators such as the dolphin fish. Needlefish and sauries are fast-moving fish that swim near the surface and prey on small fishes. Medakas, or ricefishes, are common inhabitants of brackish and freshwater in tropical Asia.

### Atlantic Flyingfish *Cypselurus heterurus*

**RANGE** W. Atlantic Ocean: S. Canada to Brazil; E. Atlantic: Denmark to N. Africa; Mediterranean Sea

**HABITAT** Surface waters: open sea and coastal

**SIZE** 11¾–17 in (30–43 cm)

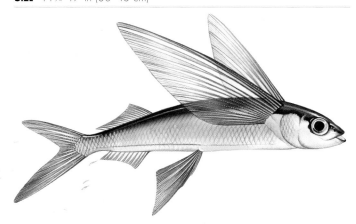

The Atlantic flyingfish is a four-winged flyingfish, with enlarged pectoral and pelvic fins to propel it on its "flights". When swimming underwater, its pectoral fins are kept folded against the body. The dorsal and anal fins are small and positioned near the tail, which has a long lower lobe. The body is fully scaled. Before a flight, the fish builds up speed in the water and then rises into the air, both pairs of fins expanded, and glides up to 300 ft (90 m) at 5 ft (1.5 m) above the surface. Most flights last about 10 seconds.

Flyingfishes breed in the spring and lay their eggs among seaweed or other debris. The eggs bear many fine threads which attach them to one another and anchor them to floating objects. Newly hatched flyingfishes have short barbels on the chin.

### Flyingfish *Exocetus volitans*

**RANGE** All oceans: tropical and subtropical areas

**HABITAT** Open sea

**SIZE** 11¾ in (30 cm)

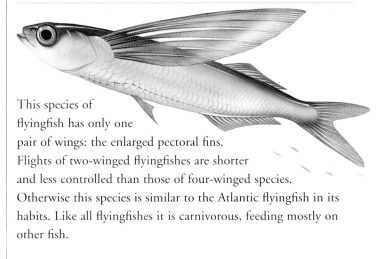

This species of flyingfish has only one pair of wings: the enlarged pectoral fins. Flights of two-winged flyingfishes are shorter and less controlled than those of four-winged species. Otherwise this species is similar to the Atlantic flyingfish in its habits. Like all flyingfishes it is carnivorous, feeding mostly on other fish.

### Wrestling Halfbeak *Dermogenys pusillus*

**RANGE** Thailand, Malaysia, Singapore, Sunda Islands

**HABITAT** Fresh water

**SIZE** 2¾ in (7 cm)

A small slender fish, with dorsal and anal fins positioned near the broad rounded tail, the wrestling halfbeak has the elongated lower jaw typical of its group. It is one of the few freshwater halfbeaks. Mosquito larvae are its main food source, and it is an important controller of these pests.

Males are aggressive and fight one another by wrestling with their jaws. The anal fin of the male is modified to form a copulatory organ for internal fertilization of the female. About 8 weeks after her eggs have been fertilized, the female gives birth to 12 to 20 live young, each of which is about ½ in (1 cm) long.

### Ballyhoo *Hemiramphus brasiliensis*

**RANGE** Atlantic Ocean: New England, USA to Brazil; Gulf of Mexico, Caribbean; off W. Africa

**HABITAT** Coastal waters

**SIZE** 17¾ in (45 cm)

The ballyhoo is a slender-bodied fish, with a greatly elongated lower jaw and small dorsal and anal fins set back on the body near the tail. It is a typical halfbeak with small pectoral fins which, although it cannot glide over the water like its relatives the flyingfishes, can skim over the surface. It is surface-living and moves in schools, feeding on sea grass and small fish. The form of its jaws may help it to scoop up food from the water surface.

## Garfish *Belone belone*

**RANGE** N. Atlantic Ocean: Iceland to Spain and Scandinavia; Mediterranean and Black Seas

**HABITAT** Surface waters, mainly offshore

**SIZE** 37 in (94 cm)

The garfish is a long, slim fish with elongate jaws, which are studded with numerous needlelike teeth. Both dorsal and anal fins are long based and set well back near the tail. An active predator, the garfish feeds on many species of small fish and crustaceans. It spawns in late spring or early summer, in coastal waters. The small, round eggs bear many fine threads which attach to floating debris or seaweed.

## Freshwater Needlefish *Belonion apodion*

**RANGE** South America

**HABITAT** Lakes, rivers

**SIZE** 2 in (5 cm)

A tiny, fragile fish, first discovered in 1966, the freshwater needlefish is one of a family of about 30 needlefishes and garfishes, most of which are marine. It is typical of its family, with its slender body and small anal and dorsal fins placed near the tail, but unlike most other species, which have elongate upper and lower jaws, only its lower jaw is long.

## Houndfish *Tylosaurus crocodilus*

**RANGE** All oceans

**HABITAT** Inshore surface waters

**SIZE** 5 ft (1.5 m)

The largest, heaviest needlefish, the houndfish has a shorter, thicker beak than most species. Houndfishes sometimes leap out of the water and skip over the surface and, because of their size

and strong, pointed jaws, can be quite dangerous to man. The houndfish feeds on fish, which it seizes crosswise in its jaws and skilfully turns to swallow headfirst.

## Saury *Scomberesox saurus*

**RANGE** N. Atlantic Ocean: N. American to European coasts; Mediterranean Sea; temperate waters in S. hemisphere, around the globe

**HABITAT** Open ocean, coastal waters

**SIZE** 15¾–19¾ in (40–50 cm)

The saury, or skipper, is a long, slim fish with elongate beaklike jaws, the lower of which is longer than the upper. Behind the saury's dorsal and anal fins are further rows of small fins. Sauries swim in shoals in surface waters, feeding on small crustaceans and small fish.

Sauries spawn in open sea. Their eggs, which are small and round and covered with many threads, float at the water surface while they develop. The young fishes hatch with short jaws of equal length; the elongate jaws develop as the fishes grow and mature.

## Ricefish/Japanese Medaka *Oryzias latipes*

**RANGE** Japan

**HABITAT** Coastal marshes, rice fields

**SIZE** 1½ in (4 cm)

The ricefish is one of a family of 8 species of fish, known as medakas, and found in Southeast Asia and Japan. It is a small, slender fish, with a flattened head and an almost straight back. The underside of the body is distinctly curved, and there is a long-based anal fin. In the male the dorsal fin is pointed, but in the female it is rounded. Medakas are useful to mankind in that they feed on mosquito larvae and other small invertebrates.

Medakas breed by laying eggs. At first, the female carries her eggs around in a mucous sheath attached to her belly, but then she deposits them among submerged plants, where they complete their development and hatch out up to 12 days after they were laid.

# CYPRINIDONTIFORM FISHES

## ORDER CYPRINODONTIFORMES

This major group of freshwater fish includes 807 species in 8 families that include rivulines, killifishes, foureye fishes, livebearers, splitfins, guppies, and pupfishes. Most are small omnivorous fish although there are also some predatory and some herbivorous species.

Cyprinodontiforms are noted for their ability to live in habitats in both temperate and tropical regions that are unsuitable for most other fish. This includes stagnant, saline or even hypersaline conditions.

Most are surface swimmers that feed on insects and vegetation that has fallen onto the water. Because of their living near the surface cyprinodontiforms are sometimes referred to as top-minnows, although they are not related to true minnows (Cyprinidae). They are also referred to as toothcarps because of the presence of small teeth in the jaws and their superficial resemblance to carp.

### Sheepshead Minnow *Cyprinidon variegatus*

**RANGE** USA coasts: Cape Cod to Texas, south to Mexico

**HABITAT** Bays, harbors, salt marshes

**SIZE** 3 in (7.5 cm)

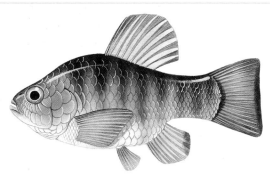

The sheepshead minnow has a short, stubby body and a high back and a prominent dorsal fin. Outside the breeding season, both males and females appear similar, but females have darker markings. Breeding males develop much brighter coloration, turning steely-blue and green, with orange or red bellies.

Sheepshead minnows feed on a wide range of tiny invertebrates and aquatic plants.

Breeding takes place between April and September and males compete for mates. The female lays her eggs a few at a time while the male clasps her round the tail and fertilizes the eggs as they are shed. The eggs have sticky threads on their surface which attach them to each other and to plants or objects on the bottom.

## Mummichog/Common Killifish

*Fundulus heteroclitus*

**RANGE** N. American coasts: Labrador to Mexico

**HABITAT** Bays, marshes, river mouths

**SIZE** 4–6 in (10–15 cm)

The stout-bodied mummichog is an adaptable and hardy little fish which is able to tolerate brackish, salt and fresh water.

It is a voracious feeder and will eat almost any available plants and animals.

Mummichogs breed between April and August in shallow water. The male chases his mate in an extensive courtship ritual and then clasps her with his fins in order to fertilize the eggs as they are laid. The sticky-surfaced eggs then sink to the bottom in a cluster.

*Aphanius dispar*

**RANGE** Indian Ocean: coasts of E. Africa and Middle East; Red Sea

**HABITAT** Coastal waters

**SIZE** 3¼ in (8 cm)

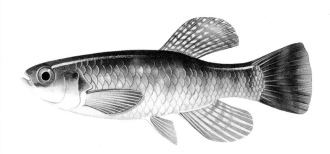

This adaptable toothcarp occurs in fresh- and saltwater pools in its range, as well as in the sea. Males and females of the species differ slightly in coloration. The males are brownish blue with dark markings near and on the tail, while females are a grayish blue with markings on their sides. This toothcarp feed on small invertebrates and algae.

The female sheds her eggs on to submerged aquatic plants. The eggs hatch out in under 2 weeks, and the young fishes feed on plant plankton and algae.

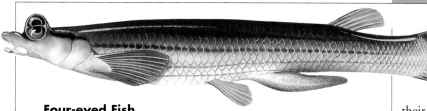

## Four-eyed Fish

*Anableps anableps*

**RANGE** S. Mexico, Central America and N. South America

**HABITAT** Coasts, estuaries, lakes

**SIZE** 11¾ in (30 cm)

The four-eyed fish has, in fact, only two eyes, which project well above the head and are divided into two parts. The top section of each eye is adapted for vision in the air and the lower for vision in water; the sections are separated by a dark band. The fish swims at the surface, the water reaching the level of the dividing bands on the eyes, and is able to watch for insect prey at the surface or in the air and any prey swimming just under water, at the same time.

Four-eyed fish bear live young and females are fertilized internally. The male's anal fin is modified into a copulatory organ which can be moved either to the left or the right, and the female's genital opening is covered by a specialized scale which opens to the left or right. It is believed that a "left-handed" male must copulate with a "right-handed" female and vice versa; fortunately it seems that the proportion of right and left mating types is more or less equal in both sexes. The eggs develop inside the mother's body, and 4 or 5 live young are born.

## Guppy *Poecilia reticulata*

**RANGE** N. South America to Brazil; Barbados, Trinidad; introduced in many tropical areas

**HABITAT** Streams, pools

**SIZE** 2¼ in (6 cm)

The guppy occurs naturally over a wide range and has been spread by humans as a pest controller, since it feeds on the aquatic larvae of mosquitos. It is an extremely abundant fish, occurring in huge numbers in brackish as well as fresh water. Females are generally larger than males and less attractively colored, with dull, brownish bodies. As well as feeding on mosquito larvae, guppies eat other insect larvae, small crustaceans and the eggs and young of other fishes.

Guppies breed throughout the year bearing litters of live young. The male's anal fin is modified as a copulatory organ for internal fertilization of the female. The young develop inside the mother and their egg membranes burst as they are born. Up to 24 young are born at a time and they achieve sexual maturity in between 4 and 10 weeks, depending on the temperature of their surroundings. This ability to mature fast and to breed many times a year leads to such large populations of guppies that they are called millions fish in some areas. Many different brilliantly colored forms are bred as aquarium fish.

## Cape Lopez Lyretail *Aphyosemion australe*

**RANGE** Africa: Gabon, Cape Lopez area

**HABITAT** Swamps, ditches

**SIZE** 2¼ in (6 cm)

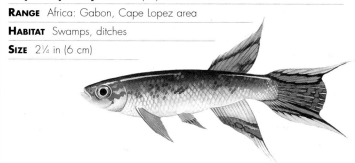

The male Cape Lopez lyretail is an attractive, brightly colored fish, with large, pointed dorsal and anal fins and a tail with extended lobes. The female is plainer, and her fins lack the decorative points and extensions.

The lyretail deposits its eggs among the mud and detritus at the bottom of its habitat. If there is then a prolonged dry season, the embryos cease their development and lie dormant in the mud, protected by their drought-resistant egg membrane. Although the parent fishes die in the drought, the eggs resume development with the arrival of rain and hatch shortly afterwards.

## Least Killifish/Dwarf Top-minnow *Heterandria formosa*

**RANGE** Streams, ponds, ditches, swamps

**HABITAT** USA, South Carolina, Florida

**SIZE** ¾–1¼ in (2–3.5 cm)

One of the smallest vertebrates at only ¾ in (2 cm) long, adult males of this species are smaller than females. The fishes live among dense aquatic vegetation and feed on mosquitoes and minute crustaceans.

Least killifish have unusual breeding habits. After mating, the eggs develop a few at a time and are fertilized inside the female by sperm that were deposited by the male at mating.

The young are born over a period of a week or more at the rate of 2 or 3 a day. This is a popular aquarium species.

# CYPRINODONTIFORM FISHES AND ATHERINIFORM FISHES

**Pike Top-minnow** *Belonesox belizanus*

**RANGE** Mexico, Central America to Honduras

**HABITAT** Muddy backwaters, marshes, lakes

**SIZE** 47 in (10–20 cm)

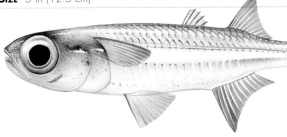

A long-bodied fish, the pike top-minnow has a pointed snout and a large mouth. It resembles a tiny pike and hunts in the same way, lurking among vegetation then dashing out quickly from its hiding place in order to seize passing prey.

Females are larger than males, sometimes reaching twice their size. These fishes are thought to have considerably reduced in number due to insecticides which have been sprayed on to the waters of their habitats in order to destroy mosquito larvae.

Female pike top-minnows produce 20 to 80 live young at a time. Although rather predatory, top-minnows are used as aquarium fish.

**Swordtail** *Xiphophorus helleri*

**RANGE** Mexico, Guatemala

**HABITAT** Springs, streams, rivers, lagoons, swamps

**SIZE** 5 in (12.5 cm)

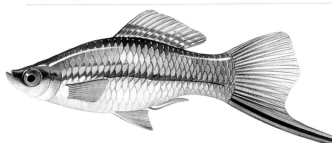

In male swordtails the lower lobe of the tail is greatly extended into a slim, bladelike projection from which the common name is derived. Females lack this tail extension and are less brightly colored.

The range of habitats of this species is reflected in the number of forms, differing in coloration, shape and tail development, which have arisen to fit them. Swordtails feed on

small aquatic invertebrates.

Like all members of the family Poeciliidae, the swordtail produces live young. The male fertilizes the female internally, and the young fish develop inside her ovarian cavity.

The female swordtail is known to change sex, but the reasons for this are not clear. She stops producing young, develops the tail extension and male coloration and gradually becomes a totally functional male. Males do not change into females.

These little fishes have become popular aquarium fish and have been bred in a variety of colors.

## ORDER ATHERINIFORMES

These are mostly small, silvery fishes with large eyes and two dorsal fins. The 285 or so species include silversides, rainbowfishes, blueeyes, and grunions. About half of the species in the order are silversides. These plankton feeders are found in large shoals in lakes, estuaries, and shallow marine habitats.

**Hardhead Silverside** *Atherinomorus stipes*

**RANGE** N. Atlantic Ocean: Florida to Brazil, including Caribbean

**HABITAT** Inshore waters

**SIZE** 5 in (12.5 cm)

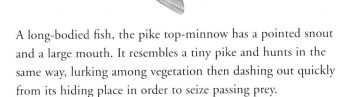

The hardhead silverside has an elongated, cylindrical body and two dorsal fins. The first dorsal fins consists of spines. The hardhead silverside's eyes are large relative to its body size. The coloration of this species is variable. During the day it is almost transparent, with a narrow silvery stripe running down its body. Then when night falls the color darkens.

These silversides are abundant, and they occur in large shoals. They lay eggs bearing threads, which anchor them to aquatic plants while they develop.

*Phenacostethus smithi*

**RANGE** Thailand

**HABITAT** Fresh water: muddy pools, ditches, canals

**SIZE** 1 in (2 cm)

One of the tiniest of fishes, this abundant species occurs in small schools and feeds on microscopic planktonic organisms. It has minute scales and two dorsal fins (one of which is just a spine) and a disproportionately long anal fin. Since the body is virtually transparent, the internal organs are visible.

These fishes have no pelvic fins, but the male has a complex copulatory organ, positioned just behind the chin, that involves some of the pelvic structure. The female's urogenital opening is in the same position and is covered by a specialized scale. The fishes spawn from May to December, the male clasping the female and fertilizing the eggs as they are laid.

### California Grunion *Leuresthes tenuis*

**RANGE** Pacific Ocean: coasts of California and Baja California

**HABITAT** Inshore waters

**SIZE** 7 in (18 cm)

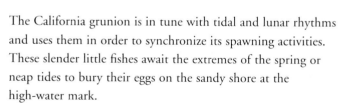

The California grunion is in tune with tidal and lunar rhythms and uses them in order to synchronize its spawning activities. These slender little fishes await the extremes of the spring or neap tides to bury their eggs on the sandy shore at the high-water mark.

They spawn at night between March and August, but the spawning peaks between May and June. Once the high-water mark is reached by the waves, the grunion swim ashore in huge numbers, mate and lay their eggs in shallow scrapes which they dig in the sand. The next wave covers the eggs with sand and carries the fish from the beach back into the sea. Two weeks later, at the extreme high of the next high tides, the eggs are exposed, which triggers hatching. The spawning cycle is thus entirely predictable and is associated with the tidal rhythms.

The vast numbers of California grunion that gather in order to take part in the fortnightly spawning runs attract many predators, including man. Fishermen are allowed to take only a limited quantity of the fishes.

### Sandsmelt *Atherina presbyter*

**RANGE** E. Atlantic Ocean: coasts of Britain, Ireland, France, Spain, Portugal and N. Africa

**HABITAT** Inshore waters, estuaries

**SIZE** 6–8 in (15–2 cm)

Sandsmelts are small schooling fishes which are found worldwide, mostly in tropical and warm temperate seas. This species is one of the few found in northern waters and is fairly typical of its family with its long, slender body and two widely spaced dorsal fins; the first dorsal fin has seven or eight spines. Schools of sandsmelts are most common on sandy or muddy bottoms, and young fishes may sometimes be found in coastal rock pools.

The jaws of sandsmelts are highly protrusible, and small crustaceans form their main food, although they occasionally eat tiny fish. Sandsmelts are themselves preyed upon by larger fishes and by seabirds such as terns.

Breeding starts between late spring and midsummer. Sandsmelts often spawn in shore pools, laying eggs that bear long threads, which anchor them to seaweed. The newly hatched young are about ⅓ in (7 mm) long.

### Crimson-spotted Rainbowfish *Melanotaenia fluviatilis*

**RANGE** Australia: South Australia, New South Wales, Queensland

**HABITAT** Rivers, streams

**SIZE** 3 in (9 cm)

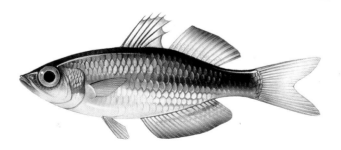

The colorful crimson-spotted rainbowfish occurs over a vast area and is one of about 53 species of rainbowfish all found in Australia or New Guinea. In early summer it lays its eggs, which become safely anchored to aquatic plants by means of fine threads and hatch in about 9 days. This rainbowfish is a popular aquarium species.

# LAMPRIDIFORM FISHES, WHALE FISHES AND BERYCIFORM FISHES

## LAMPRIDIFORMES

There are about 19 species of marine fish in this little-studied, relatively little-known order. The lampridiformes include the opahs, crestfishes, oarfishes and ribbonfishes. Many of these fish are extremely large. The oarfish (*Regalecus*), for example, may sometimes exceed 20 ft (6 m) in length.

Most are without scales, and have laterally flattened bodies, but some species have fragile, modified scales. The opah is deep-bodied, but most other species are elongate, resembling flattened eels. They have no true spines in their fins.

### Oarfish *Regalecus glesne*

**RANGE** Atlantic, Pacific and Indian Oceans: temperate and tropical areas

**HABITAT** Open sea at 980–2,000 ft (300–600 m)

**SIZE** Up to 23 ft (7 m)

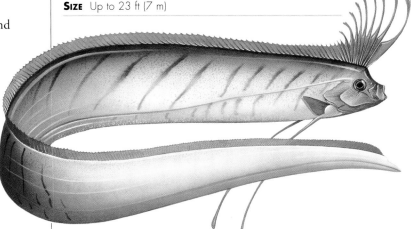

The oarfish has a long, ribbonlike body, which is extremely compressed at the sides. The dorsal fin originates just behind the snout and runs the length of the body; its first few rays are elongate and form a crest. There is no anal fin, but the pelvic fins, tipped with flaps of skin, are long and slender. The oarfish swims with rippling movements and is thought to have given rise to many tales about sea serpents.

The oarfish has a small, protrusible mouth and no teeth and feeds on shrimplike crustaceans. There are thought to be only 1 or 2 species of these strange-looking fishes.

### Opah *Lampris guttatus*

**RANGE** Worldwide except Antarctic; most common in temperate and tropical seas

**HABITAT** Open sea, mid-waters at 330–1,300 ft (100–400 m)

**SIZE** 5 ft (1.5 m)

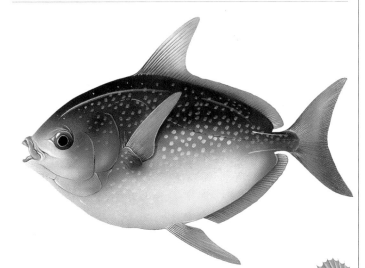

A striking, colorful fish, the opah is predominantly bright blue, dotted with white on the upper part of its body. It has well-developed red fins. An adult opah may weigh as much as 161 lb (73 kg) .

The opah has a protrusible mouth and it is toothless, but despite its lack of armory and its apparently awkward shape, it is a successful predator, feeding mainly on squid and fish such as hake and blue whiting.

Little is known of the biology and habits of this fish, and it is rarely seen.

### Dealfish *Trachipterus arcticus*

**RANGE** N.E. Atlantic Ocean: Greenland and Iceland to Madeira and N. Africa

**HABITAT** Open sea, mid-depths

**SIZE** 8¼ ft (2.5 m)

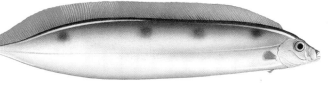

The dealfish has a long, laterally compressed body, with a distinctive red dorsal fin running almost its entire length. It has tiny pelvic fins, no anal fin and an upturned tail fin. There are several dark blotches on its silvery sides. It has a protrusible mouth and eats fish, squid and crustaceans. It may sometimes move in small schools but is more often found alone.

*Atelopus japonicus*

**RANGE** Indian and Pacific Oceans:
E. African coast to Japan

**HABITAT** Deep sea, 600–1,800 ft (180–550 m)

**SIZE** 24 in (61 cm)

This fish has a long, tapering body and a relatively large head. It has threadlike pelvic fins, a high, shortbased dorsal fin and a long anal fin, which unites with the reduced tail fin. The body is soft and fragile, and the few specimens found have been damaged. There are teeth only in the upper jaw; the lower jaw is set back under the protruding snout.

This little-known fish is thought to feed on the seabed on bottom-dwelling invertebrates.

# ORDER STEPHANOBERYCIFORMES

The 86 species in this order are mainly nocturnal, predatory deep sea fish with light organs and weak or absent fin spines. Species include whalefish, gibberfish, and pricklefish.

**Whalefish** *Cetomimus indagator*

**RANGE** Indian Ocean

**HABITAT** Deep sea

**SIZE** 5½ in (14 cm)

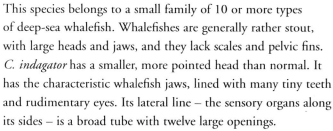

This species belongs to a small family of 10 or more types of deep-sea whalefish. Whalefishes are generally rather stout, with large heads and jaws, and they lack scales and pelvic fins. *C. indagator* has a smaller, more pointed head than normal. It has the characteristic whalefish jaws, lined with many tiny teeth and rudimentary eyes. Its lateral line – the sensory organs along its sides – is a broad tube with twelve large openings.

At the bases of the dorsal and anal fins, whalefishes have soft luminous tissue that is believed to glow in the dark. These fishes have soft, fragile bodies and have rarely been caught undamaged. Only one specimen of *C. indagator* has been found.

# BERYCIFORMES

This order includes about 123 species of marine fishes, grouped in 7 families. Forms include whalefish, squirrelfish, lanterneyes, pinecone fish, slimeheads and beardfish. Most are deep-bodied, large-eyed fishes with spiny fins. Most families contain fewer than a dozen species. The family of squirrelfishes, Holocentridae, is the largest with more than 60 species.

**Pinecone Fish** *Monocentris japonicus*

**RANGE** Indian and Pacific Oceans: South Africa to Japan

**HABITAT** Open sea at 100–600 ft (30–180 m)

**SIZE** 5 in (12.5 cm)

The body of the pinecone fish is encased in an armor of heavy, platelike scales. Its dorsal fin consists of stout spines, directed alternately to left and right, and it has large pelvic spines. Under the lower jaw it has two light-producing organs. Their luminescence is not generated by luminous cells in the fish – as in the case of photophores, possessed by some other fishes – but by luminous bacteria, living symbiotically with the fish.

Pinecone fish move in schools near to the bottom of the sea. There is only 1 other species in the family, also found in the Indian and Pacific oceans.

**Squirrelfish** *Holocentrus ascensionis*

**RANGE** Atlantic Ocean: Bermuda, Gulf of Mexico to Brazil; vicinity of Ascension Island

**HABITAT** Coastal waters in tropical and warm temperate areas

**SIZE** 24 in (61 cm)

This brightly colored squirrelfish is common on coral reefs or in rocky-bottomed areas. Its scales are large and rough, and it has a strong spine on the gill cover. It hides in crannies and rock crevices during the day and emerges at night to feed, mainly on small crustaceans.

Squirrelfishes make a variety of sounds by vibrating the swim bladder with the aid of specialized muscles. The sounds are believed to be part of territorial and breeding behavior.

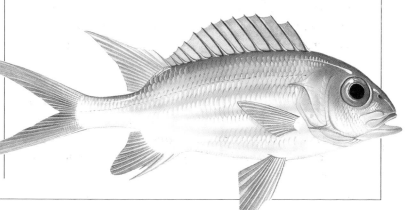

# BERYCIFORM FISHES

*Adioryx xantherythrus*

**RANGE** Pacific Ocean: Hawaiian Islands

**HABITAT** Coral reefs

**SIZE** 7 in (18 cm)

This Hawaiian squirrelfish resembles the other members of its family, with its reddish and pink body and stout dorsal spines. It is a nocturnal fish, remaining hidden in the reef during the day and emerging at night to feed on small invertebrates.

Like the rest of the squirrelfishes, this species is able to produce sounds with its swim bladder which are believed to form part of courtship behavior.

*Anomalops kaptoptron*

**RANGE** S. Pacific Ocean: Indonesian coasts

**HABITAT** Shallow offshore waters

**SIZE** 11¾ in (30 cm)

One of a small family of 3 species known as lanterneyes, this is a heavy, deep-bodied fish with stout dorsal spines. Its head is broad and strong, and it has the large eyes characteristic of the order. Active at night, it swims in small shoals.

Lanterneyes are among the few shallow-water fishes to possess luminous organs. Beneath each eye there is an oval bar, which appears white in daylight but shines brightly at night. Inside the bar-shaped organ are many tubes containing luminous bacteria, which live symbiotically with the fish and give off light. If the fish needs to dispense with its light for a while, the organs can be rotated so that the luminous sides are turned downward and masked. The fish blinks its lights as it swims, but it is not known whether this is to communicate with other fishes, to attract prey, or to help it navigate.

**Roughie** *Hoplostethus atlanticus*

**RANGE** N. Atlantic Ocean

**HABITAT** Deep sea at 1,650–3,300 ft (500–1,000 m)

**SIZE** 11¾ in (30 cm)

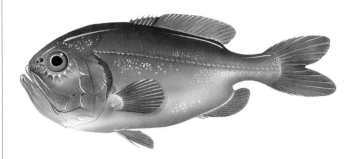

The brightly colored roughie has a large head and deep body, compressed at the sides, and there are strong spines on its belly and preceding its dorsal fin. Its mouth is large and upturned, and the jaws are equipped with many tiny, closeset teeth. Although little is known of its habits, the roughie is thought to feed mainly on crustaceans.

Fishes, such as the roughie, that belong to the family trachichthyidae are also known as slimeheads because of the many mucus-secreting cavities on their heads.

*Photoblepharon palpebratus*

**RANGE** Indian and Pacific Oceans

**HABITAT** Shallow offshore waters

**SIZE** 3¼ in (8 cm)

A stout fish, with prominent fins and a forked tail, *P. palpebratus* is active only at night. It is a member of the lanterneye family and, like its relatives, has a light organ beneath each eye which appears white in daylight but shines at night. Inside the organ are tubes containing luminous bacteria, which live on the fish and in return produce light. To turn the light off, the fish raises a fold of dark skin across the organ.

Local fishermen remove the lanterneye's light organs, which remain luminous for many hours, and use them as fishing lures.

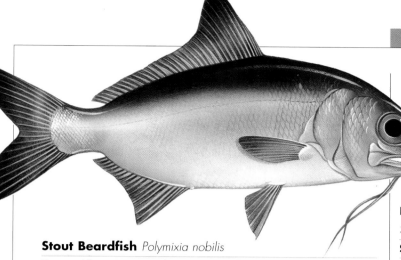

prey by slowly stalking it until it can engulf the victim within its vast jaws.

### John Dory *Zeus faber*

**RANGE** E. Atlantic Ocean: N. Scotland to South Africa; Mediterranean Sea

**HABITAT** Inshore waters at 33–164 ft (10–50 m)

**SIZE** 15¾–26 in (40–66 cm)

The John dory is identified by its deep body and large head with protrusible, steeply sloping jaws. There are nine or ten stout spines in the front portion of the dorsal fin, and three or four preceding the anal fin. On each side, above the pectoral fin, there is a characteristic, light bordered black patch.

Usually a solitary fish, the John dory may occasionally move in small schools. It is not a fast swimmer and catches prey by stealth rather than speed. Keeping its flattened body head on and, therefore, harder to spot, it approaches prey slowly until close enough to engulf it in its huge mouth. Small fish and crustaceans make up the bulk of the fish's diet.

Although rarely caught in large numbers, the John dory is highly thought of as a food fish in Europe. An almost identical species of dory, *Z. japonicus*, occurs in the Indian and Pacific oceans.

### Stout Beardfish *Polymixia nobilis*

**RANGE** All oceans, tropical areas

**HABITAT** Deep water

**SIZE** 9¾ in (25 cm)

Beardfishes are found in tropical and subtropical regions of the Atlantic, Indian and Pacific oceans, usually at depths of 600 to 2,000 ft (180 to 640 m). A deep-bodied fish, the stout beardfish has a pair of long barbels dangling from its lower jaw which may help it to find food on the seabed. The coloration of its fully scaled body is variable, but its tail fin and the tip of the dorsal fin are usually dark, almost black. The almost identical species, *P. japonicus*, is found in the Sea of Japan.

## ZEIFORMES

There are about 39 species in this order, which includes the dories, the boarfishes and some lesser-known deep-sea species. All are marine fishes. Typically zeiformes have laterally compressed, deep bodies and large, prominent eyes. There are usually heavy spines in the anterior parts of the dorsal and anal fins. Most have jaws that open very wide.

### Boarfish *Capros aper*

**RANGE** E. Atlantic Ocean: Ireland to Senegal; Mediterranean Sea

**HABITAT** Rocky-bottomed open sea at 330–1,300 ft (100–400 m)

**SIZE** 4–6¼ in (10–16 cm)

This small relative of the dories also has a deep, laterally compressed body. The head is pointed, with a small mouth, but the jaws are protrusible and lined with fine teeth. Each pelvic fin bears a strong spine, and there are long, stout spines in the first dorsal fin. Small, finely toothed scales cover the body, making it rough to the touch. Like all members of its family, the boarfish is reddish in coloration.

Boarfishes feed on crustaceans, worms and mollusks. They spawn in the summer, and the eggs float freely in surface waters until they hatch.

### American John Dory *Zenopsis ocellata*

**RANGE** W. Atlantic Ocean: Nova Scotia to Chesapeake Bay

**HABITAT** Offshore waters

**SIZE** 24 in (61 cm)

The American John dory, like its European relative, has a deep, greatly compressed body. Its protruding lower jaw is steeply angled, the tip being almost on a line with the eyes. There are nine or ten stout spines in the first dorsal fin. The anal fin bears three or four short, stout spines. Adults are silvery in color, but the young fish has several irregular dark spots on each side. These gradually disappear as the fish matures, most adults having only a single spot on each side near the gill opening. Like all dories, this species catches its

# GASTEROSTEIFORM FISHES

## ORDER GASTEROSTEIFORMES

The 260 or so species in this order include some of the most unusual and well-known of the bony fish, including sticklebacks, seahorses, and pipefish.

The sticklebacks and their relatives the tubesnouts are spiny-finned fishes found in both the sea and freshwater in the northern hemisphere. Sticklebacks are territorial nest-builders that are easily recognised by the presence of between 3 and 16 spines along the back. Within 2 of the 8 species of sticklebacks – the threespine stickleback, *Gasterosteus aculeatus*, and the ninespine stickleback, *Pungitius pungitius* – there is enormous diversity over their ranges.

The 225 species of unusually-shaped pipefishes and seahorses cannot move quickly and depend on armor and secretive behavior to camouflage them from predators. Most inhabit shallow marine waters.

### Threespine Stickleback *Gasterosteus aculeatus*

**RANGE** N. America: Pacific and Atlantic coasts and fresh water; Europe: coasts and fresh water, north to Arctic Circle; N. Asia; N. Pacific Ocean: Bering Strait to Korea

**HABITAT** Coastal waters, lakes, rivers

**SIZE** 2–4 in (5–10 cm)

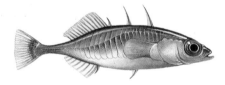

A small fish, with three characteristic spines on its back, this stickleback is scaleless but it is armored with bony plates. It feeds on almost any available small creatures, such as crustaceans, worms, mollusks, fish eggs and larvae, and even on some plant material.

In the breeding season – spring and early summer in North America and Europe – the male stickleback develops a bright red belly. He makes a nest on the bottom from plant fragments, glued together with mucous secretions. He then displays, to attract several females to his nest, where they lay eggs, which he immediately fertilizes. The male then guards the eggs carefully, driving away any predators and fanning water into the nest in order to aerate the eggs, which hatch in about 3 weeks.

### Fifteenspine Stickleback *Spinachia spinachia*

**RANGE** Coasts of Scandinavia, Britain, N. Europe

**HABITAT** Shallow, coastal waters

**SIZE** 6–7½ in (15–19 cm)

A slender, long-bodied fish, with a pointed snout, this stickleback is identified by the 14 to 17 (usually 15) spines on its back. It lives only in the sea, generally in areas where there is abundant seaweed, and feeds on small crustaceans.

The male makes a nest from scraps of marine plants, stuck together with his mucous secretions, and then attracts a series of females into his nest to lay their eggs. He fertilizes and then guards the eggs until they hatch 18 to 21 days later.

### Fourspine Stickleback *Apeltes quadracus*

**RANGE** W. Atlantic Ocean: E. coast of N. America, Nova Scotia to Virginia

**HABITAT** Coastal waters, brackish and fresh water

**SIZE** 2¼ in (6 cm)

Found in salt and fresh water, the fourspine stickleback prefers areas with plenty of seaweed. Its body is naked, lacking the plates of the threespine stickleback, but there are bony ridges on each side of the belly. Small crustaceans are its main food.

Like other sticklebacks, these fishes spawn in spring and early summer, and the male builds a nest in which females lay eggs. The male guards the eggs until they hatch.

### Tubesnout *Aulorhynchus flavidus*

**RANGE** Pacific Ocean: coast of N. America from Alaska to Baja California

**HABITAT** Inshore waters

**SIZE** 6¼ in (16 cm)

The tubesnout has a long, cylindrical body which tapers toward the tail. The small mouth is at the tip

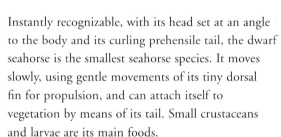

of the long, rigid snout. There is one normal dorsal fin, placed opposite the anal fin, but in front of this are 24 to 26 isolated spines, which make up the first dorsal fin. Tubesnouts move in large shoals of hundreds, or even thousands, of individuals and feed on small crustaceans, as well as on other items of plankton.

The female deposits her eggs in a nest of algae, which is stuck together with threads of mucus, extruded by the male.

### Winged Dragon *Pegasus volitans* DD
**RANGE** Indian and Pacific Oceans, E. Africa to N. Australia
**HABITAT** Sandy-bottomed shallow waters
**SIZE** 5½ in (14 cm)

A curious fish, the winged dragon has a broad, flattened body, surrounded with bony rings, and a tapering tail. The snout is long and flattened, with a small mouth on the underside. The pectoral fins are broad and winglike, while the other fins are all relatively small.

### Shrimpfish *Aeoliscus strigatus*
**RANGE** Indian and Pacific Oceans to N. Australia
**HABITAT** Coastal waters, open sea
**SIZE** 6 in (15 cm)

The shrimpfish has a flat, compressed body with a sharp-edged belly. At the end of its body is a long spine, formed by part of the tail fin. The fish frequently swims in a vertical position, with its elongate snout held downward, propelling itself with its tail and anal fins. It is often found among the spines of sea urchins, where dark stripes along the sides of its body, which mimic the spines, provide camouflage. They also conceal the fish's eyes, which might otherwise reveal its presence.

### Greater Pipefish *Syngnathus acus*
**RANGE** E. Atlantic Ocean: coasts of Norway to N. Africa; Mediterranean and Adriatic Seas
**HABITAT** Shallow waters with sandy or muddy bottoms
**SIZE** 11¾–18½ in (30–47 cm)

The body of the greater pipefish is encased in bony armor, which forms distinct segments. Its snout is long and tubular, with a small mouth at the tip, and the main means of propulsion is the pronounced dorsal fin. It feeds on small crustaceans and other tiny planktonic creatures, as well as on young fish.

Breeding occurs from May to August. Like all pipefishes, the male incubates the eggs in a brood pouch, which in this species is a double fold of skin positioned under the tail. The eggs are incubated for about 5 weeks, and on hatching, the perfectly formed young are released through a slit, where the folds of the pouch meet.

### Dwarf Seahorse
*Hippocampus zosterae* VU
**RANGE** W. Atlantic Ocean: Florida through Gulf of Mexico to Caribbean
**HABITAT** Shallow waters
**SIZE** 1½ in (4 cm)

Instantly recognizable, with its head set at an angle to the body and its curling prehensile tail, the dwarf seahorse is the smallest seahorse species. It moves slowly, using gentle movements of its tiny dorsal fin for propulsion, and can attach itself to vegetation by means of its tail. Small crustaceans and larvae are its main foods.

The breeding season extends from February to October, and the female lays 50 or more eggs, which she places in the male's brood pouch.

### Weedy Seadragon *Phyllopteryx taeniolatus* DD
**RANGE** Coasts of S. Australia
**HABITAT** Shallow waters
**SIZE** 18 in (46 cm)

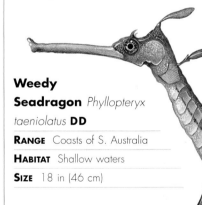

Although little is known of the habits of this strange seahorse, the many leaflike flaps of skin on its body are presumed to give it a protective resemblance to fronds of seaweed.

Like all seahorses, the male incubates the eggs on a flap of skin beneath his tail.

# SWAMP EELS, FLYING GURNARDS AND SCORPAENIFORM FISHES

## SYNBRANCHIFORMES ORDER

There are about 87 species in this order, 7 of which are marine. They are grouped in 3 families – swamp eels, spiny eels and chaudiriid eels. Swamp eels are not, however, true eels but have an eellike body shape and extremely reduced fins. Their gill system is minute and is linked with a variety of organs for breathing air and techniques of doing so.

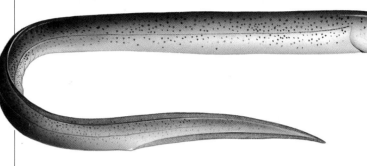

### Rice Eel *Monopterus alba*
**RANGE** Japan, N. China to Thailand and Burma
**HABITAT** Rivers, ponds, rice fields
**SIZE** 35¾ in (91 cm)

The rice eel has an elongate, scaleless body and lacks pectoral and pelvic fins. The dorsal and anal fins are low and join with the tail fin. There are one or two gill openings on the throat, but the fish, commonly lives in stagnant, oxygen-poor water, and often breathes air at the surface. In dry seasons, rice eels burrow into the mud and stay alive until rains arrive, provided their skin remains moist.

The male rice eel makes a nest by blowing a cluster of bubbles of air and mucus. The eggs are shed among these bubbles, and the whole structure floats freely, guarded by the male.

### Spiny Eel *Mastacembelus armatus*
**RANGE** India, Sri Lanka, S.E. Asia, China, Sumatra, Java, Borneo
**HABITAT** Swamps, rivers, lakes
**SIZE** 29½ in (75 cm)

A slender, eellike fish, the spiny eel has a row of sharp, spines preceding its dorsal fin. It has no pelvic fins, and the dorsal and anal fins are near the tail. The head is narrow and pointed, and the upper part of the snout extends into a fleshy appendage. This eel eats insects and crustaceans; adults eat fish.

## DACTYLOPTERIFORMES FLYING GURNARD ORDER

This order contains 1 family of 7 species of marine fishes, found in tropical and warm temperate areas of the Atlantic and Indo-Pacific Oceans. They have large pectoral fins, but there is no evidence that these fish fly above the water.

### Flying Gurnard *Dactylopterus volitans*
**RANGE** W. Atlantic Ocean: Bermuda through Caribbean to Argentina; E. Atlantic: Portugal to W. Africa; Mediterranean Sea
**HABITAT** Bottom of shallow waters
**SIZE** 11¾–16 in (30–40.5 cm)

A bottom-dwelling fish, the flying gurnard uses its long winglike pelvic fins to "walk" over the seabed searching for crustaceans. If alarmed, the gurnard may spread its fins, revealing the blue spots on their surfaces.

## SCORPAENIFORMES SCORPIONFISH ORDER

This large, widely distributed order contains 24 families and nearly 1,300 species of fish, most of which are marine. Body form is variable, but most species are thick-set and spiny.

### Rascasse *Scorpaena porcus*
**RANGE** Mediterranean and Black Seas; N. Atlantic Ocean: Biscay to Madeira
**HABITAT** Shallow waters
**SIZE** 9¾ in (25 cm)

The rascasse lurks amid seaweed-covered rocks, where its camouflaging coloration and the weedlike flaps of skin on its head make it almost invisible. Its dorsal fin is spiny, with venom glands at the sides of the spines. The fish breed in spring or early summer. Eggs are shed in a mass of gelatinous mucus. Rascasse are an essential ingredient of the French fish-stew *bouillabaisse*.

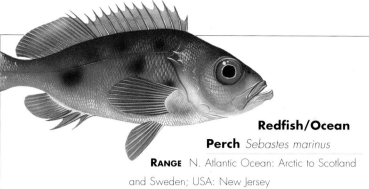

## Redfish/Ocean Perch *Sebastes marinus*

**RANGE** N. Atlantic Ocean: Arctic to Scotland and Sweden; USA: New Jersey

**HABITAT** Deep water: 330–1,300 ft (100–400 m)

**SIZE** 31¾ in–3¼ ft (81 cm–1 m)

A heavy-bodied fish, with a large head and a protuberant lower jaw, the redfish has a strongly spined dorsal fin and three spines on the anal fin. By day it stays close to the bottom, rising to surface waters at night to feed on fish such as herring and cod.

Redfishes bear live young. In the north of their range the male fertilizes the female internally in late summer. Females then migrate south during winter and give birth to up to 40,000 larval young the next May or June. The young are about ⅗₀ in (8 mm) long at birth and eat plankton at first, then crustaceans.

## Lionfish *Pterois volitans*

**RANGE** Indian and Pacific Oceans

**HABITAT** Shallow waters, reefs

**SIZE** 15 in (38 cm)

The lionfish has long, fanlike pectoral fins, branched dorsal fin and brightly striped body. This eye-catching coloration warns potential enemies that the lionfish's grooved spines are equipped with potent venom, which can have serious, perhaps fatal, effects, even in humans.

## Stonefish *Synanceia verrucosa*

**RANGE** Indian and Pacific Oceans: Africa and Red Sea to N. Australia

**HABITAT** Shallow water, coral reefs

**SIZE** 11¾ in (30 cm)

About 20 species of stonefish occur in the Indo-Pacific. All have needlelike dorsal-fin spines, equipped with venom glands that produce the most deadly of all fish venoms. Wounds from a stonefish can kill any human unlucky enough to tread on the spines. This species is typical of its family, with its rough, scaleless body, large,

upward-turning head and protuberant eyes. As its name suggests, the stonefish's coloring and shape camouflage it perfectly as it lies half-buried among stones or in rock crevices.

## Tub Gurnard *Trigla lucerna*

**RANGE** E. Atlantic Ocean: Norway, British Isles to N. Africa; coasts of Black, Adriatic and Mediterranean Seas

**HABITAT** Inshore waters, sandy and muddy bottoms

**SIZE** 19¾–29½ in (50–75 cm)

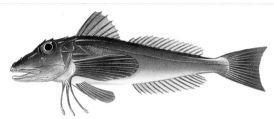

A member of the sea robin family, the tub gurnard has a bony head, pointed snout and well-formed fins. Several rays of the pectoral fins are elongate and free, and they are used by the fish to search for food on the bottom and as props on which to rest. It normally eats bottom-living crustaceans, mollusks and fish.

Tub gurnards are fished commercially in many areas.

## Northern Sea Robin *Prionotus carolinus*

**RANGE** W. Atlantic Ocean: Bay of Fundy to Venezuela

**HABITAT** Seabed, coastal waters

**SIZE** 16 in (41 cm)

The northern sea robin is typical of its family, with its large head covered with bony plates and its fanlike pectoral fins. The lowest three rays of the pectoral fins are free, and they are used to feel for prey, such as fish and crustaceans, on the seabed. Coloration varies from grayish to brown, but the sea robin always has dark, saddlelike markings across its back.

Much of the sea robin's life is spent on the bottom, often supported on its pectoral fins. It quickly buries itself if threatened, leaving the top of its head and eyes exposed. Sea robins can make loud sounds by vibrating their swim-bladders with specialized muscles. They are particularly noisy in the breeding season, which lasts from June to September. The eggs are shed and float at the surface until they hatch.

# SCORPAENIFORM FISHES CONTINUED

## Sablefish *Anoplopoma fimbria*

**RANGE** Pacific Ocean: Japan to Bering Sea, south to Baja California

**HABITAT** Inshore waters, open sea

**SIZE** Up to 3¼ ft (1 m)

The sablefish is a long, slender fish with two well-separated dorsal fins. The head is smooth, lacking the spines and ridges of the related scorpionfishes. Adult sablefishes usually live near the bottom in areas of continental shelf, but young fishes swim in surface waters, often in the open ocean. Sablefishes spawn in winter and early spring.

## Kelp Greenling *Hexagrammos decagrammus*

**RANGE** Pacific coast of N. America: Alaska to California

**HABITAT** Shallow, rocky-bottomed water, kelp beds

**SIZE** 20¾ in (53 cm)

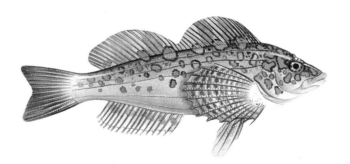

The kelp greenling is one of 11 species of greenling, all found in the North Pacific. Its head is smooth with no spines or ridges, and it has large pectoral fins and a long based dorsal fin which is notched halfway along its length. Males and females differ slightly in appearance, males having blue spots on the foreparts and females reddish-brown spots. Kelp greenlings are unusual in that they have five lateral lines (series of sensory organs) on each side of the body; most fishes have only one.

Kelp greenlings eat worms, crustaceans and small fish, and they themselves are preyed on by larger fishes and fish-eating birds. They spawn in autumn, laying clusters of eggs among the rocks. The young fishes swim in the surface waters of open sea.

## Bullrout/Shorthorn Sculpin *Myoxocephalus scorpius*

**RANGE** N. Atlantic Ocean: Labrador to Cape Cod; N. European coasts: Britain, Scandinavia, Iceland

**HABITAT** Shallow inshore waters to 200 ft (60 m)

**SIZE** 9¾–23½ in (25–60 cm)

Known as the shorthorn sculpin in the USA and the bullrout in Britain, this fish is one of the larger sculpins. It has a broad head, large fins and small spines near its gills and along each side. Females are usually larger than males and have creamy-yellow markings on the belly, where males have orange spots. A bottom-dwelling fish, it feeds mainly on bottom-living crustaceans, as well as on worms and small fish.

It breeds in winter, depositing its sticky-surfaced eggs in clusters among seaweed or in rock crevices. The male guards the eggs until they hatch some 4 to 12 weeks later, depending on the temperature of the water.

## Bullhead *Cottus gobio*

**RANGE** Europe: Sweden and Finland to England and Wales, south to the Pyrenees, Alps, former Yugoslavia

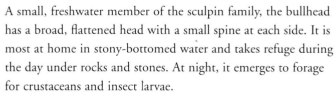

**HABITAT** Streams, small rivers, lakes

**SIZE** 4 in (10 cm)

A small, freshwater member of the sculpin family, the bullhead has a broad, flattened head with a small spine at each side. It is most at home in stony-bottomed water and takes refuge during the day under rocks and stones. At night, it emerges to forage for crustaceans and insect larvae.

Bullheads spawn in spring, from March to May. The male makes a shallow cavity under a rock so that the female can shed her eggs on the underside of the rock. The eggs are guarded by the male until they hatch 3 to 4 weeks later. On hatching, the tiny fishes disperse to find shelter among stones.

## Cabezon *Scorpaenichthys marmoratus*

**RANGE** N. Pacific Ocean: Alaska to Baja California

**HABITAT** Shallow inshore waters to 200 ft (60 m)

**SIZE** 30 in (76 cm)

One of the largest sculpins, the cabezon has a heavy body, smooth, scaleless skin and a deeply notched dorsal fin. Its head and mouth are broad and there is a prominent flap on the snout. Coloration is very variable, but the skin is generally mottled with pale patches. Although most common in rocky bottomed waters, it also lives over sandy bottoms and in kelp beds. Crabs are its main food. It also eats crustaceans and small fish.

Cabezons spawn during the winter from November to March, often using communal sites. A breeding female carries as many as 100,000 eggs which she deposits in masses on rocks. Males guard the eggs until they hatch.

## Oilfish/Baikal Cod *Comephorus baicalensis*

**RANGE** Russia: Lake Baikal

**HABITAT** Deep water

**SIZE** 7½ in (19 cm)

This strange freshwater sculpin is one of a family of only 2 species. It is a long-bodied fish, with no pelvic fins but with long-based dorsal and anal fins. Its head is covered with transparent, delicate skin and it has a large mouth. Although it lives in deep water, it migrates upward at night to feed near the surface on small crustaceans.

Female baikal cod bear live young in the summer in the surface waters of the lake. The other species, *C. dybotwski*, also lives in Lake Baikal.

## Sturgeon Poacher *Agonus acipenserinus*

**RANGE** N. Pacific Ocean: N. American coast, Bering Sea to California

**HABITAT** Coastal muddy-bottomed water at depths of 60–180 ft (18–55 m)

**SIZE** Up to 11¾ in (30 cm)

An elongate, extremely slender fish, the sturgeon poacher has a body armor of non-overlapping bony plates. It has several spines on its large sturgeonlike head and clusters of slender barbels

around its mouth. It lives near or on the seabed and feeds mainly on crustaceans and marine worms. Although a common, abundant species, it has no commercial value.

## Lumpsucker *Cyclopterus lumpus*

**RANGE** N. Atlantic Ocean: Arctic to Scandinavia, Iceland, British Isles; Newfoundland to New Jersey, USA

**HABITAT** Shallow waters to 650 ft (200 m), usually on seabed

**SIZE** 11¾–23½ in (30–60 cm)

The lumpsucker has a round, deep body, studded with rows of spined plates along the sides. Its skin is scaleless. The ventral fins are modified to form the powerful suction disk on its belly with which the lumpsucker attaches itself to the seabed or to rocks and other debris. It feeds on small crustaceans, jellyfishes and other invertebrates, as well as some small fish. Females are usually larger than males.

In late winter or spring, lumpsuckers gather in pairs in shallow coastal waters in order to spawn around the low-tide mark. The female lays as many as 200,000 sticky-surfaced eggs which sink to the bottom in a spongy mass. The male then guards the egg clusters and keeps water flowing through them until they hatch.

The young fishes remain in the coastal shallows during the summer and move out to deeper waters in their first winter.

## Seasnail/Snailfish *Liparis liparis*

**RANGE** N. Atlantic Ocean: Arctic to coasts of Scandinavia, Iceland, British Isles; Greenland to Virginia, USA

**HABITAT** Inshore waters at 16½–490 ft (5–150 m)

**SIZE** 4–7 in (10–18 cm)

A relative of the lumpsuckers, the seasnail or snailfish, is a round-bodied fish with long dorsal and anal fins, both connected with the tail fin. The skin is slimy and scaleless, and on the belly is a strong suction disk with which the seasnail attaches itself to the seabed or to seaweed. It feeds mainly on small crustaceans and worms.

Seasnails spawn in winter or spring. The eggs settle in clusters on seaweed or other objects on the seabed and hatch in 6 to 8 weeks.

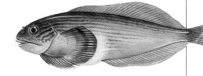

# PERCHLIKE FISHES

## PERCIFORMES PERCHLIKE FISH ORDER

This is the largest and most varied of all fish orders and contains more species than any other vertebrate order. There are 148 families and at least 9,300 species known. The five largest families are the sea basses (Serranidae) with 450 species; cichlids (Cichlidae) with 1,300 species; gobies (Gobiidae) with 1,875 species; wrasses (Labridae) with 500 species and combtooth blennies (Blenniidae) with 345 species.

Perciform fishes have found niches for themselves in almost every conceivable aquatic habitat and in so doing have evolved a diverse range of body forms and habits. They include species as different as the barracuda, the angelfish, the swordfish and the Siamese fightingfish. It is difficult to generalize about such a widely divergent order, but there are a few broad similarities. All forms have one or two dorsal fins. In forms with one dorsal fin, it is elongate and spiny at the front, while in fishes with two dorsal fins, the first is generally spiny and the second soft rayed. Most perciform fishes have pelvic fins, which are placed in close proximity to the head. Each pelvic fin usually has a spine and five rays. The body scales are generally of the type known as ctenoid – they have a rounded front edge and a serrated trailing edge.

Perhaps as many as three-quarters of the species live in waters close to the shore. There are 18 suborders of perchlike fish.

## PERCOIDEI PERCOID SUBORDER

This is the largest perciform suborder with over 2,850 species in 71 families. Many have an elongate body, large mouth and eyes, and two dorsal fins. Mostly inshore predatory fish, the group includes sea bass, bluefish, perch, sunfish, and snappers.

### Snook *Centropomus undecimalis*
**RANGE** Caribbean, north to Florida and South Carolina; south to Brazil
**HABITAT** Coastal waters, estuaries, bays, brackish water
**SIZE** 4½ ft (1.4 m)

One of the largest and most common of the 30 species in the snook family (Centropomidae), this fish has a long, tapering body, a slightly flattened snout and a protruding lower jaw. It eats mainly crustaceans and fish, and adults can

tolerate a wide variety of habitats including almost fresh water.

Snooks spawn from June to November; young fishes, less than a year old, usually live in coastal lagoons and streams. They are mature in their third year. The snook is a popular species with marine fishermen.

### Nile Perch *Lates niloticus*
**RANGE** Africa: Congo, Volta and Niger river systems, Lake Chad
**HABITAT** Rivers, lakes
**SIZE** 6½ ft (2 m)

This widely distributed member of the snook family has been introduced into many man-made lakes and is fished commercially and for sport. It is one of the most important food fish in some areas of Africa. A large, heavy-bodied fish, the Nile perch has the spiny first dorsal fin characteristic of the perchlike fishes and three spines on the anal fin. It eats mainly fish. Introduction of the Nile perch into Lake Victoria in the 1960s caused the elimination of many cichlid species.

### Striped Bass *Roccus saxatilis*
**RANGE** N. America: Atlantic coast from Gulf of St. Lawrence to N. Florida; Gulf of Mexico; Pacific coast from Washington to California
**HABITAT** Inshore waters, estuaries, bays, deltas
**SIZE** Up to 4 ft (1.2 m)

A distinctive fish, the striped bass may vary in coloration but always has seven or eight dark stripes along its sides. It has a long head and body, a pointed snout and projecting lower jaw. The female is usually larger and heavier than the male, and large specimens may weigh up to 66 lb (30 kg). They feed on fish and crustaceans. Originally a native of the Atlantic coast, the striped bass was first introduced to the Pacific coast in 1886 and is now well established. It is a member of the temperate perch family Percichthyidae.

In the breeding season, April to July, striped bass enter estuaries and ascend rivers to spawn. The female is courted by a number of males and sheds her eggs into the water, where they drift until they hatch about 3 days later. A mature female may produce several million eggs in a season.

## Murray/Trout Cod *Maccullochella macquariensis* **EN**

**RANGE** Australia: New South Wales, Queensland

**HABITAT** Rivers, lakes; introduced in reservoirs

**SIZE** 6 ft (1.8 m)

The Murray cod has a long powerful body, usually with mottled markings on its back and sides, and an elongate snout. It eats mainly crustaceans and fish and is itself an important commercial food fish. It is a member of Percichthyidae, the temperate perch family.

Murray cod often spawn over trees and branches, which have fallen into the water. The eggs adhere to the surface of the bark and branches.

## Giant Sea Bass *Stereolepis gigas*

**RANGE** Pacific Ocean: off coasts of California and Mexico

**HABITAT** Inshore waters

**SIZE** 7 ft (2.1 m)

The giant sea bass is a huge fish. Some specimens weigh over 550 lb (250 kg). It is known to live for about 70 to 75 years and eats fish and crustaceans. It is fished commercially and for sport.

Giant sea bass mature at about 11 to 13 years old, at a weight of about 50 lb (23 kg). They spawn in summer, and the young fishes are reddish in color and deeper bodied than adults. They gradually take on the adult appearance and coloration as they mature.

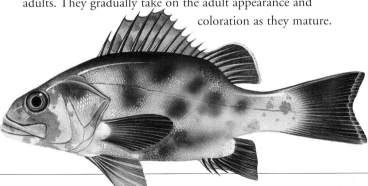

## Jewfish *Epinephelus itajara*

**RANGE** W. Atlantic Ocean: coasts of Florida, Bermuda, Bahamas, West Indies; Pacific Ocean

**HABITAT** Coastal waters, around ledges, caves and wrecks

**SIZE** 8 ft (2.4 m)

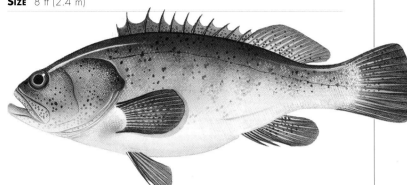

One of the largest of the fishes known as groupers (all members of the sea bass family, Serranidae), the jewfish weighs as much as 700 lb (318 kg). It has a robust body and broad head and is usually dark brown, with irregular dark spots and bars on the body. It lurks around underwater crevices and feeds on crustaceans, fish and even turtles. Jewfishes are sought-after food fish and are popular with sporting fishermen.

## Black Grouper *Mycteroperca bonaci*

**RANGE** W. Atlantic Ocean: New England, USA, south through Gulf of Mexico and Caribbean to Brazil

**HABITAT** Coastal waters, deeper waters over rocky bottoms

**SIZE** 4 ft (1.2 m)

The black grouper is a fairly common grouper, which may weigh up to 50 lb (23 kg). Its appearance is typical of the Serranidae family to which it belongs. There are irregular dark markings on the sides of its body. It is a good food fish and is caught commercially.

## Coney *Cephalopholis fulvus*

**RANGE** W. Atlantic Ocean: Florida, USA, south through the Caribbean and Gulf of Mexico to Brazil

**HABITAT** Coastal waters, coral reefs

**SIZE** 11¾ in (30 cm)

One of the smallest but most abundant groupers, the coney varies from red to yellow or brown in coloration but is usually marked with blue spots. It has two black spots on its tail. Crustaceans are its main diet. It is a highly valued food species.

# PERCHLIKE FISHES CONTINUED

## Soapfish *Rypticus saponaceus*

**RANGE** E. Atlantic Ocean: off tropical W. Africa and Ascension Island; W. Atlantic: Florida to Brazil

**HABITAT** Shallow, coastal waters

**SIZE** 11¾ in (30 cm)

Soapfishes belong to the family Seranidae. The skin of the soapfish is slimy with body mucus, which creates a frothy effect, like soapsuds, in the water. This mucus is toxic and its presence deters predators. The soapfish is usually brownish, with some gray blotches on the body. There are several spines preceding the dorsal fin. Active at night, it feeds on fish and crustaceans and shelters in rock crevices during the day.

## Pumpkinseed *Lepomis gibbosus*

**RANGE** S. Canada; USA: North Dakota and Great Lakes, east to Atlantic coast, south to Texas and Florida; introduced on the west coast of the USA and in Europe

**HABITAT** Brooks, clear ponds with plenty of vegetation

**SIZE** 6–9 in (15–23 cm)

The attractive pumpkinseed is a sunfish, belonging to the Centrarchidae family of about 29 species of sunfish. Aids to its identification are the black gill cover, surrounded with orange or red, the blue lines radiating from the snout and eye region and the three anal spines. It feeds on snails and aquatic insects, as well as small and larval fish.

Breeding takes place between May and July in sandy-bottomed water. The male fish hollows out a shallow nest with his tail and then attracts one or more females to lay eggs in his nest. He guards the eggs while they incubate for between 5 and 10 days, depending on the temperature of the water, and continues to look after the young fishes until they are able to disperse and fend for themselves. Pumpkinseeds may breed near one another in small colonies.

## Rock Bass *Ambloplites rupestris*

**RANGE** S. Canada: Lake Winnipeg, east to coast; USA: Great Lakes, east to Vermont, south to Gulf Coast; introduced in other areas of USA

**HABITAT** Rocky-bottomed streams, lake shallows

**SIZE** 6–10 in (15–25.5 cm)

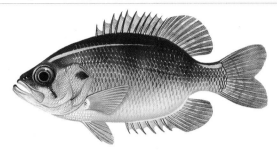

This sunfish lives among rocks and stones, where it feeds on insects, crayfish and fish. It is a sturdy, deep-bodied fish, with a large mouth and a protruding lower jaw.

The male rock bass excavates a nest at the bottom, often amid the roots of aquatic plants. The female lays about 5,000 eggs in the nest, which is then guarded by the male. He defends the young fishes when they first hatch.

## Largemouth Bass *Micropterus salmoides*

**RANGE** S.E. Canada; USA: Great Lakes area, south to Gulf of Mexico; introduced in other areas of USA and in Europe and Africa

**HABITAT** Shallow lakes, ponds, rivers

**SIZE** 10–18 in (25.5–46 cm)

A member of the sunfish family, the largemouth bass is usually greenish and silvery in coloration, with a dark band along each side; its dorsal fin is divided almost in two by a notch. A predatory fish, it feeds on crustaceans and other invertebrates when young, gradually progressing to fish, frogs and larger invertebrates when mature.

Spawning takes place in spring or early summer, depending on temperature and latitude. The male excavates a nest in sand or gravel in shallow water and attracts a female to his nest to lay her eggs, usually a few hundred. The male fertilizes the eggs and may then attract more females to his nest. The sticky-surfaced eggs attach themselves to the bottom of the nest and are guarded by the male until they hatch, 7 to 10 days after laying.

## Perch *Perca fluviatilis*

**RANGE** Europe: Britain, east across Scandinavia and Russia to Siberia; south to N. Italy, Black and Caspian Seas; introduced in Ireland, Australia, New Zealand and South Africa

**HABITAT** Lakes, ponds, slow rivers

**SIZE** 13¾–20 in (35–51 cm)

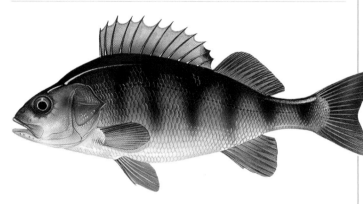

This fish is a member of the perch family (Percidae), which contains 162 fresh water species. It is a deep-bodied fish with two dorsal fins, the first joined to the second only by a membrane at the base. There is a characteristic black mark at the end of the spiny fin. The perch lives among aquatic vegetation, submerged tree roots or other debris, where its barred markings help to camouflage it. It feeds on fish.

Perch spawn in shallow water during April and May. The eggs are shed in long strings, which wind around plants or other objects, and they hatch in about 8 days. Young perch feed on plankton and then on insects and larger crustaceans until they are old enough to adopt the adult diet.

## Orangethroat Darter

*Etheostoma spectabile*

**RANGE** Central USA: Mississippi and Missouri river systems

**HABITAT** Streams

**SIZE** 3¼ in (8 cm)

The orangethroat darter is one of the many species of darter found in the USA, all of which are members of the perch family (Percidae). It feeds on insects and planktonic crustaceans.

Breeding males develop some orange coloration on throat and breast, while females and non-breeding males have pale throats. The male of a pair selects a nesting site, and the female excavates a shallow nest and deposits several hundred eggs, which are fertilized and guarded by the male.

## Conchfish *Astrapogon stellatus*

**RANGE** Tropical W. Atlantic Ocean, from Bahamas south through Caribbean

**HABITAT** Shallow waters

**SIZE** 2 in (5 cm)

The conchfish is one of approximately 320 species of cardinalfish (Apogonidae) found in tropical and subtropical seas. It is a tiny fish, with some dark and some silvery coloration and dark spots along its sides.

Some cardinalfish live in rock crevices or empty shells, but the conchfish lives inside the shell of a live conch, *Strombus gigas*, a large mollusk. The conch is unaffected by the association, but the fish gains the benefit of shelter.

## Zander *Stizostedion lucioperca*

**RANGE** C. and E. Europe: Sweden and Finland, south to Black and Caspian Seas, east to Russia; introduced in England and W. Europe

**HABITAT** Large lakes, slow rivers

**SIZE** 23½ in–4¼ ft (60 cm–1.3 m)

A member of the perch family, the zander has the characteristic two dorsal fins of that group; the first spiny fin is just separated from the second. The zander prefers to inhabit cloudy water and does most of its hunting at dawn and dusk, remaining near the bottom at other times. It feeds on almost any species of fish.

Zanders spawn between April and June in either sandy or stony-bottomed water. The eggs are laid in a shallow nest, where they are guarded by the male.

# PERCHLIKE FISHES CONTINUED

**Bluefish** *Pomatomus saltatrix*

**RANGE** Atlantic, Indian and N. Pacific Oceans:

tropical and warm temperate areas

**HABITAT** Coastal waters, open ocean

**SIZE** Up to 4 ft (1.2 m)

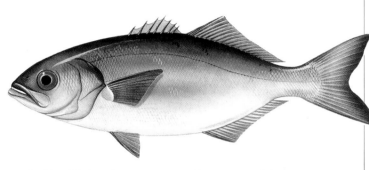

The bluefish has the reputation of being one of the most predatory of fish, killing more prey than it can eat and feeding voraciously on almost any fish, including smaller individuals of its own species.

It is a sturdy fish, with a forked tail, fully scaled body and large jaws equipped with formidable teeth.

Schools of bluefishes of a similar size travel together, often following shoals of prey fish. Young bluefishes, which are known as snappers, also form their own shoals, and, in general, the smaller the fish, the bigger the shoal.

**Cobia** *Rachycentron canadum*

**RANGE** Atlantic, Indian and W. Pacific Oceans:

tropical areas

**HABITAT** Open sea, occasionally inshore waters and estuaries

**SIZE** 6 ft (1.8 m)

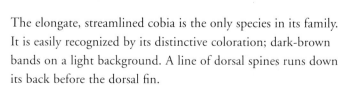

The elongate, streamlined cobia is the only species in its family. It is easily recognized by its distinctive coloration; dark-brown bands on a light background. A line of dorsal spines runs down its back before the dorsal fin.

The cobia is an active predator, feeding mainly on fish but it will also consume crabs, squid and shrimps.

**Remora** *Remora remora*

**RANGE** Atlantic, Indian and N. Pacific Oceans:

tropical and warm temperate areas

**HABITAT** Wherever taken by, generally, offshore hosts

**SIZE** 6–18 in (15–46 cm)

The remora is one of the 7 or 8 species of sharksucker in the family Echeneidae. By means of a specialized sucking disk on the top of the head, sharksuckers attach themselves to sharks or other large fishes, whales or turtles and travel with them wherever they go. The disk is formed from a modified spiny dorsal fin and contains two rows of slatlike ridges divided by a central bar. The remora presses the disk flat against the host fish and creates a partial vacuum by moving the ridges, thus making it virtually impossible to remove it.

While some sharksuckers use many different types of host, others, including the remora, are adapted to only a few specific hosts. The remora seems nearly always to be associated with the blue shark. It feeds mainly on the parasites that live on the shark but may leave its host briefly to catch small fish or crustaceans.

**Sharksucker** *Echenis naucrates*

**RANGE** Atlantic, Indian and W. Pacific Oceans: tropical areas

**HABITAT** Wherever taken by host

**SIZE** Up to 36¼ in (92 cm)

The largest member of the Echeneidae family, the sharksucker is a long-bodied fish, with distinctive white-bordered black stripes down each side of the body, from snout to tail. On top of its rather flattened head is the powerful sucking disk, with which it attaches itself to a host so firmly that it is almost impossible to remove. Attached in this way, the sharksucker rides around effortlessly and presumably gains some protection from the larger animal; this species uses a wide range of hosts, including sharks, large rays and turtles. Sharksuckers were once used for catching sea turtles. The fish, with a line tied to its tail, was released near the turtle and would generally make straight for it and fasten itself to the tail. The fishermen could then gradually pull in the turtle, the sharksucker holding firm.

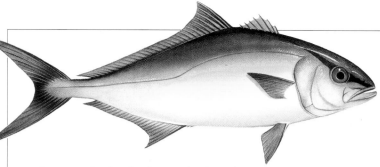

deeply forked tail. It is a member of the pompano and jack family, Carangidae, and like so many of that family is a game fish, popular with sport fishermen.

## Greater Amberjack *Seriola dumerili*

**RANGE** W. Atlantic Ocean: New England to Brazil; E. Atlantic: Mediterranean Sea to coast of W. Africa

**HABITAT** Surface inshore waters

**SIZE** Up to 6 ft (1.8 m)

The greater amberjack is one of the large family, Carangidae, which includes about 140 species of fish, such as jacks and pompanos. It is a fairly deep-bodied fish, with a dark-blue or green back and lighter, golden or whitish sides. There is a distinctive dark line running from the snout through the eye to the top of the head. It feeds on many species of fish.

## Crevalle Jack *Caranx hippos*

**RANGE** Probably worldwide in tropical and subtropical waters

**HABITAT** Juveniles in inshore waters, adults offshore, especially around reefs

**SIZE** 31½ in–3¼ ft (80 cm–1 m)

The exact distribution of this species is unknown because of confusion between similar species in the Carangidae family. However, it is certainly abundant on both sides of the Atlantic. The crevalle jack has a high, rounded forehead and a prominent dark spot on each gill cover; there are also dark spots on each pectoral fin. Its body is dark blue or metallic green on the back, with silvery or yellowish underparts. Fish are its main food, but crustaceans and some other invertebrates are also eaten.

## Rainbow Runner *Elagatis bipinnulata*

**RANGE** Atlantic, Indian and N. Pacific Oceans: tropical and subtropical waters

**HABITAT** Open sea

**SIZE** Up to 4 ft (1.2 m)

Identified by its beautiful coloration, the rainbow runner has a blue back and yellow and blue stripes along the sides shading to a whitish belly. Its body is slender, tapering sharply toward the

## Florida Pompano *Trachinotus carolinus*

**RANGE** W. Atlantic Ocean: Cape Cod to Brazil

**HABITAT** Shallow waters close to shore

**SIZE** 18–25 in (46–63.5 cm)

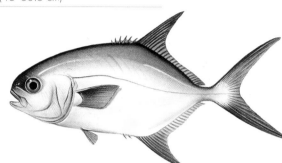

The Florida pompano closely resembles the permit, *T. falcatus*, but has a less strongly arched profile and lacks the elongate dorsal-fin spine of the permit. It has a rounded snout and a fairly deep body, which tapers sharply before the forked tail. Mollusks and crustaceans are its main foods, for which it roots around in the sand and mud of the seabed. It is itself considered an excellent food fish and is caught commercially.

Spawning is believed to take place offshore between March and September, depending on latitude. The young fishes then move inshore, where they feed on bottom-living invertebrates and small fish. The Florida pompano and the permit both belong to the Carangidae family.

## Lookdown *Selene vomer*

**RANGE** W. Atlantic Ocean: New England, south to Bermuda and to Uruguay; E. Atlantic: off W. Africa

**HABITAT** Shallow sandy- or muddy-bottomed waters

**SIZE** 11¾ in (30 cm)

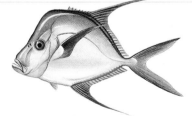

The lookdown is an extremely unusual-looking fish, which has a large head and a small, dramatically tapering body. The head arches up steeply above the snout and is almost one and a half times as deep as it is long. Both dorsal and anal fins have long extensions, which point back toward the sharply forked tail.

# PERCHLIKE FISHES CONTINUED

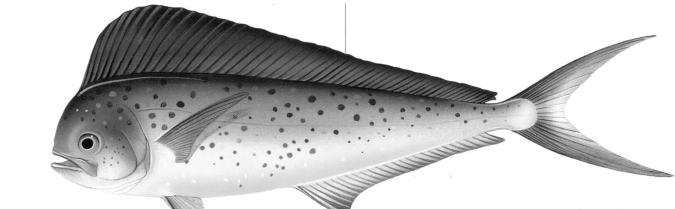

## Dolphinfish

*Coryphaena hippurus*

**RANGE** Atlantic, Pacific, Indian Oceans:
tropical and warm temperate areas

**HABITAT** Open sea

**SIZE** Up to 5 ft (1.5 m)

Immediately identifiable by the long dorsal fin that originates
over its head, the dolphinfish is extremely beautiful, with its
vivid blue, green and yellow coloration. As males grow older,
their foreheads become increasingly steep, almost vertical, and
they may grow larger than females; otherwise males and females
look alike. Dolphinfishes move in small schools and feed on a
variety of fish, squid and crustaceans. They often frequent the
waters around patches of floating seaweed or other debris, which
may harbor potential prey.

Dolphinfishes are popular game fish and excellent to eat.
They belong to the family Coryphaenidae, which contains only
1 other species, the pompano dolphinfish, *C. equisetis*; this fish is
similar in appearance but smaller than *C. hippurus*. They are also
known simply as dolphins, but the name dolphinfish is preferable
in order to distinguish them from mammalian dolphins.

## Ray's Bream *Brama brama*

**RANGE** N. Atlantic Ocean: Iceland and Scandinavia to
N. Africa; Mediterranean Sea; off coasts of Chile, South Africa,
Australia, New Zealand

**HABITAT** Open sea

**SIZE** 15¾–27½ in (40–70 cm)

Ray's bream, a member
of the Bramidae (Pomfret)
family, which contains
18 species, has a deep
body that tapers sharply toward the

long, deeply forked tail. It migrates into the northern part of
its range in summer, but such migrations are irregular and
appear to be dependent on suitable water temperatures.

An unselective predator, it feeds on almost any fish or
crustaceans available.

## Mutton Snapper *Lutjanus analis*

**RANGE** W. Atlantic Ocean: Florida and Bahamas, south to Caribbean,
Gulf of Mexico and Brazil

**HABITAT** Coastal waters, bays

**SIZE** Up to 30 in (76 cm)

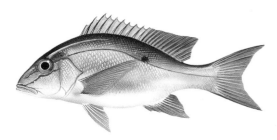

Common off American coasts, the mutton snapper is one of the
approximately 125 species in the snapper family, Lutjanidae. It is
a brightly colored fish, with a green and reddish or pink body
and some blue markings; there is a black spot below the dorsal
fin on both sides of the body. Like most snappers, it has large,
caninelike teeth. Mutton snappers often frequent shallow waters,
where there are mangroves or turtle grass, and feed on the fish
and crustaceans found among the vegetation.

Some snappers are among the fishes that are known to cause
the ciguatera type of fish poisoning, which can be fatal to
humans who eat the flesh of affected fish. The poison originates
in certain algae. Herbivorous fishes may feed on this algae and
they are in turn eaten by carnivorous fishes, with no
apparent ill effects to the predators. The flesh of the predator
fish becomes toxic, however, and the poison can then affect
any human consumer.

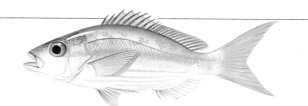

## Yellowtail Snapper *Ocyurus chrysurus*

**RANGE** W. Atlantic Ocean: New England to Brazil, including Gulf of Mexico and Caribbean

**HABITAT** Offshore waters, near coral reefs

**SIZE** 30 in (76 cm)

One of the snapper family (Lutjanidae), the yellowtail snapper is an attractive fish, with a bright yellow tail and a yellow stripe along each side. Its body is slender and its dorsal fin long and low. Yellowtail snappers feed near the bottom on crustaceans and fish but also occur offshore above reefs. They are popular with anglers and are excellent food fish.

## Tripletail *Lobotes surinamensis*

**RANGE** Atlantic, Indian and W. Pacific Oceans: tropical and warm temperate areas

**HABITAT** Coastal surface waters

**SIZE** 3¼ ft (1 m)

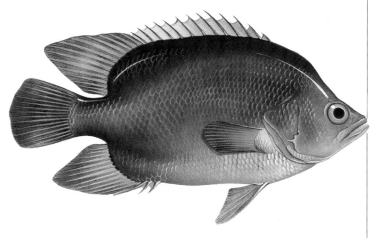

Although never common, the tripletail is a widely distributed fish, which occurs on both sides of the Atlantic. It belongs to the tripletail family (Lobotidae) which includes only about 4 species. It has a deep, heavy body and is usually dark brown in color, although some individuals may be yellow and brown. The large, rounded lobes of the dorsal and anal fins, which project back toward the tail, give the fish the appearance of having three tails, hence the name.

Young tripletails often live close to the shore in bays and estuaries, where they float on their sides among dead mangrove and other leaves. Their curving posture and brownish-yellow coloration imitate the movement and appearance of the leaves and are an excellent example of protective mimicry.

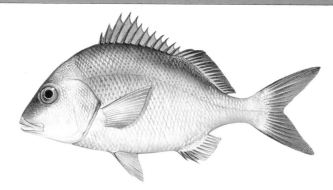

## Margate *Haemulon album*

**RANGE** W. Atlantic Ocean: Bahamas and Florida, south through Caribbean to Brazil

**HABITAT** Shallow inshore waters, often near reefs

**SIZE** 24¾ in (63 cm)

The margate is one of about 150 species in the grunt family, Haemulidae. These marine fishes occur in tropical waters and are related to the snappers but lack their large teeth. They are known as grunts because of the noise that they make by grinding their pharyngeal teeth together; the resulting sounds are amplified by the swim bladder. The margate is fairly typical of its family, with its high, spiny dorsal fin, which is continuous with the rayed dorsal fin. It is usually grayish in color, with darker dorsal and tail fins, but coloration does vary.

Small groups of margates often frequent reefs and wrecks, where they feed on small fish and also forage on the seabed for bottom-living invertebrates. This is the largest of the Atlantic grunts and is caught commercially.

## Black Margate *Anisotremus surinamensis*

**RANGE** W. Atlantic Ocean: Florida and the Bahamas, south through Gulf of Mexico and Caribbean

**HABITAT** Inshore waters, near rocks and reefs

**SIZE** Up to 24 in (61 cm)

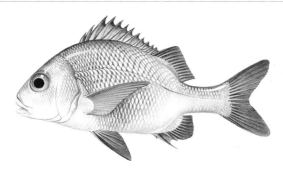

The black margate, a member of the grunt family, Haemulidae, is typical of its group in its body shape and continuous dorsal fin. It is grayish in color, with a dark spot on each scale on the back; the fins are dark gray. Most active at night, it feeds on crustaceans sea urchins and fish, often foraging in small groups. By day it shelters in caves or crevices.

# PERCHLIKE FISHES CONTINUED

### Scup *Stenotomus chrysops*

**RANGE** Atlantic coast of N. America: Cape Cod
(sometimes Nova Scotia) to Florida

**HABITAT** Sandy-bottomed inshore and offshore waters

**SIZE** 18 in (46 cm)

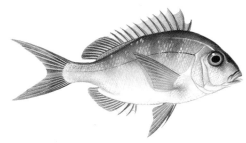

An abundant fish in the Atlantic, the scup, also called the
northern porgy, is one of the 100 species in the porgy family,
Sparidae. It has a deep, laterally compressed body, a deeply
forked tail and spines on both dorsal and anal fins. Its scales are
silvery, with indistinct dark bars on the sides of the body. Most
of its feeding is done on the bottom, and the scup takes
crustaceans, worms and some bottom-living fish.

In spring, adults spawn in waters close to the shore, often in
bays; the eggs float freely until they hatch. In winter, scups move
farther offshore and toward the south of their range.

### Jolthead Porgy *Calamus bajonado*

**RANGE** Caribbean, Gulf of Mexico; W. Atlantic Ocean:
coasts of North and South America from New England to Brazil

**HABITAT** Coastal waters, near reefs

**SIZE** 24 in (61 cm)

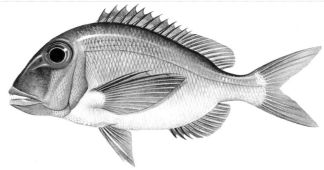

One of the larger members of the family Sparidae, the jolthead
porgy is a distinctive fish, with a high, rounded forehead. Its
scales have a silvery sheen, and there are some blue markings
around the eyes, which are placed characteristically high. Small
schools of jolthead porgies feed near the shore on invertebrates
such as sea urchins, mollusks and crustaceans. They are good
food fish, which are fished for by anglers and commercial
fishermen.

### Sheepshead *Archosargus probatocephalus*

**RANGE** W. Atlantic Ocean: Nova Scotia, south to Gulf of Mexico
(now rare in north of range)

**HABITAT** Tidal streams, bays, seabed near jetties

**SIZE** 11¾–30 in (30–76 cm)

Sometimes called the
convict fish, the
sheepshead is
identified by the
broad black bars down
each of its silvery sides. These
bars vary in shape and number and are
most prominent in younger fishes. Otherwise the sheepshead is
typical in appearance of the porgy family, to which it belongs,
with its large head, thick lips and spiny dorsal and anal fins. It
feeds on crustaceans and mollusks, which it crushes with its
broad, flat teeth. It is itself an excellent food fish and is caught
in large quantities.

Spawning takes place in spring, and the eggs float freely until
they hatch only 3 or 4 days later, provided the temperature is
sufficiently high.

### Snapper *Chrysophrys auratus*

**RANGE** Pacific Ocean: coasts of New Zealand,
Australia, Lord Howe Island

**HABITAT** Seabed, rocky reefs

**SIZE** 4¼ ft (1.3 m)

The snapper, a member of the porgy family, Sparidae, undergoes
slight changes of appearance and behavior as it matures. Young
snappers are pale pink in color, with dark bands, and live in
large schools in shallow water close to the shore, often in bays.
Adults are redder, with bright blue spots dotting the fins, back
and sides. They frequent the seabed and rocky reefs in deeper
waters but may come into shallow coastal waters in summer. In
the oldest specimens, the forehead becomes rather humped, and
the lips particularly fleshy; these older fishes
tend to be solitary. The snapper is a
valuable food fish.

### Red Sea Bream

*Pagellus bogaraveo*

**RANGE** Atlantic Ocean: coasts of S. Norway, Britain, Europe, N. Africa, Canary Islands; Mediterranean Sea

**HABITAT** Inshore waters, deeper waters at 330–650 ft (100–200 m)

**SIZE** 13¾–20 in (35–51 cm)

Quite common in the south of their range, red sea bream are rare in the north, and those fishes which do occur are mostly summer migrants. A member of the porgy family, Sparidae, the fish is distinguished by the reddish flush to its body and fins, the dark spot above its pectoral fin and its short, rounded head. Young fishes are paler in color than adults and may lack the dark spot. The young red sea breams form large schools and frequent shallow inshore waters, feeding on small crustaceans. Adults live farther offshore in deeper waters and form smaller groups; they feed on fish, and also on crustaceans.

Little is known of the breeding habits of the red sea bream, but it is thought to spawn in summer or autumn, depending on the area: the farther south, the earlier it spawns. Red sea bream are good-quality food fish and are caught commercially.

### Gilthead Bream *Sparus aurata*

**RANGE** Atlantic Ocean: coasts of Ireland, S. England, Europe, N. Africa, Canary Islands; Mediterranean and Black Seas

**HABITAT** Shallow sandy-bottomed or muddy-bottomed waters at about 100 ft (30 m)

**SIZE** Up to 27½ in (70 cm)

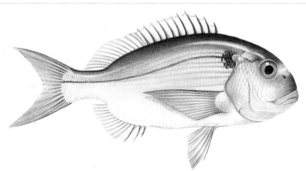

A golden stripe, which runs between the eyes of this fish, is the origin of its common name; the stripe fades on death. The gilthead is a fairly deep-bodied fish, with a markedly rounded snout and high-set eyes; there is a dark spot on each side, well above the pectoral fin. It feeds largely on mollusks and crustaceans, and its teeth are adapted to deal with this hard-shelled prey – those in the front of the jaws are pointed and curved for breaking into the shells, while those at the sides are broad and flattened for crushing and grinding down food. Because of their diet, giltheads can prove a menace on commercial oyster and mussel beds.

Like all sea breams, the gilthead is a member of the porgy family, Sparidae. Breeding takes place in winter in offshore waters, deeper than the giltheads normally frequent. They are not believed to breed in the north of their range.

### Sweetlip Emperor *Lethrinus chrysostomus*

**RANGE** Off N. coast of Australia, Great Barrier Reef

**HABITAT** Inshore waters, reef areas

**SIZE** 36 in (91 cm)

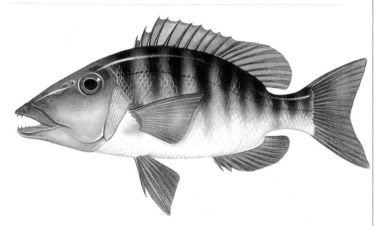

The sweetlip emperor belongs to the family Lethrinidae, known as scavengers and emperors. The sweetlip has a rather large head for its body, a long snout and scaleless cheeks. Its coloration is striking, with deep-red fins, dark barring on the sides and vivid red patches around the eyes. It can attain a weight of 20 lb (9 kg) and is a valuable food fish.

### Spangled Emperor *Lethrinus nebulosus*

**RANGE** Indian and Pacific Oceans: Red Sea and E. Africa to N. Australia and W. Pacific islands

**HABITAT** Coral reefs, open ocean

**SIZE** 30 in (76 cm)

The name of the attractively colored spangled emperor is well deserved. Identifying characteristics are the scattering of blue spots on its dorsal and anal fins, the blue on many of the scales on its sides and the blue lines on each side of the face, running from the eye toward the snout. A member of the family Lethrinidae, the fish has the long snout, thick lips and dorsal and anal spines typical of the group. Like several of the larger members of this family, it is a valuable food fish.

# PERCHLIKE FISHES CONTINUED

### White Seabass *Cynoscion nobilis*

**RANGE** Pacific Ocean: Alaska to Mexico

**HABITAT** Near kelp beds, shallow to deep waters

**SIZE** 24 in–6 ft (61 cm–1.8 m)

The white seabass is not a true sea bass, but a member of the drum family Sciaenidae. There are about 270 species of drum, so called because many of them can make sounds by vibrating their swim bladders with specialized muscles; in some species only the male makes sounds, and in others, both male and female can "drum". Most species of drum have a deeply, often almost completely, divided dorsal fin.

A large, elongate fish, the white seabass has a rather pointed head and large mouth, with the lower jaw projecting slightly beyond the upper. The two parts of its dorsal fin just touch. It moves in large schools and feeds on many kinds of fish and on crustaceans and squid. Spawning takes place in spring and summer, and young fishes generally live in quiet, inshore waters.

White seabass are important to sport and commercial fishermen along the Pacific coast of America. An almost identical but much larger fish, the totoaba, (*Totoaba macdonaldii*), occurs farther south, off the coast of Mexico. It is critically endangered.

### Spotted Seatrout *Cynoscion nebulosus*

**RANGE** Atlantic Ocean: coast of USA from New York to Florida; Gulf of Mexico

**HABITAT** Coastal bays, estuaries; deeper waters in winter

**SIZE** 17¾–24 in (45–61 cm)

Although called "seatrout" because of its troutlike spots, the spotted seatrout belongs to the drum family, Sciaenidae. It has an elongate body and pointed head, with a slightly protruding lower jaw; its dorsal fin is deeply notched. Like many drums, the spotted seatrout can make sounds by vibrating its swim bladder. It feeds on crustaceans and fish.

Spawning takes place in sheltered coastal bays, from March to November. Once hatched, larval and juvenile fishes stay in the protection of marine vegetation, where they find plentiful supplies of food. In winter, they move into deeper waters. Spotted seatrout are caught for sport and commercially.

### Black Drum *Pogonias cromis*

**RANGE** W. Atlantic Ocean: coasts from New England to Argentina

**HABITAT** Bays, coastal lagoons

**SIZE** 4–6 ft (1.2–1.8 m)

Identified by its short, deep body, somewhat flattened belly and arched back, the black drum is one of the largest members of the drum family and is known to weigh as much as 146 lb (66 kg). Several short barbels hang from its lower jaw. A bottom-feeding fish, the black drum eats crustaceans and mollusks, which it is able to crush with the large, flat teeth in its throat. Oysters are a particularly favored food, and black drums can do much harm to commercial oyster beds.

### Jackknife-fish *Equetus lanceolatus*

**RANGE** W. Atlantic Ocean: coasts of North and South Carolina, Bermuda to Brazil; Gulf of Mexico, Caribbean

**HABITAT** Rocky- or coral-bottomed waters more than 50 ft (15 m) deep

**SIZE** 9 in (23 cm)

An unusual member of the drum family, the jackknife-fish is an extremely distinctive species, strikingly marked with three black stripes, bordered with white. One of these stripes curves down from the high dorsal fin to the tail fin disrupting the normal outline of the fish. Such markings are a form of camouflage, intended to confuse and distract the observer and to delay recognition.

A solitary species, the jackknife-fish hides among rocks or in crevices in the coral reef during the day and feeds at night.

## Freshwater Drum *Aplodinotus grunniens*

**RANGE** N. America: S. Canada through the Great Lakes and Mississippi river system to Gulf of Mexico; south to Mexico and Guatemala

**HABITAT** Large rivers, lakes

**SIZE** Up to 4 ft (1.2 m)

One of the few freshwater species in the drum family, this fish has a humped back and a long-based dorsal fin. As befits a bottom-feeder, its mouth is low slung; its main foods are mollusks, crustaceans and some insect larvae, all of which it crushes with the large, flattened teeth in its throat, spitting out the shells and swallowing the soft bodies. It produces sounds by vibrating its swim bladder and is one of the few freshwater fishes to do so.

Spawning takes place in April, May or June in shallow gravel-bottomed or sandy-bottomed water. Females may shed from 10,000 to 100,000 eggs, which hatch in about 2 weeks.

## Meagre *Argyrosomus regius*

**RANGE** Indian Ocean; E. Atlantic Ocean: Britain to Senegal; Mediterranean Sea

**HABITAT** Shore line to deeper waters to 1,150 ft (350 m), estuaries

**SIZE** 5–6½ ft (1.5–2 m)

One of the giants of the drum family, the meagre is an elongate fish, with a rounded snout and large mouth. It is a common fish in southern waters and occasionally strays to northern European seas. It moves in shoals, eating fish, and usually occurs in sandy-bottomed water.

## Spotted Goatfish *Pseudupeneus maculatus*

**RANGE** W. Atlantic Ocean: New Jersey to Brazil; Gulf of Mexico, Caribbean

**HABITAT** Shallow waters, reefs, turtle grass beds

**SIZE** 11 in (28 cm)

There are 55 species of goatfish, or red mullet, which occur worldwide in tropical and warm temperate seas. These fishes have elongate bodies and two widely spaced dorsal fins.

The spotted goatfish is typical of the family and has the characteristic feature of two long, sensory chin barbels, used for finding food on the seabed. With these barbels, the goatfish forages over the substrate for the small invertebrate animals on which it feeds.

## Red Mullet *Mullus surmuletus*

**RANGE** Mediterranean Sea, E. Atlantic Ocean: Britain, south to Canary Islands and N. Africa

**HABITAT** Sandy-, muddy-, sometimes rocky-bottomed waters to 300 ft (90 m)

**SIZE** 15¾ in (40 cm)

The red mullet is a Mediterranean species, which sometimes occurs farther north, presumably as a summer migrant. It has a steeply rounded forehead and, like the other members of the family Mullidae, two sensory barbels on its chin, which it uses to search the seabed for food, mostly bottom-living invertebrates. Once prey is found, the red mullet will dig to uncover it. Red mullets usually travel in small schools of fewer than 50. They can change color quite dramatically, varying between reddish-brown, red and yellowish-brown. In the daytime, they are usually brownish, with several yellow stripes along the sides; at night, these lines break up into a marbled pattern. In deeper water, red mullets are a deep red, but color variations also occur when the fishes are alarmed.

Spawning takes place between July and September. The female sheds her eggs on the seabed, but once they hatch, the young live at the surface.

## Archerfish *Toxotes jaculator*

**RANGE** India, S.E. Asia, Philippines, Indonesia, N. Australia

**HABITAT** Inshore waters, estuaries, lower reaches of rivers

**SIZE** 9 in (23 cm)

The archerfish in the family Toxotidae are so called because of their habit of shooting down insects by spitting water at them. The archerfish holds water in its throat and, with its tongue, makes the mouth opening into a narrow tube. By then using its tongue as a valve and compressing the gill covers to propel the water, the drops are ejected with some force and great accuracy. The fish has excellent vision, and its large mobile eyes allow it to look upward above the water surface. It shoots at insects on plants overhanging the water and also feeds on aquatic insects and small invertebrates.

# PERCHLIKE FISHES CONTINUED

## Foureye Butterflyfish *Chaetodon capistratus*

**RANGE** W. Atlantic Ocean: Cape Cod, south to Caribbean and Gulf of Mexico

**HABITAT** Coral reefs, rocky-bottomed and sandy-bottomed waters

**SIZE** 6 in (15 cm)

The approximately 114 species in the family Chaetodontidae – the butterflyfishes – are among the most colorful inhabitants of coral reefs.

The foureye butterflyfish is typical of the family, with its deep, laterally compressed body, so thin that it resembles a disk. This body shape is ideal for twisting and turning among the coral "forests" and utilizing the many crevices for shelter.

The black spots, on each side near the tail, presumably mislead predators into thinking that these are the vulnerable eye areas, while the actual eyes have additional protection from the dark bands that run through and help to conceal them. The butterflyfishes feed by grazing on the coral reef, eating polyps or pieces of seaweed.

## Copperband Butterflyfish *Chelmon rostratus*

**RANGE** Indian and Pacific Oceans: E. Africa to India, Indonesia, Australia, Japan and Philippines

**HABITAT** Coral reefs, rocky areas

**SIZE** 7¾ in (20 cm)

Also known as the beaked butterflyfish, this fish has an elongated, beaklike snout, with which it is able to reach into crevices in the coral to find food. The beak is equipped with tiny, sharp teeth. It is an attractive fish, with coppery bands running down each side of the body, presumably as a camouflaging device. There is a black spot near the dorsal fin, which confuses predators into thinking that this is the vulnerable head area.

## Forceps Butterflyfish *Forcipiger longirostris*

**RANGE** Indian and Pacific Oceans: tropical areas from Hawaii to Indonesia and Comoro Islands

**HABITAT** Coral reefs, rocky areas

**SIZE** 7 in (18 cm)

The forceps butterflyfish has a long, beaklike snout, with a small mouth at the tip, which it pokes into crevices and crannies in the coral to find food. With its jaws like forceps, it picks out tiny invertebrates and polyps from the densely packed coral heads.

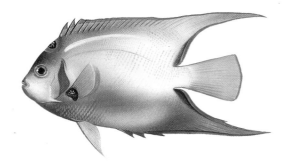

## Queen Angelfish *Holacanthus ciliaris*

**RANGE** Tropical W. Atlantic Ocean: Florida and Bahamas, south to Brazil including Gulf of Mexico

**HABITAT** Coral reefs

**SIZE** Up to 18 in (46 cm)

The brilliantly colored queen angelfish belongs to the family Pomacanthidae. Angelfish are very similar to butterflyfish but have a characteristic spine near each gill cover. It has a deep, slim body, a blunt snout and greatly elongated lobes to dorsal and anal fins that extend past the tail fin.

## Imperial Angelfish *Pomacanthus imperator*

**RANGE** Tropical Indian and Pacific Oceans: Red Sea, E. Africa to Indonesia, Philippines, Australia and Polynesia

**HABITAT** Coral reefs, rocky areas

**SIZE** Up to 15 in (38 cm)

The adult imperial angelfish is a striking fish, with attractive yellow and blue markings and a dark, masklike area over the eyes. Young fishes, however, are much darker, with blue and white stripes on the body and a whitish spot near the tail. The stripes are believed to lead a predator's eye toward the light spot and away from the vulnerable head area. The fish's slightly protuberant mouth enables it to graze over the coral.

### Schomburgk's Leaffish *Polycentrus schomburgkii*
**RANGE** N.E. South America, Trinidad
**HABITAT** Freshwater streams, pools
**SIZE** 4 in (10 cm)

The leaffish is a member of the family Nandidae, a group of about 10 species of freshwater fish. Typical of its family, it has a laterally compressed body and many dorsal and anal spines, its mouth is large and protrusible. Although small, it is a voracious predator, lurking among vegetation, where it is well camouflaged by its leaflike appearance, to watch for prey and then dashing out to attack.

### Bermuda Chub *Kyphosus sectatrix*
**RANGE** W. Atlantic Ocean: Cape Cod, south to Bermuda, Caribbean and Brazil; E. Atlantic: off coast of W. Africa; Mediterranean Sea
**HABITAT** Rocky-bottomed waters, reefs
**SIZE** Up to 30 in (76 cm)

The sea chubs of the family Kyphosidae are found worldwide in tropical and warm temperate waters. Most of the 42 or so species live in shallow water and feed on algae. The Bermuda chub is typical of its family, with its deep body and small head and mouth. Its coloration varies, but it is generally gray, with narrow dark bands running the length of the body and yellow markings on the head. Plants are its main food, but it also eats small invertebrates.

Although the range extends to Cape Cod, adult Bermuda chub are rarely found north of Florida. Young fishes are probably carried farther north by the Gulf Stream.

### Australian Salmon *Arripis trutta*
**RANGE** S. Pacific Ocean: waters around S. and W. Australia, Tasmania, New Zealand
**HABITAT** Shallow inshore waters, often near river mouths
**SIZE** 36in (91 cm)

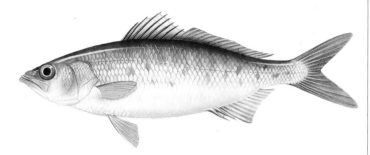

The Australian salmon is one of a family (Arripidae) of only 2 species, both confined to Australian waters. It is not related to the salmons of the northern hemisphere. It has a tapering, cylindrical body, a long dorsal fin and distinctive yellow pectoral fins, its sides are spotted with dark markings which are particularly plentiful on young fishes. Shrimplike crustaceans and small fish are its main foods.

### Tigerfish *Therapon jarbua*
**RANGE** Indian and Pacific Oceans: Red Sea, E. African coast to S. China, Philippines, N. Australia
**HABITAT** Inshore waters, estuaries
**SIZE** 11¾ in (30 cm)

The tigerfish belongs to a family of about 45 species or more of grunters (Traponidae). A distinctive fish, it is identified by the dark, curving stripes on its sides. Like all grunters, it has many small teeth and is predatory, feeding on small fish. Although generally a marine species, it will enter fresh water on occasion. Tigerfishes can produce sounds by vibrating the swim bladder using specialized muscles.

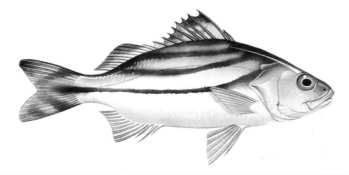

# PERCHLIKE FISHES CONTINUED

## LABROIDEI LABROID SUBORDER

There are over 2,200 species of labroids in 6 families including the Cichlidae (cichlids), Embiotocidae (surfperches), Pomacentridae (damselfishes), Labridae (wrasses), and Scaridae (parrotfishes). The latter 3 families contain many species that are present in large numbers in coral reefs. The cichlids form a highly diverse family of lake-dwelling species, and also include many popular aquarium species.

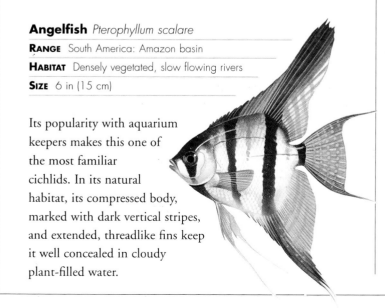

**Discus Fish** *Symphysodon discus*
**RANGE** Tropical South America: Amazon and other large river systems
**HABITAT** Heavily vegetated backwaters and pools
**SIZE** 7¾ in (20 cm)

One of the most handsome members of the family Cichlidae, the discus fish has a laterally compressed body, marked with irregular red stripes. These stripes, and the dark vertical bars that cross them, help to camouflage the fish among the vegetation and dappled light of its forested habitat.

The discus fish lays its eggs on gravel bottoms and then moves the newly hatched young to submerged vegetation. About 3 days after hatching, the young swim to one of their parents, attach themselves to its body or fins and feed on slime secreted by the adult's skin. They feed in this way for 5 weeks or more.

**Angelfish** *Pterophyllum scalare*
**RANGE** South America: Amazon basin
**HABITAT** Densely vegetated, slow flowing rivers
**SIZE** 6 in (15 cm)

Its popularity with aquarium keepers makes this one of the most familiar cichlids. In its natural habitat, its compressed body, marked with dark vertical stripes, and extended, threadlike fins keep it well concealed in cloudy plant-filled water.

**Nile Mouthbrooder** *Oreochromis niloticus*
**RANGE** N. Africa, south to Congo basin and E. Africa
**HABITAT** Rivers, dammed-up pools
**SIZE** 19¾ in (50 cm)

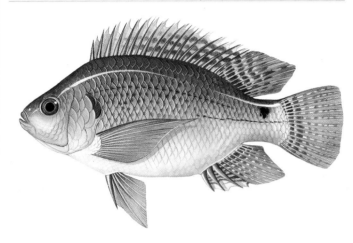

A large cichlid, the Nile mouthbrooder is a sturdy fish, with a long-based dorsal fin. It has a small mouth and tiny teeth and feeds mainly on plankton, although insects and crustaceans are also part of its diet.

Like many cichlids, this fish carries its developing eggs inside its mouth, thus keeping them safe and aerated at the same time. The female of this species broods the eggs, and even after the young fish are hatched, they will return to her mouth when danger threatens.

**Ring-tailed Pike Cichlid** *Crenicichla saxatilis*
**RANGE** South America: Venezuela, Amazon basin to Paraguay and Uruguay
**HABITAT** Rivers, pools
**SIZE** 14¼ in (36 cm)

A large, elongate fish, the ring-tailed pike cichlid has a distinctive black stripe running the length of its body. Its tail and dorsal fins are black-edged, and there is a black spot on the tail fin. Male and female fishes have the same markings, but males have pointed dorsal and anal fins and females have more rounded fins. An active predator, it snaps up prey in its large mouth as a pike does.

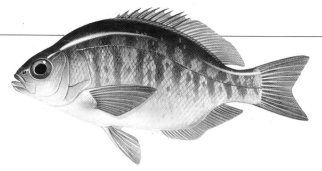

## Barred Surfperch *Amphistichus argenteus*

**RANGE** USA: California, south to Baja California, Mexico

**HABITAT** Coastal waters

**SIZE** Up to 16 in (41 cm)

The barred surfperch belongs to the family Embiotocidae, which contains about 24 species, all but one are found in the North Pacific. Most members of the family do frequent the surf area of coasts, hence the common name. A deep-bodied fish, its sides are marked with gold or bronze vertical bars and spots. It feeds on small crabs and other crustaceans and mollusks.

Surfperches bear live young. The male fertilizes the female internally by means of the modified front portion of the anal fin, and the young develop inside her body, protected and nourished by ovarian fluid. The brood size varies from 4 to 113, depending on the size of the mother, but the average is about 33. Most young are born from March to July and are mature at about 2 years old, when they are just over 5 in (12.5 cm) long.

## Kelp Perch *Brachyistius frenatus*

**RANGE** Pacific coast of N. America: Vancouver to California

**HABITAT** Shallow waters along rocky coasts, kelp beds

**SIZE** 7¾ in (20 cm)

A member of the surfperch family, Embiotocidae, the kelp perch has handsome coppery coloration on its sides, each scale having a dark spot. It feeds on crustaceans. It bears live young – the male fertilizes the female internally, and the young develop inside her body.

## Sergeant Major *Abudefduf saxatilis*

**RANGE** Worldwide, warm temperate and tropical seas

**HABITAT** Inshore waters, coral reefs

**SIZE** 9 in (23 cm)

The sergeant major belongs to the damselfish family, Pomacentridae, which contains over 315 species of marine fish, found all over the world in warm temperate and tropical areas. A deep-bodied fish, its coloration changes according to the depth of water it is in; in shallow water, it is yellow with dark barring, but in deeper water or caves, it turns blue with darker blue vertical bars.

The eggs are laid on a rock or in a rock crevice, on a surface cleared of any algal plant growth. The male fish guards the eggs until they hatch.

## Clown Anemonefish

*Amphiprion percula*

**RANGE** W. and central Pacific Ocean

**HABITAT** Coral reefs

**SIZE** 2¼ in (6 cm)

Unmistakable with its broad bands of white and orange and its dark-rimmed fins, the clown anemonefish belongs to the damselfish family, Pomacentridae. Like the others in its genus, it has developed a relationship with large sea anemones, living among their stinging tentacles and even remaining inside when the anemone draws in its tentacles. Thus the fish shelters from predators, and, at the same time, it is protected from the anemone's poison by its own body mucus. It feeds on tiny crustaceans and other organisms, which are taken during brief dashes from its refuge.

The eggs are laid on rock or coral near the anemone and are guarded by both parents.

## Beaugregory *Pomacentrus leucostictus*

**RANGE** W. Atlantic Ocean: coasts of Florida and Bermuda; Caribbean; Pacific coast of Mexico

**HABITAT** Inshore waters, coral reefs

**SIZE** 6 in (15 cm)

A member of the family Pomacentridae, the beaugregory is a handsome, rich orange-brown and blue fish, dotted with yellow spots. Like most members of its family, it is an active little fish, which darts around coral and rock crevices, feeding on algae, tiny crustaceans, worms and other small invertebrates.

# PERCHLIKE FISHES CONTINUED

### Ballan Wrasse *Labrus bergylta*

**RANGE** E. Atlantic Ocean: Norway and
Britain, south to N. Africa; Mediterranean Sea

**HABITAT** Rocky coasts

**SIZE** 19¾–23½ in (50–60 cm)

There are several hundred species of wrasse. Like many wrasses,
this species has interesting breeding behavior. After displays, the
pair builds a nest of weeds, bound together with mucus and
lodged in a rock crevice. Once the eggs are laid, the male
fertilizes them and guards them until they hatch.

### Tautog *Tautoga onitis*

**RANGE** W. Atlantic Ocean:
Nova Scotia to South Carolina

**HABITAT** Coastal waters, around
rocky shores and mussel beds

**SIZE** Up to 36 in (91.5 cm)

The tautog is a rather dull-colored fish, with a blunt snout and
a well-rounded body. Adults eat various invertebrates, mostly
barnacles, mussels, crabs and snails, which they crush with their
strong jaws and teeth. Young fishes eat worms and small
crustaceans.

Spawning occurs in the spring and summer, in deep water.
The eggs float at the surface and gradually drift inshore as they
develop and hatch. The young spend their first few months in
shallow waters, where there is plenty of seaweed for protection.

### Hogfish *Lachnolaimus maximus* **VU**

**RANGE** W. Atlantic Ocean: Bermuda and North Carolina to Brazil;
Gulf of Mexico, Caribbean

**HABITAT** Coastal waters, coral reefs

**SIZE** 35¾ in (91 cm)

The first three spines of the hogfishes' dorsal fins are greatly
elongated and thickened. The tips of the dorsal and anal fins are
pointed. The hogfish's thick lips protrude
slightly, and its forehead curves steeply
above the mouth. Coloration is variable
in this species, but males tend to
be more intensely colored
than females. Hogfishes
eat mollusks, crabs and
sea urchins.

### California Sheepshead

*Pimelometopon pulchrum*

**RANGE** Pacific Ocean: Monterey Bay,
California to Gulf of California

**HABITAT** Rocky coasts, around kelp and mussel beds

**SIZE** Up to 36 in (91.5 cm)

This distinctive wrasse has a deep body and a heavy, bulbous
head. In the breeding season, the male develops a prominent
bump on the forehead. The dorsal fin spines are shorter than the
rayed portion of the fin, and the lobes of the dorsal, anal and tail
fins are pointed. The middle of the male's body is red and the
front and back black or purple. The female is reddish all over,
sometimes with black markings.

The California sheepshead eats crustaceans and
mollusks and is believed to spawn in summer.

### Slippery Dick

*Halichoeres bivittatus*

**RANGE** W. Atlantic Ocean: Bermuda and
North Carolina to Brazil; Caribbean

**HABITAT** Coastal waters, coral reefs

**SIZE** Up to 9 in (23 cm)

The slippery dick is a common inhabitant of coral reefs. It eats
crustaceans, sea urchins worms and mollusks. The species is
characterized by two black lines running along the body.

### Rainbow Parrotfish

*Scarus guacamaia* **VU**

**RANGE** W. Atlantic
Ocean: Bermuda and Florida
through Caribbean to Argentina

**HABITAT** Coastal waters, coral reefs

**SIZE** 4 ft (1.2 m)

The rainbow parrotfish is one of approximately 83 species in the
family Scaridae. It has a robust, heavy body and a large head. It
has strong, beaklike jaws, formed from fused teeth, with which
it scrapes algae and coral off reefs to eat. Farther back in the
throat, the fish has large grinding teeth.

In common with some other parrotfish species, the rainbow
parrotfish sometimes secretes a cocoon of mucus around its body
at night. This natural "sleeping-bag" protects the fish from
predators while it sleeps.

### Blue Parrotfish *Scarus coeruleus*

**RANGE** W. Atlantic Ocean: North Carolina
to Brazil, including Gulf of Mexico and Caribbean

**HABITAT** Coral reefs

**SIZE** 4 ft (1.2 m)

The lower jaw of the blue parrotfish is far shorter than the upper; older males develop a prominent bump on the snout. The blue parrotfish feeds in the same manner as the rest of the family Scaridae, scraping algae and coral off reefs with its beaklike jaws; the food is then broken down for digestion by the grinding teeth, farther back in the throat.

### Stoplight Parrotfish *Sparisoma viride*

**RANGE** Caribbean

**HABITAT** Coral reefs

**SIZE** 9¾–19½ in (25–50 cm)

Males of this common parrotfish species are larger than females and differ in coloration. Males are bluish-green, while females are red and reddish-brown. These parrotfishes feed on algae and other plant material which they scrape from rocks and coral with their teeth.

## ZOARCOIDEI: ZOARCOID SUBORDER

A group of marine fishes found primarily in the North Pacific but also in the North Atlantic and the tropical regions of both oceans. Most of the 320 species of zoarcoids are offshore or deep sea dwellers although some species are found in tidal pools. The 9 families in the suborder include the eelpouts, pricklebacks, wrymouths, gunnels, and wolf-fishes.

### Ocean Pout *Macrozoarces americanus*

**RANGE** N. Atlantic Ocean: Labrador to Delaware

**HABITAT** Seabed, 50–600 ft (15–183 m)

**SIZE** 36½ in (93 cm)

The ocean pout is one of a small family collectively known as eelpouts. Their classification has been the subject of dispute, and

some authorities have placed them with the blennies rather than the codfishes. Typical of the eelpouts, the elongate ocean pout has long anal and dorsal fins joined to the tail fin. Its head is broad and flattened and it has thick, protuberant lips. It is a bottom-living species and eats crustaceans, sea urchins, brittle stars and other small invertebrates. In autumn, ocean pouts migrate into deeper, offshore waters to spawn. A female may shed 4,000 or more eggs, massed together in a gelatinous substance, which lie on the bottom and hatch after 2 or 3 months. Some eelpouts, such as the European species *Zoarces viviparus*, give birth to live young.

### Wrymouth *Cryptacanthodes maculatus*

**RANGE** W. Atlantic Ocean: Labrador to New Jersey

**HABITAT** Muddy seabed

**SIZE** 35½ in (90 cm)

A bottom-living fish, the wrymouth lives buried in mud, sometimes making a complex system of tunnels. It eats fish, crustaceans and mollusks. Rather eellike in appearance, the wrymouth has an elongate, scaleless body, with dorsal and anal fins continuous with the tail fin but no pelvic fins. Its head is flattopped, with the eyes set high, and its mouth slants obliquely, the lower jaw extending beyond the upper. Also known as the ghostfish, the wrymouth belongs to the family Cryptacanthodidae.

### Butterfish *Pholis gunnellus*

**RANGE** W. Atlantic Ocean: Labrador to Massachusetts; E. Atlantic: N. coast of France, north to Barents Sea; coasts of Iceland and S. Greenland

**HABITAT** Rocky shores, intertidal pools, sometimes in deeper waters

**SIZE** 9¾ in (25 cm)

This widely distributed fish has a slender, elongate body, brownish in color, and a distinctive row of white-edged black spots along the bottom of its longbased dorsal fin. It is a member of the family Pholididae (Gunnels), which contains fish found in the cooler waters of the North Pacific and Atlantic. Small crustaceans, worms and mollusks are its main foods, and since the butterfish is so abundant near the shore, it is itself an important item of diet for many seabirds.

Spawning takes place in winter when eggs are laid in clusters among stones near the shore and the parents guard the eggs until they hatch.

# PERCHLIKE FISHES CONTINUED

## Atlantic Wolffish *Anarhichas lupus*

**RANGE** W. Atlantic Ocean: Labrador to Cape Cod, sometimes New Jersey; across to E. Atlantic: Iceland and Spitsbergen to N. France

**HABITAT** From shallow waters down to 980 ft (300 m)

**SIZE** 3¼–4 ft (1–1.2 m)

One of about 6 species in the family Anarhichadidae, the Atlantic wolffish has a huge head, fanglike teeth and long dorsal and anal fins. It eats mollusks, such as clams, and crustaceans, which it breaks open with its sharp fangs and crushes with the broad teeth farther back in its mouth.

Spawning takes place in winter. The sticky eggs are shed in clumps on the seabed, where they may adhere to stones.

## NOTOTHENIOIDEI: ICEFISH SUBORDER

Commonly referred to as icefishes, the 120 notothenioid species are the dominant fish group of the Antarctic. They show many adaptations to their cold water habitat.

## Antarctic Cod *Notothenia coriiceps*

**RANGE** Antarctic coasts

**HABITAT** Coastal waters

**SIZE** 24 in (61 cm)

Almost three-quarters of fishes in the arctic belong to the notothenioidae family. Some have a special protein in their blood, which lowers its freezing point, and so they are able to survive temperatures as low as 28°F (–1.9°C).

Young antarctic cod are blue and silver at first, turning reddish as juveniles. This cod is a bottom-dweller and eats algae, mollusks, small crustaceans and worms.

## Icefish *Chaenocephalus aceratus*

**RANGE** Antarctic area off South Georgia, South Orkneys, South Shetlands

**HABITAT** Shallow waters to 1,100 ft (340 m)

**SIZE** 23½ in (60 cm)

The icefish is one of about 16 species in the family Channichthyidae, all found in the Antarctic. These fishes lack the oxygen-carrying pigment hemoglobin, which is common to all other vertebrates. Their blood appears whitish, almost clear. Oxygen is taken through the gills in the normal way for fishes but is carried within the body dissolved in the blood plasma. These fishes are sluggish, and need relatively little oxygen, so they are able to obtain sufficient oxygen from the cold, well-oxygenated waters that they inhabit.

An elongate, slender fish, the icefish has a large head, with beaklike jaws. It spends much of its time close to the bottom, eating fish and crustaceans.

## TRACHINOIDEI: TRACHINOID SUBORDER

Most of the 210 or so species in this suborder are bottom dwellers that bury themselves in sand to ambush passing prey. They include weeverfish, stargazers, and sand eels.

## Sand Eel/Sand Lance *Ammodytes tobianus*

**RANGE** E. Atlantic Ocean: Iceland and Norway to S. Portugal and Spain

**HABITAT** Inshore waters to depths of about 100 ft (30 m)

**SIZE** 7¾ in (20 cm)

Sand eels are so called because of their habit of burrowing extremely rapidly into clean, sandy bottoms, but they also swim in shoals near the surface. There are about 12 species in the sand eel family, Ammodytidae, all of which are thin, elongate fishes, with long dorsal and anal fins. Typically, the head is pointed, with a protruding lower jaw. The sand eel feeds on plankton and is itself an important food fish for many larger fishes.

Some sand eels spawn in autumn, others in spring, but all shed their eggs on the seabed, where they adhere to the sand.

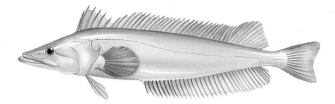

## Lesser Weever *Echiichthys vipera*

**RANGE** European Atlantic coasts, Britain to N. Africa; Mediterranean sea

**HABITAT** Shallow, sandy-bottomed waters

**SIZE** 5½ in (14 cm)

A bottom-living fish, the lesser weever lies half-buried in the sand with only its head visible. If disturbed, it erects its dorsal-fin spines, which contain tissue that produces highly toxic venom; there are more venom-producing spines on the gill covers. These spines can cause extremely painful wounds, but are used only in defence and as a warning signal. The lesser weever eats small bottom living crustaceans and fish. It is one of about 6 species in the family Trachinidae, all of which have venomous spines.

## Northern Stargazer *Astroscopus guttatus*

**RANGE** Atlantic coast of N. America: New York to North Carolina

**HABITAT** Shallow, sandy-bottomed waters

**SIZE** Up to 12 in (30.5 cm)

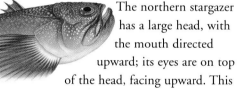

The northern stargazer has a large head, with the mouth directed upward; its eyes are on top of the head, facing upward. This structure allows the stargazer to lie partially buried on the seabed with only its eyes and mouth exposed, waiting for prey such as fish and crustaceans. Behind the eyes is a specialized area of electric organs, capable of producing charges of over 50 volts.

Spawning is believed to take place in spring or early summer, offshore. The young fishes gradually drift inshore to shallower waters, where they settle to the bottom-dwelling life of adults.

# BLENNIOIDEI: BLENNIOID SUBORDER

The 730 fish in this suborder, which include the blennies, are small marine fishes of tropical and subtropical regions.

## Giant Kelpfish *Heterostichus rostratus*

**RANGE** Pacific coast of N. America: British Columbia to Baja California

**HABITAT** Inshore shallow waters, near kelp beds

**SIZE** Up to 24 in (61 cm)

The giant kelpfish is the largest of the family Clinidae, which contains about 75 species of primarily tropical marine fish. It is distinguished by its elongate body, sharp, pointed head and longbased dorsal and anal fins, but its coloration is extremely variable, according to its surroundings. Fishes living in eel grass are bright green, others are dark green, brown, orange, yellow or reddish; their coloration always blends with the aquatic vegetation or other background of their habitat.

## Shanny *Lipophrys pholis*

**RANGE** N. European coasts: S. Norway and Scotland, south to Portugal and Madeira

**HABITAT** Rocky shores, rock pools

**SIZE** Up to 7 in (18 cm)

The combtooth blenny family, Blenniidae, to which the shanny belongs, contains about 345 species of mostly marine, shore-living fish. The shanny is typical of the family, with its scaleless skin, rounded head and rows of fine sharp teeth – these teeth are the origin of the family's common name. The shanny's diet includes algae, barnacles, crustaceans and fish.

The eggs are laid in clusters under a rock or in a crevice and are guarded by the male until they hatch.

## Redlip Blenny *Ophioblennius atlanticus*

**RANGE** W. Atlantic Ocean: North Carolina to Bermuda and south to coast of Brazil; Gulf of Mexico, Caribbean

**HABITAT** Rocky- or coral-bottomed waters

**SIZE** 4¾ in (12 cm)

Characterized by its steep, rounded snout bearing tufts and tentacles, red lips and red-edged dorsal fin, the redlip blenny is a common fish in its range. It is a member of the combtooth blenny family, Blenniidae, and is typical of the family in its bottom-living, secretive habits. It feeds on small invertebrates.

The eggs are laid amid coral or under rocks and are guarded by the male. The young fishes live in surface waters, farther offshore than adults.

# PERCHLIKE FISHES CONTINUED

### Batfish *Platax pinnatus*

**RANGE**  Indian and Pacific Oceans: Red
Sea, E. Africa to Philippines,
Indonesia, Australia

**HABITAT**  Coastal waters;
lagoons when young, reefs
as adults

**SIZE**  30 in (76 cm)

A member of the
spadefish family,
Ephippidae, the batfish
has a deep, laterally
compressed body and high
dorsal and anal fins. Juvenile
batfish are black, with fins
outlined in orange. The fins look
similar to some aquatic flatworms
and mollusks, which fishes find unpleasant to eat. Batfish swim
on their sides, with undulatory movements, heightening this
similarity. They probably gain protection from this.

### Scat *Scatophagus argus*

**RANGE**  Indian and Pacific Oceans: E. Africa to
India, Indonesia and W. Pacific Islands

**HABITAT**  Coastal waters; fresh and brackish water

**SIZE**  11¾ in (30 cm)

The scat is one of the 3 or so species in the Scatophagidae family
which means, literally, "dung-eaters". The scat is often found
near sewer outputs and is believed to feed on feces, but it
normally eats plant material. Adults are spotted with brownish
blotches. Young fishes have dark, barred markings on their sides.

### Blue-lined Spinefoot *Siganus virgatus*

**RANGE**  Indian and Pacific Oceans: India and Sri Lanka to Indonesia and
N. Australia, north to Philippines, China and Japan

**HABITAT**  Inshore waters, edges of coral reefs

**SIZE**  10 in (25.5 cm)

This is one of 27 or so species in the
rabbitfish, or spinefoot, family, Siganidae.
Spinefoots have many strong, sharp venomous
spines, capable of inflicting serious wounds. This species has a
typically blunt, rounded head and strong jaws. It grazes on algae.

### Blue Tang *Acanthurus coeruleus*

**RANGE**  W. Atlantic Ocean: New York and
Bermuda, south to Caribbean and Brazil

**HABITAT**  Coastal waters, coral reefs

**SIZE**  12 in (30.5 cm)

The brilliantly colored blue tang is one
of the 72 or so species in the surgeonfish
family, Acanthuridae. The fishes have extremely
sharp, movable spines on each side of the tail that are thought to
resemble a surgeon's scalpels. Normally the spines lie flat in a
groove, but if the fish is disturbed or alarmed, they are erected
and can inflict serious wounds on an enemy as the tail is lashed
to and fro. The blue tang uses these spines only for defensive
purposes, since it feeds entirely on algae, which it removes from
rocks with its sharp-edged teeth.

Although fairly typical of its family, the blue tang has a
particularly deep body and steep profile. Its coloration changes
as it matures. Young fishes are bright yellow, with blue spots
near the eyes; they then become blue over much of the front of
the body, with a yellow tail. Fully grown adults are a deep rich
blue all over, with narrow, dark blue lines running the
length of the body.

### Moorish Idol *Zanclus cornutus*

**RANGE**  Indian and Pacific Oceans: E. Africa to Hawaiian
Islands

**HABITAT**  Shallow waters, coral reefs

**SIZE**  7 in (18 cm)

The spectacular moorish idol is an unmistakable fish, with its
extremely bold coloration and projecting snout. Its body is deep
and compressed, and its dorsal and anal fins are pointed and
swept back, making the fish appear deeper than it is long. The
dorsal fin has a long, filamentous extension. Adults develop
protuberances over the eyes that enlarge with age.
Although it is a member of the surgeonfish
family, Acanthuridae, the moorish idol lacks
the formidable tail spines of its relatives.
The young fish, however, does have a
sharp spine at each corner of the
mouth. These spines drop off as
the fish matures. Indeed, young
and adults appear so different that
they were originally thought to be
separate species.

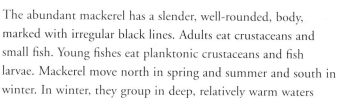

### Striped-face Unicornfish *Naso lituratus*

**RANGE** Indian and Pacific Oceans: E. Africa to
Australia and Hawaiian Islands

**HABITAT** Coastal waters, coral reefs

**SIZE** 16 in (41 cm)

The unicornfish is a member of the surgeonfish family, but it
has fixed, forward-pointing spines, not erectile spines, on each
side of its tail. This species does not develop a horn on its
forehead as it matures. Males do, however, have long, distinctive
streamers on the lobes of the tail
fin. Unicornfishes swim in
small schools and graze
on algae and coral.

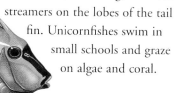

## MUGILOIDEI: MULLET SUBORDER

The 80 or so mullet species form the only family in this
suborder. Mullets are inshore fish that have thick,
streamlined bodies and two dorsal fins, the anterior being spiny
and the posterior soft. They live in large shoals.

### Striped Mullet *Mugil cephalus*

**RANGE** Worldwide, tropical and warm temperate seas

**HABITAT** Open sea, inshore waters, estuaries

**SIZE** Up to 35¾ in (91 cm)

The striped mullet is one of
the gray mullet family,
Mugilidae, which contains
species that live in salt, brackish

and fresh water. It has a typically rounded,
heavily scaled body and widely spaced dorsal fins. It eats the
minute algae and planktonic animals contained in the bottom
detritus, by sucking up the detritus, filtering it through its gills
and crushing the remaining material in its muscular stomach. A
good deal of sand and mud is also taken into the gut.

## SCOMBROIDEI: SCOMBROID SUBORDER

There are 1,365 species of scombroids in 6 families –
barracudas, snake mackerel, cutlassfishes, mackerel and
tunas, sailfishes and marlins, and swordfish. Most are voracious
predators that move at fast speed, and are prized by anglers.

### Great Barracuda *Sphyraena barracuda*

**RANGE** Worldwide, tropical seas except E. Pacific Ocean;
best known in Caribbean and W. Atlantic Ocean

**HABITAT** Coastal lagoons, coral reefs; adults farther offshore

**SIZE** Up to 6 ft (1.8 m)

There are about 18 species of barracuda found in tropical and
subtropical areas of the Atlantic, Indian and Pacific oceans. The
great barracuda is characteristic of the family, with its long,
slender body, pointed head and jutting jaw studded with
formidable teeth. An aggressive predator, it eats fish but has been
known to attack humans if disturbed or provoked. Barracudas
are generally solitary, but may gather in groups before spawning.

### Atlantic Cutlassfish *Trichiurus lepturus*

**RANGE** Atlantic Ocean: tropical and temperate waters,
including Gulf of Mexico and Caribbean; Mediterranean Sea

**HABITAT** Surface waters of open sea

**SIZE** 5 ft (1.5 m)

The Atlantic cutlassfish has an elongate,
ribbonlike body, with a pointed head and large jaws,
armed with formidable teeth. Its dorsal fin runs
the length of its silvery body to the end of the tail. A voracious
predator, it eats fish and squid. It is a member of the
Trichiuridae family.

### Atlantic Mackerel *Scomber scombrus*

**RANGE** W. Atlantic Ocean: Gulf of St. Lawrence to North Carolina;
E. Atlantic: Iceland, Scandinavia, south to N. Africa; Mediterranean Sea

**HABITAT** Offshore surface waters

**SIZE** 16–26 in (41–66 cm)

The abundant mackerel has a slender, well-rounded, body,
marked with irregular black lines. Adults eat crustaceans and
small fish. Young fishes eat planktonic crustaceans and fish
larvae. Mackerel move north in spring and summer and south in
winter. In winter, they group in deep, relatively warm waters
along the edge of the continental shelf. Mackerel are one of
about 50 species in the Scombridae family.

In summer a medium-sized female may produce as many as
450,000 eggs, shed in no particular place, which float until they
hatch about 4 days later.

# PERCHLIKE FISHES CONTINUED

### Yellowfin Tuna *Thunnus albacares*

**RANGE** Worldwide, tropical and warm temperate seas

**HABITAT** Offshore surface waters, inshore waters

**SIZE** Up to 6½ ft (2 m)

The yellowfin tuna has long pectoral fins, small, yellow finlets behind the dorsal and anal fins and yellow markings along its sides. Its body is typically, spindle-shaped. Yellowfin tuna eat fish, crustaceans and squid. Like most Scombridae, they make seasonal migrations. Spawning takes place at any time of year in the tropics and in late spring and summer elsewhere. Each year females are believed to produce at least two batches of over a million eggs.

### Wahoo *Acanthocybium solanderi*

**RANGE** Worldwide in tropical seas

**HABITAT** Open sea

**SIZE** Up to 6½ ft (2 m)

Unlike most of the family Scombridae, the wahoo is not a schooling fish. It usually occurs alone or in small groups. Its body is longer and more slender than most tunas, and it has a long, narrow snout, equipped with many strong teeth. It eats a range of fish and squid and it can reach extremely high speeds when in pursuit of prey – reputedly up to 41 mph (66 km/h).

The wahoo is not abundant and is not fished commercially, but it is popular with anglers.

### Skipjack Tuna *Euthynnus pelamis*

**RANGE** Worldwide in tropical seas, seasonally in temperate areas

**HABITAT** Offshore surface waters

**SIZE** 3¼ ft (1 m)

A member of the family Scombridae the skipjack has the streamlined body typical of the fast swimming tunas. It has dark stripes on the lower half of its body. An extremely abundant fish, it swims in huge schools, containing up to 50,000 fishes, and is an important commercial fish. Skipjacks eat fish, squid and crustaceans.

### Sailfish *Istiophorus platypterus*

**RANGE** Worldwide, tropical and warm temperate seas

**HABITAT** Surface waters, open sea and sometimes closer to shore

**SIZE** 12 ft (3.6 m)

The high, saillike dorsal fin is the outstanding characteristic of the sailfish but it also has elongate jaws, which are rounded, not flattened like those of the swordfish. It is one of the 10 species in the family Istiophoridae, all of which are spectacular, fast-swimming fishes. The sailfish has a varied diet and seems to eat almost any available type of fish and squid. It makes regular seasonal migrations, moving from cooler to more tropical waters in winter.

Sailfishes spawn in open sea, each female shedding several million eggs, which float in surface waters until they hatch. Those few that survive grow extremely quickly.

### Blue Marlin *Makaira nigricans*

**RANGE** Worldwide, tropical and warm temperate seas

**HABITAT** Offshore waters, open sea

**SIZE** 10–15 ft (3–4.6 m)

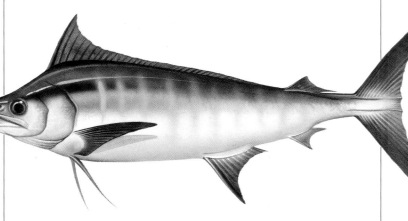

An extremely impressive fish, the blue marlin weighs at least 400 lb (180 kg) on average and can be more than twice as heavy. It has the elongate, rounded snout common to all members of the family Istiophoridae, with which it is thought to stun prey such as schooling fishes and squid.

Blue marlins are among the fastest of all fishes and have perfectly streamlined bodies and the high, crescent-shaped tails characteristic of the high-speed species. They make regular seasonal migrations, moving toward the Equator in winter and away again in summer.

## Striped Marlin *Tetrapturus audax*

**RANGE** Indian and Pacific Oceans: warm temperate waters, less common in tropical waters

**HABITAT** Open sea, inshore waters

**SIZE** 10 ft (3 m)

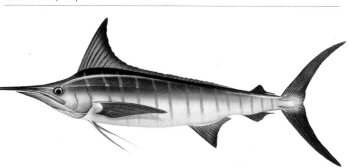

A steely-blue fish, marked with blue or white vertical bars, the striped marlin is distinguished from the blue marlin by its higher dorsal fin. Otherwise it is similar in appearance, with its elongate, beaklike snout and streamlined body. It feeds on fish and occasionally squid, both surface and deepwater species. Like all marlins, it is a member of the family Istiophoridae.

## Swordfish *Xiphias gladius* **DD**

**RANGE** Worldwide, temperate and tropical seas

**HABITAT** Open sea, surface and deep waters

**SIZE** 6½–16 ft (2–4.9 m)

The huge and spectacular swordfish is the only member of the family Xiphiidae. It has a greatly elongated, flattened snout, and its dorsal fin is sickle-shaped and placed farther back from the head than that of the similar sailfish. Swordfishes can also be distinguished from marlins and sailfishes by their flattened bills and lack of pelvic fins. Adult swordfishes are generally solitary and do not form schools, except in the spawning season. They are fast, active predators and feed on a variety of small fish, as well as squid. The exact function of the sword is not clear; it may be used to strike at schooling fishes, or it may be simply a result of body streamlining.

In the northern hemisphere swordfishes make seasonal migrations, in winter moving south and into deeper waters. The elongated snout is not present in young fishes but develops gradually, as they mature.

# STROMATEOIDEI: STROMATEOID SUBORDER

The 65 species in this suborder are found in tropical and warm temperate seas and include driftfishes, medusafishes, squaretails, and butterfishes. Juvenile fishes of these species are commonly associated with jellyfish or floating objects which provide protection as well as food.

## Man-o'-war Fish *Nomeus gronovii*

**RANGE** Tropical areas of Indian and Pacific Oceans; tropical W. Atlantic Ocean and Caribbean

**HABITAT** Lives in association with the Portuguese man-o'-war jellyfish

**SIZE** 8½ in (22 cm)

Best known for its habit of living among the long, stinging tentacles of the Portuguese man-o'-war, *Physalia physalis*, this little fish seems to be immune to the Physulia's stinging cells or may even inhibit their operation. The jellyfish is usually thought to be unaffected by the fish's presence, but the details of the relationship are poorly known, and it is possible that the fish removes debris from its host's body.

The small man-o'-war fish is one of about 15 species in the family Nomeidae.

## Butterfish *Peprilus triacanthus*

**RANGE** W. Atlantic Ocean: Gulf of St. Lawrence to S. Florida

**HABITAT** Coastal waters, bays, estuaries

**SIZE** 12 in (30.5 cm)

The attractively colored butterfish has a deep, but laterally compressed, body, a deeply forked tail and long dorsal and anal fins; adults have no pelvic fins. It feeds on crustaceans, squid and small fish. Butterfishes swim in small schools, and some appear to move northward in summer, returning south, but farther offshore, in winter. They belong to the family Stromateidae, which contains about 13 species of marine fish.

# PERCHLIKE FISHES AND FLATFISHES

## ANABANTOIDEI: GOURAMI SUBORDER

The 80 species of gouramis are freshwater fish that include several species that are well-known aquarium fish.

### Climbing Perch *Anabas testudineus*

**RANGE** India, Sri Lanka, S.E. Asia, Indonesia, Philippines, S. China

**HABITAT** Rivers, canals, ditches, ponds

**SIZE** 10 in (25.5 cm)

The climbing perch often inhabits stagnant, poorly oxygenated water. This, combined with its small gills, means that it must obtain some of its oxygen from the air. In each gill chamber is a labyrinthine organ, well supplied with blood vessels. Air taken in through the mouth passes through this auxiliary breathing organ, where oxygen is absorbed. This fish has an astonishing capacity for movement on land, made feasible by its capacity for breathing air. Using its tail for leverage and its pectoral fins and spiny gill covers as props, it hauls itself considerable distances between bodies of water, usually because its previous home has dried up. It is thought to feed on insects and small crustaceans.

The climbing perch is one of about 40 members of the family Anabantidae. It is an important food fish in much of its range.

### Paradisefish
*Macropodus opercularis*

**RANGE** China, S.E. Asia

**HABITAT** Ditches, rice fields

**SIZE** 3½ in (9 cm)

The paradisefish normally lives in poorly oxygenated water but, like the other members of the family Belontiidae, has auxiliary breathing organs in each gill chamber for extracting oxygen from the air. These operate in a similar manner to those of the climbing perch. A colorful little fish, it has greatly extended fins, those of the male being particularly long.

Its breeding habits are common to many of its family. The male makes a floating nest by blowing bubbles of air and mucus. The female sheds her eggs, which he fertilizes and transfers to the nest by spitting them into the bubbles.

### Siamese Fightingfish *Betta splendens*

**RANGE** Thailand

**HABITAT** Ponds, ditches, slow rivers

**SIZE** 2¼ in (6 cm)

The Siamese fightingfish has long been bred in captivity to take part in staged fights. Many forms with extremely long fins have been developed. Male fishes may be green, blue or red, but females are usually yellowish-brown. In the wild, males are brown or green. Wild fishes fight for dominance or to maintain territory, but much of the contest takes the form of ritualized threat displays, rather than actual combat.

The Siamese fightingfish often lives in oxygen-poor water. It takes in air at the surface using auxiliary breathing organs in its gill chambers. Mosquito larvae are a major food and they are extremely important as controllers of these insect pests.

In the breeding season, the male fish selects a suitable nest site and blows a bubble nest from air and mucus, which both protects the eggs and keeps them at the well-oxygenated water surface. As the eggs are shed, they are fertilized by the male, who spits them into the nest. The male guards and maintains the nest.

### Gourami *Osphronemus goramy*

**RANGE** Probably Indonesia; introduced in China, S.E. Asia, India, Sri Lanka, Philippines

**HABITAT** Ponds, swamps, streams

**SIZE** 24 in (61 cm)

A large, heavy-bodied fish, with a greatly extended pelvic fin ray, the gourami is the only species in its family, Osphronemidae. It is related to the Siamese fightingfish family and has auxiliary breathing organs in its gill chambers, to allow it to take in air at the surface. It often lives in oxygen-poor waters. The male makes a bubble nest and guards the eggs and larvae.

## CHANNOIDEI: SNAKEHEAD SUBORDER

Snakeheads are voracious predators. The 21 species form a single family found in freshwater habitats in tropical Africa and Asia.

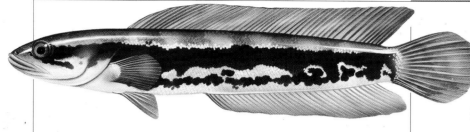

### Snakehead *Ophicephalus striatus*

**RANGE** India, Sri Lanka, S.E. Asia, China, Philippines, Indonesia

**HABITAT** Lakes, rivers, canals, ditches, swamps

**SIZE** 3¼ ft (1 m)

An elongate fish, with long dorsal and anal fins, the snakehead is one of about 10 species in the family Channidae. It generally lives in oxygen-poor waters and has accessory organs in its gill chambers with which it can utilize oxygen from the air. It can live for prolonged periods out of water as long as its skin stays moist, and can survive dry spells by burrowing into mud.

Before spawning, parents clear a surface area of vegetation, and the eggs float there for 3 days, guarded by the male until they hatch.

# PLEURONECTIFORMES: FLATFISH ORDER

This group contains 11 families and about 570 species, all but 3 of which are marine. The typical flatfish has a compressed body, and spends much of its life on the seabed. Young flatfishes swim normally, but as they develop, the eye on one side migrates so that both eyes are on the upper surface. The fishes lie and swim with the eyed side uppermost. Bone structure, nerves and muscles undergo complex modifications to achieve this change. All flatfishes are bottom-feeding predators.

### Adalah *Psettodes erumei*

**RANGE** Red Sea, Indian Ocean from E. Africa to N. Australia, into W. Pacific Ocean

**HABITAT** Shallow waters down to 300 ft (90 m)

**SIZE** Up to 24 in (61 cm)

The adalah is one of the 2 species in the most primitive flatfish family, Psettodidae. It is thicker bodied and less dramatically compressed than other flatfishes, and the migrated eye is on the edge of the head, rather than on the top side. Some individuals have eyes on the left, some on the right. The adalah and its fellow species, *P. belcheri*, also differ in that they have spiny rays in front of the dorsal fins. These fish live on the seabed but also swim in midwaters.

### Turbot *Scophthalmus maximus*

**RANGE** E. Atlantic Ocean: Scandinavia and Britain, south to N. Africa; Mediterranean Sea

**HABITAT** Shallow inshore waters to depths of 260 ft (80 m)

**SIZE** 3¼ ft (1 m)

The turbot is an extremely broad flatfish, with a large head and mouth; the female is bigger than the male. Its scaleless body varies in coloration but is usually brownish, with dark speckles that camouflage it on the seabed. The right eye is generally the one to migrate, so turbots have both eyes on the left side. Adults are active predators, feeding largely on fish. Young turbots feed also on crustaceans.

Spawning takes place in spring or summer, and females produce as many as 10 million eggs, comparatively few of which reach adulthood. Eggs and larvae float in surface waters while they develop, but by the time the young fish is 1 in (2.5 cm) long, it has adopted the adult body form and started its bottom-dwelling life. Turbot is one of the finest and most commercially valuable of all marine food fish.

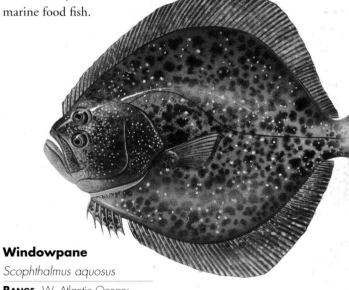

### Windowpane
*Scophthalmus aquosus*

**RANGE** W. Atlantic Ocean: Gulf of St. Lawrence to South Carolina

**HABITAT** Coastal waters to depths of about 230 ft (70 m)

**SIZE** 18 in (46 cm)

The windowpane is an extremely thin-bodied flatfish, white on the underside and brown with dark spots on the upper. The right eye is generally the one to migrate, so most individuals have both eyes on the left side. Young fishes feed on crustaceans, but adults normally eat fish. Although edible, this species is too thin-bodied to be of commercial value.

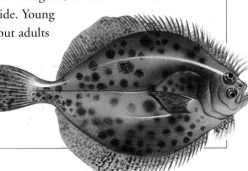

# FLATFISHES CONTINUED

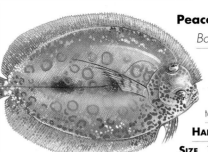

### Peacock Flounder

*Bothus lunatus*

**RANGE** W. Atlantic Ocean: Bermuda and Florida through Gulf of Mexico and Caribbean to Brazil

**HABITAT** Shallow coastal waters

**SIZE** 18 in (46 cm)

An attractive fish, with scattered blue markings, the peacock flounder is one of the family of lefteye flounders, so called because both eyes are generally on the left side of the head. The eyes of males are more widely separated than those of females. Another characteristic feature is the dorsal fin, which begins well forward in front of the eyes. Even though it is a fairly common fish, the peacock flounder is rarely seen, spending much of its life partially buried in sand on the seabed.

### Summer Flounder *Paralichthys dentatus*

**RANGE** W. Atlantic Ocean: Maine to South Carolina

**HABITAT** Coastal waters, bays, harbours; farther offshore in winter

**SIZE** Up to 3¼ ft (1 m)

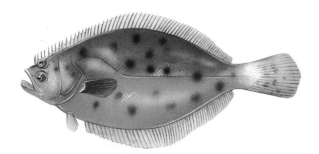

The summer flounder is a slender, active flatfish, with both eyes normally on the left side of its head. It feeds on crustaceans, mollusks and fish and will pursue prey in mid-waters and even to the surface. However, despite the fact that it is a relatively fast swimmer, much of its life is spent lying half-buried on the seabed. Its coloration varies according to the type of bottom it is lying on, but it is generally grayish-brown, with dark spots. In summer, it lives in shallow waters close to the shore, moving farther offshore to deeper waters in the winter.

Spawning takes place between late autumn and early spring, depending on the latitude. The eggs are thought to float in surface waters, and the young fishes drift inshore, where they live in shallow water while they develop.

### California Halibut *Paralichthys californicus*

**RANGE** Pacific Ocean: coast of California, sometimes as far north as Oregon

**HABITAT** Sandy-bottomed coastal waters

**SIZE** 5 ft (1.5 m)

The California halibut is a member of the lefteye flounder family, but perhaps as much as half the population have both eyes on the right side. It feeds on fish, particularly anchovies, and has a large mouth and strong teeth. The halibut, in turn, is eaten by rays, sea lions and porpoises and is also an important commercial food fish for man.

Spawning occurs in spring and early summer, and the growth rate of the young is fairly slow.

### Atlantic Halibut *Hippoglossus hippoglossus* **EN**

**RANGE** N. Atlantic Ocean: New Jersey, north to Greenland, Iceland and Barents Sea, south to English Channel

**HABITAT** Sandy-bottomed, gravel-bottomed and rocky-bottomed waters at 330–5,000 ft (100–1,500 m)

**SIZE** 6½–8 ft (2–2.4 m)

One of the largest of all flatfishes, the Atlantic halibut is identified by its size, its slender, yet thickset, body and its slightly concave tail. It may attain a top weight of 700 lb (316 kg), although fishes of such size are probably rare today. Its mouth and teeth are large, and both eyes are on the right side in almost all individuals. Females are generally larger than males and tend to live longer. Despite its size, the halibut is an active and voracious predator and pursues prey in mid-water, rather than remaining confined to the seabed. Fish are the main food of adults, but young halibuts also feed on crustaceans.

Spawning occurs in winter and spring, each female shedding as many as 2 million eggs. The eggs drift near the surface of deep water until they hatch after 9 to 16 days. Their growth rate is slow, and halibut are not sexually mature until they are 10 to 14 years of age. Adults migrate northward after spawning.

The Atlantic halibut has long been an important commercial species, but its slow growth rate and late maturity make the population extremely vulnerable to overfishing. Its numbers are now greatly reduced.

### Starry Flounder *Platichthys stellatus*

**RANGE** N. Pacific Ocean: California to Alaska and Bering Sea, south to Japan and Korea

**HABITAT** Coastal waters, bays, estuaries; also deeper waters down to 900 ft (275 m)

**SIZE** 36 in (91.5 cm)

Identified by the distinctive pattern of dark and light bars on the fins, the starry flounder has a dark-brown body on the eyed side, scattered with sharp spines. Although a member of the righteye flatfish family, Pleuronectidae, more than half of the population has both eyes on the left side. This flounder feeds on worms, crustaceans, mollusks and fish.

Spawning takes place in late winter and spring, usually in shallow waters. Young fishes may enter brackish water or river mouths. Females are mature in their third year, males in their second. Starry flounders are caught commercially, particularly off the coasts of Japan and Korea.

### Plaice *Pleuronectes platessa*

**RANGE** E. Atlantic Ocean: Scandinavia, south to N. Africa and Mediterranean Sea; coasts of Iceland and S. Greenland

**HABITAT** Shallow waters down to 165 ft (50 m), sometimes to 650 ft (200 m)

**SIZE** 19¾–35¾ in (50–91 cm)

The plaice is characterized by the rich brown color, dotted with prominent orange spots, of its eyed side; the underside is white. A member of the righteye flatfish family, Pleuronectidae, the plaice has both eyes on the right side of the body; reversed

specimens (those with eyes on the left) are rare. A bottom-dweller, it lives on mud, sand or gravel on the seabed and feeds on mollusks, worms and crustaceans. Even adults often come right inshore to the tidal zone to find food.

Spawning usually takes place from January to March. Eggs hatch in 10 to 20 days, depending on water temperature. The larvae live at the surface for up to 6 weeks before adopting the bottom-dwelling life, when they are about ½ in (1.25 cm) long. By this time, the structural adjustments and the migration of the eye have been completed. Males are mature at 2 to 6 years, females at 3 to 7 years. Plaice may live for up to 30 years.

Plaice is an important commercial fish in northern Europe.

### Dab *Limanda limanda*

**RANGE** E. Atlantic Ocean: White Sea, coasts of Scandinavia and Britain to Biscay; coasts of Iceland

**HABITAT** Shallow sandy-bottomed waters

**SIZE** 9¾–16½ in (25–42 cm)

A small flatfish, the dab has toothed scales on its eyed side, which give its body a rough texture. The blind side is white and has toothed scales only at the edges of the body. Both eyes are on the right side and exceptions are rare. The dab feeds on the seabed on almost any bottom-living invertebrates, especially crustaceans, worms and mollusks. It makes seasonal migrations, moving inshore in spring and offshore in autumn.

The dab spawns in spring and early summer, and the eggs and larvae float in surface waters until they adopt the adult form and bottom-dwelling habits, when about ¾ in (2 cm) long. By this time, the structural modifications and migration of the eye to the right side are complete.

This extremely abundant fish is an important commercial species in Europe, despite its small size.

# FLATFISHES CONTINUED

## Greenland Halibut *Reinhardtius hippoglossoides*

**RANGE** N. Atlantic Ocean: Arctic Ocean, Norwegian Sea, Iceland, Greenland, coasts of N. America as far south as New Jersey; N. Pacific Ocean: Bering and Okhotsk Seas, south to California and Japan

**HABITAT** Deep waters at 650–6,600 ft (200–2,000 m)

**SIZE** 31½ in–4 ft (80 cm–1.2 m)

An active predator, the Greenland halibut hunts in mid-water rather than on the seabed, feeding on fish, crustaceans and squid. In keeping with its habits, it is more symmetrical in body form than most flatfishes and has a blind side almost as dark as its eyed side. Although both eyes are on the right side, the upper eye is at the edge of the head, giving a larger field of vision than is usual for flatfishes. The large jaws are equipped with strong, fanglike teeth.

Spawning occurs in deep water in summertime; eggs and larvae float freely until the metamorphosis to adult form is complete.

## Winter Flounder *Pseudopleuronectes americanus*

**RANGE** W. Atlantic Ocean: Labrador to Georgia

**HABITAT** Shallow coastal waters, bays, estuaries, down to 300 ft (90 m)

**SIZE** 11¾–24 in (30–61 cm)

The winter flounder is most common in shallow waters over muddy sand, but the fish is also found over gravel or hard bottoms. In normal specimens, both eyes are on the right side, which is usually reddish-brown in color. The underside is white, but there are a few fishes with darker undersides. Winter flounders feed on the sea bottom on worms, crustaceans and mollusks and are thought to damage valuable soft-shelled clams by feeding on their breathing siphons.

In autumn, the flounders migrate to inshore waters, moving offshore again in spring.

Spawning takes place in winter and early spring, each female shedding up to half a million eggs. Unlike the eggs of most flatfishes, which float, these eggs sink to the bottom, where they stick to each other and to other objects. They hatch in about 2 weeks.

Winter flounders are important food fish, and are caught both commercially and by anglers.

## American Plaice *Hippoglossoides platessoides*

**RANGE** W. Atlantic Ocean: Greenland, Labrador, south to Rhode Island; E. Atlantic: Iceland, Barents Sea, south to English Channel

**HABITAT** Depths of 130–600 ft (40–180 m)

**SIZE** 11¾–24 in (30–61 cm)

Also known as the long rough dab, this plaice has toothed scales on its eyed side, which give the skin a rough texture. Both of the eyes are on the right side, which is brown or reddish-brown. The underside is white.

American plaice live on sand or mud bottoms, feeding on bottom-living invertebrates, such as sea urchins, brittle stars, crustaceans, mollusks and worms.

Spawning takes place in summer in the north of the range and in spring in the south. Each female produces up to 60,000 eggs, which are buoyant and float near the surface until they hatch.

### Sole *Solea solea*

**RANGE** E. Atlantic Ocean: Norway and Britain,
south to N. Africa and Mediterranean Sea

**HABITAT** Shallow coastal waters; winters farther offshore in deeper waters

**SIZE** 11¾–23½ in (30–60 cm)

The sole is the most abundant member of the family Soleidae in Europe and it is an important commercial food fish. Like other flatfishes, soles pass through a symmetrical larval stage, but as they develop, one eye migrates around to the other side of the head – the left eye usually moves to the right side. This, and other structural adaptations, fit the sole for an adult life spent partially buried on the seabed, eyed side uppermost.

The sole is a fairly slender-bodied flatfish. It is medium-brown on its upper side and white on its blind side. Its dorsal and anal fins extend as far as the tail fin.

Normally a night time feeder, the sole eats crustaceans, worms, mollusks and sometimes fish, often coming near to the water surface in search of prey. It may be active during the day in dull weather, but it usually spends daylight hours buried in sand or mud.

Soles make seasonal migrations, moving into shallow waters in spring and offshore again in winter. They spawn in spring and early summer, the eggs floating at the surface of the water until they hatch. Larvae live at the surface at first but by the time they are about ½ in (1.25 cm) long, they have metamorphosed into adult form and have drifted into shallow coastal waters, where they begin life on the seabed.

### Naked Sole *Gymnachirus melas*

**RANGE** W. Atlantic Ocean: coasts of
Massachusetts, south to Florida, Bahamas
and Gulf of Mexico

**HABITAT** Coastal waters,
most common in depths of
100–150 ft (30–45 m)

**SIZE** 9 in (23 cm)

The naked sole is a thickset flatfish, with scaleless skin marked with dark stripes on the eyed side. Both eyes are on the right in most individuals. Much of their life is spent on the sandy seabed, but they can swim well if necessary.

### Long Tongue-sole *Cynoglossus lingua*

**RANGE** Indian Ocean: E. Africa to India and Sri Lanka; W. Pacific Ocean

**HABITAT** Coastal waters, estuaries

**SIZE** 17 in (43 cm)

The long tongue-sole has an extremely narrow body for a flatfish but it is well adapted to life on the seabed, where it lives virtually buried in sand or mud with only its eyes showing. Both eyes are on the left side of the body, and the mouth, too, is situated on the left, low down, just below the eyes. The fish has no pectoral fins, and only the left pelvic fin is developed, the dorsal and anal fins join with the small, pointed tail fin. On the eyed side, the scales have toothed edges, giving a rough texture to the body.

There are about 86 species in the tongue-sole family, Cynoglossidae; most species are marine and are found in tropical and subtropical seas.

### Blackcheek Tonguefish *Symphurus plagusia*

**RANGE** W. Atlantic Ocean: New York, south to Florida,
Bahamas and Gulf of Mexico

**HABITAT** Sandy bays, estuaries

**SIZE** 8 in (20.5 cm)

A member of the tongue-sole family of flatfishes, this fish is typical of the group, with a body that is broadest at the front and tapers to a pointed tail. Its dorsal and anal fins unite with the tail, but it has no pectoral fins, and only the left pelvic fin is developed. Both of the eyes are on the left of the head, and the small mouth is set low and is contorted to the left. The eyed side is pale brown, with some dark markings and a dark spot near the eyes. The blind side is creamy white. Like all flatfishes, the tonguefish passes through a larval stage when its eyes are symmetrical – one on each side of the head – before the metamorphosis to adult form occurs and the eye migrates.

# TETRAODONTIFORM FISHES

## TETRAODONTIFORMES ORDER

This order of spiny-finned fishes contains about 340 species, only about 8 of which live in fresh water. Common names, such as pufferfish, porcupinefish, boxfish, trunkfish and triggerfish, give an idea of the strange body forms of the fishes contained in the order; most of them are rotund, deep or boxlike in shape. Some accentuate this plumpness by inflating the body with water as a defensive mechanism, and in species such as the porcupinefish, this swelling erects an array of sharp body spines. Others, such as the triggerfishes, enlarge the body by expanding a flap on the belly.

Many tetraodontiformes produce sounds, either by grinding their teeth or by vibrating the swim bladder with specialized muscles.

### Gray Triggerfish *Balistes carolinensis*

**RANGE** Atlantic Ocean: from W. Africa to Portugal in E. (seasonally north to Britain), across to Argentina and north to Nova Scotia in W.

**HABITAT** Open sea

**SIZE** 16 in (41 cm)

The gray triggerfish, a member of the family Balistidae, has a compressed, but deep, body and a slightly protruding snout, armed with sharp, incisorlike teeth. Its anal and second dorsal fins are prominent, and the first dorsal fin consists of three spines, the first of which is strong and thick and, when erect, is locked into place by the second spine. This "trigger" must be released before the spine can be flattened again. If the triggerfish is alarmed or pursued, it can take refuge in a crevice and wedge itself in by means of this "locking" spine, which makes it extremely hard to remove. It lacks pelvic fins but does possess a pelvic spine. It is thought to feed on crustaceans.

Young gray triggerfishes float among Sargassum weed in the open sea and hence become widely distributed.

### Queen Triggerfish *Balistes vetula*

**RANGE** W. Atlantic Ocean: Florida, (sometimes New England) to Brazil, including Gulf of Mexico and Caribbean

**HABITAT** Inshore waters, coral reefs

**SIZE** 22 in (56 cm)

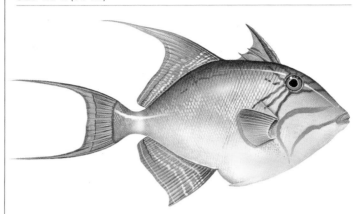

The attractive queen triggerfish is easily distinguished from other species by the slender extensions on its dorsal and tail fins and by its striking blue and yellow coloration. Like other triggerfishes, it has three dorsal spines, the first of which can be locked into an erect position by the second spine. It feeds on a variety of invertebrates, particularly sea urchins.

### Clown Triggerfish *Balistoides conspicillum*

**RANGE** Indian and Pacific Oceans: E. Africa to India, S.E. Asia, N. Australia and Japan

**HABITAT** Rocky coasts, coral reefs

**SIZE** 13 in (33 cm)

A dramatically patterned fish, the clown triggerfish has large, light spots on the lower half of its body, contrasting with the dark coloration on its back. Its mouth is circled with bright orange, and there are green markings on its back and on its tail fin. Its second dorsal and anal fins are smaller than those of many triggerfishes, but the first of the dorsal spines is robust and can be locked into an erect position by the second spine, in the manner common to all members of the family Balistidae.

## Black-barred Triggerfish *Rhinecanthus aculeatus*

**RANGE** Indian and Pacific Oceans: E. Africa through S.E. Asia to
Hawaiian Islands

**HABITAT** Shallow waters on the outer edges of reefs

**SIZE** 12 in (30.5 cm)

The black-barred triggerfish, a member of the family Balistidae,
has a strongly compressed body and a rather elongate snout. Its
coloration is distinctive but variable, although there are always
dark and light bands running down to the anal fin. In addition
to the three dorsal spines, typical of the triggerfish family, there
is a patch of spines on each side of its tail, surrounded by an area
of black. This triggerfish is capable of making quite loud sounds
by rubbing together bones supporting the pectoral fin. The
sounds are amplified by the fish's swim bladder.

## Sargassum Triggerfish *Xanichthys ringens*

**RANGE** W. Atlantic Ocean: North Carolina
through Caribbean to Brazil; probably
also occurs in tropical areas of Indian
and W. Pacific Oceans

**HABITAT** Open sea

**SIZE** 10 in (25.5 cm)

A small, fairly soberly colored member of the family Balistidae,
the sargassum triggerfish is marked with dark, broken stripes
along the length of its body. Like other triggerfishes, it has no
pelvic fins, but it does have a pelvic spine. The young of this
species tend to live under patches of floating Sargassum weed at
the water surface.

## Scrawled Filefish *Aluterus scriptus*

**RANGE** Atlantic, Pacific and Indian Oceans: tropical seas

**HABITAT** Inshore waters, seabed

**SIZE** 35¾ in (91 cm)

The scrawled filefish is one of a group of about 95 species of
filefish, which make up a subfamily of the
triggerfish family. This
filefish is long and

much more slender than most other members of its family, and
its snout is long and sharppointed. It has one dorsal spine, and
its dorsal and anal fins are small and soft. There are small spines
on its scales giving the body a prickly texture, which is the
origin of the fish's common name.

Bottom-living invertebrates and algae are the scrawled
filefish's main foods. and it forages on the seabed with its nose
down. It often feeds in clumps of eelgrass, where, with its
head-down posture, undulating fins and mottled greenish
coloration, it is perfectly camouflaged.

## Planehead Filefish *Monacanthus hispidus*

**RANGE** W. Atlantic Ocean: Cape Cod
(sometimes as far north as Nova Scotia) to
Florida and Caribbean, south to Brazil

**HABITAT** Inshore waters

**SIZE** 6–10 in (15–25.5 cm)

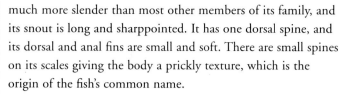

The planehead filefish has a compressed, deep body, covered
with small, spiny scales, which give it a rough texture. A
distinguishing feature is the fish's single dorsal spine, which has
a toothed rear edge. There is also a large pelvic spine.

## Scrawled Cowfish *Lactophrys quadricornis*

**RANGE** W. Atlantic Ocean: New England to Brazil,
including Gulf of Mexico and Caribbean

**HABITAT** Coastal waters, among beds of eel grass

**SIZE** 18 in (46 cm)

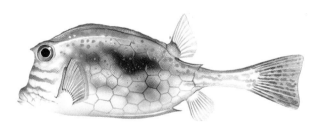

A member of the boxfish family, the scrawled cowfish has a bony
shell, which is composed of fused plates, encasing most of its
body. Only the mouth, eyes, gill and ventral openings, and fins
are free of this rigid shell. On its head is a pair of
forward-pointing spines, and there is another,
backward-pointing pair at the rear of the shell near the tail –
hence the scientific name meaning "four-horned".

Well protected by its body armor, the scrawled cowfish
swims slowly, by means of paddlelike movements of the fins,
but spends much of its life hidden amid eelgrass or close to the
seabed. Bottom-living invertebrates and aquatic plants are the
main part of its diet.

# TETRAODONTIFORM FISHES CONTINUED

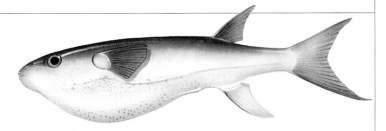

### Blue-spotted Boxfish *Ostracion tuberculatus*

**RANGE** Indian and Pacific Oceans: E. Africa to S.E. Asia, Australia, Philippines and W. Pacific Islands

**HABITAT** Coastal waters, coral reefs

**SIZE** 18 in (46 cm)

Like all members of the boxfish family Ostraciidae, the blue-spotted boxfish has a body encased in a bony shell, composed of fused plates. Mouth, eyes, fins, and gill and ventral openings are the only breaks in this armor, which effectively protects the fish from predators. This boxfish feeds on a variety of bottom-living invertebrates, and although it normally swims quite slowly, it can make a rapid spurt by moving its strong, flexible tail.

### Sharpnose Puffer *Canthigaster rostrata*

**RANGE** W. Atlantic Ocean: Bermuda and Bahamas, south to Brazil, including Gulf of Mexico and Caribbean; E. Atlantic: St. Helena, W. Africa, Canary Islands, Madeira

**HABITAT** Coastal waters, coral reefs, tidal pools, eelgrass beds

**SIZE** 4¼ in (11 cm)

A member of the pufferfish family, Tetraodontidae, the sharpnose puffer, like most of its relatives, is a stout round-bodied little fish. A characteristic dark ridge runs along the middle of its back, and its head and body are scattered with blue markings. Its varied diet includes worms, crustaceans sea urchins crustaceans and aquatic plants.

### Pufferfish *Lagocephalus lagocephalus*

**RANGE** Tropical and subtropical Atlantic Ocean, occasionally as far north as Britain; Indian and Pacific Oceans

**HABITAT** Surface waters in open sea

**SIZE** 24 in (61 cm)

This pufferfish, a member of the family Tetraodontidae, has a body that is stout behind the head and tapers sharply toward the forked tail. Like most puffers, it is capable of inflating its body with water, and when it does this, the small spines embedded in its belly stand erect as a defensive device. The skin on its back is smooth. Again, like all puffers, it has beaklike jaws, formed by one pair of partially fused teeth in each jaw. It is believed to feed on fish, crustaceans and squid, although little is known about its habits.

### Bandtail Puffer *Sphoeroides spengleri*

**RANGE** W. Atlantic Ocean: New England to Brazil; E. Atlantic: Azores, Madeira, Canary and Cape Verde Islands

**HABITAT** Shallow inshore waters, sea grass beds, tidal inlets

**SIZE** 12 in (30.5 cm)

An elongate puffer, the bandtail has a long, blunt snout and large eyes for its size. It is identified by the row of dark spots running from head to tail; there are also barred markings on its tail. Like all puffers, it has the ability to inflate its body enormously with water until it is like a balloon, in order to deter its predators. Any enemy would find it extremely difficult to swallow or even bite the blown-up body. The skin is covered with tiny spines, which stick out when the body is inflated. Once the danger is past, the puffer quickly deflates.

### Common Pufferfish *Tetraodon cutcutia*

**RANGE** India, Burma, Malaysia

**HABITAT** Rivers

**SIZE** 6 in (15 cm)

One of the few freshwater puffers, the common pufferfish has a rotund body attractively colored with green and patches of yellow. When threatened, it inflates its body with water until it is virtually globular, but it does not have skin spines. With its plump, rather rigid, body the puffer moves slowly, using undulations of its small dorsal and anal fins, but it compensates for this lack of speed by its defensive techniques. It feeds on bottom-dwelling invertebrates and on fish. Common puffers are very popular aquarium fishes and have been bred in captivity. The female sheds her eggs on the bottom, where they are guarded by the male, who lies over them until they hatch.

Many members of the puffer family are considered to be good food fish, despite the fact that their internal organs – and occasionally even the flesh – are extremely toxic and can cause fatal poisoning. In Japan, chefs are specially trained in the cooking of puffers, known as *fugu*, but there are still cases of poisoning.

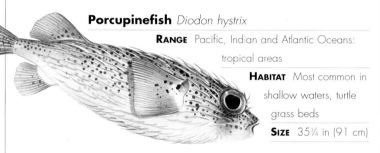

### Porcupinefish *Diodon hystrix*

**RANGE** Pacific, Indian and Atlantic Oceans: tropical areas

**HABITAT** Most common in shallow waters, turtle grass beds

**SIZE** 35¾ in (91 cm)

Similar to its relatives the pufferfishes in that it can inflate its body, the porcupinefish is covered with long, sharp spines; these spines normally lie flat but stand out when the body is inflated. It is clearly almost impossible for any predator to tackle this globular pin cushion, and this method of defence compensates the fish for its lack of speed and mobility. It swims slowly, with undulations of its small dorsal and anal fins; it lacks pelvic fins.

The porcupinefish has two fused teeth in each jaw, making a sharp, birdlike beak with which it crushes hardshelled prey such as crabs, mollusks and sea urchins.

### Striped Burrfish *Chilomycterus schoepfi*

**RANGE** W. Atlantic Ocean: Cape Cod to Florida, south through Gulf of Mexico and Caribbean to Brazil

**HABITAT** Shallow inshore waters

**SIZE** Up to 10 in (25.5 cm)

One of the approximately 15 species in the porcupinefish family, Diodontidae, the striped burrfish has an oval body, studded with stout, thornlike spines. The body can be inflated with water, but the spines are fixed in an erect position. The upper part of the body is marked with dark, irregular stripes, and there are a couple of dark patches on the sides.

Crustaceans and mollusks are the main foods of the striped burrfish which has fused, beaklike teeth, strong enough to crush their hard shells.

### Ocean Sunfish *Mola mola*

**RANGE** Atlantic, Pacific and Indian Oceans: temperate and tropical areas

**HABITAT** Open sea

**SIZE** Up to 13 ft (4 m)

The extraordinary ocean sunfish is a member of the small, largely unstudied family Molidae, which contains 3 species. Quite unlike any other fish, it has an almost circular body, which ends rather abruptly in a curious frill, consisting of a series of lobes that form a modified tail. Both dorsal and anal fins are short based and high and placed near the end of the body. The ocean sunfish's pectoral fins are rounded, and it lacks pelvic fins. Its mouth is small for so large a fish and contains two fused teeth in each jaw, making a strong beak.

The fish feeds largely on small planktonic organisms, such as tiny jellyfishes and comb jellies, but also eats crustaceans and fish.

Although they are so huge and so widely distributed, ocean sunfishes are little known. They are so called because of the belief that they bask in the sun in surface waters, but fishes observed basking in this way may, in fact, be sick or disabled.

# LUNGFISHES AND COELACANTH

## COELACANTHIFORMES COELACANTH ORDER

The lobe-finned fishes (Class Sarcopterygii) are the fishes that are most closely related to the amphibians, reptiles, and other tetrapods. Their lobed fins, like tetrapod limbs, are supported by an internal skeleton attached to the pelvic or pectoral girdle. The few extant members of the class include the coelacanth and the lungfishes. There is a single living species of coelacanth in the order Coelacanthiformes, an order which was once widespread and abundant. Coelacanths were only known as 90-million-year-old fossils until one was caught by a fisherman off the coast of South Africa in 1938. This living species was so like its fossil relatives as to be unmistakably a coelacanth and has enabled scientists to learn about the bodies of animals hitherto known only from skeletons.

### Coelacanth *Latimeria chalumnae* **EN**

| | |
|---|---|
| **RANGE** | Indian Ocean, off Comoro Islands |
| **HABITAT** | Rocky or coral slopes |
| **SIZE** | 6¼ ft (1.9 m) |

Coelacanths are heavy-bodied fishes, with fleshy lobes at the base of all fins except the first dorsal fin; the pectoral fins can be turned through 180 degrees. Such fishes, known as the crossopterygians, were once widespread.

The internal structure of the coelacanth has many features which throw light on the evolution of fishes; for example, the heart is extremely simple compared with that of other fishes and is similar to the early fish heart which theorists had predicated. The kidneys, unlike those of any other vertebrate, are positioned on the underside of the body.

Modern coelacanths are carnivores, believed to feed mainly on fish. There has been much disagreement about their breeding methods, but now, since the discovery of a female with 5 almost fully developed young in her oviduct, they are known to be ovoviviparous: they bear fully formed young by means of eggs that hatch inside the mother.

## CERATODIFORMES AUSTRALIAN LUNGFISH ORDER

There is only a single living species in this order, which has some relationship with the other lungfish order. All lungfishes have lunglike breathing organs which they can use to take breaths of air at the surface, when under water, they inhale water as other fishes do. Lungfishes are related to early air-breathing fishes and are the only remaining representatives of formerly abundant orders. How closely the lungfishes are related to terrestrial vertebrates is the subject of considerable debate.

### Australian Lungfish *Neoceratodus forsteri*

| | |
|---|---|
| **RANGE** | Australia: Queensland |
| **HABITAT** | Rivers |
| **SIZE** | 5 ft (1.5 m) |

First discovered in 1870, the Australian lungfish differs from other lungfishes in that it has only one lung. It lives in permanent waters, so does not generally undergo estivation, the period of dormancy in a mud burrow to withstand drought that is characteristic of African and South American lungfishes. In captivity it is mainly carnivorous and feeds on almost any animal food. The fishes spawn from August to October in shallow water.

The lungfish occurs naturally only in the Burnett and Mary rivers, but is being introduced into other rivers, including the Upper Brisbane, the Albert and the Coomera rivers in an attempt to protect the species.

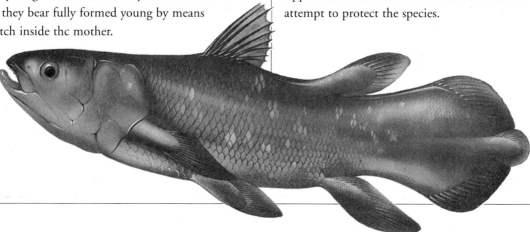

# LEPIDOSIRENIFORMES AFRICAN AND SOUTH AMERICAN LUNGFISH ORDER

This order contains 2 related families one with only a single species, the South American lungfish, and the other with 4 species of African lungfishes. The close relationship of these 2 families is one of the pieces of evidence suggesting that Africa and South America were once joined. While the Australian lungfish, with its flipperlike fins, single lung, and flattened body, most resembles fossil forms of lungfish, the South American and African lungfishes have eellike bodies, fins reduced to filaments, and paired lungs. Both families live in swampy areas where summer droughts are likely to occur. If swamps dry up, these fish dig burrows in the mud in which they survive in a dormant state until the waters return. During this dormant period, known as estivation, the lungfish's metabolism is reduced to a very low level. Estivating lungfishes survive by metabolising their own muscles. Muscle tissue is restored once the rains fall, and the lungfish emerges from its burrow and starts feeding.

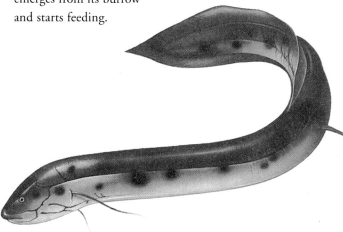

### South American Lungfish *Lepidosiren paradoxa*

| **RANGE** | Central South America |
|---|---|
| **HABITAT** | Swamps, weeded river margins |
| **SIZE** | 50 in (1.25 m) |

The South American lungfish has a pair of lunglike organs connected with its oesophagus. This fish usually lives in oxygen-poor, swampy areas of the Amazon and Paraná river systems and the large swamps of the Chaco region. Because of its lungs it is able to supplement the oxygen obtained from the water by breathing air at the surface.

The swamps this lungfish inhabits are periodically flooded and then undergo a dry season. The fish survives the dry period by digging itself a burrow in which it lives,

breathing air, while the swamp dries out. Once the surroundings become really arid, the fish closes the burrow entrance with mud, curls up and covers itself with a protective covering of mucus secretion to conserve moisture. Its body slows down to a state of dormancy, but it continues to breathe air. When the rains return, the lungfish emerges from its burrow. This form of inactivity in a hot climate is known as estivation.

During the rainy season, lungfish pairs spawn in burrows made by the male. He guards the eggs and then the young. During this time his pelvic fins develop branched, well-vascularised projections that may supply additional oxygen to the incubating male and, by diffusion, to the developing young. The newly hatched South American lungfish have adhesive glands by which they hang from vegetation, and external gills that make them resemble salamander tadpoles. Both these larval features are lost after 6 to 8 weeks, by which time the 1.5 in (4 cm) long fins can breathe air.

### African Lungfish *Protopterus aethiopicus*

| **RANGE** | E. and C. Africa |
|---|---|
| **HABITAT** | Rivers, lakes |
| **SIZE** | 6½ ft (2 m) |

The African lungfish has a pair of lungs connected to its esophagus and can breathe air at the water surface. It has normal, but poorly developed, gills. Like other lungfish species, the air breathing apparatus of African lungfishes is equivalent to the lungs of terrestrial vertebrates. They come to the surface to breathe about every 30 minutes.

This species lives mostly in permanent waters, but if there is a long dry period and the water level drops, it can burrow and estivate in much the same way as the South American lungfish. The other 3 African species live in swamps ancl must estivate during the regular dry seasons.

In the breeding season the male makes a hole in which one or more females lay eggs. He then guards the eggs and the young when they hatch and will chase away and attack any predators.

*P. aethiopicus* is a predatory fish that feeds mainly in the inshore parts of the lakes in which it lives on crabs, mollusks and fishes, including catfishes and cichlids.

# ANIMALS A-Z

In this alphabetical listing of all the animals in the encyclopedia, all species are listed by their common names where possible. Where animals have more than one common name, for example, the caribou/reindeer, both of these names are listed.

## Mammals

Aardvark
Aardwolf
Addax
Agile Mangabey
Agouti
Angwantibo
Anoa, lowland
Anteater,
     *giant, silky*
Antechinus, *brown*
Antelope,
     *beira, four-horned, roan,*
     *royal*
Ape, *barbary*
Aplodontia
Armadillo,
     *giant, nine-banded,*
     *pink fairy*
Ass,
     *African, Asiatic wild*
Aye-aye

Baboon,
     *chacma, hamadryas, olive*
Babirusa
Badger,
     *American, Chinese ferret,*
     *Eurasian, hog, stink*
Baiji
Bandicoot,
     *brown, eastern barred,*
     *rabbit*
Banteng
Barbastelle
Bat,
     *American false vampire,*
     *Australian false vampire,*
     *big brown, common*
     *long-eared, Cuban flower,*
     *Egyptian free-tailed,*
     *Egyptian rousette, Egyptian*
     *slit-faced, fisherman, fish-*
     *eating, flower-faced,*
     *Franquet's fruit, greater false*
     *vampire, greater fruit,*
     *greater horseshoe, greater*
     *mouse-tailed,*
     *hammerheaded, harpy fruit,*
     *heart-nosed, hog-nosed,*
     *Honduran disc-winged,*
     *Jamaican fruit-eating, large*
     *Malay leaf-nosed, leaf-*
     *chinned, lesser horseshoe,*
     *little big-eared, little brown,*
     *long-tongued, long-tongued*
     *fruit, mastiff, Mexican*
     *funnel-eared, moustached,*
     *New Zealand short-tailed,*
     *Old World sheath-tailed,*
     *painted, Persian trident,*
     *Philippine horseshoe,*
     *pipistrelle common,*
     *proboscis, Queensland*
     *blossom, red, short-tailed*
     *leaf-nosed, smoky, spear-*
     *nosed, sucker-footed, tail-less*
     *leaf-nosed, tent-building,*
     *tomb, trident leaf-nosed,*
     *tube-nosed fruit, two-lined,*
     *vampire, velvety free-tailed,*
     *white, Wroughton's*
     *free-tailed, yellow-winged,*
     *yellow-shouldered*

Bear,
     *American black, Asiatic*
     *black, big brown, grizzly,*
     *polar, spectacled, sun*
Beaver,
     *American, Eurasian,*
     *mountain*
Bighorn, *American*
Binturong
Bison,
     *American, European*
Blackbuck
Blackcap, *bush*
Boar, *wild*
Bobcat
Bongo
Bonobo
Bontebok
Boutu
Buffalo, *African bigmouth*
Bushbaby,
     *greater, lesser*

Capybara
Camel, *bactrian*
Capuchin, *white-fronted*
Caracal
Caribou
Cat,
     *African golden, leopard,*
     *pampas, Pallas's, wild*
Cavy, *rock*
Chamois
Cheetah
Chevrotain,
     *lesser Malay, water*
Chimpanzee, *pygmy*
Chinchilla-rat
Chipmunk, *eastern*
Civet, *African*
Congo water
Coati
Colobus,
     *Angolan black and white,*
     *olive, red*
Colocolo
Colugo
Cottontail, *desert*
Coyote
Coypu
Cusimanse

Degu
Deer,
     *Chinese water, pampas,*
     *Père David's, red, roe,*
     *tufted, white-tailed*
Desman, *Russian*
Dhole
Dibatag
Dik-dik, *Kirk's*
Dingo
Dog,
     *bush, hunting*
Dolphin,
     *bottlenose, common,*
     *Ganges, Indo-Pacific*
     *humpbacked, Risso's, striped,*
     *whitefin*
Dormouse,
     *African, desert,*
     *edible, fat, Japanese,*
     *Malabar spiny*
Douroucouli
Drill
Dromedary
Dugong
Duiker,
     *collared, bay, yellow*
Dunnart, *fat-tailed*

Echidna,
     *long-beaked, short-beaked*
Eland
Elephant,
     *African, Asian*
Elk

Fanalouc
Ferret, *black-footed*
Fossa

Fox,
     *red, Arctic, crab-eating,*
     *fennec*
Gaur
Gazelle, *Thomson's*
Gelada
Genet, *small-spotted*
Gerbil,
     *fat-tailed, great,*
     *greater short-tailed,*
     *Indian, large,*
     *North African,*
     *South African pygmy*
Gerenuk
Guenon, *red-bellied*
Gundi
Gibbon,
     *black, hoolock, Kloss's, lar,*
     *pileated*
Giraffe
Glider,
     *greater, pygmy*
Gopher,
     *northern pocket, plains,*
     *pocket*
Goral, *common*
Gorilla
Grison
Grysbok, *cape*
Guanaco
Guinea pig

Haartebeest
Hamster,
     *common, dwarf, golden*
Hanuman langur
Hare,
     *brown, hispid, snowshoe,*
     *spring*
Hare-wallaby, *spectacled*
Hedgehog,
     *desert, Western European*
Hippopotamus, *pygmy*
Hog, *giant forest*
Hog-nosed bat family
Honey possum family
Horse, *Przewalski's wild*
Howler,
     *black, red*
Hutia
Hyena,
     *brown, spotted, striped*
Hyrax,
     *large-toothed rock, small-*
     *toothed rock, tree*

Ibex
Impala
Indri

Jack rabbit, *black-tailed*
Jaguar
Jerboa,
     *great, northern three-toed*

Kangaroo,
     *red, Lumholtz's tree*
Kangaroo-mouse, *pale*
Kangaroo-rat, *desert*
Kinkajou
Klipspringer
Koala
Kob, *Uganda*
Kowari
Kudu, *greater*

Langur,
     *Hanuman, snub-nosed*
Lechwe
Lemming,
     *Norway, southern bog*
Lemur,
     *Philippine flying, ring-*
     *tailed, ruffed, woolly*
Leopard
Leopard,
     *clouded, snow*
Linsang,
     *African, banded*
Lion, *mountain*

Loris,
     *slender, slow*
Lynx
Macaque,
     *bonnet, Japanese,*
     *stump-tailed*
Manatee, *American*
Mandrill
Mangabey,
     *agile, white-cheeked*
Mara
Marmoset,
     *Goeldi's, pygmy, silvery*
Marsupial mole, *Southern*
Marten, *American*
Meerkat
Mole,
     *cape golden, European,*
     *giant golden, hairy-tailed,*
     *Hottentot golden, Pacific,*
     *star-nosed*
Mole-rat,
     *cape dune, lesser, giant,*
     *naked*
Mole-vole, *southern*
Mongoose,
     *banded, bushy-tailed,*
     *Indian, marsh, white-tailed*
Monkey,
     *Allen's swamp, black spider,*
     *common woolly,*
     *De Brazza's, Diana, night,*
     *patas, proboscis, vervet,*
     *woolly spider*
Moonrat, *mindanao*
Moose
Mouflon
Mountain goat
Mouse,
     *African climbing, American*
     *climbing, Californian*
     *pocket, deer, eastern shrew,*
     *fat, forest spiny pocket,*
     *four-striped grass, golden,*
     *harvest, hopping, house,*
     *meadow jumping, Mexican*
     *spiny pocket, mosaic-tailed,*
     *northern birch, northern*
     *grasshopper, silky pocket,*
     *South American field,*
     *western harvest, wood*
Mouse-lemur, *russet*
Mulgara
Muntjac, *Chinese*
Musk deer, *forest*
Muskrat
Myoxida

Narwhal
Nilgai
Noctule
Numbat
Nutria
Nyala

Ocelot
Okapi
Olingo
Onager
Opossum,
     *water, pale-bellied mouse,*
     *short-tailed, shrew, Virginia*
Orang-utan
Oribi
Oryx, *Arabian*
Otter,
     *African clawless, Eurasian,*
     *giant, sea*
Otter-civet
Ox, *musk*

Paca
Pacarana
Pademelon, *red-legged*
Palm civet,
     *African, banded, masked*
Panda,
     *red, giant, lesser*
Pangolin,
     *giant, tree*

Peccary,
     *chaco, collared,*
     *white-lipped*
Pig,
     *bearded, bush*
Pika, *northern*
Pipstrelle, *common*
Planigole, *pygmy*
Platypus
Polecat, *western*
Porcupine,
     *Asian brush-tailed, crested,*
     *Indonesian, long-tailed,*
     *North American, tree,*
     *upper Amazon*
Porpoise,
     *common, Dall's,*
     *finless, harbour*
Possum,
     *brush-tailed, honey*
Potoroo
Potto
Prairie dog, *black-tailed*
Pronghorn
Pudu, *northern*
Rat,
     *African grass, Arizona*
     *cotton, armoured, Baja*
     *California rice, bamboo,*
     *black, brown, cane, crested,*
     *dassie, fat sand, fish-eating,*
     *giant pouched, gliding spiny,*
     *greater bandicoot, karroo,*
     *long-tailed pouched,*
     *Madagascan, Norway,*
     *rough-tailed giant, spiny*
     *rice, stick-nest, swamp,*
     *white-tailed*

Quokka
Quoll

Rabbit,
     *brush, European, pygmy,*
     *Sumatran short-eared,*
     *swamp, volcano*
Raccoon
Raccoon-dog
Rat-kangaroo,
     *musky, rufous*
Ratel
Reedbuck, *southern*
Reindeer
Rhebok
Rhinoceros,
     *black, Indian, square-*
     *lipped, Sumatran, white*
Rockhare, *greater red*

Sable
Saiga
Saki,
     *black-barred, monk*
Salano
Sassaby
Sea lion,
     *Australian, California,*
     *steller*
Seal,
     *bearded, common, crabeater,*
     *gray, harp, hooded, leopard,*
     *Mediterranean monk,*
     *northern elephant, northern*
     *fur, South American fur,*
     *Weddell*
Serow
Serval
Sheep, *Barbary*
Shrew,
     *armored, feather-tailed tree,*
     *giant Mexican, giant otter,*
     *madras tree, masked,*
     *mountain tree, mouse,*
     *Philippine tree, pygmy*
     *white-toothed, short-eared*
     *elephant, short-tailed, Sri*
     *Lankan long-tailed*
Siamang
Sifaka, *Verreaux's*

Skunk,
*striped, hog-nosed, western spotted*
Sloth,
*three-toed, two-toed*
Solenodon, *Cuban*
Springbok
Squirrel,
*monkey, African giant, African ground, African palm, Beecroft's flying, black giant, European red, gray, Indian striped palm, northern flying, Prevost's, red giant flying, thirteen-lined ground, Zenker's flying*
Stoat
Sugar glider

Tahr, *Himalayan*
Takin
Talapoin
Tamandua, *northern*
Tamarin,
*black and red, emperor, golden lion*
Tasmanian Devil
Tayra
Tapir,
*Brazilian, Malayan*
Tarsier, *western*
Tenrec,
*streaked, rice, tail-less, greater, gehog, long-tailed shrew*
Tiger
Titi, *dusky*
Tree shrew,
*Bornean smooth-tailed, common, feather-tailed, Philippine*
Tsessebi
Tuco-tuco

Uakari, *bald*

Vicuña
Viscacha, *plains*
Vole,
*bank, European water, meadow, sagebrush*

Wallaby,
*bridled, nail-tailed, New Guinea forest, swamp, yellow-footed rock*
Walrus
Warthog
Water rat, *Australian*
Waterbuck,
*common, Defassa*
Water buffalo, *Asian*
Weasel, *east*
Whale,
*Baird's beaked, blue, bowhead, Cuvier's beaked, dwarf sperm, Greenland right, gray, humpback, killer, long-finned pilot, minke, northern bottlenose, pygmy sperm, sei, Shepherd's beaked, Sowerby's beaked, sperm, white*
Wildebeest, *blue*
Wolf,
*gray, maned*
Wolverine
Wombat, *common*
Woodchuck
Woodrat, *white-throated*

Yak, *wild*
Yapok

Zebra,
*common, Grevy's*
Zokor, *common Chinese*
Zorilla

# Birds

Accentor, *hedge*
Akepa
Akiapolaau
Albatross,
*light-mantled sooty, wandering*
Alethe, *firecrested*
Amazon, *yellow-crowned*
Anhinga
Ani, *smooth-billed*
Antbird,
*ocellated, white-cheeked*
Antpitta, *chestnut-crowned*
Antshrike,
*barred, great*
Antwren, *streaked*
Apalis, *yellow-breasted*

Apostlebird
Aracari, *curl-crested*
Astrapia, *ribbon-tailed*
Auk, *little*
Auklet, *crested*
Avadavat, *red*
Avocet, *pied*

Babbler,
*blackcap mountain, brown*
Bailleui
Barbet, *coppersmith*
Bananaquit,
*crimson-breasted, double-toothed*
Bateleur
Batis, *black-headed*
Bay owl, *oriental*
Bee-eater, *European*
Bellbird, *bearded*
Berrypecker, *black*
Bird of Paradise,
*blue, king, king of Saxony's*
Bishop, *red*
Bittern, *American*
Blackbird, *Eurasian*
Blackcap,
Bluebird,
*Asian fairy, eastern*
Boatbill, *yellow-breasted*
Boat-billed heron
Bobolink
Bobwhite, *northern*
Boobook
Booby, *brown*
Bowerbird,
*MacGregor's, satin*
Bristlebill, *common*
Bristlehead, *Bornean*
Broadbill, *green*
Budgerigar
Bulbul,
*black Madagascar, garden, hook-billed, red-whiskered, white-throated*
Bullfinch, *Eurasian*
Bunting,
*painted, reed, snow*
Bush-shrike, *gray-headed*
Bushrunner, *arklike*
Bushtanager, *collared*
Bustard,
*black, great*
Butcherbird, *black*
Buttonquail, *little*
Buzzard, *common*

Cacique, *yellow-rumped*
Canebill, *giant*
Catbird, *gray*
California, *thrasher*
Caracara
Cardinal, *northern*
Cassowary, *southern*
Chachalaca, *plain*
Chaffinch
Chanting-Goshawk, *dark*
Chickadee, *blackcapped*
Chicken, *prairie*
Chlorophonia, *blue-crowned*
Cicadabird, *slender-billed*
Cock-of-the-rock, *Andean*
Cockatiel
Cockatoo, *sulphur-crested*
Condor, *California*
Coot, *American*
Coquette, *frilled*
Cordon-bleu, *red-cheeked*
Cormorant,
*great, flightless, long-tailed*
Corncrake
Cotinga, *spangled*
Coua, *running*
Coucal, *buff-headed*
Courser, *cream-colored*
Cowbird, *brown-headed*
Crane,
*black crowned, whooping*
Creeper, *spotted*
Crescentchest, *elegant*
Crossbill, *red*
Crow, *American*
Cuckoo,
*African emerald, channel-billed, collared, common, drongo, striped, yellow-billed*

Cuckoo-shrike,
*ground, red-shouldered*
Cuckoo roller
Curassow,
*great, nocturnal*
Curlew, *stone*
Currawong, *pied*

Dacnis, *blue*
Dickissel
Dipper, *American*
Diver, *red-throated*
Dove,
*blue-headed quail, common ground, mourning, rock*
Dovekie
Drongo,
*fork-tailed, greater racquet-tailed, pygmy*
Duck,
*Falklands steamer, mandarin, Muscovy, ruddy, white-faced whistling*
Dunnock

Eagle,
*bald, golden, harpy*
Edible-nest swiftlet
Egret,
*cattle, great*
Eider, *common*
Elaenia, *yellow-bellied*
Emu
Euphonia, *white-vented*

Fairywren, *superb*
Falcon,
*brown, peregrine*
Falconet, *collared*
Fantail,
*rufous, yellow-bellied*
Figbird
Finch,
*gouldian, plush-capped, purple, white-naped brush, zebra*
Finchbill, *crested*
Finfoot, *African*
Firefinch, *red-billed*
Flamingo, *greater*
Flicker,
*northern, common*
Flowerpecker, *crimson-breasted*
Flycatcher,
*Asian paradise, bar-winged shrike, blue-throated, citrine canary, cliff, gray silky, ochre-bellied, pale, piratic, royal, rufous-tailed, jungle, scissor-tailed, spotted, vermilion, white-tailed crested, willow*
Forest falcon, *barred*
Forktail, *white-crowned*
Francolin, *red-necked*
Friarbird, *little*
Frigatebird, *magnificent*
Frogmouth,
*Ceylon, tawny*
Fruiteater, *barred*
Fulmar, *northern*
Fulvetta, *brown-cheeked*

Gannet, *northern*
Gerygone, *white-throated*
Gnatcatcher, *blue-gray*
Gnateater, *black-cheeked*
Go-away bird, *gray*
Goldfinch, *Eurasian*
Gonolek, *crimson-breasted*
Goose,
*Canada, graylag, magpie*
Goshawk, *northern*
Grackle, *common*
Grassbird, *little*
Grasswren, *eyrean*
Grebe,
*great crested, little*
Greenbul,
*yellow-bellied, yellow-breasted*
Greenlet, *tawny-crowned*
Grosbeak,
*pine, rose-breasted*
Ground-hornbill, *southern*
Grouse, *black*
Guan, *crested*
Guillemot
Guineafowl, *helmeted*
Gull,
*black-headed, herring, ivory*
Gyrfalcon

Hammerkop
Harrier,
*hen, northern*
Hawk,
*African harrier, black-collared, Cooper's, red-tailed*
Hemispingus, *black-capped*
Heron,
*boat-billed, black, black-crowned night, gray*
Hillstar, *Andean*
Hobby, *Eurasian*
Hoatzin
Honey-buzzard, *European*
Honeycreeper, *purple*
Honeyeater,
*brown, cardinal, fuscous, strong-billed*
Honeyguide,
*black-throated, greater*
Hoopoe
Hornbill,
*great Indian, helmeted, red-billed, southern-ground*
Hornero, *rufous*
Huet-huet, *chestnut-throated*
Hummingbird,
*bee, giant, long-tailed Sylph, ruby-throated, ruby-topaz, sword-billed*
Hypocolius, *gray*

Ibis, *glossy*
Ibisbill
Iora, *common*

Jacamar, *rufous-tailed*
Jacana,
*American, northern*
Jay,
*blue, Eurasian, green, Tibetan ground*
Junco, *dark-eyed*
Junglefowl, *red*

Kagu
Kakapo
Kauai O-o
Kea
Kestrel, *common*
Kingbird, *eastern*
Kingfisher,
*African pygmy, belted, common, common paradise, mangrove, shovel-billed, white-collared*
Kinglet, *golden-crowned*
Kiskadee, *great*
Kite,
*Brahminy, everglade, red, snail*
Kittiwake, *black-legged*
Kiwi, *brown*
Koel,
*Asian, common*
Kokako
Kookaburra, *laughing*

Lammergeier
Lapwing, *northern*
Lark,
*red-capped, bifasciated, clotbey, desert, greater hoopoe, greater short-toed, horned, shore, singing, thick-billed*
Laughing thrush, *white-crested*
Leafbird, *gold-fronted*
Leaflove
Leiothrix, *red-billed*
Limpkin
Longbill, *pygmy*
Longclaw, *yellow-throated*
Loon, *red-throated*
Lora, *common*
Lorikeet, *rainbow*
Lorius lory
Lory, *black-capped*
Lovebird,
*peach-faced, rosy-faced*
Lyrebird, *superb*

Macaw, *scarlet*
Magpie,
*Australian, black-billed, Ceylon, common*
Magpie-lark
Malachite, *scarlet-tufted*
Malkoha, *small green-billed*
Mallard
Malleefowl
Manakin,
*blue-backed, wire-tailed*

Manatee, *American*
Manucode, *crinkle-collared*
Martin,
    *purple, sand, white-eyed river*
Meadowlark, *eastern*
Melidectes, *long-bearded*
Merganser, *red-breasted*
Mesite, *white-breasted*
Minivet, *scarlet*
Mistletoebird
Mockingbird,
    *northern, Charles, Galápagos*
Monarch,
    *black-naped, spectacled*
Moorhen, *common*
Morepork
Motmot, *blue-crowned*
Mousebird, *speckled*
Murre, *common*
Murrelet, *marbled*
Myna, *hill*
Myzornis, *fire-tailed*

Needletail, *brown-backed*
Nicator,
    *common, yellow-spotted*
Nightjar,
    *Eurasian, great-eared, lyre-tailed, standard-winged*
Noddy, *brown*
Nunbird, *black-fronted*
Nuthatch,
    *coral-billed, red-breasted*

Oilbird
Openbill, *Asian*
Oriole,
    *golden, northern*
Oropendola,
    *Wagler's, chestnut-headed*
Osprey
Ostrich
Ovenbird
Owl,
    *Australian , barn, brown fish, burrowing, eastern screech, elf, Eurasian pygmy, great horned, little, long-eared, northern hawk, oriental bay, snowy, tawny,*
Owlet-nightjar, *Australian*
Oxpecker, *yellow-billed*
Oystercatcher, *common Eurasian*

Palmchat
Palmcreeper, *point-tailed*
Parakeet,
    *monk, rose-ringed, sun*
Pardalote, *spotted*
Palila
Parrot,
    *eclectus, gray, owl, yellow-headed*
Parrotbill,
    *bearded, spot-breasted*
Parrotfinch, *blue-faced*
Parrotlet, *spectacled*
Partridge,
    *crested, red-legged*
Parula, *northern*
Pauraque
Peacock-pheasant, *gray*
Peafowl,
    *blue, Congo, Indian*
Peewee, *eastern wood*
Pelican,
    *brown, great white*
Penduline-tit, *yellow*
Penguin,
    *emperor, Galápagos, little*
Peppershrike, *rufous-browed*
Petrel,
    *black storm, common subantarctic diving, European storm, mottled, ringed storm, white-faced storm, Wilson's storm*
Phalarope, *red*
Pheasant,
    *common, golden*
Philentoma,
    *maroon-breasted*
Phoebe, *eastern*

Piapiac
Piculet,
    *rufous, white-barred, whitebrowed*
Pigeon,
    *band-tailed, rock*
Piculet,
    *white-barred*
Pipit,
    *golden, water, meadow*
Pitohui, *rusty*
Pitta,
    *garnet, Indian*
Plantcutter,
    *rufous-tailed*
Plains-wanderer
Plover,
    *American golden, crab, Egyptian, ringed,*
Poorwill, *common*
Potoo, *common*
Pranticole,
    *collared, common*
Prinia, *graceful*
Prion, *broad-billed*
Ptarmigan
Puffback, *black-backed*
Puffbird, *white-necked*
Puffin, *Atlantic*
Pygmy parrot, *red-breasted*
Pygmy-tyrant, *short-tailed*

Quail,
    *California, common, painted*
Quelea, *red-billed*
Quetzal, *resplendent*

Rail,
    *water, giant wood*
Razorbill
Redpoll,
    *common, mealy*
Redshank,
    *common, painted*
Redstart, *painted*
Reed-warbler, *long-billed*
Reedling
Rhabdornis, *stripe-sided*
Rhea, *greater*
Rifleman
Roadrunner, *greater*
Robin,
    *American, flame, oriental magpie*
Rockfowl, *white-necked*
Rockthrush, *cape*
Roller,
    *European, short-legged ground*
Rook
Rosella, *crimson*
Ruff
Rush-tyrant, *many-colored*

Saltator, *buff-throated*
Sandgrouse, *Pallas's*
Sapsucker, *yellow-bellied*
Saw-wing, *blue*
Scaup, *greater*
Screamer, *northern*
Scrub bird, *noisy*
Scrubfowl, *common*
Scrubwren, *white-browed*
Scythebill, *red-billed*
Secretary bird
Seedsnipe, *least*
Seriema, *red-legged*
Serpent eagle, *crested*
Sharpbill
Shearwater, *manx*
Sheathbill, *snowy*
Shelduck, *common*
Shoebill
Shortwing,
    *blue, white-browed*
Shoveller, *northern*
Shrike,
    *black-faced cuckoo, great gray, long-crested helmet, magpie, northern, white helmet*
Shrike-thrush, *gray*
Shrike-tit, *crested*
Shrike-vireo, *chestnut-sided*
Sickle-billed vanga
Sicklebill, *white-tipped*

Silktail
Silver-eye
Sitella, *varied*
Skimmer, *black*
Skua, *great*
Skylark,
    *common, Eurasian*
Snipe,
    *common, greater painted*
Snowcock, *Himalayan*
Snowfinch, *white-winged*
Solitaire, *Andean*
Spadebill, *white-crested*
Sparrow,
    *chipping, gray-headed, house, Java, rock, savannah*
Spatuletail, *marvellous*
Speirops, *Principe Island*
Spiderhunter, *long-billed*
Spinetail,
    *red-faced, stripe-breasted*
Spurfowl, *red*
Starling,
    *metallic, red-winged, shining, superb*
Stilt, *black-winged*
Stonechat, *common*
Stork, *white*
Sugarbird, *cape*
Sunbittern
Sunbird,
    *crimson, olive-backed, purple-throated, red-tufted, ruby-cheeked, superb, wattled false, yellow-backed*
Sungrebe
Swallow,
    *bank, barn, golden, white-browed wood, white-breasted wood*
Swallow-tanager
Swan, *tundra*
Swift,
    *African palm, common, crested tree, gray-rumped tree, white-throated*
Swiflet, *edible nest*

Tahiti reed-warbler
Tailorbird,
    *common, long-tailed*
Takahe
Tanager,
    *magpie, paradise, scarlet, white-shouldered, silver-beaked*
Tawny frogmouth
Tawny owl
Tern, *common*
Thrasher, *California*
Thick-knee, *beach*
Thornbill, *yellow-rumped*
Thrush,
    *austral, cinnamon quail, island, olive, white's*
Tinamou, *great*
Tit,
    *great, long-tailed, red-throated, sultan*
Toco toucan
Tody, *Jamaican*
Tody-flycatcher, *common*
Topaz, *crimson*
Toucan, *plate-billed mountain*
Toucanet,
    *emerald, saffron, spot-billed*
Towhee, *rufous-sided*
Tragopan, *Temminck's*
Treecreeper,
    *brown, common, Eurasian*
Trembler, *brown*
Triller, *white-winged*
Trogon,
    *coppery-tailed, elegant, narina, red-headed*
Tropicbird, *red-tailed*
Trumpeter,
    *gray-winged, common*
Turaco, *red-crested*
Turkey, *common*
Turnstone, *ruddy*
Tyrant,
    *great shrike, white-headed marsh*
Tyranulet, *torrent*

Umbrella bird, *Amazonian*

Vanga, *hook-billed*
Veery
Verdin
Vireo, *red-eyed*
Vulture,
    *bearded, Egyptian, king, lappet-faced, palm-nut, turkey*

Wagtail,
    *forest, pied, white, yellow*
Wallcreeper
Warbler,
    *black-and-white, brownish-flanked bush, Ceylon bush, chestnut-crowned, chestnut-headed, golden-crowned, golden-winged, grasshopper, mourning, willow, yellow*
Wattle-eye,
    *brown-throated, common*
Waxwing, *bohemian*
Weaver,
    *sociable, white-billed buffalo*
Whalebird
Wheatear, *northern*
Whimbrel
Whipbird, *eastern*
Whistler, *golden*
Whistling duck, *white-faced*
White-eye,
    *gray-backed, Japanese*
Whydah, *paradise*
Willie wagtail
Wire-tail, *Des Murs'*
Wood peewee, *eastern*
Woodcock, *American*
Woodcreeper,
    *barred, long-billed, olivaceous*
Woodhoopoe, *green*
Woodpecker,
    *blond-crested, Eurasian green, golden-backed, goldentailed, great slaty, great spotted, greater flame-backed, ground, ivory-billed*
Wren,
    *Bewick's, cactus, house, long-billed marsh, rock, winter*
Wrentit
Wrybill
Wrymouth
Wryneck, *northern/Eurasian*

Xenops, *plain*

Yellowhammer
Yuhina, *stripe-throated*

Zitting cisticola

# Reptiles

Adder,
    *puff, saw-scaled*
Agama, *common*
Agamid, *Arabian toad-headed*
Alligator snapping turtle
Alligator, *American*
Anaconda
Anole, *green*
Armadillo lizard
Asp, *bibron's burrowing*

Bandy-bandy
Batagur
Boa,
    *constrictor, emerald tree, rubber*
Boomslang
Bushmaster

Caiman, *spectacled*
Chameleon,
    *brookesia spectrum, European, flap-necked, Jackson's, Meller's, Rhampholeon marshalli*
Chuckwalla
Cobra,
    *king, Indian*
Cottonmouth
Crocodile,
    *estuarine, Nile, West African dwarf*

Dibamus novaeguineae
Dragon,
    *bearded, flying*

Edge snout, *Somali*
Fer-de-Lance
Fimbrias klassi

Galliwasp
Gavial
Gecko,
    *Brook's, green day, Kuhl's, leaf-tailed, leopard, marbled, phelsuma vinsoni, Tokay, web-footed, white-spotted*
Gila monster
Grass snake

Hawksbill

Iguana,
    *common, Fijian banded, forest, Galápagos land, Madagascan, marine, rhinoceros, spiny-tailed*

Jungle runner

Kingsnake, *common*
Komodo dragon

Leatherback
Lizard,
    *armadillo, basilisk, Bosc's fringe-toed, Caiman, California legless, collared, desert night, eastern fence, Essex's mountain, Florida worm, frilled, girdled, green, imperial flat, plated, southern alligator, Texas horned, Transvaal snake, two-legged worm, viviparous, wall, white-bellied worm, worm*

Mabuya
Mamba, *eastern green*
Manushi
Massasauga
Mastigure, *princely*
Matamata
Monitor,
    *earless, Gould's, Nile*

Python,
    *carpet, Indian*

Racerunner, *strand*
Rattlesnake, *eastern diamondback*
Ridley, *Pacific*

Sandfish
Sand racer, *Algerian*
Scaly-foot,
    *hooded, aprasia striolata, delma nasuta*
Shield-snout, *South African*
Shieldtail,
    *Blyth's landau, red-blotched*
Sidewinder
Skink,
    *brown, cordylosaurus subtessellatus, emoia cyangaster, feylinia cussori, Florida sand, great plains, legless, leilopisma infrapunctatum, prickly forest, round-bodied, spiny-tailed, Sundeval's, western blue-tongued*
Slider, *pond*
Snake,
    *anomalepis sp., banded sea, common garter, De Vis's banded, eastern brown, eastern coral, egg-eating, elephant-trunk, false coral, glass, gopher, mangrove, paradise tree, rat, red-bellied, Schlegel's blind, slug, smooth, snail-eating, spotted water, sunbeam, vine, western blind, white-bellied mangrove, whip dark-green*
Snake-lizard, *Burton's*

Tegu, *common*
Terrapin,
    *diamondback, river*
Teyu
Thorny devil
Tortoise,
    *African pancake, bowsprit,*
    *Galápagos giant, gopher,*
    *leopard, Schweigger's,*
    *serrated hingeback,*
    *spur-thighed*
Tuatara, *Cook Strait*
Turaco, *red-crested*
Turtle,
    *alligator snapping, Arrau*
    *river, big-headed, Central*
    *American river, common*
    *musk, Eastern box,*
    *European pond, false map,*
    *flapshell Zambesi, green,*
    *loggerhead, Murray river,*
    *New Guinea plateless river,*
    *pig-nose, snapping, softshell*
    *Indian, softshell Nile,*
    *softshell spiny, softshell*
    *Zambesi, wood, yellow mud*

Viper,
    *Asiatic pit, aspic, common,*
    *desert sidewinding, gaboon,*
    *horned*

Water dragon,
    *eastern, Soa-soa*
Worm, *slow*

Xenosaurus *sp.*

## Amphibians

Axolotl

Bullfrog,
    *South African, South*
    *American*

Caecilian,
    *Panamanian, Sao Tome,*
    scolecomorpus kirkii,
    *Seychelles, South American,*
    *sticky,* typhlonectes
    compressicauda
Congo eel, *two-toed*

Frog,
    *arum lily, bush squeaker,*
    *common, corroboree,*
    cyclorana cultripes,
    *Darwin's, eastern narrow-*
    *mouthed, glass, gold, gold*
    *spiny reed, golden arrow-*
    *poison, green and gold bell,*
    *Hochstetter's, horned, Lutz's*
    *phyllomedusa, marsh,*
    *marsupial, mottled*
    *burrowing, Natal ghost,*
    *northern cricket, northern*
    *leopard, parsley, Seychelles,*
    *sheep, South African rain,*
    *striped grass, termite,*
    *Wallace's flying*

Hellbender

Mudpuppy

Newt,
    *eastern, great crested,*
    *rough-skinned, warty*

Olm

Peeper, *spring*
Phyllomedusa, *Lutz's*

Salamander,
    *amber-colored, Asian,*
    *California slender,*
    *dusky, fire, marbled,*
    *Pacific giant, red,*
    *red-backed, sharp-ribbed,*
    *slimy, spotted, spring,*
    *Texas blind, tiger,*
    *yellow-blotched,*
    *dicamptodontid*
Siren,
    *dwarf, greater*
Spadefoot,
    *European, western*

Toad,
    *African clawed, American,*
    *Boulenger's arrow poison,*
    *common, giant, green,*
    *Mexican burrowing,*
    *midwife, natterjack,*
    *oriental fire-bellied,*
    *Surinam*
Treefrog,
    *common gray, European*
    *green*

## Fish

Adalah
Adioryx xantherythrus
Alewife
Amberjack, *greater*
Anchovy, *European*
Anemonefish, *clown*
Angelfish,
    *imperial, queen*
Angler
Anomalops kaptoptron
Archerfish
Aruana
Aphonius dispar
Atelopus japonicus

Bagnus docmac
Ballyhoo
Barbel
Barb, *tiger*
Barber-eel
Barracuda, *giant*
Bass,
    *striped, rock, largemouth*
Batfish
Batfish, *shortnose*
Beardfish, *stout*
Beluga
Beaugregory
Bichir
Bitterling
Blenny, *redlip*
Bluefish
Boarfish
Bonefish
Boulengerella lucius
Bowfin
Boxfish, *blue-spotted*
Bream,
    *gilthead, ray's, Red sea*
Buffalo, *bigmouth*
Bullhead
Bullrout
Bummalow
Burbot
Burrfish, *striped*
Butterfish
Butterflyfish,
    *copperband, forceps,*
    *four-eye*

Cabezon
Candirú
Carp
Carp, *grass*
Cascadura
Catfish,
    *African glass,*
    *Australian freshwater,*
    *blue, brown, electric,*
    *gafftopsail, glass,*
    *Mekong, pungas, sea,*
    *upside-down, walking*
Cavefish, *northern*
Channoidei
Charr, *Arctic*
Chub, *Bermuda*
Cichlid, *ring-tailed pike*
Cobia
Cod,
    *Antarctic, Baikal, trout*
Coelacanth
Conchfish
Coney
Cowfish, *scrawled*
Crevalle jack
Cuiu-cuiu
Curimbata
Cusk-eel, *New Providence*
Cutlassfish, *Atlantic*

Dab
    *Dace, pearl*
Darter, *orange-throat*
Dealfish
Discus fish
Dogfish,
    *sandy, spiny*
Dolphinfish
Drum,
    *black, freshwater*
Eel,
    *conger, electric, European,*
    *gulper, rice, sand, spiny*
Elephant-snout fish
Emperor,
    *sweetlip, spangled*

Fallfish
Fightingfish, *Siamese*
Filefish,
    *planehead, scrawled*
Flounder,
    *peacock, starry, summer,*
    *winter*
Flyingfish
Flyingfish, *Atlantic*
Football-fish
Four-eyed fish
Frogfish, *longlure*

Gar, *longnose*
Garfish
Goatfish, *spotted*
Goldeye
Goldfish
Gourami
Grayling
Greenling, *kep*
Grenadier, *rough-head*
Grouper, *black*
Grunion, *California*
Gudgeon
Guitarfish, *Atlantic*
Guppy
Gurnard,
    *flying, tub*
Gymnarchus niloticus

Haddock
Hagfish
Hake,
    *European, white*
Halfbeak, *wrestling*
Halibut,
    *Atlantic, California,*
    *Greenland*
Hammerhead, *smooth*
Hoplosthethus atlanticus
Harlequin fish
Hatchetfish
Hellbender
Herring,
    *Atlantic, wolf*
Hogfish
Houndfish

Icefish

Jackknife-fish
Jaraqui
Jewfish
John dory
John dory, *American*
Jollytail
Jolthead porgy

Kelpfish, *giant*
Killifish,
    *common, least*
Knifefish, *banded*

Ladyfish
Lake trout
Lampern
Lamprey,
    *river, sea*
Lance, *sand*
Lanternfish
Leaffish, *Schomburgk's*
Ling
Ling, *New Zealand*
Linophryne arborifera
Lionfish
Lizardfish, *red*
Loach,
    *coolie, spined, stone*
Lookdown
Lumpsucker

Lungfish,
    *African, Australian,*
    *South American*
Lyretail, *Cape Lopez*

Mackerel, *Atlantic*
Mahseer
Mako
Mandi
Man-o'-war fish
Manta, *Atlantic*
Margate, *black*
Marlin,
    *blue, striped*
Meagre
Medaka, *Japanese*
Menhaden, *Atlantic*
Midshipman, *Atlantic*
Milkfish
Minnow
Minnow, *sheeps-head*
Monkfish
Moorish idol
Moray, *chain*
Mouthbrooder, *Nile*
Mullet,
    *red, striped*
Mummichog
Murray

Needlefish, *freshwater*

Oarfish
Oilfish
Opah

Pacu
Paddlefish
Paradisefish
Parrotfish,
    *blue, rainbow, stoplight*
Pearlfish
Perch
Perch,
    *climbing, kelp, nile, ocean*
Phenacostethus smithi
Photoblepharon palpebratus
Pike, *northern*
Pilchard
Pinecone fish
Pipefish, *greater*
Piranha, *red*
Pirarucu
Plaice
Plaice, *American*
Poacher, *sturgeon*
Pollock, *walleye*
Pompano, *Florida*
Porbeagle
Porcupinefish
Porgy, *jolthead*
Pout, *ocean*
Powan
Puffer,
    *bandtail, sharpnose*
Pufferfish, *common*
Pumpkinseed

Rainbowfish, *crimson-spotted*
Rascasse
Rat-fish
Ray,
    *Atlantic torpedo/electric,*
    *eagle*
Redfish
Redhorse, *northern*
Remora
Ricefish
Roach
Robin, *northern sea*
Rockling, *three-barbed*
Roughie
Runner, *rainbow*

Sablefish
Sailfish
Saithe
Salmon,
    *Atlantic, Australian, sockeye*
Sand-smelt
Sand lance
Sardine
Sardinha
Sargassumfish
Saury
Sawfish, *greater*
Scat
Sculpin, *shorthorn*
Scup

Sea bream, *red*
Seabass,
    *white, giant*
Seadragon, *weedy*
Seahorse, *dwarf*
Seatrout, *spotted*
Sergeant major
Shad, *twaite*
Shanny
Shark,
    *basking, blue, bluntnose*
    *six-gilled, bull, common*
    *saw, Greenland,*
    *Port Jackson, thresher,*
    *whale, white, saw*
Sharksucker
Sheepshead, *California*
Shiner, *common*
Shrimpfish
Silverside, *hardhead*
Skate
Slippery dick
Smalltooth
Smelt
Snail, *sea*
Snakehead
Snapper,
    *mutton, yellow-tail*
Snipe-eel
Snook
Soapfish
Soapfish
Sole,
    *long-tongue, naked*
Spinefoot, *blue-lined*
Spiny-eel
Spurdog
Squawfish, *northern*
Squirrelfish
Stargazer, *northern*
Stickleback,
    *fifteen-spined, four-spined,*
    *three-spined*
Stingray, *southern*
Stonefish
Stoneroller
Sturgeon,
    *common, poacher*
Sucker, *white*
Surfperch, *barred*
Sunfish, *ocean*
Surubim
Swordfish
Swordtail

Tadpole, *madtom*
Tarpon
Tautog
Tang, *blue*
Tench
Tetra,
    *flame, Mexican, neon*
Tiger, *sand*
Tigerfish, *giant*
Tonguefish, *black-cheek*
Top-minnow,
    *dwarf, pike*
Triggerfish,
    *black-barred, clown, gray,*
    *Sargassum*
Tripletail
Trout, *rainbow*
Trout-perch
Trout, *lake,*
Tubesnout
Tuna,
    *skipjack, yellowfin*
Turbot

Unicornfish, *striped-face*

Vieja
Viperfish, *Sloane's*

Wahoo
Weever, *lesser*
Wels
Whalefish
Whiting
Whiting, *blue*
Windowpane
Winged dragon
Wolf-fish, *Atlantic*
Wrasse, *ballan*
Wrymouth

Zander

# GLOSSARY

**Abdomen**
The part of an animal's body that lies between the **thorax** and pelvis in vertebrates. In mammals, the abdomen is separated from the thorax by the diaphragm.

**Adaptation**
Part of the process of evolutionary change that animals undergo to occupy a **niche**. Changes can concern the structure, physiology, development or behavior of animals, and are driven by **natural selection**.

**Adult**
A fully developed and mature individual, capable of breeding.

**Air Sac**
Non-respiratory air bags connected to the lungs of a bird.

**Albino**
An animal lacking coloring, or pigment, and therefore having pale or white skin or fur, and pink eyes. This characteristic is passed down in the **genes**.

**Alimentary canal**
The passage that extends from the mouth to the anus, for the digestion and absorption of food and elimination of waste matter.

**Algae**
Primitive marine and aquatic plants that lack a system of roots, stems, and leaves.

**Amphibian**
**Cold-blooded** animals belonging to the class Amphibia, such as frogs, which live on land but breed in water.

**Anadromous**
Fish, such as salmon and certain species of herring, which migrate from the sea to freshwater to spawn.

**Anal fin**
Fin that lies along the underside of the body, behind the anus in fishes. The anal fin works in conjunction with other fins for swimming and turning.

**Alpine**
Of the Alps in Europe; or any mountainous region having an altitude of over 4,500 ft (1,500m)

**Anatomy**
The study of the internal structure of plants and animals. Also the physical structure of an animal or plant, or any of its parts.

**Antarctic**
Pertaining to the south polar region.

**Aquatic**
Living mainly or wholly in water.

**Arboreal**
Living mainly in or among trees.

**Archipelago**
A large group of islands.

**Arctic**
Pertaining to the north polar region.

**Asexual reproduction**
Reproductive process that is not **sexual**; the parent organism splits into two or more organisms, or produces buds.

**Avian**
Pertaining to birds.

**Baleen**
Horny slats that hang vertically from the roof of a whale's mouth, with fringed inner edges for filtering food.

**Barbel**
A fleshy, thin, antenna-like protuberance found around the mouth of many species of fish

**Basking**
A form of temperature regulation whereby some animals, especially reptiles, expose themselves to sun to raise their body temperature.

**Bill**
The beak of a bird or the jaws of a fish.

**Bioluminescence**
The production of light by some organisms, such as the hatchetfish, by biochemical means.

**Biome**
A community of plants and animals occupying a large geographical area. For example, **rain forest**, **desert**, or **tundra**.

**Bipedal**
Walking on two legs. Some primates may travel bipedally for short distances; only humans exhibit habitual bipedalism.

**Bipolar**
Occurring in both polar regions.

**Bird**
A class of animals called Aves, consisting of feathered, warm-blooded **tetrapods** with forelimbs adapted for flying. Examples include eagles, ostriches, and parrots.

**Bisexual**
Pertaining to animals and plants that have both male and female reproductive organs. Also known as **hermaphrodite**.

**Blubber**
A layer of fatty insulating tissue found directly beneath the outer layer of skin (**epidermis**) in marine mammals.

**Brackish**
Water that is a mixture of seawater and freshwater. May be found in river estuaries where seawater enters the river mouth.

**Brood**
The eggs or offspring of a single female from one mating; any group of young animals being cared for by an adult.

**Browser**
A **herbivore** that feeds on the leaves and shoots of shrubs and trees, as opposed to grasses.

**Buccal cavity**
The cheek or mouth cavity leading to the pharanx, and (in vertebrates) the esophagus.

**Calf**
A young cow or bull, buffalo, seal or whale.

**Camouflage**
When an animal conceals itself by adopting the color and texture of its surroundings, either physically or by concealing itself in a suitable place.

**Canine teeth**
In **carnivorous** mammals, the two long and pointed teeth in the upper and lower jaws, behind the **incisors** that are used for seizing and holding prey. In Pinnipedia, a suborder that includes sea lions and walruses, they can take the form of tusks.

**Canopy**
In forests, an almost continuous layer of foliage at the level of the tree tops, produced by the intermingling of vegetation. The crowns of some trees may project above the canopy layer and are known as emergents.

**Carapace**
A skeletal shield of bone or chitin (tough fibrous material) covering the bodies of reptiles such as tortoises or terrapins.

**Carcass**
The dead or rotting flesh of an animal, which is a source of food for scavengers.

**Carnassial teeth**
An opposing pair of teeth adapted especially to shear with a scissor-like, cutting edge.

**Carnivore**
A flesh-eating animal (but not necessarily a member of the order Carnivora).

**Cartilage**
Strong elastic connective tissue between bones; also called gristle.

**Cementum**
Hard material coating the roots of teeth in mammals. In some **species** it is laid down in layers annually, and the number of layers can be used to help determine an animal's age.

**Cell**
The basic structural unit of all living organisms.

**Chromosome**
An assembly of **genes** (units of **DNA**), which determine hereditary characteristics.

**Cladogram**
A diagram used to show how groups of organisms have evolved from a common ancestor.

**Class**
A **taxonomic** rank superior to **order**, but subordinate to **phylum**.

**Clutch**
The number of eggs laid, and simultaneously incubated, by a female.

**Cock**
A male bird, crab, lobster or salmon.

**Cold-blooded**
An animal with no internal temperature mechanism, such as a **reptile** or an

**amphibian**, whose body temperature is determined by external temperatures.

**Colony**
A **population** of animals living and breeding together in one place.

**Communal**
Cooperative behavior between animals, such as can be found in the nest building of some birds.

**Coniferous forest**
Forest comprising largely evergreen conifers, such as pines, spruces, and firs. Usually found in northern latitudes.

**Conservation**
Preservation of the environment and natural resources.

**Continental shelf**
An area of relatively shallow water adjacent to a continental land mass and rarely deeper than 600 ft (200m).

**Coral reef**
An organic marine reef composed of solid coral and coral sand.

**Courtship**
Communication between individual animals of opposite sexes of a species to facilitate breeding.

**Crepuscular**
Mainly active during the twilight hours around dawn and dusk.

**Crest**
A prominent tuft of feathers on the heads of some species of bird.

**Cue**
A signal produced by an animal to elicit a response in another individual, for example, in **courtship**.

**Deciduous forest**
Temperate and tropical forest with moderate rainfall and marked seasons. Trees normally shed their leaves during cold or dry periods.

**Dentition**
The arrangement of the animal's teeth, which varies according to the species.

**Desert**
An area with low average rainfall, with sparse scrub, or grassland vegetation, or no vegetation at all.

**Detritus**
Dead organic or inorganic material.

**Digit**
A finger or a toe.

**Dispersal**
Movement of animals away from their home range as they reach maturity. Distinct from dispersion, where animals or food sites are distributed or scattered.

**Display**
Conspicuous behaviour to convey specific information to others, usually to other members of a species. May be visual or vocal, and used as a threat to **predators** or in **courtship**.

**Distal**
Farthest point away from center of the body, for example, the tip of an animal's tail.

**DNA**
Deoxyribonucleic acid, a long molecule resembling a chain made up of four kinds of link, the sequence of which codes hereditary information.
**Genes** are units of DNA. The DNA molecule consists of two strands joined in a spiral, an arrangement known as a double helix.

**Dormancy**
A period of inactivity. For example, many bears are dormant for a period during winter. This is not true **hibernation** as the animal's pulse rate and body temperature do not drop significantly.

**Dorsal**
The upper surface or plane of an animal's body.

**Dorsal fin**
In fishes, the **fin** that lies along the spine on the upper side of the body. The dorsal fin works in conjunction with the other fins in swimming, turning and balancing.

**Eardrum**
A thin membrane in the middle ear which vibrates in response to airborne sounds.

**Echolocation**
A process used by Cetaceans (whales, dolphins), bats and some species of birds to detect distant or invisible objects (in darkness), by means of sound waves that are reflected back to the emitter from the object.

**Eclipse plumage**
Dull plumage of birds, which is superseded by more striking plumage in the breeding season.

**Ecology**
The study of plants and animals in relation to their natural environmental setting.

**Ecosystem**
A part of the environment in which both living and non-living elements exist and interact.

**Eft**
A lizard or newt.

**Egg tooth**
A specially modified tooth that a new-hatched reptile or bird uses to break free of the egg on hatching.

**Elongate**
Relatively long. For example, canine teeth are elongate compared to adjacent teeth.

**Embryo**
The developing egg until it hatches. Or the early stages of a developing mammal. Once the mammalian embryo begins to resemble an adult animal, it is known as a **fetus**.

**Emigration**
The departure of an animal, or animals, from its group or from its place of birth, often on reaching maturity. Also known as **dispersal**.

**Enamel**
A hard substance that forms the outer layer of a vertebrate tooth.

**Environment**
External surroundings; the physical, biological, and chemical influences that act on an individual organism.

**Enzyme**
An organic substance produced by living cells that catalyses biochemical changes.

**Epidermis**
The outermost layer of cells comprising the outer layer of skin of a mammal, or the outer tissue of stems or leaves in plants.

**Equator**
A theoretical line around the Earth's surface midway between the north and south poles. Equatorial regions are those areas located at, or lying close to, the equator.

**Estrus**
When female mammals are receptive to mating and are attracted to males. Also when ovulation occurs and mature eggs are released from the ovaries.

**Estuary**
The mouth of a river where the tide enters, the resulting body of water is a mixture of **freshwater** and seawater.

**Eutherian**
Pertaining to mammals whose **embryos** receive nourishment from the placenta.

**Evolution**
The act or process of gradual change where the characteristics of a **species** or **population** alter over many generations.

**Excretion**
The elimination of waste products from the body.

**Extant**
Living, still in existence, and therefore not **extinct**.

**Extinct**
According to available evidence, no longer in existence, having died out.

**Family**
A **taxonomic** rank superior to **genus**, but subordinate to **order**.

**Fang**
In carnivorous mammals, a **canine** tooth. In snakes, a modified tooth carrying poison.

**Fauna**
All of the animal life of a region, geological period, or special environment.

**Feces**
The remains of indigestible food excreted from an animal's bowels.

**Feral**
A wild or undomesticated animal, descended from domestic animals.

**Fertilization**
The process of union of two sex cells (**gametes**) to form a new animal. In mammals, reptiles, and birds, fertilization takes place within the female's body, whereas in most species of fish and amphibians, fertilization takes place externally.

**Fetus**
An **embryo** of a mammal in the later stages of development, when it shows the features of the fully developed animal.

**Filter feeders**
Animals, such as certain whale species, that obtain their food from straining or filtering water to sift out small organic particles.

**Fin**
A flat, projecting organ, used by fishes and other aquatic animals, such as whales and seals, to swim, turn, and balance in the water.

**Fish**
Streamlined **vertebrates** adapted to life in the water. Examples include hagfish, sharks, salmon, and coelacanth.

**Fledgling**
A young bird that has recently learned to fly.

**Flora**
The plant life of a particular region, geological period or special environment.

**Fluke**
In Cetaceans (whales, dolphins) and Dugongs, the flat, horizontal tail fins.

**Forage**
To search for food.

**Fossil**
The remains of dead organisms, or their imprint, which have been preserved in rocks. Fossils therefore reveal the history of life on earth in the fossil record. Palaeontology is the study of fossils and the fossil record.

**Freshwater**
Water that is not saline, as found in a river or lake.

**Fusiform**
Streamlined. Sometimes referred to as "torpedo-shaped." Cetaceans (whales, dolphins) are said to have fusiform-shaped bodies, aiding propulsion in water.

**Gamete**
A sex cell. When sexual **fertilization** takes place, the male sex cell or **sperm** fuses with the female sex cell or **ovum**.

**Gelatinous**
A substance having a jelly-like consistency.

**Generalist**
An animal that does not rely on specialized strategies for feeding or surviving, as distinct from a **specialist** animal that does.

**Gene**
A unit of **DNA** carrying hereditary information that is passed on from generation to generation. An assembly of genes make up a **chromosome**.

**Genital**
Pertaining to the genitalia, the reproductive organs.

**Genus**
A taxonomic rank superior to **species**, but subordinate to **family**.

**Gestation**
The period from conception to birth in mammals. Elephants have the longest gestation period of any animal, that is, 22 months.

**Gills**
Organs found in fish and other animals that are completely or mainly aquatic to obtain oxygen from the surrounding water. Consists of membranes through which exchange of oxygen and carbon dioxide takes place.

**Grazers**
Herbivorous animals that feed on grasses (if land-based) or other plant material, such as **algae** or plankton (if **aquatic**).

**Gregarious**
Sociable animals that often live in large groups, such as many species of **Old World** and **New World** monkey.

**Guano**
Phosphate deposits resulting from the accumulation of bird excrement or droppings.

**Gut**
Forming part of the **alimentary canal**, the gut is a hollow tube for the digestion and absorption of food, and for the elimination of waste material.

**Habitat**
The place or **environment** in which an animal or plant lives. Usually described in terms of the predominant vegetation of the area, and by its physical features and characteristics.

**Harem group**
A group of animals consisting of one dominant mature male and two or more breeding females. A common social arrangement among mammals.

**Hen**
A female bird.

**Herbaceous**
Pertaining to herbs; resembling leaves.

**Herbivore**
An animal that feeds mainly on plants, or parts of plants, for its source of energy.

**Hermaphrodite**
An animal which has both male and female sex organs, or which functions as both male and female at the same time. Some hermaphrodites alter their sex at different stages of their lives.

**Herpetology**
The scientific study of **reptiles** and **amphibians**.

**Hibernation**
A period of sleep-like inactivity for some mammals, reptiles, and amphibians, usually during winter. The animal reduces its normal physiological processes in order to minimize energy requirements.

**Hierarchy**
The pattern or structure of divisions within a social group or **population**, whereby some animals come to dominate others. Dominant individuals have control over the resources available in terms of access to food and mates.

**Higher primate**
The more advanced primates – monkeys, apes, and man – are also known as anthropoids.

**Homing**
The capability of an animal, or group of animals, to return to its original location following **migration**.

**Hoof**
The horny sheath that encases **digits** and bears the weight of certain **ungulate** mammals.

**Hormone**
A chemical substance produced by glands that regulates and controls many bodily functions, such as growth, digestion, and sexual development.

**Host**
The organism which a **parasite** organism lives on and receives food or shelter from.

**Hybrid**
The offspring resulting from crossbreeding two different species. Hybrids are often sterile;

the best known example is a mule, the result of crossbreeding a horse and a donkey.

**Hyoid arch**
One of the bony arches that supports the gills in primitive vertebrates.

**Implantation**
The process in which the early **embryo** becomes attached to the wall of the uterus in mammals, resulting in the development of the complex network of blood vessels linking the **embryo** to the mother's **placenta**.

**Incisors**
Chisel-shaped teeth in **carnivores**, used for cutting rather than tearing or grinding. In certain animals, such as rodents, the incisor teeth continue to grow throughout life as they are worn down by use.

**Incubation**
The period between the laying of eggs and their hatching. During incubation the eggs are kept warm by a parent.

**Insectivore**
An animal whose primary source of food is arthropods – insects and spiders. Not necessarily of the mammal order Insectivora.

**Introduced**
Species which are brought by man, either accidentally or deliberately, from regions where they occur naturally to other regions where they previously were not represented.

**Intertidal zone**
Intermediate area of shore that is exposed between high and low water marks.

**Juvenile**
The growth stage of development spanning the period between an infant and a full-grown **adult**.

**Juvenile plumage**
The plumage of a young bird, when it departs from the nest. Later replaced by **adult plumage**.

**Keratin**
A tough fibrous protein that produces an impervious outer layer in the **epidermis** of mammals, birds, amphibians, and reptiles. Thicker layers of keratin form the major part of hair, scales, feathers, nails, claws, and horns.

**Kingdom**
The second highest **taxonomic** category in the hierarchy of classification, one of which is Animalia – the animals.

**Krill**
Crustaceans that are an abundant source of food for marine mammals, particularly baleen whales.

**Lactation**
Discharge of milk from the mammary glands in mammals, occurring after the birth of young. Lactation is controlled by **hormones**.

**Larynx**
The upper part of the wind pipe which contains the vocal chords, used to produce vocal sounds.

**Larva/Larvae**
A pre-adult stage in species where the young of an animal has a completely different appearance and way of life from the adult. Amphibians and some fish have a larval stage.

**Lek**
A traditional "display ground," used year after year, where animals of one sex display themselves to members of the opposite sex in order to attract potential mates.

**Lateral**
On or toward the right or left side of the body.

**Life cycle**
The sequence of different stages in an animal's life. In **vertebrates**, the production of sex cells (**gametes**) is followed by fertilization and the development of an **embryo**, followed by birth or hatching, growth to adulthood, and repetition of the cycle.

**Litter**
A number of young produced by an animal at one time.

**Longevity**
A record or estimate of an animal's life span. May refer to the maximum recorded longevity or to the average life expectancy at birth.

**Lower primate**
A primitive primate known as a Prosimian.

**Lung**
An internal chamber, nearly always air-filled, used for the exchange of respiratory gases between the **environment** and the animal's body. The structure varies from a simple, unfolded chamber in some amphibians to the complex systems of tubes in mammals and birds.

**Mammal**
**Vertebrate** animals that are warm-blooded, breathe air using **lungs**, and give birth to live young. Mammals live in the air, land, and water. Examples include bats, monkeys, and dolphins.

**Mammillae**
Nipples or teats belonging to female mammals through which milk is passed to the young from the mother.

**Mammary glands**
The milk-producing organs in female mammals.

**Mandible**
The lower bone of the jaw, or the lower part of a bird's bill.

**Mangrove forest**
Tropical forests containing salt-tolerant trees and shrubs, located on the shores of **estuaries** and river deltas.

**Marine**
Living in the sea.

**Marsupial**
Unlike **eutherian** mammals, marsupial mammals such as kangaroos, wombats, and bandicoots have a very short gestation period, after which the immature young finish their development inside a pouch on the mother's belly.

**Mating**
Pairing of individuals for reproductive purposes.

**Maturation**
The attainment of sexual maturity, that is reaching reproductive age.

**Membrane**
Thin tissue covering or connecting organs and other bodily structures.

**Metabolic rate**
The speed at which chemical changes in the body occur.

**Metabolism**
The chemical changes in living cells by which energy is supplied for vital processes and other activities, for example, the production of protein from amino acids, and the extraction of energy from foods.

**Metamorphosis**
A transformation in the shape and structure (**morphology**) of an animal. For example, metamorphosis occurs when a tadpole is transformed into an adult frog.

**Microplankton**
**Plankton** so small they are not easily visible to the naked eye.

**Migration**
The seasonal movement of a population from one area to another – often over large distances – for the purpose of feeding or breeding.

**Mimicry**
A species development of a superficial similarity to another species or to natural objects in its environment, often for protective purposes.

**Molar teeth**
In mammals, cheek teeth used for crushing and chewing food. The biting surface is made up of a series of ridges and the teeth have several roots.

**Monogamous**
Having only one mate per breeding season.

**Morphology**
A branch of biology that deals with the structure and shape of animals and plants.

**Moult**
The shedding of fur, feathers, or skin. Reptiles shed their outer dead layers of skin when they grow; moulting in mammals and birds occurs seasonally.

**Musk gland**
A gland used for secreting musk, a strong smelling odor produced by animals such as badgers and musk deer. Such secretions usually occur during the breeding season.

**Nasal plugs**
Found in toothed whales, these are muscular flaps at the base of the nasal passage used to close the airway when diving. May be used to produce sounds.

**Natal range**
Home **range** into which an individual animal is born.

**Natural Selection**
The key evolutionary process whereby animals with the most appropriate **adaptations** are more successful at reproducing than others.

**Nerve cell**
Specialized cells which transmit information in the form of electrical signals. All types of animal behavior, from a blink of the eye to complicated body movements, are controlled by the action of the nerve cells.

**New World**
A term used to describe the western hemisphere, the Americas, and the animals from those regions, as distinct from the **Old World**.

**Niche**
Role of a **species** within its **community**, defined in terms of its lifestyle, that is, food, competitors, predators, and other resource requirements.

**Nocturnal**
Mainly active during the night.

**Nomadic**
Moving from place to place, not settled or resident in any particular area.

**Nomenclature**
A system used for naming and classifying animals and plants using **scientific names**.

**Old World**
A term used to describe the eastern hemisphere, Europe, Africa, Asia and Australasia and the animals from those regions, as distinct from the **New World**.

**Olfactory**
The sense of smell which relies on the receptors inside the nasal cavity.

**Omnivore**
An animal which feeds on both plant and animal material. The digestive system is specially adapted to cope with both sources of food.

**Operculum**
Any type of hard cover or flap used for protection of tissue, such as the flaps that protect fishes' **gills**.

**Opportunistic**
A type of feeding behavior. Many species of **carnivore** are opportunistic feeders, taking advantage of circumstances to exploit varied food resources.

**Opposable**
A finger or toe which can be used in conjunction with other **digits.**

**Order**
A **taxonomic** division superior to a **family**, but subordinate to a **class**.

**Ornithology**
The scientific study of birds.

**Ovum**
An egg or female sex cell (**gamete**). Develops into a new individual of the same **species** on **fertilization** by the male sex cell or **sperm**.

**Oviduct**
The tube between the ovaries and the uterus used to carry eggs. **Fertilization** and early development occur in the oviduct of mammals and birds.

**Oviparous**
Egg-laying animals. The young hatch outside the body of the female.

**Ovoviviparous**
An animal that produces eggs, but retains them inside the body until the release of the live young.

**Pair-bond**
Prolonged association between a mating pair of animals for breeding purposes. In some species, the association may last until the death of one partner.

**Palaeontology**
One of the earth sciences, a branch of geology which deals with the scientific study of **fossils** and the fossil record.

**Palmate**
Palm-shaped.

**Pampas**
Extensive grassland plain found in South America.

**Parasite**
A relationship between two organisms, whereby one, the parasite, obtains its food from the other, the **host**.

**Passerine**
In birds, where one toe is directed backward and the others are directed forward.

**Patagium**
A membrane found in bats and flying squirrels, situated along the sides of the body between the fore and hind limbs, that helps them glide through the air.

**Pectoral fin**
A pair of fins in fishes, situated immediately behind the head on either side of the body, which work in conjunction with other fins for swimming, turning, and balancing.

**Pelvic fin**
A pair of fins in fishes, situated in the pelvic region (on the underside of the body), which work in conjunction with the other fins for swimming, turning, and balancing.

**Photophores**
If fish, an organ which can produce **bioluminescent** light.

**Phylogenetic**
Pertaining to the **evolutionary** relationships within and between groups of animals.

**Phylum**
A **taxonomic** rank superior to a **class**, but subordinate to a **kingdom**.

**Physiology**
The scientific study of processes and metabolic functions of living organisms.

**Pigment**
The natural coloring of living tissue.

**Placenta**
The organ that develops inside the uterus, allowing the exchange of oxygen, food, and waste to and from the **fetus** in **eutherian** mammals during **gestation**. The placenta is discharged after birth.

**Plankton**
Tiny water-borne organisms, eaten by whales and some fishes.

**Plastron**
The lower section of the shell of tortoises and turtles, connected to the **carapace** by a bony bridge.

**Plumage**
The feather covering of birds.

**Pod**
Name for a family group of Cetaceans (whales and dolphins), which may remain together for life.

**Polar**
Pertaining to the north or south polar regions of the earth.

**Polygamous**
Mating of one male with several females or one female with several males.

**Polygynous**
Mating of one male with several females during the breeding season.

**Polyandrous**
Mating of one female with several males.

**Population**
A group of animals of the same **species** that live separately from other similar groups.

**Pouch**
Female **marsupial** mammals have a pouch on their abdomen in which the young complete their development, following a short **gestation** period.

**Prairie**
The grassland steppe of North America, treeless and flat.

**Predator**
Any animal which hunts for live prey to feed on. Predation is the killing of one **species** by another for food.

**Prehensile**
Capable of grasping or seizing, as in monkeys' or lizards' tails and the trunks of elephants.

**Premolar teeth**
The cheek teeth of mammals, in front of the **molars** and behind the **canine teeth**, which are normally preceded by milk teeth and are used for chewing and crushing food.

**Primary forest**
A mature forest that has lain undisturbed for a long period.

**Primate**
A member of the order of animals that includes lemurs, monkeys, apes, and humans. Primates have larger brains than other animals and their **digits** are adapted for grasping and holding.

**Proboscis**
A protruding organ used for sensing and food-gathering, such as an elephant's trunk.

**Progeny**
Offspring.

**Protein**
A long chain molecule made of amino acids, essential to all living organisms.

**Protrusible**
Capable of protruding, jutting out, as in the tongue of a lizard or other reptile.

**Quadrumanous**
An animal that uses both hands and feet for grasping or holding.

**Quadruped**
An animal that walks on four legs.

**Rain forest**
Tropical or subtropical forest that receives high levels of year-round rainfall and supports rich and diverse **flora** and **fauna**.

**Race**
A subgroup of a **species** in the hierarchy of classification of living things.

**Range**
Area in which an individual animal or a social group usually lives. The range may not be exclusive to the animal or group, and may overlap with the range of other animals or groups of animals. It typically contains regular areas for feeding and resting/sleeping.

**Receptive**
A female mammal that is ready to mate.

**Regeneration**
Having the capability to regrow an organ or limb after accidental loss.

**Reingestion**
The extraction of the maximum amount of energy from food by digesting it more than once. The animal brings up food from the stomach for further chewing.

**Reproduction**
The process by which living organisms produce other organisms similar to themselves by **sexual** or **asexual** means.

**Reptile**
**Vertebrate** animals that are **cold-blooded**, breathe air using lungs, and lay eggs. They need an external heat source to maintain their body temperature and are therefore found in the hotter regions of the Earth.
Examples include lizards, snakes, and turtles.

**Respiration**
The system of breathing that involves the exchange of oxygen and carbon dioxide between an organism and its **environment**.

**Retractile**
Capable of being pulled back into the animal's body, for example, claws.

**RNA**
Ribonucleic acid, a long molecule that is used in several ways to carry out a cell's genetic instructions. RNA is chemically similar to **DNA**.

**Rostrum**
The upper jaw in Cetaceans or the forward projection of the snout in fish.

**Rufous**
Reddish-brown in color.

**Ruminant**
An animal, such as a camel or cow, with a complex stomach designed for chewing the cud, or regurgitating its food in order to chew it again.

**Saddle**
Distinctive markings on the back of whales and dolphins.

**Salivary gland**
A gland for the secretion of saliva that aids the digestive function.

**Savanna**
Grassland areas of the tropics and subtropics with few scattered trees and receiving seasonal rainfall. A transition zone from forest to open grassland.

**Scales**
Modified skin in the form of overlapping plates that serve as the outer protective covering in reptiles and fish.

**Scavenger**
An animal that feeds mainly on dead animal **carcasses**.

**Scientific name**
The precise Latin name of a **species** of animal, as distinct from its common name.

**Scent mark**
A place where chemical secretions from **scent glands** are left. Scent marks act as a form of communication between animals, often for breeding or territorial purposes.

**Scent gland**
Organs that secrete chemical "messages" to other animals.

**School**
A large number of fishes or Cetaceans (whales, dolphins) swimming together.

**Scrub**
A pattern of vegetation characterized by shrubs and low trees.

**Sedentary**
Animals that habitually remain in one place, or occupy a small range and do not migrate.

**Sexual dimorphism**
Differences between males and females of the same **species** in terms of size, color, and so on.

**Sexual reproduction**
The process by which living organisms produce new organisms similar to themselves by sexual means.

**Siblings**
Brothers and sisters, that is, animals who share one or both parents.

**Simian**
A monkey or ape, or having their characteristics; used colloquially to mean any of the **higher primates**.

**Shoal**
A large number of fishes swimming together.

**Skeleton**
The internal structure in an animal that provides support for the body and protects internal organs. In higher vertebrates, the skeleton consists of a system of bones.

**Solitary**
Animals which habitually live on their own, as distinct from social animals which live in family groups.

**Sonar**
Part of the facility of **echolocation** used by bats and some marine mammals to help them navigate.

**Spatulate**
Shaped like a spatula, that is, broad and rounded in shape.

**Spawn**
In **aquatic** animals, the act of producing and laying eggs.

**Specialist**
An animal that uses specialized strategies or techniques for feeding or surviving, as opposed to a **generalist**.

**Species**
A species is the basic **taxonomic** rank comprising a set of individuals having common attributes which can interbreed to produce fertile offspring. Related species are grouped together in a **genus**.

**Sperm**
The male sex cell (**gamete**), also known as spermatazoon (plural spermatazoa).

**Spermatophores**
A case enclosing the **sperm** in certain amphibians.

**Sphagnum**
Moss found in boggy areas in temperate regions, forming peat as it decays.

**Steppe**
Large areas of open grassland, known as **prairie** in North America; steppe lands receive low rainfall and may experience wide temperature variation.

**Subfamily**
A division of a **family**.

**Suborder**
A division of an **order**.

**Subadult**
Developmental stage between a **juvenile** and an **adult** animal.

**Subspecies**
A division of a **species**.

**Swim bladder**
A fish's gas-filled bladder that helps maintain buoyancy. Certain fish use them for breathing.

**Taxonomy**
The study of the classification of plants and animals. Animals that share common features are grouped together. The categories are: **species**, **genus**, **family**, **order**, **class**, **phylum**, **kingdom**; these can be divided further into subspecies, subfamily and so on.

**Temperate**
A climate that does not experience either hot or cold extremes.

**Testis**
The organ in which **sperm** are made in most mammals.

**Tetrapod**
Any **vertebrate** with four limbs.

**Terrestrial**
Living on the land.

**Territory**
An area defended from intruders by an individual or group of animals.

**Thorax**
In mammals, the chest or middle part of the body between the head and the **abdomen**.

**Thermoregulation**
The regulation and maintenance of body temperature in mammals.

**Toxin**
Any poisonous substance of animal or plant origin.

**Trachea**
The windpipe in air-breathing **vertebrates**, used to carry air from the throat to the bronchi.

**Transluscent**
Partially, but not completely transparent.

**Tropical zone**
Located between 15 and 23.5 degrees in the southern and northern hemispheres.

**Tundra**
A region of sparse vegetation and extremely low temperatures, where only lichens and mosses are able to grow.

**Ultrasonic**
Very high-frequency sound produced by some marine mammals, possibly as a form of communication.

**Ungulates**
Hoofed herbivorous mammals. Examples include horses, deer, cows, goats, and pigs.

**Venom**
A **toxic** secretion produced by some animals, used to kill their prey.

**Vertebrate**
Any animal with a backbone – mammals, birds, reptiles, amphibians, and fish. More than 40,000 species of vertebrates exist.

**Vestigal**
An organ which is no longer useful and is consequently diminished in size.

**Viviparous**
Giving birth to live young, as opposed to laying eggs.

**Vocalization**
The production of songs, calls and other vocal sounds by animals.

**Warm-blooded**
Animals that regulate body temperature independent of external temperature. Examples include mammals and birds.

**Yolk sac**
A sac containing the yolk of the egg, which contains food for the use of the **embryo**.

# THREATENED SPECIES

Animals appearing in the encyclopedia that have been designated threatened species by the World Conservation Union (IUCN) in its Red List of Threatened Animals are listed here. See Volume 1, page 13 for more information on the individual categories of threat.

## Mammals
### Critically Endangered

African Ass
*Equus africanus*

African Civet
*Viverra civetta*

Black Rhinoceros
*Diceros bicornis*

Eastern Shrew Mouse
*Pseudohydromys murinus*

Golden Lion Tamarin
*Leontopithecus rosalia*

Mediterranean Monk Seal
*Monachus monachus*

Sumatran Rhinoceros
*Dicerorhinus sumatrensis*

Sumatran Short-eared Rabbit
*Nesolagus netscher*i

Wroughton's Free-tailed Bat
*Otomops wroughtoni*

### Endangered

Addax
*Addax nasomaculatus*

African Elephant
*Loxodonta africana*

Arabian Oryx
*Oryx leucoryx*

Arizona Cotton Rat
*Sigmodon arizonae*

Asian Elephant
*Elephas maximus*

Asian Water Buffalo
*Bubalus arnee*

Aye-aye
*Daubentonia madagascariensis*

Bactrian Camel
*Camelus bactrianus*

Banteng
*Bos javanicus*

Black Gibbon
*Hylobates concolor*

Blue Whale
*Balaenoptera musculus*

Bridled Nail-tailed Wallaby
*Onychogalea fraenata*

Chaco Peccary
*Catagonus wagneri*

Chimpanzee
*Pan troglodytes*

Cuban Solenodon
*Solenodon cubanus*

Desert Dormouse
*Selevinia betpakdalaensis*

Drill
*Mandrillus leucophaeus*

European Bison
*Bison bonasus*

Fanalouc
*Eupleres goudotii*

Ganges Dolphin
*Platanista gangetica*

Giant Armadillo
*Priodontes maximus*

Giant Golden Mole
*Chrysospalax trevelyani*

Giant Panda
*Ailuropoda melanoleuca*

Golden Hamster
*Mesocricetus auratus*

Gorilla
*Gorilla gorilla*

Grevy's Zebra
*Equus grevyi*

Hispid Hare
*Caprolagus hispidus*

Hog-nosed Bat
*Craseonycteris thonglongyai*

Hunting Dog
*Lycaon pictus*

Indian Rhinoceros
*Rhinoceros unicornis*

Indri
*Indri indri*

Japanese Macaque
*Macaca fuscata*

Lesser/Red Panda
*Ailurus fulgens*

Lowland Anoa
*Bubalus depressicornis*

Mindanao Moonrat
*Podogymnura truei*

Otter-civet
*Cynogale bennettii*

Pacarana
*Dinomys branickii*

Pink Fairy Armadillo
*Chlamyphorus truncatus*

Pygmy Chimpanzee/ Bonobo
*Pan paniscus*

Rabbit-bandicoot
*Macrotis lagotis*

Ruffed Lemur
*Varecia variegata*

Sei Whale
*Balaenoptera borealis*

Snow Leopard
*Uncia uncia*

Southern Marsupial Mole
*Notoryctes typhlops*

Sri Lankan Long-tailed Shrew
*Crocidura miya*

Steller Sea Lion
*Eumetopias jubatus*

Tiger
*Panthera tigris*

Volcano Rabbit
*Romerolagus diazi*

Woolly Spider Monkey
*Brachyteles arachnoides*

### Vulnerable

American Manatee
*Trichecus manatus*

Asiatic Black Bear
*Ursus thibetanus*

Australian False Vampire Bat
*Macroderma gigas*

Babirusa
*Babyrousa babyrussa*

Bald Uakari
*Cacajao calvus*

Barbary Ape
*Macaca sylvanus*

Barbary Sheep
*Ammotragus lervia*

Barbastelle
*Barbastella barbastellus*

Beira Antelope
*Dorcatragus megalotis*

Blackbuck
*Antilope cervicapra*

Bornean Smooth-tailed Tree Shrew
*Dendrogale melanura*

Boutu
*Inia geoffrensis*

Bush Dog
*Speothos venaticus*

Cheetah
*Acinonyx jubatus*

Chinchilla
*Chinchilla laniger*

Clouded Leopard
*Neofilis nebulosa*

Colocolo
*Dromiciops gliroides*

Common Chinese Zokor
*Myospalax fontanierii*

Common Porpoise/Harbor Porpoise
*Phocoena phocoena*

Dhole
*Cuon alpinus*

Diana Monkey
*Cercopithecus diana*

Dibatag
*Ammodorcas clarkei*

Dugong
*Dugong dugon*

Eastern Barred Bandicoot
*Perameles gunnii*

Flower-faced Bat
*Anthops ornatus*

Fossa
*Cryptoprocta ferox*

Four-horned Antelope
*Tetracerus quadricornis*

Gaur
*Bos frontalis*

Giant Anteater
*Myrmecophaga tridactyla*

Giant Otter
*Pteronura brasiliensis*

Goeldi's Marmoset
*Callimico goeldii*

Himalayan Tahr
*Hemitragus jemlahicus*

Humpback Whale
*Megaptera novaeangliae*

Hutia
*Geocapromys ingrahami*

Kloss's Gibbon
*Hylobates klossii*

Lesser Horseshoe Bat
*Rhinolophus hipposideros*

Lesser Mole-rat
*Spalax leucodon*

Lion
*Panthera leo*

Long-tailed Pouched Rat
*Beamys hindei*

Madras Tree Shrew
*Anathana elliotti*

Malayan Tapir
*Tapirus indicus*

Mouflon
*Ovis orientalis*

Mountain Tree Shrew
*Tupaia montana*

Mulgara
*Dasycercus cristicauda*

New Zealand
Short-tailed Bat
*Mystacina tuberculata*

Northern Fur Seal
*Callorhinus ursinus*

Numbat
*Myrmecobius fasciatus*

Onager/Asiatic Wild Ass
*Equus hemionus*

Orang-utan
*Pongo pygmaeus*

Philippine Flying
Lemur/Colugo
*Cynocephalus volans*

Philippine Tree Shrew
*Urogale everetti*

Pileated Gibbon
*Hylobates pileatus*

Proboscis Monkey
*Nasalis larvatus*

Pygmy Hippopotamus
*Hexaprotodon liberiensis*

Quokka
*Setonix brachyurus*

Red-bellied Guenon
*Cercopithecus erythrogaster*

Ring-tailed Lemur
*Lemur catta*

Russian Desman
*Desmana moschata*

Saiga
*Saiga tatarica*

Salano
*Salanoia concolor*

Serow
*Capricornis sumatraensis*

Short-eared Elephant Shrew
*Macroscelides proboscideus*

Slender Loris
*Loris tardigradus*

Spectacled Bear
*Tremarctos ornatus*

Sperm Whale
*Physeter catodon*

Springhare
*Pedetes capensis*

Stick-nest Rat
*Leporillus conditor*

Stump-tailed Macaque
*Macaca arctoides*

Sucker-footed Bat
*Myzopoda aurita*

Takin
*Budorcas taxicolor*

Verreaux's Sifaka
*Propithecus verreauxi*

White Whale
*Delphinapterus leucas*

Wild Yak Bos
*grunniens*

Wolverine
*Gulo gulo*

# Birds
## Critically Endangered

California Condor
*Gymnogyps californianus*

Kauai O-o
*Moho braccatus*

White-eyed River Martin
*Pseudochelidon sirintarae*

## Endangered

Akepa
*Loxops coccineus*

Akiapolaau
*Hemignathus wilsoni*

Blue-headed Quail Dove
*Starnoenas cyanocephala*

Charles/Galapagos
Mockingbird
*Nesomimus trifasciatus*

Gouldian Finch
*Chloebia gouldiae*

Kagu
*Rhynochetos jubatus*

Kokako
*Callaeas cinerea*

Palila
*Loxioides bailleui*

Takahe
*Porphyrio mantelli*

Whooping Crane
*Grus americana*

## Vulnerable

Blue Bird of Paradise
*Paradisaea rudolphi*

Brown Kiwi
*Apteryx australis*

Congo Peafowl
*Afropavo congensis*

Corncrake
*Crex crex*

Flightless Cormorant
*Phalacrocorax harrisi*

Galápagos Penguin
*Spheniscus mendiculus*

Great Bustard
*Otis tarda*

Java Sparrow
*Padda oryzivora*

Long-billed/Tahiti Reed-
warbler
*Acrocephalus caffer*

Malleefowl
*Leipoa ocellata*

Marvelous Spatule-tail
*Loddigesia mirabilis*

Noisy Scrub-Bird
*Atrichornis clamosus*

Plains-wanderer
*Pedionomus torquatus*

Principe Island Speirops
*Speirops leucophoeus*

Ribbon-tailed Astrapia
*Astrapia mayeri*

Short-legged Ground Roller
*Brachypteracias leptosomus*

Silktail
*Lamprolia victoriae*

Southern Cassowary
*Casuarius casuarius*

Wandering Albatross
*Diomedea exulans*

White-breasted Mesite
*Mesitornis variegata*

White-necked Rockfowl
*Picathartes gymnocephalus*

Wrybill
*Anarhynchus frontalis*

# Reptiles, Amphibians, and Fish
## Critically Endangered

Common Sturgeon
*Acipenser sturio*

Hawksbill
*Eretmochelys imbricata*

## Endangered

Atlantic Halibut
*Hippoglossus hippoglossus*

Batagur/River Terrapin
*Batagur baska*

Beluga
*Huso huso*

Central American River Turtle
*Dermatemys mawii*

Coelacanth
*Latimeria chalumnae*

Fijian Banded Iguana
*Brachylophus fasciatus*

Gavial
*Gavialis gangeticus*

Green Turtle
*Chelonia mydas*

Leatherback
*Dermochelys coriacea*

Loggerhead Turtle
*Caretta caretta*

Mekong Catfish
*Pangasianodon gigas*

Murray/Trout Cod
*Maccullochella macquariensis*

Pacific Ridley
*Lepidochelys olivacea*

Smalltooth/Greater Sawfish
*Pristis pectinata*

## Vulnerable

African Pancake Tortoise
*Malacochersus tornieri*

Alligator Snapping Turtle
*Macroclemys temmincki*

Armadillo Lizard
*Cordylus cataphractus*

Axolotl
*Ambystoma mexicanum*

Basking Shark
*Cetorhinus maximus*

Bluntnose Six-gilled Shark
*Hexanchus griseus*

Cod
*Gadus morhua*

Dwarf Seahorse
*Hippocampus zosterae*

Florida Sand Skink
*Neoseps reynoldsi*

Galápagos Giant Tortoise
*Geochelone nigra*

Galápagos Land Iguana
*Conolophus subcristatus*

Gila Monster
*Heloderma suspectum*

Gopher Tortoise
*Gopherus polyphemus*

Haddock
*Melanogrammus aeglefinus*

Hogfish
*Lachnolaimus maximus*

Komodo Dragon
*Varanus komodensis*

Marine Iguana
*Amblyrhynchus cristatus*

Narrow-headed/Indian
Softshell
*Chitra indica*

New Guinea Plateless River/
Pig-Nose Turtle
*Carettochelys insculpta*

Olm
*Proteus anguinus*

Paddlefish
*Polyodon spathula*

Porbeagle
*Lamna nasus*

Rainbow Parrotfish
*Scarus guacamaia*

Rhinoceros Iguana
*Cyclura cornuta*

Seychelles Frog
*Sooglossus sechellensis*

Spur-thighed Tortoise
*Testudo graeca*

Texas Blind Salamander
*Typhlomolge rathbuni*

West African Dwarf
Crocodile
*Osteolaemus tetraspis*

White Shark
*Carcharodon carcharias*

Wood Turtle
*Clemmys insculpta*

# WORLD ZOOS & AQUARIUMS

## North America

### CANADA
**QUEBEC**
MONTREAL
Biodome de Montreal, 4777 Ave.
Pierre-de-Coubertin, Montreal, PQ,
Canada H1V 1B3.
Phone: 514-868-3000
Email: biodome@ville.montreal.qc.ca
Speciality: Recreated ecosystems of
the Americas and polar regions.

### UNITED STATES OF AMERICA
**CALIFORNIA**
LOS ANGELES
The Los Angeles Zoo, 5333 Zoo
Drive, Los Angeles, CA 90027.
Phone: 213-666-4650.
Speciality: California Condor
Recovery Program.

SAN DIEGO
San Diego Zoological Garden,
Zoological Society of San Diego,
POB 551, 2920 Zoo Drive,
San Diego, CA 92112-0551.
Phone: 619-231-1515.
Speciality: Rare Chinese animals.

**COLORADO**
DENVER
Denver Zoological Gardens, 2300
Steele St, Denver, CO 80205.
Phone: 303-331-4102.
Email: zoodirector@denverzoo.org
Speciality: African ungulates, tropical
reptiles and amphibians.

**DISTRICT OF COLUMBIA**
WASHINGTON
National Zoological Park,
Smithsonian Institution, Washington
DC 20008-2589.
Phone: 202-673-4717.

**FLORIDA**
MIAMI
Miami Seaquarium, 4400
Rickenbaker Causeway, Miami,
FL 33149.
Phone: 305-361-5705.
Speciality: Marine mammals.

ORLANDO
Sea World of Florida, 7007 Sea
World Drive, Orlando,
FL 32821.
Phone: 407-363-2351
Speciality: Marine mammals, sharks,
fish, aquatic birds.

TAMPA
Busch Gardens Zoological Park, POB
9158, Tampa, FL 33674-9158.
Phone: 813-987-5250.
Speciality: African ungulates
and birds.

**HAWAII**
HONOLULU
Honolulu Zoo,151 Kapuhulu Ave,
Honolulu, HI96815.
Phone: 808-971-7174.
Speciality: Galapagos tortoise and
Hawaiian bird species.

**ILLINOIS**
CHICAGO
Chicago Zoological Park (Brookfield
Zoo), 3300 Golf Road, Brookfield,
IL 60513.
Phone: 708-485-0263
Speciality: Tropic world, habitat
Africa, and seven seas dolphinarium.

**MARYLAND**
BALTIMORE
Baltimore Zoo, Druid Hill Park,
Baltimore, MD 21217, USA.
Phone: 410-396-7102.

**MASSACHUSETTS**
BOSTON
Franklin Park Zoo, One Franklin
Park Road, Boston,
MA 02121.
Phone: 617-442-2002
Speciality: Tropical forest species.

**MICHIGAN**
DETROIT
Detroit Zoological Park & Belle Isle
Zoo & Aquarium,
8450 W 10 Mile Road, POB 39,
Royal Oak,
MI 48068-0039.
Phone: 248-398-0903.
Speciality: Penguins, great apes,
amphibian conservation.

**MINNESOTA**
MINNEAPOLIS/ST PAUL
Minnesota Zoological Garden,
13000 Zoo Blvd, Apple Valley,
MN 55124.
Phone: 612-431-9200.
Speciality: Animals indigenous to
Minnesota and the Asian tropics.

**MISSOURI**
ST. LOUIS
St Louis Zoological Park,
Forest Park, St. Louis,
MO 63110.
Phone: 314-781-0900

**NEW YORK**
BRONX
Bronx Zoo/Wildlife Conservation
Park & St Catherine's Wildlife
Survival Center, Wildlife
Conservation Society,
185th Street & Southern
Boulevard, Bronx,
NY 10460-1099.
Phone: 718-220-5100.

**PENNSYLVANIA**
PHILADELPHIA
Philadelphia Zoological Gardens,
Zoological Society of Philadelphia,
PA 19104-1196.
Phone: 215-243-1100.
Speciality: Primates, small mammals,
amphibians.

**TEXAS**
DALLAS
Dallas Zoo, 650 South R. L.
Thornton Freeway, Dallas,
TX 75203-3013.
Phone: 214-670-6825.
Speciality: Herpetological collection.

**WASHINGTON**
SEATTLE
The Seattle Aquarium,
1483 Alaskan Way, Pier 59,
Seattle,
WA 98101-2059.
Phone: 206-386-4300.

Woodland Park Zoological Gardens,
5500 Phinney Ave. North,
Seattle, WA 98103-5897,
USA.
Phone: 206-684-4880.

## International

### AUSTRALIA
MELBOURNE
Royal Melbourne Zoological
Gardens, POB 74, Parkville,
Victoria 3052,
Australia.
Phone: 03-9285-9330
Email: melbzoo@zoo.org.au.

SYDNEY
Sydney Aquarium, Aquarium Pier,
Darling Harbour, Sydney, NSW
2000, Australia.
Phone: 02-9262-2300
Email: wrasse @magna.com.au
Speciality: Australian aquatic life.

### BRAZIL
RIO DE JANEIRO
Fundacao Jardim Zoologico da
Cidade do Rio de Janeiro-Riozoo,
Parque da Quinta da Boa
Vista s/n. São Cristóvão,
CEP 20940-040, Brazil.
Phone: 55- 21-567-6196.
Speciality: Threatened species, bats
and Brazilian mammals.

### CHINA
BEIJING
Beijing Zoological Park,
137 Xi Zhi Wai Street Beijing -
100044,
People's Republic of China.
Phone: 010-6831-4411.

### FRANCE
PARIS
Menagerie du Jardin des Plantes,
Museum National d'Histoire
Naturelle, 57 rue Cuvier,
75231 Paris Cedex 05,
France
Phone: 1-40-79-37-94.
Speciality: Wild goats, African
primates, birds of prey.

### GERMANY
BERLIN
Tierpark Berlin-Friedrichsfelde
GmbH, Am Tierpark 125,
D-!0307 Berlin,
Germany.
Phone: 030-515310.

MUNICH
Munchener Tierpark
Hellabrunn AG, Tierpark Str, 30,
81543 München,
Germany.
Phone: 089-625-0816. Email:
munichzoo@compuserve.com

### NETHERLANDS
AMSTERDAM
Stichting Koninklijk Zoologisch
Genootschap Natura Artis Magistra,
Plantage Kerlaan 38-40,
1018 CZ Amsterdam,
Netherlands.
Phone: 31- 20-5233400.

### RUSSIA
MOSCOW
Moscow Zoo, Moskva, Bolshaya
Gruzinskaya ul. 1, Russia 123242.
Phone: 095-255-60-34

### SPAIN
MADRID
Zoo-Aquarium de la Casa
de Campo,
Casa de Campo, s/n-28011
Madrid, Spain.
Phone: 34-1-711-99-50. Email:
zoomad@genio.infor.es
Speciality: Gorillas and pandas,
dolphinarium and aquarium.

### SWITZERLAND
BASLE
Zoologischer Garten Basel,
Binningerstrasse 40,
CH-4054 Basel,
Switzerland.
Phone: 061-295-3535
Speciality: Primates

### UNITED KINGDOM
LONDON
London Zoo, Regent's Park,
London NW1 4RY,
United Kingdom.
Phone: 0171-722-3333.

# CONSERVATION ORGANIZATIONS

## United States of America

**Center for Marine Conservation**
1725 DeSales Street, N.W., Suite 600, Washington, DC 20036.
Phone: 202-429-5609
Exists to promote informed citizen participation in reversing the degradation of the world's oceans.
Web site: http://www.cmc-ocean.org/

**Greenpeace USA**
1436 U Street, N.W., Washington D.C. 20009
Phone: 1-800-326-0959
The U.S. chapter of the international environmental organization that seeks to expose environmental problems for a peaceful future.
Web site: http://www.greenpeaceusa.org/

**National Audubon Society**
700 Broadway, New York, NY 10003.
Focuses on the preservation of natural ecosystems for birds and other wildlife in the Americas.
Web site: http://www.audubon.org/

**National Fish and Wildlife Association**
1120 Connecticut Ave., NW, Suite 900, Washington, DC 20036
Phone: 202-857-0166
Dedicated to preserving natural resources through environmental education, habitat protection, and public policy development.
Web site: http://www.nfwf.org/

**The Conservation Fund**
1800 N. Kent Street, Suite 1120, Arlington, VA 22209-15.
Phone: 703-525-6300
Seeks sustainable conservation solutions for the 21st century, emphasizing the integration of economic and environmental goals.
Web site: http://www.conservationfund.org/

**Woods Hole Oceanographic Institution**
Co-op Building, MS 16, Woods Hole, MA 02453.
Phone: 508-289-2252
Email: Information@whoi.edu
Marine scence research facility committed to conserving the diversity of marine life.
Web site: http://www.whoi.edu/

**Wildlife Conservation Society**
2300 Southern Blvd., Bronx, NY 10460.
Headquartered at New York's Bronx Zoo, this society works to save wildlife and lands throughout the world.
Web site: http://www.wcs.org/

## International

**Earthtrust: Wildlife Conservation Worldwide**
25 Kaneohe Bay Drive, Suite 205, Kailua, HI 96734, USA.
Phone: 808-254-2866
Dedicated to protecting the world's threatened wildlife and its habitats.
Web site: http://www.earthtrust.org/

**Econet Links**
A Web site listing of links to environmental organization sites, with site descriptions.
Web site: http://www.igc.org/igc/members/en.html

**International Rivers Network**
1847 Berkeley Way, Berkeley, CA 94703, USA.
Phone: 510-848-1155 Email: irnweb@irn.org
Works to halt destructive river development projects and to promote sound river management options worldwide.
Web site: http://www.irn.org

**Land Conservation**
A number of Web sites concentrating on the conservation of coastal areas, dunes, the Arctic, forests, and other areas.
Web site: http://www.webdirectory.com/Land_Conservation/

**The International Biopark Foundation**
PO Box 69069, Oro Valley, Arizona, USA.
Phone: 520-531-5581
Dedicated to the conservation of natural environments, wildlife, and indigenous peoples.
Web site: http://www.biopark.org/

**The World Conservation Union**
IUCN, rue Mauverney, 28, 1196 Gland, Vaud, Switzerland.
A global network of 895 institutions that aims to influence and assist in conserving the integrity and diversity of nature.
Web site: http://www.iucn.org/

**WebDirectory: Wildlife**
A collection of Web sites detailing organizations concerned with mammals and reptiles, ecology, rehabilitation, and other areas of general interest.
Web site: http://www.webdirectory.com/Wildlife/

**World Wildlife Fund**
1250 Twenty-Fourth Street, N. W., P. O. Box 96555, Washington, DC 20077-7787.
Exists to protect the world's threatened wildlife and the habitats they need to survive.
Web site: http://www.worldwildlife.org/

# BIBLIOGRAPHY

## General

Burton, DeVere (1996)
*Ecology of Fish and Wildlife*
Delmar Publishers, Albany, New York

Colbert, Edwin Harris, and Morales, Michael (1991)
*Evolution of the Vertebrates: A History of Backboned Animals Through Time*
John Wiley and Sons, New York

Crawley, Michael J. (1992)
*Natural Enemies: The Population Biology of Predators, Parasites and Diseases*
Blackwell Science Inc., Cambridge, Massachusetts

Dorit, Robert L. (1991)
*Zoology*
Saunders College Publishing, Philadelphia

Fleagle, John G. (1999)
*Primate Adaptation and Evolution*
Academic Press, New York

Hildebrand, M., Bramble, D. M., Liem, K. F., and Wake, D. B. (Editors) (1985)
*Functional Vertebrate Morphology*
Harvard University Press, Cambridge, Massachusetts

Kingdon, Jonathan (1989)
*East African Mammals: An Atlas of Evolution in Africa*
University of Chicago Press, Chicago

Kricher, John (1997)
*A Neotropical Companion: An Introduction to Animals, Plants and Ecosystems of the New World Tropics*
Princeton University Press, Princeton, New Jersey

Maier, Richard (1998)
*Comparative Animal Behavior: An Evolutionary and Ecological Approach*
Allyn & Bacon, Needham Heights, Massachusetts

MacInnes, Joseph (Editor) (1992)
*Saving the Oceans*
Key Parker Books, Canada

Norton Bryan G., Hutchins, Michael, Stevens, Elizabeth F., and Maple, Terry L. (Editors) (1995)
*Ethics on the Ark*
Smithsonian Institution Press, Washington D.C.

Pough, F. Harvey (1999)
*Vertebrate Life*
Prentice Hall, New York

## Mammals

*Book of Mammals* (1998)
National Geographic Society, Washington, D.C.

Clutton-Brock, T. H. (1980)
*Malayan Forest Primates*
Plenum, New York

Estes, Richard Despartes (1990)
*Behavior Guide to African Mammals*
University of California Press, California

Geist, Valerius (1996)
*Deer of the World: Their Evolution, Behavior, and Ecology*
Stackpole Books, Pennsylvania

Mech, L. David (1988)
*The Arctic Wolf Ten Years with the Pack*
Voyageur Press, Minnesota

Nichols, Michael, and Ward, Geoffrey C. (1998)
*The Year of the Tiger*
National Geographic Society, Washington, D.C.

Nowak, R. M., and Paradiso, J. L. (Editors) (1983)
*Walker's Mammals of the World* (4th edition)
John Hopkins University Press, Baltimore

Rosing, Norbert (1994)
*The World of the Polar Bear*
Firefly Books, Buffalo, New York

Gill, Peter, and Gibson, Linda (1997)
Reader's Digest *Explores Whales, Dolphins, and Porpoises*
Reader's Digest Association Inc., Pleasantville, New York

## Birds

*Book of North American Birds* (1990)
Reader's Digest Association Inc.
Pleasantville, New York

Buckley, P. A., and Cooke, F. (Editor) (1987)
*Avian Genetics: A Field and Ecological Approach*
Academic Press, New York

Cramp, S., and Perrins, C. M. (1994)
*Birds of Europe, the Middle East and North Africa*
Oxford University Press, New York

Farraud, J. Jr. (1983)
*The Audubon Society Master Guide to Birding* (3 vols.)
Alfred A. Knopf, New York

Hagemeïjer, Ward J. M., and Blair, Michael J. (Editors)
(1997) *EBCC Atlas of European Breeding Birds: Their
Distribution and Abundance*
Academic Press, San Diego, California

Morse, Douglas H. (1990)
*American Warblers: An Ecological and
Behavioral Perspective*
Harvard University Press, Cambridge, Massachusetts

Parmalee, David Freeland (1992)
*Antarctic Birds: Ecological and Behavioral Approaches*
University of Minnesota Press, Minnesota

Ridgely, Robert S., and Tudor, Guy (1981)
*The Birds of South America*
Oxford University Press Inc., New York

Scholz, Floyd (1993)
*Birds of Prey*
Stackpole Books, Pennsylvania

*The Origin and Evolution of Birds* (1996)
Yale University Press, New Haven, New York

## Reptiles and Amphibians

Beebee, T. J. C. (1997)
*Ecology and Conservation of Amphibians*
Chapman and Hall, New York

Bishop, Sherman C. (1994)
*Handbook of Salamanders*
Comstock Publishing Association with
Cornell University Press, Ithaca, New York

Breen, John F. (1994)
*Encyclopedia of Reptiles and Amphibians: Habits and Care*
tfh Publications Inc., New Jersey

Coburn John (1994)
*The Mini-Atlas of Snakes of the World*
tfh Publications Inc., New Jersey

Coggar, Dr. Harold G., and Zweiful, Richard G. (Editors)
*Encyclopedia of Reptiles and Amphibians*
Academic Press, San Diego, California

Crother, Brian I. (Editor) (1999)
*Caribbean Amphibians and Reptiles*
Academic Press, New York

Ernst, Carl A. (1994)
*Venomous Reptiles of North America*
Smithsonian Institution, Washington D.C.

Feder, Martin E, and Burggren, Warren W. (Editors) (1992)
*Environmental Physiology of the Amphibians*
University of Chicago Press, Chicago

Pritchard, Dr. Peter C.H. (1979)
*Encyclopedia of Turtles*
tfh Publications Inc., New Jersey

Pursall, Brian (1994)
*Mediterranean Tortoises*
tfh Publications Inc., New Jersey

Ricciuti, Edward, and Marketa, Vincent (Editors),
Behler John L. (1994)
*Amphibians (Our Living World)*
Blackbirch Press Inc., Woodbridge, Connecticut

Walls, Jerry G. (1994)
*Jewels of the Rainforest Poison: Frogs of the Family
Dedrobatidae*
tfh Publications Inc., New Jersey

Walls Jerry G. (1992)
*The Living Boas*
tfh Publications Inc., New Jersey

Zimmerman, Elke (1986)
*Reptiles and Amphibians: Care, Behavior, Reproduction*
tfh Publications Inc., New Jersey

## Fish

Bardach, John E, Ryther, John H, and McLarney,
William O. (1998)
*Aquaculture: The Farming and Husbandry of Freshwater
and Marine Organisms*
John Wiley & Sons Inc., New York

Gosner Kenneth L. (1978)
*Petersen Field Guide to the Atlantic Seashore*
Houghton Mifflin Co., Boston, New York

Kaplan, Eugene H. (1982)
*Petersen Field Guide to Coral Reefs*
Houghton Mifflin Co., Boston, New York

Michael, S. W. (1983)
*Sharks and Rays of the World*
Sea Challengers, Monterey, California

Moss, Brian (1998)
*Ecology of Fresh Waters: Man and Medium,
Past to Future*
Blackwell Science Inc., Cambridge, Massachusetts

Nelson, Joseph S. (1994)
*Fishes of the World* (3d edition)
John Wiley & Sons Inc., New York

Page, Lawrence M., and Burr, Brooks M. (1991)
*Petersen Field Guide to Freshwater Fishes*
Houghton Mifflin Co., Boston, New York

# CLASSIFICATION

## CLASS MAMMALIA: MAMMALS
Subclass Prototheria: Egg-laying Mammals

### Order Monotremata: Monotremes
Family Tachyglossidae: Echidnas
Family Ornithorhynchidae: Platypus

Subclass Theria: Live-bearing Mammals
Infraclass Metatheria: Marsupials

### Order Didelphimorpha
Family Didelphidae: Opossums

### Order Paucituberculata
Family Caenolestidae: Shrew Opossums

### Order Microbiotheria
Family Microbiotheriidae: Colocolo

### Order Dasyuromorpha
Family Myrmecobiidae: Numbat
Family Dasyuridae: Marsupial Carnivores and Insectivores

### Order Peramelemorpha
Family Peramelidae: Bandicoots and Bilbies
Family Peroryctidae: New Guinean Bandicoots

### Order Notoryctemorpha
Family Notoryctidae: Marsupial Moles

### Order Diprotodonta
Family Phascolarctidae: Koala
Family Vombatidae: Wombats
Family Phalangeridae: Phalangers
Family Potoroidae: Rat Kangaroos
Family Macropodidae: Kangaroos, Wallabies
Family Burramyidae: Pygmy Possums
Family Pseudocheiridae: Ring-tailed and Greater Gliding Possums
Family Petauridae: Striped and Lesser Gliding Possums
Family Tarsipedidae: Honey Possums
Family Acrobatidae: Pygmy Gliding Possum, Feather-tailed Possum

Infraclass Eutheria: Placental Mammals

### Order Xenarthra: Edentates
Family Myrmecophagidae: Anteaters
Family Bradypodidae: Three-toed Sloths
Family Megalonychidae: Two-toed Sloths
Family Dasypodidae: Armadillos

### Order Pholidota
Family Manidae: Pangolins

### Order Lagomorpha
Family Ochotonidae: Pikas
Family Leporidae: Rabbits

### Order Rodentia
Family Sciuridae: Squirrels
Family Geomyidae: Pocket Gophers
Family Heteromyidae: Pocket mice
Family Aplodontidae: Mountain Beaver
Family Castoridae: Beavers
Family Anomaluridae: Scaly-Tailed Squirrels
Family Pedetidae: Spring Hare
Family Muridae:
    Subfamily Sigmodontinae: New World Rats and Mice
    Subfamily Cricetinae: Hamsters
    Subfamily Calomyscinae: Mouse-like Hamster
    Subfamily Mystromyscinae: White-tailed Rat
    Subfamily Spalacinae: Blind Mole-rats
    Subfamily Myospalacinae: Eastern Asiatic Mole-rats
    Subfamily Rhizomyinae: Mole- and Bamboo Rats
    Subfamily Lophiomyinae: Crested Rats
    Subfamily Platacanthomyinae: Spiny Dormice
    Subfamily Nesomyinae: Madagascan Rats
    Subfamily Otomyinae: African Swamp Rats
    Subfamily Arvicolinae: Voles and Lemmings
    Subfamily Gerbillinae: Gerbils
    Subfamily Petromyscinae: Rock Mice, Swamp Mouse
    Subfamily Dendromurinae: African Climbing Mice
    Subfamily: Cricetomyinae: African Pouched Rats
    Subfamily Murinae: Old World Rats and Mice
Family Dipodidae: Jerboas and Jumping Mice
Family Myoxidae: Dormice
Family Ctenodactylidae: Gundis
Family Hystricidae: Old World Porcupines
Family Erethizontidae: New World Porcupines
Family Caviidae: Guinea Pigs
Family Hydrochaeridae: Capybara
Family Dinomyidae: Pacarana
Family Dasyproctidae: Agoutis
Family Agoutidae: Pacas
Family Chinchillidae: Chinchillas and Viscachas
Family Capromyidae: Hutias
Family Myocastoridae: Coypu
Family Octodontidae: Octodonts
Family Ctenomyidae: Tuco-tucos
Family Abrocomidae: Chinchilla-rats
Family Echimyidae: Spiny Rats
Family Thryonomyidae: Cane Rats
Family Petromuridae: Dassie Rat
Family Bathyergidae: African Mole-Rats

### Order Macroscelidea
Family Macroscelididae: Elephant Shrews

**Order Insectivora: Insectivores**
Family Solenodontidae: Solenodons
Family Tenrecidae: Tenrecs
Family Chysochloridae: Golden Moles
Family Erinaceidae: Hedgehogs, Moonrats
Family Soricidae: Shrews
Family Talpidae: Moles, Desmans

**Order Scandentia**
Family Tupaiidae: Tree Shrews

**Order Primates: Primates**
Family Cheirogaleidae: Mouse Lemurs, Dwarf Lemurs
Family Lemuridae: Lemurs
Family Megaladapidae: Sportive Lemurs
Family Indridae: Indri, Sifakas, Avahi
Family Daubentoniidae: Aye-aye
Family Loridae: Lorises, Pottos
Family Galagonidae: Galagos
Family Tarsiidae: Tarsiers
Family Callitrichidae: Marmosets and Tamarins
Family Cebidae: New World Monkeys
Family Cercopithecidae: Old World Monkeys
Family Hylobatidae: Gibbons
Family Hominidae: Apes and Humans

**Order Dermoptera**
Family Cynocephalidae: Flying Lemurs or Colugos

**Order Chiroptera: Bats**
Family Pteropodidae: Fruit Bats
Family Rhinopomatidae: Mouse-tailed Bats
Family Emballonuridae: Sheath-tailed Bats
Family Craseonycteridae: Hog-nosed Bat
Family Nycteridae: Slit-faced Bats
Family Megadermatidae: False Vampire Bats
Family Rhinolophidae: Horseshoe Bats
Family Noctilionidae: Fisherman Bats
Family Mormoopidae: Moustached Bats
Family Molossidae: Free-tailed Bats
Family Phyllostomidae: New World Leaf-nosed Bats
Family Vespertilionidae: Evening Bats
Family Natalidae: Funnel-eared Bats
Family Furipteridae: Smoky Bats
Family Thyropteridae: Disc-winged Bats
Family Myzopodidae: Old World Sucker-footed Bat
Family Mystacinidae: New Zealand Short-tailed Bats

**Order Carnivora: Carnivores**
Family Canidae: Dogs, Foxes
Family Ursidae: Bears, Pandas
Family Procyonidae: Raccoons
Family Mustelidae: Mustelids
Family Viverridae: Civets
Family Herpestidae: Mongooses
Family Hyaenidae: Hyenas
Family Felidae: Cats

Family Otariidae: Sea Lions, Fur Seals
Family Odobenidae: Walrus
Family Phocidae: True Seals

**Order Tubulidentata**
Family Orycteropodidae: Aardvark

**Order Artiodactyla: Even-toed Ungulates**
Family Suidae: Pigs
Family Tayassuidae: Peccaries
Family Hippopotamidae: Hippopotamuses
Family Camelidae: Camels
Family Tragulidae: Mouse Deer
Family Moschidae: Musk Deer
Family Cervidae: Deer
Family Giraffidae: Giraffes
Family Antilocapridae: Pronghorn
Family Bovidae: Bovids

**Order Cetacea: Whales**
Family Platanistidae: River Dolphins
Family Phocoenidae: Porpoises
Family Delphinidae: Dolphins
Family Monodontidae: Narwhal, White Whale
Family Physeteridae: Sperm Whales
Family Ziphiidae: Beaked Whales
Family Eschrichtiidae: Grey Whale
Family Balaenopteridae: Rorquals
Family Balaenidae: Right Whales

**Order Perissodactyla: Odd-toed Ungulates**
Family Equidae: Horses
Family Tapiridae: Tapirs
Family Rhinocerotidae: Rhinoceroses

**Order Hyracoidea**
Family Hyracoidea: Hyraxes

**Order Proboscidea**
Family Elephantidae: Elephants

**Order Sirenia: Sea Cows**
Family Dugongidae: Dugong
Family Trichechidae: Manatees

**CLASS AVES: BIRDS**
**Order Struthioniformes: Ratites**
Family Struthionidae: Ostrich
Family Rheidae: Rheas
Family Casuariidae: Cassowaries, Emu
Family Apterygidae: Kiwis

**Order Tinamiformes: Tinamous**
Family Tinamidae: Tinamous

**Order Craciformes: Curassows, Guans, Megapodes**
Family Cracidae: Curassows, Guans, Chachalacas

Family Megapodiidae: Megapodes

**Order Galliformes: Gamebirds**
Family Phasianidae: Quails, partridge, francolins, pheasants, grouse, turkey
Family Numididae: Guineafowl
Family Odontophoridae: New World Quail

**Order Anseriformes: Waterfowl**
Family Anhimidae: Screamers
Family Anseranatidae: Magpie goose
Family Dendrocygnidae: Whistling ducks
Family Anatidae: Geese, swans, ducks

**Order Turniciformes: Buttonquail**
Family Turnicidae: Buttonquail

**Order Piciformes: Barbets and woodpeckers**
Family Indicatoridae: Honeyguides
Family Picidae: Woodpeckers
Family Megalaimidae: Asian barbets
Family Lybiidae: African barbets
Family Ramphastidae: New World barbets and toucans

**Order Galbuliformes: Jacamars and Puffbirds**
Family Galbulidae: Jacamars
Family Bucconidae: Puffbirds

**Order Bucerotiformes: Hornbills**
Family Bucerotidae: Hornbills
Family Bucorvidae: Ground-hornbills

**Order Upupiformes: Hoopoes**
Family Upupidae: Hoopoe
Family Phoeniculidae: Wood-hoopoes
Family Rhinopomastidae: Scimitar-bills

**Order Trogoniformes: Trogons**
Family Trogonidae: Trogons

**Order Coraciiformes: Kingfishers, Rollers, Bee-eaters**
Family Coraciidae: Rollers
Family Brachypteraciidae: Ground-rollers
Family Leptosomidae: Cuckoo-roller
Family Momotidae: Motmots
Family Todidae: Todies
Family Alcedinidae: Alcedinid kingfishers
Family Dacelonidae: Dacelonid kingfishers
Family Cerylidae: Cerylid kingfishers
Family Meropidae: Bee-eaters

**Order Coliiformes: Mousebirds**
Family Coliidae: Mousebirds

**Order Cuculiformes: Cuckoos**
Family Cuculidae: Old World cuckoos
Family Centropodidae: Coucals

Family Coccyzidae: American cuckoos
Family Opisthocomidae: Hoatzin
Family Crotophagidae: Anis and guira cuckoos
Family Neomorphidae: Roadrunners and ground-cuckoos

**Order Psittaciformes: Parrots**
Family Psittacidae: Parrots

**Order Apodiformes: Swifts**
Family Apodidae: Swifts
Family Hemiprocnidae: Crested-swifts

**Order Trochiliformes: Hummingbirds**
Family Trochilidae: Hummingbirds

**Order Musophagiformes: Turacos**
Family Musophagidae: Turacos

**Order Strigiformes: Owls and Nightjars**
Family Tytonidae: Barn owls
Family Strigidae: True owls
Family Aegothelidae: Owlet nightjars
Family Podargidae: Australian frogmouths
Family Batrachostomidae: Asiatic frogmouths
Family Steatornithidae: Oilbird
Family Nyctibiidae: Potoos
Family Eurostopodidae: Eared-nightjars
Family Caprimulgidae: Nightjars

**Order Columbiformes: Pigeons**
Family Columbidae: Pigeons

**Order Gruiformes: Cranes and Rails**
Family Eurypygidae: Sunbittern
Family Otididae: Bustards
Family Gruidae: Cranes
Family Heliornithidae: Limpkins and sungrebes
Family Psophiidae: Trumpeters
Family Cariamidae: Seriemas
Family Rhynochetidae: Kagu
Family Rallidae: Rails
Family Mesitornithidae: Mesites

**Order Ciconiiformes: Waterbirds and Birds of Prey**
Family Pteroclididae: Sandgrouse
Family Thinocoridae: Seedsnipes
Family Pedionomidae: Plains wanderer
Family Scolopacidae: Woodcock, snipe, sandpipers
Family Rostratulidae: Painted snipe
Family Jacanidae: Jacanas
Family Chionididae: Sheathbills
Family Burhinidae: Stone curlews
Family Charadriidae: Oystercatchers, avocets, plovers
    Subfamily Recurvirostrinae: Oystercatchers, avocets, stilts, ibisbill
    Subfamily Charadriinae: Plovers, lapwings
Family Glareolidae: Coursers, pratincoles, crab plover

Family Laridae: Skuas, skimmers, gulls, terns, auks
  Subfamily Larinae: Skuas, skimmers, gulls, terns
  Subfamily Alcinae: Auks
Family Accipitridae: Osprey, birds of prey (eagles, kites, hawks, buzzards, harriers, Old World vultures)
Family Sagittariidae: Secretarybird
Family Falconidae: Falcons
Family Podicipedidae: Grebes
Family Phaethontidae: Tropicbirds
Family Sulidae: Gannets, boobies
Family Anhingidae: Anhingas
Family Phalacrocoracidae: Cormorants
Family Ardeidae: Herons, egrets, bitterns
Family Scopidae: Hammerkop
Family Phoenicopteridae: Flamingos
Family Threskiornithidae: Ibises, spoonbills
Family Pelecanidae: Pelicans, shoebills
Family Ciconiidae: New World vultures, storks
  Subfamily Cathartinae: New World Vultures
  Subfamily Ciconiinae: Storks
Family Fregatidae: Frigatebirds
Family Spheniscidae: Penguins
Family Gaviidae: Divers or loons
Family Procellariidae: Shearwaters, petrels, albatrosses, storm petrels
  Subfamily Procellariinae: Petrels, shearwaters, diving petrels
  Subfamily Diomedeinae: Albatrosses
  Subfamily Hydrobatinae: Storm petrels

**Order Passeriformes: Songbirds**
*Suborder Tyranni: Primitive passerines*
Family Acanthisittidae: New Zealand wrens
Family Pittidae: Pittas
Family Eurylaimidae: Broadbills
Family Philepittidae: Asities
Family Sapayoidae: Sapayoa
Family Tyrannidae: Tyrant flycatcher, cotinga, and manakin family
  Subfamily Pipromorphinae: MionectIne flycatchers
  Subfamily Tyranninae: Tyrant flycatchers
  Subfamily Tityrinae: Tityras, becards
  Subfamily Cotinginae: Cotingas, plantcutters, sharpbill
  Subfamily Piprinae: Manakins
Family Thamnophilidae: Antbirds
Family Furnariidae: Ovenbirds, woodcreepers
  Subfamily Furnariinae: Ovenbirds
  Subfamily Dendrocolaptinae: Woodcreepers
Family Formicariidae: Ground antbirds
Family Conopophagidae: Gnateaters
Family Rhinocryptidae: Tapaculos
Family Climacteridae: Australian treecreepers
*Suborder Passeri: Advanced passerines*
Family Menuridae: Lyrebirds, scrub-birds
Family Ptilonorhynchidae: Bowerbirds
Family Maluridae: Fairywrens, emuwrens, grasswrens
Family Meliphagidae: Honey-eaters
Family Pardalotidae: Pardalotes, bristlebirds, scrubwrens,

thornbills
Family Eopsaltriidae: Australian robins
Family Irenidae: Leafbirds, fairy-bluebirds
Family Orthonychidae: Logrunners
Family Pomatostomidae: Australasian babblers
Family Laniidae: Shrikes
Family Vireonidae: Vireos
Family Corvidae: Crow family
  Subfamily Cinclosomatinae: Quail thrushes, whipbirds
  Subfamily Corcoracinae: Australian chough, apostlebird
  Subfamily Pachycephalinae: Sittellas, mohouas, shrike tits, whistlers
  Subfamily Corvinae: Crows, magpies, birds-of paradise, currawongs, wood-swallows, orioles, cuckoo-shrikes
  Subfamily Dicrurinae: Fantails, drongos, monarchs
  Subfamily Aegithiniae: Ioras
  Subfamily Malacotinae: Bush-shrikes, helmet-shrikes, vangas
Family Callaetidae: New Zealand wattlebirds
Family Picathartidae: Rock-jumpers, rockfowl
Family Bombycillidae: Palmchat, silky-flycatchers, waxwings
Family Cinclidae: Dippers
Family Muscicapidae: Thrushes, Old World flycatchers, chats
  Subfamily Turdinae: Thrushes
  Subfamily Muscicapinae: Old World flycatchers, chats
Family Sturnidae: Starlings, mockingbirds
Family Sittidae: Nuthatches, wallcreeper
Family Certhiidae: Wrens, treecreepers, gnatcatchers
  Subfamily Troglodytinae: Wrens
  Subfamily Certhiinae: Treecreepers
  Subfamily Polioptilinae: Gnatcatchers
Family Paridae: Penduline-tits, titmice
  Subfamily Remizinae: Penduline tit
  Subfamily Parinae: Titmice
Family Aegithalidae: Long-tailed tits
Family Hirundinidae: River martins, swallows, martins
Family Regulidae: Kinglets
Family Pycnonotidae: Bulbuls
Family Hypocoliidae: Hypocolius
Family Cisticolidae: African warblers
Family Zosteropidae: White-eyes
Family Sylviidae: Warblers
  Subfamily Acrocephalinae: Leaf-warblers
  Subfamily Megalurinae: Grass-warblers
  Subfamily Garrulacinae: Laughingthrushes
  Subfamily Sylviinae: Babblers, parrotbills, typical warblers
Family Alaudidae: Larks
Family Nectariniidae: Sugarbirds, flowerpeckers, sunbirds
Family Melanocharitidae: Berrypeckers, longbills
Family Paramythiidae: Paramythias
Family Passeridae
  Subfamily Passerinae: Sparrows
  Subfamily Motacillinae: Wagtails, pipits
  Subfamily Prunellinae: Dunnocks
  Subfamily Ploceinae: Weavers
  Subfamily Estrildinae: Grass finches, parasitic whydahs
Family Fringillidae
  Subfamily Peucedraminae: Olive warbler

Subfamily Fringillinae: Chaffinches, cardueline finches, Hawaiian honeycreepers
Subfamily Emberizinae: Buntings, wood warblers, tanagers, cardinals, icterids

## CLASS REPTILIA: REPTILES
### Order Chelonia: Turtles and Tortoises
Family Emydidae: Emydid Turtles
Family Testudinae: Tortoises
Family Trionychidae: Softshell Turtles
Family Carettochylidae: Plateless River Turtle
Family Dermatemydidae: Central American River Turtle
Family Kinosternidae: American Mud and Musk Turtles
Family Cheloniidae: Marine Turtles
Family Dermochelyidae: Leatherback Turtle
Family Chelydridae: Snapping Turtles
Family Pelomedusidae: Greaved Turtles
Family Chelidae: Matamatas

### Order Sphenodontia
Family Sphenodontidae: Tuataras

### Order Squamata: Lizards and Snakes

### Lizards
Family Iguanidae: Iguanas
Family Agamidae: Agamid Lizards
Family Chamaeleonidae: Chameleons
Family Gekkonidae: Geckos
Family Pygopodidae: Scaly-footed Lizards
Family Dibamidae: Old World Burrowing Lizards
Family Gymnophthalmidae: Microteiid Lizards
Family Teiidae: Teiid Lizards
Family Lacertidae: Lacertid Lizards
Family Xantusiidae: Night Lizards
Family Scincidae: Skinks
Family Cordylidae: Girdled and Plated Lizards
Family Xenosauridae: Crocodile Lizards
Family Anguidae: Slow Worms and Alligator Lizards
Family Varanidae: Monitors
Family Helodermatidae: Gila Monsters

### Amphisbaenians (Worm Lizards)
Family Bipedidae: Bipeds
Family Trogonophiidae: Trogonophiids
Family Amphisbaenidae: Amphisbaenids

### Snakes
Family Leptotyphlopidae: Thread Snakes
Family Typhlopidae: Blind Snakes
Family Anomolepididae: Dawn Blind Snakes
Family Uropeltidae
Family Aniliidae: Pipe Snakes
Family Xenopeltidae: Sunbeam Snake
Family Loxocemidae: Loxocemid Snake
Family Boidae: Boas and Pythons
Family Boyleriidae: Round Island Snakes

Family Tropidophiidae: Neotropical Ground Boas
Family Acrochordidae: Wart Snakes
Family Atractaspidae: Burrowing Asps
Family Colubridae: Colubrid Snakes
Family Elapidae: Cobras and Sea Snakes
Family Viperidae: Vipers and Pit Vipers

### Order Crocodilia: Crocodiles, Alligators and Gavial
Family Crocodylidae: Crocodiles
Family Alligatoridae: Alligators
Family Gavialidae: Gavial

## CLASS AMPHIBIA: AMPHIBIANS
### Order Anura: Frogs and Toads
Family Ascaphidae: Tailed Frogs
Family Leiopelmatidae: New Zealand Frogs
Family Discoglossidae: Discoglossid Frogs
Family Pipidae: Pipid Frogs
Family Rhinophrynidae: Mexican Burrowing Frog
Family Pelodytidae: Parsley Frogs
Family Pelobatidae: Spadefoot Toads
Family Centrolenidae: Glass Frogs
Family Heleophrynidae: Ghost Frogs
Family Bufonidae: Bufonid Toads
Family Brachycephalidae: Gold Frogs
Family Hylidae: Treefrogs
Family Pseudidae: Pseudid Frogs
Family Rhinodermatidae: Mouth-brooding Frogs
Family Leptodactylidae: Leptodactylid Frogs
Family Myobatrachidae: Myobatrachid Frogs
Family Sooglossidae: Sooglossid Frogs
Family Dendrobatidae: Poison-dart Frogs
Family Hyperoliidae: Reed Frogs
Family Microhylidae: Narrow-mouthed Frogs
Family Ranidae: True Frogs
Family Rhacophoridae: Rhacophorid Treefrogs

### Order Caudata: Salamanders and Newts
Family Sirenidae: Sirens
Family Amphiumidae: Congo Eels
Family Plethodontidae: Lungless Salamanders
Family Rhyacotritonidae: Rhyacotritonid Salamanders
Family Proteidae: Olms and Mudpuppies
Family Salamandridae: Newts and Salamanders
Family Ambyostomatidae: Mole Salamanders
Family Dicamptodontidae: Dicamptodontid Salamanders
Family Cryptobranchidae: Giant Salamanders
Family Hynobiidae: Asiatic Land Salamanders

### Order Gymnophonia: Caecilians
Family Rhinatrematidae: Rhinatrematid Caecilians
Family Ichthyophidae: Ichthyophid Caecilians
Family Uraeotyphlidae: Uraeotyphlid Caecilians
Family Scolecomorphidae: Scolecomorphid Caecilians
Family Caeciliaidae: Caeciliaid Caecilians
Family Typhlonectidae: Typhlonectid Caecilians

FISH
**Class Myxini**
Order Myxiniformes: Hagfishes

**Class Cephalaspidomorphi**
Order Petromyzontiformes: Lampreys

**Class Chondrichthyes: Cartilaginous Fish**
Order Heterodontiformes: Bullhead, Horn Sharks
Order Lamniformes: Sand Tigers, Goblin Sharks, Megamouth Sharks
Order Carchariniformes: Cat Sharks, Hound Sharks, Requiem Sharks
Order Orectolobiformes: Wobbegons, Nurse Sharks, Whale Sharks
Order Squatiniformes: Angel Sharks
Order Hexanchiformes: Frilled Sharks, Cow Sharks
Order Squaliformes: Bramble Sharks, Sleeper Sharks, Dogfish Sharks
Order Pristiphoriformes: Saw Sharks
Order Rajiformes: Rays, Skates, Sawfishes
Order Chimaeriformes: Chimaeras

**Class Osteichthyes: Bony Fish**
**Subclass Actinopterygii: Ray-finned Fishes**
Order Polypteriformes: Bichirs
Order Acipenseriformes: Sturgeons, Paddlefishes
Order Lepisosteiformes: Gars
Order Amiiformes: Bowfin
Order Osteoglossiformes: Bonytongues, Butterflyfish, Mooneyes
Order Elopiformes: Tarpons, Tenpounders
Order Albuliformes: Bonefishes, Halosaurs, Spiny Eels
Order Anguilliformes: Freshwater Eels, Moray Eels, Conger Eels
Order Saccopharyngiformes: Bobtail Snipe Eels, Swallowers, Gulpers
Order Clupeiformes: Herrings, Anchovies
Order Gonorynchiformes: Milkfish, Beaked Sandfishes, Snake Mudhead
Order Cypriniformes: Carps, Minnows, Loaches
Order Characiformes: Characins, Trahiras, Headstanders
Order Siluriformes: Catfishes
Order Gymnotiformes: Knifefishes, Electric Eel
Order Esociformes: Pikes, Mudminnows
Order Osmeriformes: Smelts, Slickheads, Noodlefishes
Order Salmoniformes: Salmon, Trout, Chars
Order Stomiiformes: Bristlemouths, Marine Hatchetfishes, Lightfishes
Order Atelopodiiformes: Jellynose Fishes
Order Aulopiformes: Telescope fishes, Greeneyes, Barracudinas
Order Myctophiformes: Lanternfishes
Order Percopsiformes: Trout-perches, Cavefishes
Order Ophidiiformes: Carapids, Cuskeels, Brotulas
Order Gadiformes: Cods, Hakes
Order Batrachoidiformes: Toadfishes
Order Lophiiformes: Anglerfishes
Order Beloniformes: Flying fishes, Needlefishes, Halfbeaks
Order Cyprinodontiformes: Killifishes, Rivulines, Splitfins, Pupfishes
Order Atheriniformes: Rainbow Fishes, Blueeyes, Silversides
Order Lampridiformes: Crestfishes, Oarfishes, Ribbonfishes
Order Stephanoberyciformes: Whalefishes, Gibberfishes
Order Beryciformes: Beardfishes, Lanterneyes, Squirrelfishes
Order Zeiformes: Dories, Oreos
Order Gasterosteiformes: Sticklebacks, Sand Eels, Tubesnouts
Order Synbranchiformes: Swamp Eels, Spiny Eels
Order Dactylopteriformes: Flying Gurnards
Order Scorpaeniformes: Scorpionfishes, Velvetfishes, Sculpins
Order Perciformes: Perchlike Fishes
    Suborder Percoidei: Percoid Fishes
    Suborder Elassomatoidei: Pygmy Sunfishes
    Suborder Labroidei: Cichlids, Damselfishes, Wrasses, Parrotfish
    Suborder Zoarcoidei: Eelpouts, Wrymouths, Gunnels, Wolffishes
    Suborder Notothenioidei: Icefishes
    Suborder Trachinoidei: Sand Lances, Weeverfishes, Stargazers
    Suborder Blennioidei: Blennies
    Suborder Icosteodei: Ragfish
    Suborder Kurtoidei: Nurseryfishes
    Suborder Acanthuroidei: Spadefishes, Scats, Rabbitfishes, Surgeonfishes
    Suborder Mugiloidei: Mullets
    Suborder Scombrolabracoidei: Scombrolabracoid Fishes
    Suborder Scombroidei: Barracudas, Mackerel, Tunas, Marlin
    Suborder Stromateoidei: Medusafishes, Squaretails, Butterfishes
    Suborder Anabantoidei: Gouramis
    Suborder Channoidei: Snakeheads
Order Pleuronectiformes: Flounders, Soles
Order Tetraodontiformes: Puffers, Triggerfishes, Porcupinefishes

**Subclass Sarcopterygii: Lobe-finned Fishes**
Order Ceratodontiformes: Australian Lungfishes
Order Lepidosireniformes: African and South American Lungfishes
Order Coelacanthiformes: Coelacanth

# INDEX

# ACKNOWLEDGEMENTS

The Publishers received invaluable help during the preparation of the Animal Encyclopedia from: Heather Angel, who lent us reference slides, Angus Bellairs, who gave advice, Dr H. G. Cogger, who lent us reference slides; Rosanne Hooper and Zilda Tandy who assisted with research, Dr Pat Morris of Royal Holloway College, London and Dr Robert Stebbings of the Institute of Terrestrial Ecology, Huntingdonshire, who both helped with reference on the Mammal section, Ed Wade, who helped with reference on the Fish section, the staff of the Herpetology Department of the British Museum (Natural History), London, particularly Colin McCarthy and Barry Clarke, who allowed us access to specimens and reference, the staff of the Ornithology Department of the British Museum (Natural History) outstation at Tring, particularly Peter Colston, who gave assistance with the specimen collection, the staff of the Science Reference Library, London, the IUCN Conservation Monitoring Centre, Cambridge, England, for data on threatened species, and the Zoological Society of London, which allowed us to reproduce information from its *International Zoo Yearbook*.

We acknowledge the contribution of Professor Carl Gans in his book *Reptiles of the World* (Bantam 1975).